Alexander Mackenzie

History of the Camerons

With genealogies of the principal families of the name

Alexander Mackenzie

History of the Camerons
With genealogies of the principal families of the name

ISBN/EAN: 9783337322120

Printed in Europe, USA, Canada, Australia, Japan

Cover: Foto ©ninafisch / pixelio.de

More available books at **www.hansebooks.com**

HISTORY
of the
CAMERONS

WITH

GENEALOGIES OF THE PRINCIPAL FAMILIES
OF THE NAME.

BY

ALEXANDER MACKENZIE, F.S.A., Scot.,

EDITOR OF THE "CELTIC MAGAZINE"; AUTHOR OF "THE HISTORY AND GENEALOGIES OF
THE CLAN MACKENZIE"; "THE HISTORY OF THE MACDONALDS AND LORDS OF THE
ISLES"; "THE HISTORY OF THE MATHESONS"; "THE PROPHECIES OF
THE BRAHAN SEER"; "THE HISTORICAL TALES AND LEGENDS OF
THE HIGHLANDS"; "THE HISTORY OF THE HIGHLAND
CLEARANCES"; "THE SOCIAL STATE OF THE ISLE
OF SKYE IN 1882-83"; ETC., ETC.

Pro Rege et Patria.

INVERNESS: A. & W. MACKENZIE.
MDCCCLXXXIV.

PREFACE.

The completion of the History of the Camerons brings me to the end of another task, in a similar field to that traversed in my *History of the Mackenzies*, my *History of the Macdonalds and Lords of the Isles*, and, on a more limited scale, in my *History of the Mathesons*. The present work, no doubt, like its predecessors, contains errors, and not a few blemishes of execution and style; but, when the materials available are taken into consideration, these defects will be readily condoned by those who best understand the difficulties that had to be overcome, and by those who know how very little help could be afforded even by the heads of the leading families of the clan, however willing they may have been to give it.

The portion of the book devoted to the career of General Sir Allan Cameron of Erracht, K.C.B., has been re-written from a series of articles, on that distinguished soldier, that appeared, anonymously, in the first volume of the *Celtic Magazine;* and for the sketch of Colonel John Cameron of Fassiefern, distinguished in the same field, I am mainly indebted to the account of his life, by the Rev. Archibald Clerk, LL.D., of Kilmallie; to whom I am also under obligation for the valuable papers from which are taken the interesting Appendices at the end of the volume. My thanks are also due to Mrs. Mary Mackellar, the well-known Gaelic bard, and a few others for valuable genealogical notes, and other information.

The Index, which, I have no doubt, will be much appreciated by those consulting the book, is the unaided work of my eldest boy, Hector Rose Mackenzie, who has already shown a very considerable and intelligent interest in the History, Traditions, and Folk-Lore of the Highlands.

A. M.

INVERNESS, *August*, 1884.

CONTENTS.

TITLE	iii
PREFACE	v
CONTENTS	vii
LIST OF SUBSCRIBERS	ix
ORIGIN OF THE CAMERONS—Various authorities	1-9
I. ANGUS	9
II. GILLESPICK, or ARCHIBALD	10
III. JOHN CAMERON	10
IV. ROBERT CAMERON	10
V. SIR JOHN DE CAMERON	11
VI. SIR ROBERT DE CAMERON	11
VII. JOHN DE CAMERON	11
VIII. JOHN DE CAMERON—"Ochtery"	11
IX. ALLAN CAMERON—"MacOchtery"	12-21
X. EWEN CAMERON	21-25
XI. DONALD CAMERON—"Domhnull Dubh MacAilein"	25-32
XII. ALLAN CAMERON—"Ailean MacDhomh'uill Duibh"	32-34
XIII. EWEN CAMERON—"Eoghainn MacAilein"	34-48
XIV. EWEN CAMERON—"Eoghainn Beag"	48-60
XV. DONALD CAMERON—"Domhnull Dubh MacDhomhnuill"	60-61
XVI. ALLAN CAMERON—"Ailean MacIan Duibh"	61-94
XVII. SIR EWEN CAMERON—The Famous "Eoghainn Dubh"	94-212
XVIII. JOHN CAMERON, son of Sir Ewen	212-214
XIX. DONALD CAMERON—The "Gentle Lochiel"	214-250
XX. JOHN CAMERON	250-253
XXI. CHARLES CAMERON	254
XXII. DONALD CAMERON	254-256
XXIII. DONALD CAMERON	256-258
XXIV. DONALD CAMERON, now of Lochiel	258
LOCHIEL ARMS—Deed of Registration in Lyon Office	258-260
DR. ARCHIBALD CAMERON OF LOCHIEL AND HIS DESCENDANTS	261-280

CONTENTS.

FASSIEFERN, THE CAMERONS OF	281-284
FASSIEFERN, COLONEL JOHN CAMERON OF	284-308
WORCESTER, THE CAMERONS OF	309-317
ERRACHT, THE CAMERONS OF	318-320
ERRACHT, GENERAL SIR ALLAN CAMERON OF, K.C.B.	320-374
INVERAILORT, THE CAMERONS OF	375-380
CALLART, THE CAMERONS OF	381-384
LUNDAVRA, THE CAMERONS OF	385-390
GLENEVIS, THE CAMERONS OF	391-398
SPEYSIDE, THE CAMERONS OF	399-402
DAWNIE, THE CAMERONS OF	403-405
BARCALDINE, THE CAMERONS OF	406-408
CAMERON, SIR RODERICK W., FAMILY OF	409-412
CUILCHENNA, THE CAMERONS OF	413-414
KINLOCHIEL, CLUNES, CAMISKY, AND STRONE, THE CAMERONS OF	414-415
APPENDIX I., ACTION OF REDUCTION AND DECLARATOR—The Trustees of Donald Cameron of Lochiel against Allan Cameron of Erracht.	417-457
APPENDIX II.—Rents of all the Farms on the Estate of Lochiel at Martinmas, 1787, with the names of all the Tenants at that date	458-460
APPENDIX III.—Rental and new Valuation of the Estate of Lochiel, made by Lieutenant Allan Cameron of Lundavra in, or about, 1789	461-462
INDEX	465

LIST OF SUBSCRIBERS.

Aitken, Dr., District Asylum, Inverness.
Allan, William, Esq., Scotland House, Sunderland.
Bain, Donald, Esq., Inverness.
Bell, A. R., Esq., bookseller, Inverness.
Brown, Neil, Esq., merchant, Greenock.
Buccleuch, His Grace the Duke of (Large Paper Copy).
Burgess, J. W. Cameron, Esq., Inverness.
Bute, The Most Noble The Marquis of (Large Paper Copy).
Cameron, A Canadian (100 Copies).
Cameron, A. H. F., Esq., M.D., Liverpool (2 Copies).
Cameron, Alexander, Esq., Ballater, Aberdeen.
Cameron, Alexauder, Esq., Highfield, Elgin.
Cameron, Allan Gordon, Esq., Tunbridge Wells (2 Copies, 1 Large Paper).
Cameron, D., Esq., St. Peters, Cape Breton, Nova Scotia.
Cameron, D. A., Esq., Achnacarry House, Nairn.
Cameron, D. A., Esq., Nokomai, New Zealand.
Cameron, D. E. C., Esq., Banker, Lucknow, Ontario.
Cameron, Donald, Esq., of Lochiel (2 Copies, 1 Large Paper).
Cameron, Donald, Esq., of Barcaldine, Queensland.
Cameron, Donald Charles, Esq., Cuchullin Lodge, Inverness.
Cameron, Dr. Charles H. H., Harlesden, London.
Cameron, Dr. J. A., Bawtry, Yorkshire.
Cameron, Dugald, Esq., Calton, Glasgow (1 Copy, 1 Large Paper).
Cameron, D. M., Esq., merchant, Inverness.
Cameron, Ewen, Esq., C.I.R.I.C., Ballina, Ireland (16 Copies, 2 Large Paper).
Cameron, Ewen, Esq., 105 George Street, Edinburgh.
Cameron, Ewen, Esq., National Bank, Fort-William.
Cameron, Ewen Somerled, Esq., of Barcaldine (5 Copies, 1 Large Paper).
Cameron, Geo. Fenton, Esq., M.D., London.
Cameron, H. St. George De Halberg, Esq., Provincial Bank of Ireland.
Cameron, J., Esq., St. Andrews, Fife.
Cameron, J., Esq., Shieldaig, Lochcarron.
Cameron, J. A., Esq., War Correspondent of the *Standard*.
Cameron, J. Macdonald, Lime Street, London.

Cameron, James, Esq., merchant, Inverness.
Cameron, John, Esq., Royal Academy, Inverness.
Cameron, John, Esq., Mitchell, Queensland.
Cameron, John, Esq., Ex-Provost of Kirkintilloch.
Cameron, John, Esq., S.S.C., Edinburgh.
Cameron, John Alex. Staples, Esq., Napa, Canada.
Cameron, Miss, of Invernilort (Large Paper Copy).
Cameron, Miss Isabel Macdonald, Scarborough.
Cameron, Miss Mary Emily, Innseagan, Fort-William.
Cameron, Mrs., of Barcaldine (2 Copies, 1 Large Paper).
Cameron, Neil R., Esq. (of Messrs. D. Cameron & Co.), Inverness.
Cameron, Nicol, Esq., Gowanbrae, Pollokshaws.
Cameron, P. H., Esq., S.S.C., Burntisland.
Cameron, Patrick, Esq. (Corrychoille), Edinburgh.
Cameron, Ralph A., Esq., Blackheath, London.
Cameron, Rev. Alex., Brodick, Arran.
Cameron, Rev. Geo. T., Heckington Vicarage, Lincolnshire (2 Copies).
Cameron, Rev. John, Dornoch.
Cameron, Richard Standish Le Bagge, Esq., Batavia, Java.
Cameron, Robert, Esq., Parkhead Chemical Works, Glasgow.
Cameron, Robert F., Esq., C.A., Inverness.
Cameron, Russell Bedford Colclough, Esq., Sourabaya, Java.
Cameron, Sir Roderick W., New York (20 Copies, 5 Large Paper).
Cameron, Wm., Esq., Uppertown, Glenurquhart.
Cameron, Wm. Justin Beauchamp, Esq., of Uanda, Queensland.
Campbell, Geo. J., Esq., solicitor, Inverness.
Campbell, J. L., Esq., Broughty-Ferry.
Campbell, Mrs. C. Cameron, of Monzie and Inverawe (2 Copies, 1 Large Paper).
Carey, John James, Esq., Rock Bank East, Brixham.
Carruthers, Robert, Esq., of the *Inverness Courier*.
Chisholm, Colin, Esq., Namur Cottage, Inverness.
Clarke, James, Esq., solicitor, Inverness.
Corbet, A. Cameron, Esq., Moxhull Hall, Warwickshire.
Corbet, H. G. Cameron, Esq., Clapton Park, London (Large Paper Copy).
Cran, John, Esq., F.S.A. Scot., Kirkton, Bunchrew.
Davidson, John, Esq., merchant, Inverness.
Douglas & Foulis, Messrs., booksellers, Edinburgh (2 Copies).
Elderton de Coigny, Mrs., Petersburg, Innellan.
Forbes, Duncan, Esq., of Culloden.
Fraser, James, Esq., C.E., Inverness.
Fraser, John, Esq., bookseller, Nairn (2 Copies).
Fraser-Mackintosh, C., Esq., M.P., of Lochardill, Inverness (Large Paper Copy).
Fraser, William, Esq., LL.D., Deputy-keeper of the Records, Edinburgh.
Grant, P., Esq., banker, Fortrose.
Grant, Patrick, Esq. (of Glenmoriston), London.

LIST OF SUBSCRIBERS.

Grant, Mrs. Patrick (late of Ballifeary), Farnborough, Kent.
Kerr, John, Esq., leather merchant, Inverness.
Laird, James, Esq., Charlottetown, Prince Edward Island.
Lovat, The Right Hon. Lord, Beaufort Castle (Large Paper Copy).
Malcolm, Geo., Esq., Craigard, Invergarry.
Melven, James, Esq., bookseller, Inverness (6 Copies).
Mitchell Library, Glasgow.
Macandrew, Provost, Midmills, Inverness.
MacBain, Alex., Esq., M.A., F.S.A. Scot., Raining's School, Inverness.
MacBean, W. Charles, Esq., solicitor, Inverness.
MacCallum, John, Esq., of Millburn, Inverness.
Macdonald, Alex., Esq., timber merchant, Beauly.
Macdonald, Andrew, Esq., solicitor, Inverness (Large Paper Copy).
Macdonald, Angus, Esq., St. Ignatius Mission, U.S.A.
Macdonald, Ewen, Esq., water manager, Inverness.
Macdonald, Harry, Esq., Portree.
Macdonald, John, Esq., The Exchange, Inverness.
Macdonald, John Cameron, Esq., manager of the *Times*, London.
Macdonald, Kenneth, Esq., F.S.A. Scot., Town Clerk, Inverness (Large Paper Copy).
Macdonald, Lachlan, Esq., of Skaebost (Large Paper Copy).
Macdonald, Lieutenant-General W. C. R., C.B., Pall Mall, London.
Mackay, Councillor D. J., Inverness.
Mackay, John, Esq., C.E., Hereford.
Mackay, William, Esq., solicitor, Inverness.
Mackenzie, A. C., Esq., Maryburgh.
Mackenzie, D. H., Esq., Auckland, New Zealand.
Mackenzie, Dr. F. M., Inverness.
Mackenzie, Dr. J., Government House, Madras.
Mackenzie, Gordon, Esq., Civil Service, India.
Mackenzie, John A., Esq., Burgh Surveyor, Inverness.
Mackenzie, John Whitefoord, Esq., W.S. (of Lochwards), Edinburgh.
Mackenzie, Major Colin, F.S.A. Scot., Pall Mall, London.
Mackenzie, N. B., Esq., banker, Fort-William (Large Paper Copy).
Mackenzie, Master Hector Rose, Park House, Inverness.
Mackenzie, Roderick, Esq., Aynott Villa, Wandsworth, London.
Mackenzie, Wm., Esq., merchant, Inverness.
Mackenzie, Wm., Esq., Clarence Villa, Inverness.
Mackintosh, Hugh, Esq. (of Messrs. Mactavish & Mackintosh), Inverness.
MacLachlan & Stewart, Messrs., Edinburgh (2 Copies).
MacLeish, James, Esq., Mill Street, Perth.
MacLeod, Roderick, Esq., Lonsdale Terrace, Edinburgh.
MacNair, David, Esq., Batavia, Java.
Macnee, Dr. James, Inverness.
Macpherson, Colonel Cluny, of Cluny, C.B. (Large Paper Copy).
Macpherson, Hugh, Esq. (of Messrs. Bethune & Macpherson), Inverness.
Mactavish, Alex., Esq. (of Messrs. Mactavish & Mackintosh), Inverness.
Milne, Messrs. A. & R., booksellers, Aberdeen (2 Copies).

Munro, Councillor David, Inverness.
Napier & Ettrick, Right Hon. Lord, K.T., Thirlestane, Selkirk.
Norman, Chas. Loyd, Esq., Oakley, Bromley, Kent.
Paton, Sir Noel, R.S.A., LL.D., Her Majesty's Limner for Scotland.
Reid, Donald, Esq., solicitor, Inverness.
Rose, Mrs., Thistleton House, Stoke Newington, London.
Ross, Alex., Esq., Alness.
Ross, Councillor Alex., Inverness.
Ross, James, Esq., Balbair, Edderton (2 Large Paper Copies).
Ross, James, Esq., solicitor, Inverness.
Ross, Jonathan, Esq., Town Treasurer, Inverness.
Scott, Roderick, Esq., solicitor, Inverness.
Shaw, Sheriff, Thornhill, Inverness.
Sim, Henry A., Esq., Inverness.
Simpson, ex-Provost, Inverness.
Sinton, Rev. Thos., The Manse, Invergarry.
Smart, P. H., Esq., drawing-master, Inverness.
Smith, J. Turnbull, Esq., C.A., Edinburgh.
Smith & Son, Messrs. John, booksellers, Glasgow (2 Copies, 1 Large Paper).
Stevens, B. F., Esq., bookseller, Trafalgar Square, London.
Steuart, James, Esq., Dalkeith Park, Dalkeith.
Stewart, A. G., Esq., merchant, Inverness.
Stodart, R. R., Esq., Lyon Office, Edinburgh.
Stuart, Councillor W. G., Inverness.
Sutherland, Evan C., Esq., of Skibo.
Taylor, The Rev. Duncan, The Manse, Avondale.
Taylor, Mrs. John, Greenhill Gardens, Edinburgh.
Taylor, Professor Campbell, Greenhill Park, Edinburgh.
Taylor, Rev. Neil, F.C. Manse, Dornoch.
Thin, James, Esq., bookseller, Edinburgh (2 Copies).
Trail, Wm. R., Esq., S.S.C., Edinburgh.
Tweedmouth, The Right Hon. Lord (Large Paper Copy).
University Library, Aberdeen.
Whyte, John, librarian, Inverness.
Whyte, Duncan, Esq., Duke Street, Glasgow.
Wilson, John, bookseller, King William Street, London (Large Paper Copy).
Wodehouse, Rev. Constantine G., Mongewell Rectory, Wallingford.

THE HISTORY OF THE CAMERONS.

ORIGIN.

IN an old Manuscript history of this family, printed in *The Memoirs of Sir Ewen Cameron of Lochiel*, the author says —"The Camerons have a tradition among them that they were originally descended of a younger son of the Royal Family of Denmark, who assisted at the restoration of King Fergus II., anno 404. He was called Cameron from his crooked nose, as that word imports. But it is more probable that they were of the aborigines of the ancient Scots or Caledonians that first planted the country." Skene quotes this family Manuscript in his *Highlanders of Scotland*, and agrees with its author that the clan came originally from the ancient inhabitants of the district of Lochaber. He says:—"With this last conclusion I am fully disposed to agree, but John Major has placed the matter beyond a doubt, for in mentioning on one occasion the Clan Chattan and the Clan Cameron, he says, 'Hae tribus sunt consanguineæ'. They, therefore, formed a part of the extensive tribe of Moray, and followed the chief of that race until the tribe became broken up, in consequence of the success of the Mackintoshes in the conflict on the North Inch of Perth, in 1396," after which the Camerons separated themselves from the main stem, and assumed a position of independence. Major further says that "these two tribes are of the same stock, and followed one head of their race as chief". Gregory, who agrees with these authorities, says that the Camerons, as far back as he could trace, had their seat in Lochaber, and appeared to have been first connected with the Macdonalds of Islay, in the reign of Robert Bruce, from whom Angus Og of Isla had a grant of Lochaber. "There is reason to believe," he continues, "that the Clan Cameron and Clan Chattan had a common origin, and for some time followed one chief." They have, however, been separated, according to this author, ever since the middle of the fourteenth century, if not from an earlier date. Alexander Mackintosh-Shaw, in his recently published History of the Mackintoshes, makes a sturdy attempt to upset the authorities here quoted, founding his argument mainly on a difference between the original edition of Major, printed at Paris in 1521, and the Edinburgh edition of 1740. It appears to us, that the ingenious argument used, tends rather to weaken than strengthen the position taken up by this author, and in his "Postscript," written in reply to Skene's views, as set forth in Vol. III., *Celtic Scotland*, he considerably modifies what, in the body of his work, he contended for. In the postscript he says:—" I have no wish to deny the *possibility* that the two clans were connected in their remote origin; all I say is, that no sufficient evidence of such connection has yet appeared, and, therefore, that no writer is justified in affirming the connection as a fact." Compare this with what he writes at p. 129 of the same work, where he says that the original reading of Major, and the considerations suggested by it, "afford very strong evidence that the statements of Mr. Skene as to the community of stock of Clan Chattan and Clan Cameron. . . . are in reality unfounded". Skene too has somewhat modified the opinion published by him, in 1837, in his *Highlanders of Scotland*. In that work he maintained that the famous combat on the North Inch of Perth was fought between the Mackintoshes and the Macphersons, whereas in his later work, *Celtic Scotland*, he comes to the conclusion that the combatants were the Mackintoshes and the Camerons. Thus all the leading authorities are now at one on this long-contested point.

Skene's later conclusions on the subject are important. In his recent work he informs us that when the Royal forces attacked Alexander, Lord of the Isles, in 1429, and defeated him in Lochaber, the two tribes who deserted him and went over to the Royalists were, according to Bower, the "Clan Katan and Clan Cameron"; while Maurice Buchanan gives them, "more correctly, as the Clan de Guyllequhatan and Clan Cameron". On Palm Sunday, being the 20th of March following, the Clan Chattan attacked the Clan Cameron when assembled in a church, to which they set fire, "and nearly destroyed the whole clan". Though it would seem from these statements that all the Camerons and Mackintoshes deserted the Lord of the Isles on that occasion, it is clear that this was not the case, for, after his restoration to liberty, the Hebridean chief, in 1443, granted a charter to Malcolm Mackintosh, of the lands of Keppoch, and, in 1447, conferred upon him the office of Bailie of the Lordship of Lochaber. Ample evidence is forthcoming that the Camerons were by no means totally destroyed, as stated by the chroniclers. "It would thus appear," says Skene, "that a part only of these two clans had deserted the Lord of the Isles in 1429, and a part adhered to him; that the conflict on Palm Sunday was between the former part of these clans, and that the leaders of those who adhered to the Lord of the Isles, became afterwards recognised as captains of the respective clans. It further appears that there was, within no distant time after the conflict on the North Inch of Perth, a bitter feud between the two clans who had deserted the Lord of the Isles, and there are indications that this was merely the renewal of an older quarrel, for both clans undoubtedly contested the right to the lands of Glenlui and Locharkaig in Lochaber, to which William Mackintosh received a charter from the Lord of the Isles in 1336, while they unquestionably afterwards formed a part of the territory possessed by the Camerons. By the later historians, one of the clans who fought on the North Inch of Perth, and who were termed by the earlier chroniclers Clan Qwhele, are identified with the Clan Chattan, and that this identification is well founded, so far as regards that part of the clan which adhered to the Royal cause, while that in the part of the Clan Cameron who followed the same course, and were nearly entirely destroyed on Palm Sunday, we may recognise their opponents the Clan Kay, is not without much probability." This is most likely; and the fact that Skene has found it necessary to depart so far from his earlier theory gives it greater weight, and renders it on the whole pretty conclusive.

The Clan Chattan of modern times who followed Mackintosh as Captain of the clan, consisted of sixteen septs, but the original Clan Chattan was formed of the Clan Mhuirich, or Macphersons, the Clan Daibhidh or Davidsons, "who were called the Old Clan Chattan," and six others, who came under the protection of the clan, namely, the Macgillivrays, the Macbeans, the Clan MhicGovies, the Clan Tarrel, the Clan Cheann-Duibh, and the Sliochd-Gow-chruim or Smiths. The Clan MhicGovies were a branch of the Camerons, while the Smiths were the descendants of the famous *gobha* or smith who took the place of the missing man at Perth in 1396.

On the other hand, the Camerons at that period consisted of four branches or septs, known "as the Clan Gillanfhaigh or Gillonie, or Camerons of Invermalie and Strone; the Clan Soirlie, or Camerons of Glenevis; the Clan Mhic Mhartain, or Macmartins of Letterfinlay; and the Camerons of Lochiel. The latter were the sept whose head became Captain of Clan Cameron and adhered to the Lord of the Isles, while the three former represented the part of the clan who seceded from him in 1429. Besides these, there were dependent septs, the chief of which were the Clan Mhic Gilveil or Macmillans, and these were believed to be of the race of Clan Chattan. The connection between the two clans is thus apparent. Now there are preserved genealogies of both

clans in their earlier forms, written not long after the year
1429. One is termed the 'genealogy of the Clan an Toisig,
that is the Clan Gillechattan,' and it gives it in two separate
lines. The first represented the older Mackintoshes. The
second is deduced from Gillechattan Mor, the eponymus of
the clan. His great grandson Muireach, from whom the
Clan Mhuirich takes its name, had a son Domnall or
Donald, called 'an Caimgilla,' and this word when aspirated
would form the name Kevil or Quhevil. The chief seat of
this branch of the clan can also be ascertained, for Alexander, Lord of the Isles and Earl of Ross, confirms a
charter granted by William, Earl of Ross, in 1338, of the
lands of Dalnafert and Kinrorayth or Kinrara, under
reservation of one acre of ground near the Stychan of the
town of Dalnavert, where was situated the manor of the
late Seayth, son of Ferchard, and we find a 'Tsead, son of
Ferquhar,' in the genealogy at the same period. Moreover,
the grandson of this Seayth was Disiab or Shaw, who thus
was contemporary with the Shaw who fought in 1396.
With regard to the Clan Cameron, the invariable tradition
is, that the head of the Macgillonies or Macgillanaigh led
the clan who fought with the Clan Chattan during the long
feud between them, and the old Genealogy terms the
Camerons Clan Maelanfhaigh, or the race of the servant
of the prophet, and deduces them from a common ancestor,
the Clan Maelanfhaigh and the Clan Camshron, and as the
epithet 'an Caimgilla,' when aspirated, would become
'Kevil,' so the word 'Fhaigh' in its aspirated form would
be represented by the 'Hay' of the chroniclers. John
Major probably gives the clue to the whole transaction,
when he tells us that 'these two clans'—the Clan Chattan
and Clan Cameron, which, as we have seen, had a certain
connection through their dependent septs—'were of one
blood, having but little in lordships, but following one head
of their race as principal, with their kinsman and dependents'. He is apparently describing their position
before these dissensions broke out between them, and his
description refers us back to the period when the two clans

formed one tribe, possessing the district of Lochaber as their Tuath or country, where the lands in dispute—Glenlui and Locharkaig—were probably the official demesne of the 'old Toisech, or head of the tribe'."* The ancient and common origin of the Mackintoshes and Camerons in that of the old Clan Chattan will, it is thought, be now admitted by all whose theories as to the origin of their own families will not be upset or seriously affected by the acknowledgment.

The original possessions of the Camerons were confined to the portion of Lochaber lying on the east side of the Loch and River of Lochy, held of the Lord of the Isles as superior. The more modern possessions of the clan—Lochiel and Locharkaig—lying on the west side of these waters, were at an earlier period granted by the Island lord to Macdonald of Clanranald, by whose descendants they were for many generations inhabited. Skene holds that, as the Clan Cameron is one of those whose chief bore the somewhat doubtful title of Captain, a strong suspicion exists that the Cameron chiefs were of a different branch from the older family, and had, in common with the other families among whom the title of Captain is found, been the oldest cadet, and in that capacity had superseded the elder branch at a period when the latter became reduced in position and circumstances.

The traditionary origin of the Camerons proper, clearly points to the ancient chiefs of the clan, for, continues the same author, "while they are unquestionably of native origin, their tradition derives them from a certain Cambro, a Dane, who is said to have acquired his property with the chiefship of the clan, by marriage with the daughter and heiress of Macmartin of Letterfinlay. The extraordinary identity of all these traditionary tales, wherever the title of Captain is used, leaves little room to doubt that in this case the Macmartins were the old chiefs of the clan, and the Lochiel family were the oldest cadets, whose after-position at the head of the clan gave them the title of Captain of

* *Celtic Scotland*, Vol. III., pp. 313-318.

the Clan Cameron. There is reason to think that, on the acquisition of the Captainship of the Clan Chattan, in 1396, by the Mackintoshes, the Macmartins adhered to the successful faction, while the great body of the clan, with the Camerons of Lochiel, declared themselves independent, and thus the Lochiel family gained that position which they have ever since retained."* It is supposed that another circumstance—the desertion of the Lord of the Isles by the clan at Inverlochy in 1431—helped to raise the leader of the Lochiel Camerons to the chiefship of the whole clan, at a time when the Macmartins, after the victory of the Lord of the Isles, were furiously attacked, and their leader driven to exile in Ireland, while his followers had to take refuge in the more mountainous parts of the Cameron country. The Macmartins were afterwards unable to assume their former position at the head of their house, and Cameron of Lochiel, the oldest cadet of the family, assumed the chiefship of the whole clan, with the title of Captain, and was placed at their head. The leader who is said to have first taken up this distinguished position was the renowned Donald Dubh, from whom the Cameron chiefs take their patronymic of "Mac Dhomh'uill Duibh," and of whom in his proper place.†

---

* *Highlanders of Scotland*, Vol. II., pp. 194, 195.

† The following is a curious traditional account of how the Camerons first came to Lochaber, and of the origin of their name :—

"The first man who was called by the name of Cameron, was much renowned for his feats in arms, and his prodigious strength; a monument of which is still remaining near Achnacarry, the seat of Lochiel; namely, a large stone, of upwards of 500lb. weight, which he could hoist from the ground with a straight arm, and toss it with as much ease, as a man does a cricket-bat; a plough-share he could bend round his leg like a garter; and the strongest ropes were no more in his hands than twine-thread. In short, he seems to have been a second Samson; with this difference only, that our Cameron seems not to have been so easily inveigled by the women as the Jew was, nor did his strength lie in his hair.

"This man of might was so conscious of his strength and prowess, that he thought no man upon earth was a match for him, and accordingly entered the lists with the most famous champions of that age, nor was he afraid to challenge the most renowned of them. In one of their combats, it seems, his antagonist handled him very roughly, and with a violent blow of his fist set his nose awry; for the encounter was accidental, and consequently both were unarmed; for had they fought with swords, he might have hewed it quite off, but this blunt blow only set it on one side; yet so, as that it could never be recovered to its right position. From this accident he was

According to the Manuscript of 1450, which begins the genealogy of the MacGillonie Camerons with Ewen, son of this Donald Dubh, the descent of the early family

always afterwards called Cameron, or, the Knight of the Wry Nose, as that word imports in the Highland language.

"Our hero was now arrived at the 35th year of his age, and had given many signal proofs of his valour, so that his name became terrible all over the country. But having little or no paternal estate, he began to think it highly necessary for him to join himself to some great and powerful family, the better to enable him to distinguish himself more eminently, than it was possible for him to do as a single man, without friends or relations, or at least such as were of little or no account. He had spent his life in the shire of Dumbarton; but as he had no family or inheritance to encumber him, he resolved to try his fortune in the world, and to go in search of a wife. He set out accordingly, and happened to light on that part of the country where Lochiel's estate now lies. Here he informed himself of the character and circumstances of the chief who resided there, and understood that he was a man of a large estate, had a great number of friends and dependents, and withal had a fair and excellent young lady to his daughter. This was a foundation sufficient for our wry-nose knight to build his hopes and future expectations upon. He soon made himself known to the gentleman, whose name was MacTavish, Baron of Straborgig; [? MacMartin, Baron of Letterfinlay] to whom having given an account of himself and his business (for his fame was there before) he was kindly welcomed, and treated with all the civilities imaginable. In short, a bargain was soon struck for the daughter, who was as well pleased as the father with the offer of a husband so much to her liking; for strength of body, vigorous and sinewy limbs, and undaunted courage, were, in those days, the best qualifications to recommend a man to the affections of a lady.

"The Baron of Straborgig was the more willing to marry his daughter to our knight, because by this alliance he should get a brave, bold man to head his people against the clan of MacDonalds of Glengarry, who bordering on the Lochiel estate, there were frequent birkerings and skirmishes between the two clans; for in those days all quarrels and disputes were decided by the strength of the arm, and the edge of the sword. Our knight, whose courage never flinched in the greatest dangers, led on his men boldly, and fought many bloody encounters with the MacDonalds whose chief he challenged to single combat; but MacDonald knowing his antagonist was superior to him in strength, refused, but fought it out with him in a pitched battle, in which however he was worsted, and great numbers of his people slain; and finding himself much weakened, and his clan greatly diminished since the Knight of the Wry-nose became his enemy, he proposed a compromise between the two families; which was agreed to, and the chiefs on both sides met (each attended with a numerous retinue, to prevent surprise) in a certain meadow that lay, as it were, between both estates, and which both laid a claim to. Here the matters in difference were solemnly and amicably debated; and at length the parties came to this conclusion: That MacDonald should, for him and his heirs, for ever renounce all his claim and pretence of right to such a certain district, containing about 500 acres of land, with all the royalties, privileges, and prerogatives thereunto belonging and appertaining, the contending for which had occasioned innumerable feuds and quarrels, and the effusion of a great deal of innocent blood; this he solemnly assigned and made over to the Knight of the Wry-nose, and his heirs for ever. This is the story which the Highland Bards have recorded of this great progenitor of the Camerons; and these are the means, they tell us, by which he got possession of an estate worth £100 a year."—*Life of Dr. Archibald Cameron:* London, 1753.

chiefs extends back from Donald's son in the following order:—" Ewen, son of Donald Dubh, son of Allan Millony, son of Paul, son of Gillepatrick, son of Gillemartan, son of Paul, son of Millony, son of Gilleroth,* from whom descended the Clan Cameron and Clan Millony; son of Gillemartan Og, son of Gilleniorgan, son of Gillemartan Mor, son of Gilleewen, son of Gillepaul, son of Eacada, son of Gartnaid, son of Digail, son of Poulacin, son of Art, son of Angus Mor, son of Erc, son of Telt."† This genealogy clearly refers to the "Maelanfhaigh" or Macgillonie branch of the family, and it begins with Ewen, second son of Donald Dubh, who thus appears to be the progenitor of the Macgillonie or Camerons of Strone; while Allan, the eldest son, succeeded his father Donald, and carried on the Lochiel-Cameron line of succession, which we shall now proceed to trace from its source, so far as possible with the materials at our command.

The name Cameron in ancient times was variously written, in such forms as Cameron, Cambron, Cambrun. The first of which we find any trace is,

I. ANGUS,

Who married Marion, daughter of Kenneth, thane of Lochaber, and sister of Bancho, a fact which amply proves that Angus was a person of rank and dignity, even at that early period; for Bancho, in addition to his position as a Royal Prince, was governor of one of the largest Provinces in the Kingdom, Lochaber being said to comprehend, at that time, all the lands between the River Spey and the Western Sea. Angus is alleged to have been instrumental in saving Fleance the son of Bancho, his own lady's nephew, from the cruelty of Macbeth, and to have been

---

* Skene says in a foot-note, Vol. III., *Celtic Scotland*, p. 480, "This is the Gilleroth mentioned by Fordun in 1222 as a follower of Macohecan in his insurrection, along with whom he witnesses a charter as Gilleroth, son of Gillemartan".

† Translated by Skene, and printed with the Gaelic original in *Celtic Scotland*, Vol. III., p. 480.

rewarded and highly esteemed on that account. He was succeeded by his eldest son,

II. GILLESPICK OR ARCHIBALD,

Who joined the loyalists and assisted in the restoration of Malcolm Ceanmore in 1057. For this service he was, according to the family historian, raised with many others to the dignity of a "Lord Baron," on the 25th of April in that year; but such dignities it seems were not hereditary in Scotland in those days, but ended with the lives of those on whom they were conferred, though, in many cases, they were renewed to their sons. This does not appear to have happened in the case of the Camerons, and the dignity died with its first possessor. He was succeeded by his eldest son,*

III. JOHN CAMERON,

Said to have lived in the reign of King David I., but nothing further is known regarding him. He was succeeded by his son,

IV. ROBERT CAMERON.

In a donation to the Monastery of Cambuskenneth, before 1200, in the reign of William the Lyon, Henry, Archdean of Dunkeld; Alexander, Sheriff of Stirling; Henry de Lamberton; and this Robert "Cambron," are found witnesses. He died early in the reign of Alexander II., leaving issue—

1. John, his heir and successor.
2. Robert de Cambron, whose name is mentioned with that of his brother in the Chartulary of Scoon in 1239, and is said by some, but, we think, erroneously, to have been the progenitor of the Camerons of Strone.
3. Hugo, or Hugh, or Ewen de Cambron, mentioned in the Chartulary of Arbroath in 1219, of whose posterity nothing is known.

---

* He is said to have had a second son, Angus, who had a son, Martin, from whom the Macmartins of Letterfinlay sprung. This, however, is not consistent with what has been already stated.

Robert Cameron was succeeded by his eldest son,

V. SIR JOHN DE CAMERON,

Who, as John de Cambrun, is witness to a donation in favour of the Religious House at Scoon in 1234, with Walter, son of Alan, Lord High Steward and Justiciar of Scotland; Walter Cumin, Earl of Menteith; Adam de Logan, John de Haya, and his own brother, Robert de Cambrun. He is also mentioned in connection with some marches, in the Diocese of Aberdeen, in 1233; and in 1250 he is found designed "Johannes de Cambrun, Miles," etc. He had two sons—

1. Robert, his heir and successor.

2, John, mentioned in Pryme's Collections, in 1296. He is alleged to have been progenitor of the Camerons of Glenevis, though others maintain, with more probability, that they were originally Macdonalds. Sir John died in the reign of Alexander II., and was succeeded by his eldest son,

VI. SIR ROBERT DE CAMERON,

One of those who made their submission to Edward I. of England. He is twice mentioned in Pryme's collections, first as *dominus Robertus de Cambrun*, Miles, and afterwards, in 1296, *Robertus de Cambrun*, Chevalier. He was succeeded by his son,

VII. JOHN DE CAMERON,

Who made a great figure in the reign of King Robert Bruce, in whose time the clan appears to have been numerous in Lochaber. He was one of the Highland chiefs who signed the famous letter to the Pope by the Scottish Nobility in 1320, in which they plead for the king's title to the Scottish Crown and for the Independence of Scotland. He was succeeded by his son,

VIII. JOHN DE CAMERON,

Also known as "John Ochtery". He joined David II. with a considerable body of his followers, whom he commanded in the third Division of the Scots army, at the battle of Hallidon Hill, on the 15th of July, 1333. He continued in the king's service until the English were expelled from the kingdom, and the king firmly settled in the government of Scotland.*

He married Ellen de Montealto, or Mouat,† with issue—

IX. ALLAN CAMERON,

Commonly known among his countrymen as "Allan MacOchtery," which some writers have rendered "Allan MacUchtred". This does not, however, appear to have any meaning, for no such name as Uchtred turns up before or after, so far as we can find, in the whole Genealogy of the clan. A much more likely origin will be found in the suggestion that the name means Allan "MacOchdamh Triath," or Allan son of the Eighth chief. According to the family Genealogy given here, and in the *Baronage*, where two Johns are given in succession immediately before this Allan,

---

* The only chiefs prior to this period named in the Family MS. are the first two and the last, Angus, Gillespick, and John. The others are given in Wood's edition of Douglas's *Baronage*, where at this point two Johns are given in succession. The acts ascribed to the two Johns of Douglas's *Baronage* are ascribed to one John in the Family MS. We have followed the former. It is, however, quite impossible to secure certainty on a genealogical question so remote in the case of any of our Highland clans. Referring to these discrepancies, the Editor of the "Memoirs" says that he "has been informed by one of the highest authorities on these subjects, that the earlier generations contained in Douglas's *Baronage*, when not fabulous, were not of the Locheill family, but belonged to the family of Camerons of Balligarnoch, in Perthshire, and that the founder of the Locheill branch was Donald Dubh MacAllan," the sixth chief, according to the Memoirs. "It ought, however, to be observed," he continues, "that although the author evidently labours under the impression that the first were of the Locheill branch, yet he merely asserts that they were the principal men of the name of Cameron of whom he could find any mention in history." A John Cameron is mentioned in a document, dated 10th of March, 1233, printed by Mr. Charles Fraser-Mackintosh, p. 24 of his *Invernessiana*, and, at p. 44 of the same work, Robert de Chambroun de Balgligernaucht (? Baligarny) is mentioned in a document, dated the 16th of December, 1292, by which the king grants him a pension of 50 merks, payable by the burgesses of Inverness.

† The Earl of Mar, about 1357, granted a charter, witnessed by Sir John le Grant, to John Cameron, conveying to him and Ellen de Montealto, or Mouat, his wife, in free marriage, certain lands in Strathdon.—*Antiquities of Aberdeen and Banff*, Vol. IV., p. 158. Also, *The Chiefs of Grant*, by William Fraser, LL.D., 1883, Vol. I., p. 42.

such a designation would be strictly accurate. Its value will at once be seen by those who understand Gaelic; and it certainly supports the Genealogy which gives two chiefs named John. Allan's reign was of a most turbulent character. In his time began the feuds between the Camerons and the Mackintoshes, which continued more or less inveterate for many generations after, and were only finally settled towards the end of the seventeenth century.

There are various versions current, mostly traditional, of the origin of the long-continued and bitter feuds between these two powerful families. One will be found in the *Celtic Magazine*, Vol. V., pp. 284-86, contributed by the late Patrick Macgregor, M.A., Toronto, a native of Badenoch, well acquainted with the folk-lore of the district. Others are more or less known, but the following is the most recent, and probably the most accurate.— By the marriage of Eva, only child of Dougal Dall MacGilleCattan, chief of the ancient Clan Chattan, to Angus, sixth chief of Mackintosh, in 1291, when he obtained with her, if not the headship of the clan (a question still hotly disputed), at least the lands of her father, comprising those of Glenlui and Loch Arkaig, in Lochaber. The Mackintoshes, however, do not appear to have possessed these lands at this period for any length of time, for Angus, who is said to have lived in Glenlui with his wife for a few years after his marriage, is soon an exile from his home, he having had to flee from the Lord of Isla, to Badenoch. The lands, thus becoming vacant, were occupied by the Camerons, who continued in them for some years without disturbance. William Mackintosh, the son of Angus and Eva, on attaining his majority, demanded the lands in question, and, according to one of the Mackintosh MSS., obtained, in 1337, from John of Isla, a right to the lands of Glenlui and Loch Arkaig. This right being disputed by the Camerons, Mackintosh appealed to the sword, and a great battle was fought at Drumlui, in which the Mackintoshes defeated the Camerons under Donald Alin Mhic Evin Mhic Evin. This engagement was followed by others, each clan alternately carrying the war into its opponent's country, harrying each other's lands and lifting cattle, until we finally arrive at the famous battle of Invernahavon, referred to by Mr. Mackintosh-Shaw as follows :—In 1370, according to the Mackintosh MSS.—or, as others have it, sixteen years later—the Camerons, to the number of about four hundred, made a raid into Badenoch, and were returning home with the booty they had acquired, when they were overtaken at Invernahavon by a body of the Clan Chattan led by Mackintosh in person. Although outnumbering their opponents, the Clan Chattan well-nigh experienced a signal defeat in the engagement which took place, owing to a dispute such as that which in after years contributed largely to the disaster at Culloden—a dispute as to precedence. Mackintosh was accompanied by Macpherson, head of the Clan Mhuirich, and MacDhaibhidh or Davidson of Invernahavon, with their respective septs ; and between these two chieftains a difference arose as to which of them should have command of the right wing, the post of honour. It is said that Macpherson claimed it as being the male representative of the old chiefs of the clan, while Davidson contended that, by the custom of the clans, the honour should be his, as being the oldest cadet, the representative of the oldest surviving *branch*. Taking the literal application of the custom, Davidson's claim was perhaps justifiable ; but the case was peculiar, inasmuch as Macpherson, his senior in the clan, did not hold the actual position of chief. As neither party would give way, the dispute was referred to Mackintosh, who decided in favour of Davidson, thus unfortunately offending the Clan Mhuirich, who withdrew in disgust. By awarding the command to either chieftain, Mackintosh would doubtless have given offence to the other ; but his decision against the claims of Macpherson, besides being somewhat unjust, was highly imprudent, as the Macphersons were more numerous than the Mackintoshes and the Davidsons together, and without them Mackintosh's force was inferior to that of the Camerons. The battle resulted in the total defeat of the Mackintoshes and Davidsons, the latter being almost entirely cut off. But the honour of Clan Chattan was redeemed by the Macphersons, who, generously forgetting for the time the slight that had been put upon them, and, remembering only that those who had offended them were their brother-clansmen and in distress, attacked the Camerons with such vigour that they soon changed their victory into defeat and put them to flight. The fugitives are said to have taken their flight towards Drumouchter, skirting the end of Loch-Ericht, and then turning westwards in the direction of the River Treig. According to the Rev. L. Shaw, the leader of the Camerons was Charles MacGilony, who was killed; but this is contrary to the tradition of the locality, which states that "MacDhomhnuil Duibh," the chief, commanded in person.* Charles MacGilony figures prominently in this tradition as an important man among the Camerons, and a famous archer.†

The author of *The Memoirs of Lochiel* gives the Mackintosh version of the battle. He questions their title to the disputed lands in Lochaber, and says that the Camerons considered their title so good that they fought for it "from generation to generation almost to the utter ruine of both familys". He then proceeds:—"If the Camerons had any other right to the estate in question but simple possession, I know not. All I can say of the matter is, that very few, especially in these parts, could allege a better at that time. The Mackintoshes, however, pretend that, besides the story of the marriage, they had a charter or patent to those lands from the Lord of the Isles in Anno 1337, and that it was confirmed by King David II. in February, 1359. But the Camerons, it would seem, had little regard to these rights; for, in 1370, they invaded the Mackintoshes, and having carried away a great booty of cattle, and such other goods as fell in their way, they were

---

* Domhnull Dubh was not born for years after the date of this battle, and, of course, neither his son nor himself could have been present on this occasion.

† *History of the Mackintoshes and Clan Chattan*, by Alexander Mackintosh-Shaw.

pursued and overtaken at a place called Invernahavon, by Lachlan, then Laird of Macintosh, who was routed, and who had a whole branch of his clan, called the Clan Day, cut off to a man. That unhappy tribe paid dear for the honour they had in being preferred that day to the van of the battle, in opposition to the Macphersons, who claimed it, and so far resented the injury which they thought was done them, that they would not engage at all. But Mackintosh, having something of a poetical genius, composed certain ridiculous rhymes, which he gave out were made in derision of their [the Macphersons] cowardice by the Camerons, and thereby irritated them to such a degree of fury against them, that they returned next morning, attacked and defeated them, while they were buried in sleep and security after their late victory."*

This sanguinary conflict must have made a deep impression on those engaged in it, and it may fairly be assumed, when the state of society at that remote period is taken into account, that the old enmity and the feuds between the Camerons and the Mackintoshes would be largely intensified, and become the cause of great slaughter, plunder, and annoyance, throughout a considerable portion of the Central and Western Highlands. This state of affairs naturally led up to the famous combat on the North

---

* This version of the cause that roused the Macphersons to action is given *in extenso* in *Cuairtear nan Gleann*, Vol. III., p. 331. Donald Mackintosh, in his *Collection of Gaelic Proverbs*, published in 1785, explaining one of the well-known proverbs to which the combat on the Inch of Perth gave rise, says :—

"Mackintosh, being irritated and disappointed by this behaviour of the Macphersons, on the night following, sent his own bard to the camp of the Macphersons, as if he had come from the Camerons to provoke them to fight, which he accomplished by repeating the following satirical lines :—

'Tha luchd na foille air an tom,
Is am Balg-shuileach donn na dhraip ;
Cha b' e bhur cairdeas ruinn a bh'ann
Ach bhur lamh a bhi tais.'

i.e.—'The false party are on the field, beholding the chief in danger ; it was not your love to us that made you abstain from fighting, but merely your own cowardice'.

"This reproach so stung Macpherson that, calling up his men, he attacked the Camerons that same night in their camp, and made a dreadful slaughter of them, pursued them to the foot of Binn-imhais, and killed their chief, Charles Macgilony, at a place called Coire Thearlaich, *i.e.*, Charles's Valley."

Inch at Perth, where, there is little difficulty now in concluding, the Camerons and the Mackintoshes were the contending parties.*

Allan married a daughter of Drummond of Stobhall, ancestor of the Earls of Perth and Melfort, whose sister, Annabella, was Queen of Robert III., and mother to James I. By her he had three sons—

1. Ewen, who succeeded his father.

2. Donald, who succeeded his brother Ewen, and was afterwards known as the famous Donald Dubh.

3. John, Archbishop of Glasgow, described as "a gentleman of great learning and a profound statesman". He was Chancellor of Scotland and First Minister of James I. "The offices of honour and trust that his wise and learned sovereign was pleased to confer upon him," says Drummond, "are sufficient testimonies of his genius and character, for as he was a prince of the greatest abilities of any in that age, so he directed all his views to the civilising of his country, and to the improvement of religion, learning and arts ; and as he was a great judge of men, he employed none but such as answered his ends of government. All this, though there were no other documents extant, as indeed there are many, makes it surprising that Buchanan, the most polite and elegant of all modern writers, should brand this prelate with a character the most vicious and odious that ever stained the mitre. He calls him a wretch so abandoned to his insatiable avarice that he oppressed and pillaged his tenants and vassals by all the barbarous ways of injustice and extortion ; and he adds that the Divine vengeance overtook him in a manner fitter to be repeated by John Knox and his disciples, than by a historian of his rank and character." There is a tradition that he once visited Lochaber, when, with Lochiel, he called upon young John Cameron, who then had charge of Callart. John pleased his visitors so well that the Bishop suggested to

* For an exhaustive, and, in our opinion, conclusive discussion of this point, see *The Clan Battle at Perth*, in 1396, by Alexander Mackintosh-Shaw : printed for private circulation, 1874.

Lochiel that the lands should be granted to him who, then, only had charge of them. The chief, his brother, agreed, but next morning on viewing the lands again, he seems to have regretted his generous act of the previous day, for he was overheard to say, "*Call orts* an diugh, Alein," "You have a loss to-day, Allan;" and the property, it is alleged, has ever since been called "Call-orts," or Callort, from that expression of regret.

Alexander Nisbet, in a very rare work, gives the following particulars of him. It will be seen that he erroneously states that he was descended from the Camerons of Perthshire:—"The Seal of John, Bishop of Glasgow, had the image of St. Mungo standing in a portico of the church, and below his feet the shield of arms of that prelate, charged with three bars, to shew he was of the name of Cameron, which was also timbred with a Mitre, and at the sides of the shield were two salmons with rings in their mouths; and the legend round the seal, *Sigillum Joannis Episcopi Glasguen.* [Fig. 10. Plate 2.] * And the same arms are cut in stone with a salmon below the shield, which are to be seen on the vestry of the church of Glasgow, which that Bishop built. He was descended of the Camerons of Perthshire, being educated to the Church, and put into orders, and for his learning preferred to be Provost of the Collegiat Church of Lincluden, and being qualified for a higher employment, was immediately upon the return of King James I. made Secretary to that prince, and keeper of the Privy Seal; in which station, having, no doubt, served that prince with great fidelity, in 1425, he promoted him to the Episcopal see of Glasgow, and to be Lord Chancellor of Scotland, in which high offices he continued till the death of the king, anno 1437, which he himself survived nine years, and was a great benefactor to the Church of Glasgow. He died anno 1446. Mr. George Buchanan, and Bishop Spotiswood copying from Buchanan, say, that Bishop Cameron made a very fearful exit, and endeavours to give the world a very

---

* This plate is shown opposite p. 88 of the work quoted from.

ill character of him ; but 'tis with the greatest difficulty I can believe he was such a man as they represent him, in regard our excellent king James I. who was a very good judge of men, employed him immediately in his service and conferred the highest office in the State upon him, as well as the second place in the Church, which we may very reasonably suppose, from his long continuance in both, he filled with eminent efficiency ; and the Cartulary of Glasgow, where there is a pretty exact account of the *obits* of the Bishops of that see, do not make mention of any such dismal end of the Bishop, as my friend Mr. Crawford informed me, upon his perusal of the obituary of the Metropolitan see of Glasgow, a more full account of which, and of Bishop Cameron, I have seen in a manuscript in his hands composed by himself, entitled, *Reliquiae sancti Quintigerni.*" *

Some very definite and authentic information regarding the Bishop is also given in the *Scotichronicon*, where we are told that he was of the family of Lochiel, and that he was the first Official of Lothian, in 1422. He afterwards became Confessor and Secretary to the Earl of Douglas, who presented him to the Rectory of Cambuslang. He was Provost of Lincluden in 1424 ; and " Magistro Joanne Cameron " is " Secretario regis " in the same year. He is Keeper of the Great Seal on the 25th of February and 7th of March 1425, and also in 1425-6. On February the 25th and 15th of May "an. reg. 20" he is also Provost of Lincluden and Keeper of the Privy Seal, and so he is in 1436. He is also Provost of Lincluden, and Secretary in the twenty-first year of James I. In 1426, he was elected Bishop of Glasgow ; and he is " electo et confirmato episcopo Glasguensi, et priv. sigilli custode," in 1426. He is also Bishop of this See, and Lord Chancellor, in the twenty-fourth year of King James I.; in 1428, and in 1430. In 1429, he erected six churches, within his diocese, by consent of their re-

---

* *An Essay on the Ancient and Modern Use of Armories, by Alexander Nisbet, Gent, Edinburgh : Printed by William Adams, Junior, for Mr. James MacEuen, and sold at his shop opposite to the Cross-Well. Anno DOM. MDCCXVIII.*

spective Patrons, into Prebends, the title of which erection, as contained in the *Cart. Glasg.*, is thus stated—" Erectio sex ecclesiarum parochialum in prebendas ecclesiae Glasg. facta per Joannem Cameron episcopum Glasguensem". These six churches were, Cambuslang, Torbolton, Eaglesham, Luss, Kirkmaho, and Killearn. He also fixed particular offices to particular churches, such as the Rector of Cambuslang to be perpetual Chancellor of the Church of Glasgow, the Rector of Carnwarth to be Treasurer, the Rector of Kilbride to be Chantor, etc. In 1433, he was chosen one of the Delegates from the Church of Scotland to the Council of Basil; and he accordingly set out, with a safe-conduct from the king of England, accompanied by a retinue of no less than thirty persons. And, as the Truce with England was near a close on November 30, 1437, Mr. Rymer published another safe-conduct for Ambassadors from Scotland to come into England about a Prorogation of the Peace, and the first named in it is John, Bishop of Glasgow, Chancellor of Scotland. He was Bishop of Glasgow in 1439, in 1440, and Bishop and Chancellor "anno 3tio regis Jacobi II." He is mentioned in Charters of Donation and Confirmation of the Collegiate Church of Corstorphin, founded by the Knights Forrester, 1429-44. It is thus evident, from the clearest testimony, that he remained Chancellor for the first three years of the reign of king James II., contrary to what all our historians have written of him, and this affords a strong presumption that the story concerning his tragical end is untrue. After the bishop's removal from the office of Chancellor, being then freed from public business, he began to build the great tower at his Episcopal Palace in the City of Glasgow, where his Coat-Armorial is to be seen to this day, with Mitre, Crozier, and Badges. The author of *Lives of the Officers of State*, says that he also laid out a great deal of money in carrying on the building of the Vestry, which was begun by his predecessor, Bishop Lauder, where his Arms are also to be seen. "But for all the good things Bishop Cameron did, and, which is strange," adds this writer, "he is as little beholden to the charity of our historians as any man in his time. The learned Mr. George Buchanan, and the Right Rev. Archbishop Spottiswood, from Mr. George, characterize the Bishop to have been a very worldly kind of man, and a great oppressor, especially of his vassals within the Bishopric. They tell us, moreover, that he made a very fearful exit at his country seat of Lochwood, five or six miles North-East of the City of Glasgow, on Christmas Eve of the year 1446;" and then our author says—" Indeed it is very hard for me, though I have no particular attachment to Bishop Cameron, to form such a bad opinion of the man from what good things I have seen done by him, and withal, considering how much he was favoured and employed by the best of princes—I mean king James II.—and for so long a time, too, in the first Office of the State, and in the second place in the Church, especially since good Mr. Buchanan brings no voucher to prove his assertion ; only," he says, "it had been delivered by others, and constantly affirmed to be true, which amounts to be no more, in my humble opinion, than that he sets down the story upon no better authority than a mere hearsay."* This finding may now be held as conclusive. The following extract is from the *Short Chronicle of the Reign of James II.*—" Ane thousand CCCCXLVI, thar decessit in the Castall of Glasgow, Master Jhon Cameron, Bischope of Glasgow, upon Yule ewyne, that was Bischope XIX yer." No more need be said.

Allan is said to have died in the reign of Robert III. (1390-1406), when he was succeeded by his eldest son,

X. EWEN CAMERON,

In whose time the famous combat on the Inch of Perth, between thirty picked warriors of his own clan and thirty of the Clan Mackintosh, was fought. The author of the "Memoirs" states, in a footnote to his sketch of Allan

---

*Ecclesiastical Chronicle for Scotland, by Dr. J. F. S. Gordon, Vol II., pp. 498-500. 1867.

MacOchtery, referring to this combat, that the "dun, happened in the time of Ewen his (Allan's) son, though misplaced by mistake" in the text, by himself. All that could be said of this sanguinary engagement is already so well known that little more need be detailed regarding it; but the Cameron version may be given as it appears in the Memoirs of Sir Ewen. Referring to the conflict at Invernahavon, which had in the end proved so disastrous to his clansmen, that author says:—The Camerons did not long delay to avenge themselves on their enemies, and, in a word, their conflicts were so frequent, and at the same time so fierce and bloody, that they made no small noise at Court; for the parties, besides their own strength, had many friends and allies that joined; so that they often brought considerable armies to the field.

Robert the Third then sat upon the throne. He was a prince of a mild and peaceable temper, and so valetudinary that he was obliged to manage all his affairs by his Ministers. His brother, the Duke of Albany, an active and intelligent prince, governed at Court; and two of his nobility, Thomas Dunbar Earl of March, and James Lindsay Earl of Crawford, commanded his troops. These two Generals were sent to the Highlands to settle these commotions, but finding that they could not execute their orders by force, without risking the loss of their army, they endeavoured to bring the rival chiefs to some reasonable terms of agreement; and after many overtures they fell upon a proposal that was very agreeable to both. It was in a word thus: that thirty of each side should fight before the king and court without any other arms but their swords, and that the party that should happen to be defeated should have an indemnity for all past offences; and that the conquerors, besides the estate in dispute, should be honoured with the royal favour. By this method, continued they, the plea will be determined in a manner that will testify submission and loyalty to the crown, and give the world a lasting proof of the courage and bravery of both parties.

Pursuant to this treaty, both the chiefs appeared at Court, and all preliminaries being adjusted, the king ordered a part of the North Inch, or plain, upon the banks of the river, near the City of Perth, to be enclosed with a deep ditch, in the form of an amphitheatre, with seats or benches for the spectators, his Majesty himself sitting as judge of the field.

The fame of the extraordinary combat soon spreading over the kingdom drew infinite crowds from all parts to witness so memorable an event. The combatants appeared resolute and fearless, but, when they were just ready to engage, one of the Mackintoshes, who had withdrawn himself from fear, was amissing; whereupon the king demanded that one of the Camerons should be removed, but all of them expressing a great unwillingness to be exempted, one of the spectators, named Henry Wynd, a saddler and citizen of Perth, presented himself before the king, and offered to supply the place of the absent coward on condition that, if his party came off victorious, he should have a French crown of gold for his reward.*

---

* Donald Mackintosh, already quoted, and who erroneously asserts that the combat was between the Macphersons and the Davidsons, gives the following version :—

"The day appointed being come, both parties appeared, but upon mustering the combatants, the Macphersons wanted one of their number, he having fallen sick. It was proposed to balance the difference by withdrawing one of the Davidsons, but so resolved were they upon conquering their opponents, that not one would be prevailed upon to quit the danger. In this emergency, one Henry Wynd, a foundling, brought up in an hospital at Perth, commonly called an Gobh Crom, *i.e.*, the Crooked Smith, offered to supply the sick man's place for a French crown of gold, about three half-crowns sterling money, a great sum in those days. Everything being now settled, the combatants began with incredible fury, and the Crooked Smith, being an able swordsman, contributed much to the honour of the day; victory declaring for the Macphersons, of whom only ten, besides the Gobh Crom, were left alive, and all dangerously wounded. The Davidsons were all cut off, except one man, who, remaining unhurt, threw himself into the Tay, and escaped. Henry Wynd set out from Perth, after the battle, with a horse load of his effects, and swore he would not take up his habitation till his load fell, which happened in Strathdon, in Aberdeenshire, where he took up his residence. The place is still called, Leac 'ic a Ghobhain, *i.e.*, the Smith's Dwelling. The Smiths or Gows, and Macglashans, are commonly called Sliochd a Ghobh Chruim, *i.e.*, the descendants of the Crooked Smith, but all agree that he had no posterity, though he had many followers of the first rank, to the number of twelve, who were proud of being reputed the children of so valiant a man; and the more to ingratiate themselves in his favour, they generally learned to make swords, as well as to use them, which

The parties being now equal, to it they fell, and fought, with all the rage and fury that hatred, revenge, and an insatiable thirst of glory could inspire into the breasts of the fiercest of mankind. Like lions and tigers they tore and butchered one another, without any regard to their own safety, and the reader will find it easier to imagine than to express the various passions that agitated the breasts of the spectators in the different scenes of so bloody a tragedy. The king, a good natured prince, was seized with an inexpressible horror; nor was there any present who was not shocked at the cruel spectacle. But it was observed that Henry Wynd distinguished himself above all others during this furious conflict; as he was not spirited and disordered by the same passions as the rest of the party, so he employed his strength and directed his courage with more discretion and play; and to his conduct it was principally ascribed that they at last had the advantage of their antagonists. Four of the Mackintoshes survived the battle, but they were mortally wounded, and only one of the Camerons escaped, who, having the good fortune to remain unhurt, had the address to save himself by swimming the river Tay; nor were the miserable victors in a condition to prevent him. The brave mercenary, Henry Wynd, likewise survived, without so much as a scratch on his body. His valour is still famous among his countrymen, and gave rise to a proverb, which is commonly repeated when any third person unnecessarily engages

occasioned their being called Gow, *i.e.*, Smith. His twelve apprentices spread themselves all over the Kingdom. Most of them took the name of Mackintosh; those who write otherwise own their descent from them, though many of them are Macphersons, etc.

"Smith of Ballvarry's motto, 'Caraid ann am feum,' *i.e.*, 'A friend in need,' seems to allude to the Gobh Crom's assisting the Macphersons on the above occasion. As soon as the Gobh Crom had killed a man he sat down to rest, and being perceived by the Captain, he demanded the reason. The other answered that he had performed his engagement, and done enough for his wages. The captain replied that no wages would be counted to him; he should have an equivalent for his valour; upon which he immediately got up to fight, and repeated the saying—
'*Am fear nach cunntadh rium cha chunntainn ris*'."

\self in the quarrels of others—" He comes in like Çnry Wynd, for his own hand ".*

Such was the issue of this memorable combat, which, though it did not put an end to the difference betwixt the rival clans, yet, the most fierce and turbulent among them having been destroyed, it suspended the effects of their difference for years after.†

Ewen Cameron was constantly engaged in local feuds and skirmishes. On one occasion he fought a duel in vindication of the honour of an injured lady, who, in return, celebrated his gallantry and valour in a beautiful Gaelic song, "still sung," says our author, "with pleasure by his posterity".

He was succeeded by his brother,

XI. DONALD CAMERON,

Famous among the Highlanders as *Domhnull Dubh Mac-Alein*, or Black Donald, son of Allan,—and from whom the chief of the clan takes his patronymic of "Mac-Dhomh'uill Duibh,"—at a turbulent period in the history of the Highlands. He was out with Donald, second Lord of the Isles, at the battle of Harlaw, in 1411, where

---

* Mr. Mackintosh-Shaw informs us that the Mackintosh MS. History says that the absentee on their side was seized with sickness shortly before the fight—"a not unlikely occurrence, considering the temptations which a Capital would offer to a semi-barbarous Gael". This is a very natural suggestion for a Mackintosh to make, but both Bowar and Lesly agree with the Cameron chronicler that the absentee Mackintosh became "faint-hearted," and was amissing "for fear". In reference to the after history of Henry Wynd, Mr. Shaw says that "tradition has a pleasing record that this man accompanied the remnant of the Clan Chattan champions to their country, was adopted into their clan, and became the progenitor of a family, afterwards known as *Sliochd a Ghobha Chruim* (the race of the Crooked Smith). This record is far from incredible, more especially as Bowar represents the Smith of Perth as stipulating for his subsequent maintenance if he should leave the field alive. Strathavon is said to have been the place where he took up his abode, and here as well as in the neighbouring localities, his reputed descendants have long flourished, and are still to be found. The Smiths or Gows generally appear among the septs of which the Clan Chattan of more modern times was composed, and which acknowledged the chief of Mackintosh as their chief and captain. Some families of the name of Smith have the motto, *Marte et ingenio*, which is peculiarly appropriate, if any of those bearing it are descendants of the renowned Smith of Perth."—*The Clan Battle at Perth*, pp. 16, 17.

† *Memoirs of Lochiel*, Author's Introduction, pp. 10-12.

many of his followers were slain. He joined Alexander, the third Lord of the Isles, in 1429, when the Island lord, on the head of a large force, burnt and pillaged the town of Inverness, and then retired, with his followers, to Lochaber, where he was met by king James in person, commanding a powerful body of royalists, who, taking the Lord of the Isles unexpectedly, routed his followers. On the appearance of the king, the Camerons and the Mackintoshes deserted the Lord of the Isles and joined the royalists; whereupon the Island chief sued for peace, and shortly after came to terms with the king. His friends, however, did not forgive the Camerons for deserting him and going over to the king at Lochaber, and Donald Balloch ultimately took full revenge upon the clan, compelling them to escape to their mountain fastnesses, and obliging their chief to flee for safety to Ireland, where he remained for several years; while in his absence, his lands of Lochaber, of which the Lord of the Isles was superior, were bestowed upon John Garve Maclean, progenitor and founder of the Macleans of Coll.* Domhnull Dubh, however, after a time, returned and drove the Macleans out of the district, killing their young chief, John Abrach (so called from his residence in Lochaber), who disputed the possession with him.†

Gregory, referring to these proceedings, states that John, Earl of Ross, granted the same lands at a later period to John Maclean of Lochbuy, and again to Celestine, Lord of Lochalsh. "It is natural," he says, " to suppose that the Clancameron, the actual occupants of Lochiel, would resist these various claims; and we know that John Maclean, second Laird of Coll, having held the estate for a time by force, was at length killed by the Camerons in Lochaber, which checked for a time the pretensions of the Clan Gillean. But as the whole of that powerful tribe were

---

* For a full account of the proceedings at Harlaw, Inverness, and Lochaber, see *The History of the Macdonalds and Lords of the Isles*, by the same author, pp. 60 to 87.

† Seannachie's *History of the Macleans*, p. 306. Skene calls Maclean "Ewen".

were involved in the feud—some from a desire to revenge the death of Coll, others from their obligations to support the claims of Lochbuy—the chief of the Camerons was forced to strengthen himself by acknowledging the claim of the Lord of Lochalsh [to whom the Earl of Ross had given the Cameron lands after he granted them to Maclean.] The latter [Lochalsh] immediately received Cameron as his vassal in Lochiel, and thus became bound to maintain him in possession against all who pretended to dispute his right to the estate."* The Macgillonies, curiously enough, supported the Macleans against the rest of the Camerons on this occasion. For this they suffered severely afterwards, but ultimately became reconciled to their immediate friends, and they almost all adopted the name of Cameron.

The lands of Lochiel were, according to the best authorities, " probably included in those of Louchabre in the grant of the Earldom of Moray by king Robert Bruce to Thomas Randulph, between 1307 and 1314. In the year 1372, or 1373, king Robert II. confirmed a grant by John of Yle to Reginald of Yle his son of 60 marklands in Lochabre, including Loche and Kylmald (apparently Lochiel and Kilmallie). In 1461, John of Yle, Earl of Ross and Lord of the Isles, granted to his kinsman John the son of Murdac M'Gilleoin of Lochboyg, the following lands in Locheale, in his lordship of Lochaber, namely, the lands of Banvy, Mykannich, Fyelyn and Creglwing, Corpych, Innerat, Achydo, Kilmailze, Achymoleag, Drumfarmolloch, Faneworwill, Fasfarna, Stonsonleak, Correbeg, Achitolledoun, Keanloch, Drumnasalze, Culenap, Nahohacha, Clerechaik, Mischerolach, Crew, Salachan, and the half of Lyndaly." The same authority says that the lands of Locharkaig were included in the Earldom of Moray, granted as above to Thomas Randulph, between 1307 and 1314, and that, "in 1336, John of Isla, afterwards Lord of the Isles, granted the lands of Glenluy and Locharkaig to William Mackintosh, chief of Clanchattan. From that period the lands are said to have been the subject of a

* *History of the Western Highlands and Isles of Scotland*, p. 76.

deadly feud between the Clanchattan and the Clanchameron, t for upwards of three hundred years. In 1372, or 1391, king Robert II. confirmed a grant of the lands of Locharkage, made by John Yle to Reginald of Yle his son. Between the years 1443 and 1447, Alexander, Lord of the Isles, is said to have confirmed to Malcolm Macintosh, chief of the Clanchattan, his lands in Lochaber (including Glenlui and Locharkaig), and to have granted him the office of Bailie of the district. For several years after 1497, the same lands, belonging to the Clanchattan, were forcibly held by the Clanchameron."* We shall have occasion to notice the consequent feuds and sanguinary fights between the two clans as we proceed. Meanwhile it may be well to give the family chronicler's version of the incidents to which we have just referred.

Having described the part Donald Dubh and his followers took at Harlaw and at Inverlochy, and their desertion with the Mackintoshes at the latter from the Earl of Ross to the king, he says that, "though the Camerons and Mackintoshes agreed in their principles of loyalty, yet their formal quarrel about the estate divided them as much as ever, and brought them to an engagement on Palm Sunday, which was fought with that obstinacy and fury that most of the Mackintoshes, and almost the whole tribe of the Camerons, were cut to pieces". He then gives an account of Donald Balloch's victory, shortly after, over the Royal forces, under the Earls of Mar and Caithness, when the latter was killed, and the former so severely wounded, that he made a narrow escape with his life ; and then proceeds—" Donald Balloch, having now no enemy to oppose him, he turned his fury against the Camerons, and wasted all Lochaber with fire and sword. Donald [Dubh], their chief, drew all this mischief upon him and his clan for doing their duty," and he further informs us that, in addition to his chief having deserted the Earl of Ross and joined the king on the previous occasion, he now, when Donald Balloch himself commanded the Islanders, added

* *Origines Parochiales Scotiae*, Part I., Vol. II., 181-183.

himesh cause of resentment; for he not only positively refused to assist in the present rebellion, but openly declared for the king, and was drawing his men together in order to join his generals when they were unhappily defeated by Donald and his followers from the Isles. "This double defection enraged the victorious Balloch to such a degree of fury that he came to a resolution of extirpating the whole clan, but they wisely gave way, and retreated to the mountains, till the storm blew over. Donald, their chief, was obliged to take shelter in Ireland, though some say that he went not thither till some time thereafter that he was condemned to banishment, by an unjust decree of the Earl of Ross, and the Council of Parliament, as some people affect to call it. . . . Donald, chief of the Camerons, was soon recalled from Ireland by the groans of his people, who were cruelly oppressed and plundered by a robber from the north, called Hector Bui M'Lean, who, with a party of ruffians, took the opportunity of his absence to infest the country. Being joined by a sufficient party of his clan, he pursued the robbers, who fled upon the news of his arrival, and overtook them at the head of Lochness. But Hector, with his prisoners, for he had taken many, and among them Samuel Cameron of Glenevis, head of an ancient tribe of that clan, escaped him by taking sanctuary in a strong house called Castle Spiriten, where he barbarously murdered them. In revenge of their death, Donald caused two of Hector's sons, with others of their gang who had fallen into his hands, to be hanged in view of their father, a wretch so excessively savage that he refused to deliver them by way of exchange, though earnestly pressed to it." The author then gives an account of the contentions between the Camerons and the Macleans, already referred to, in which the latter were defeated and their leader killed, at Corpach. When Donald Dubh became "master of the charters he [Maclean] had from the Earl of Ross, he destroyed them," and chased Maclean's surviving followers out of Lochaber. "Donald's next business," he continues, "was with the Mackintoshes. Alexander, the chief of that clan, had not only reconciled himself with the earl, but so far insinuated himself into his favour, that he obtained from him a charter to the disputed lands of Glenlui and Locharkaig, and sometime thereafter procured a grant of the stewartry and bailiary of all Lochaber. In a word, he took possession of the estate, which occasioned many fierce skirmishes, and the issue was that the Mackintoshes were in the end obliged to retire into their own country. The rest of his estate, which had been likewise given away, he soon recovered, and possessed in peace, during his life." *

The Lord of the Isles, shortly after his liberation, was made Justiciar of Scotland north of the Firth of Forth, and, soon after, a perfect understanding seems to have been arrived at between him and Mackintosh; while his enmity to the Camerons seems, if possible, to have become more intense than ever. The reconciliation with Mackintosh, according to a recent writer, "is the more strange, as he appears never to have forgiven the Camerons for the part they had taken against him in 1429. The unvaried loyalty exhibited by the chiefs of Mackintosh to his family previously to 1429, and the good service done his father at Harlaw by Malcolm Mackintosh himself, no doubt went a great way in inclining him to show favour to the Clan Chattan; yet so far as former loyalty was concerned, the Camerons were equally entitled to consideration. There must, therefore, have been some reason for the difference of conduct which Alexander pursued towards the two clans, for the munificence with which he treated the one, and for the rigour with which he persecuted the other. This reason may possibly lie in the fact that while Mackintosh had been openly on the side of the king for some time before Alexander's defeat in Lochaber, the chief of the Camerons had contributed, in no small degree, to that defeat, by his desertion on the eve or after the commencement of the campaign. Another reason may be that Alexander hoped,

* *Memoirs of Lochiel*, Author's Introduction, pp. 16-19.

making the Clan Chattan his instruments in hunting the Camerons, to obtain revenge on both clans at same time, by giving them a pretext for slaughtering other. However it may be, one of his first proceedings on being made Justiciar of the North, was to take measures against the Camerons. He had an excuse for pursuing them, ready to his hand, in their resistance to Mackintosh's claims on the hands of Glenlui and Locharkaig; and it was with his connivance, if not with his authority, that the Clan Chattan began, in 1441, to invade and harry the Cameron lands. In this year a sanguinary conflict took place at Craig Cailloch between the two clans, in which Mackintosh's second son, Lachlan 'Badenoch,' was wounded, and Gillichallum, his brother, killed. This was followed by a raid under Duncan, Malcolm's eldest son, in which the Cameron lands were harried. In the end, Donald Dubh, then chief of the Camerons, was forced by the inveterate animosity of the Justiciar to flee to Ireland." *

Donald Dubh is admitted on all hands to have been a man of extraordinary parts, combining great prudence with bravery, and other fighting qualities of the very highest order, and no better evidence is required of his great popularity among his own people than the fact that the chiefs of the clan continue to be styled after him in the vernacular to this day as "MacDhomh'uill Duibh". He married the heiress of Macmartin of Letterfinlay, succeeded to her property, and, at the same time, united by this marriage the Camerons and Macmartins, not only under one chief, but so completely that most of the Macmartins adopted the name of Cameron. He is said, in the "Memoirs," to have had two sons, Ewen and Donald, both of whom are there stated to have succeeded him, one after the other. This is clearly incorrect in the case of Donald. Indeed, the author himself describes him in a way which proves that even if two chiefs of the names mentioned had succeeded they could not have been brothers; for

* *History of the Mackintoshes and Clan Chattan*, by Alexander Mackintosh-Shaw.

while he calls the first " Ewen M'Coilduy," or Ewen, son of *Donald*, he calls the latter Donald Dow M'Ewen, or Donald Dubh, son of *Ewen*. This Donald does not appear on record, while Skene, Gregory, and all the best authorities agree that Donald Dubh was succeeded not by another Donald but by Allan " MacDhomh'uill Duibh ".

He married the heiress of Macmartin of Letterfinlay, with issue, at least two sons—

1. Allan, who succeeded his father, as is conclusively established by the charters quoted below.

2. Ewen, referred to in the same documents, as Donald's " brother german ". He appears to be the " Ewen, son of Donald Dubh, son of Alan " mentioned in the Manuscript of 1450, and was probably the progenitor of the later " MacGillonie " Camerons of Strone.

Donald was succeeded by his eldest son,

XII. ALLAN CAMERON,

So well known in the history and traditionary lore of his country as " Ailean MacDhomh'uill Duibh ". He became a vassal of Celestine, Lord of Lochalsh, and keeper of his Castle of Strome, in Lochcarron.* In 1472, Celestine " granted lands in Ross to Allan *the son* of Donald Duff, Captain of the Clancamroun ".† These lands comprised the twelve merk lands of Kishorn, and, in the charter, Celestine calls him, his " beloved kinsman, Allan, the son of Donald Duff, or Dow, Captain of the Clan Cameron," to whom the lands are given, and to the heirs-male lawfully begotten, or to be begotten, between him and Mariot, lawful daughter to Angus, *Dominus de Isles*, and, in default, to his other heirs-male by any subsequent marriage ; these failing, to the heirs-male of Ewen, his brother german, and failing them, to return to the granter and his heirs. The document is dated the last day of November, 1472. Allan is also described in several charters to his successors as, *the son* of Donald Dubh ; and it is quite clear, from the charter

---

* Gregory's *Highlands and Isles;* and Reg. of Great Seal, XII., 203.
† *Origines Parochiales Scotiae;* and Reg. Great Seal, Lib. XIII., No. 203.

just quoted, that he must have had a brother Ewen, though it is equally certain from Allan's designation, as Captain of the clan, during Ewen's life, that Ewen was a younger brother.

Allan MacDhomh'uill Duibh is acknowledged to have been one of the bravest warriors of his time. He is said "to have made thirty-two expeditions into his enemy's country for the thirty-two years that he lived, and three more for the three-fourths of a year that he was in his mother's womb. Whatever truth may be in this, it is certain that his good fortune failed him in the end; for being too much elated with his former successes he again made preparations for another invasion, of which his next neighbour, Keppoch (who, for I know not what reason, had conceived an enmity against Allan), having information, he advised Mackintosh of the design, and promising to follow him in the rear with all the men he could raise, he formed a plot for cutting his party to pieces. Allan had no notice of the contrivance, and, despising an enemy which he had so often insulted, proceeded to his intended invasion. Mackintosh was prepared to oppose him, but artfully delayed engaging till Keppoch came up, and attacked him in the rear. In short, the Camerons were obliged, after an obstinate fight, and the death of their chief, who was killed during the heat of the action, to give way, in their turn, to the superior numbers of the confederates." *

The family manuscript says that Allan married Marion, daughter of Angus, Lord of the Isles, and grandchild of the Earl of Ross. This is incorrect. Angus Og of the Isles, who is referred to, had no daughters that we know of, nor was he ever in reality Lord of the Isles; for he died several years before his father. He was an illegitimate son, and the only issue of his, of whom anything is known, is the famous Donald Dubh, afterwards styled Lord of the Isles; but whose legitimacy of birth has been stoutly contested. Allan, in point of fact, married Mariot, daughter of Angus Macdonald, known among the Highlanders as "Aonghas

---

* *Memoirs of Lochiel*, Author's Introduction, p. 24.

na Feairte," second of Keppoch. He is styled " Angus de Insulis," in a charter of confirmation granted to " Alano Donaldi capitanei de Clan-Cameron et heredibus inter ipsum Alanum et Mariotam Angussii de Insulis ". The lady's paternal grandfather was thus Alastair Carrach Macdonald, third son of John, first Lord of the Isles, by his second wife, Lady Margaret, daughter of King Robert II. of Scotland. Alastair Carrach himself is referred to in a complaint by William, Bishop of Moray, in 1398, as " Magnificus vir et potens, Alexander *de Insulis*, Dominus de Louchabre," * proving that the Lochaber Macdonald chiefs were also designated, at that time, *de Insulis*. This is at least as good and illustrious an ancestry as the tainted one claimed by the family genealogist from Angus Og, the bastard son of John, fourth and last Earl of Ross, and Lord of the Isles.

By Mariot Macdonald of Keppoch, Allan had issue—

1. Ewen, his heir,
2. John, from whom the Camerons of Callart ; and three daughters.†

Allan was succeeded by his eldest son,

XIII. EWEN CAMERON,

Commonly known among his own countrymen as " Eoghainn MacAilein," who was a great warrior, and became one of the most distinguished chiefs of his time. He formed a marriage alliance, through his second wife, with Mackintosh, mainly with the view of bringing about more amicable relations between the two families. In this he was disappointed; their feuds became, if possible, more intense than ever ; more sanguinary battles were fought between them, much to the loss and detriment of both ; but in the end, the Camerons, under their vigorous, judicious, and brave chief, proved quite able to hold their own.

In 1491, Ewen joined Alexander of Lochalsh, with the Clan Ranalds of Garmoran and Lochaber and the Clan

---

* *The History of the Macdonalds*, by the same author, pp. 479, 480.

† *Memoirs of Sir Ewen Cameron*. John was present at Inverness, in 1485, when Angus Og of the Isles was assassinated by an Irish Harper, Hugh Macdonald, the Sleat Scannachaid, who records the fact, describing him as " John Cameron, brother to Evan, Laird of Lochiell ".

Chattan, in his famous raid to the county of Ross, which ended in the forfeiture of the Earldom of Ross and the Lordship of the Isles. Advancing from Lochaber to Badenoch, where the Mackintoshes joined them, and thence to Inverness, where they stormed the Royal Castle, Mackintosh placing a garrison in it. They afterwards proceeded across Kessock Ferry, and plundered the lands of Sir Alexander Urquhart, Sheriff of Cromarty, from which they carried away a large booty. The Lords of Lochalsh appear at this time to have had strong claims upon the Camerons to follow them in the field; for the former were superiors, under the Lord of the Isles, of the lands of Lochiel in Lochaber,* in addition to the claims of a close marriage alliance; for, according to Hugh Macdonald, the Sleat Seannachaidh, Alexander of Lochalsh gave Ewen, Captain of Clan Cameron, who succeeded his father, Allan, as heritable keeper of the Castle of Strome in Lochcarron, one of his sisters in marriage. In 1492 the Lord of Lochalsh styles himself " Lord of Lochiel ". On the 29th of July, in the same year, "Alexander of the Isles, of Lochalch, and Lochiel, granted to Ewen, the son of Alan, the son of Donald, Captain of the Clancamroun, the lands of Cray, Salchan, Banwe, Corpach, Kilmalzhe, Achedo, Anat, Achetiley, Drumfermalach, Fanmoyrmell, Fassefarn, Corebeg, Owechan, Aychetioldowne, Chanloychiel, Kowilknap, Drumnassall, Clachak, and Clochfyne, in Lochiel."† In the following August he obtained another charter, from the same Lord of Lochalsh, of the thirty merklands of Lochiel. In 1494, James IV. confirmed to John MacGilleon of Lochbuy the lands granted to him [in Lochiel] in 1461 by John, Lord of the Isles, by whom they had been forfeited to the king. On the 24th of October, 1495, the same king confirmed to Ewen, son of Alan, the lands granted to him in 1492 by Alexander of the Isles. Under date of 1520, Ewen appears again on record in the Argyll Inventory. In 1522 the lands of Banvy and others in Lochiel, included

---

* Reg. of Great Seal, VI., 116; XIII., 203. Gregory, p. 59.
† *Origines Parochiales Scotiae;* Reg. of Great Seal, and Argyll charters.

in the grant of 1461, were resigned by Maclean of Lochbuy, and then granted by James V. to Sir John Campbell of Calder. This grant was confirmed in 1526. Two years later the same lands were resigned by Calder, and granted by the same king to Colin, Earl of Argyll. In 1528, Ewen Cameron resigned to the king the thirty merklands of Lochiel, as specified in the grant of 1492, and these, with other lands at the same time resigned by Ewen, the king granted him anew, incorporating the whole into the Barony of Lochiel. In the same year the king granted these lands, apparently, to John Maclean of Coll. In 1531, Ewen Alanson appears on record, in the Register of the Great Seal as "Captain of the *parentela* of Clancameroun". In 1536 Donald is mentioned, in the same record, as Ewen's heir. In 1539, Ewen resigned the thirty merklands of Lochiel, and James V. at once regranted them to him in life-rent, and to his grandson, Ewen Cameron, *alias* "Ewen Beg," in heritage; his eldest son, Donald above referred to, having in the meantime died during his father's lifetime. Ewen Alanson appears again on record in 1541, and, in 1546, Queen Mary granted to the Earl of Huntly the escheat of certain lands which heritably belonged to Ewen Alanson of Lochiel, including the lands of Lochiel, and the place and fortalice of Torcastle, in the Lordship of Lochaber. In 1553 the Queen granted the lands to the same Earl, these having been "forfeited by Ewen Allansoun of Locheill for the crimes of treason and lese majesty".

The following lands were, in 1492, granted by Alexander of the Isles of Lochalsh to Ewen, the son of Alan, Captain of Clan Cameron, namely, the two merklands of Achandarrach and Lundie; two of Fernaig-mhor; two of Cuilmhor and Achamore; two of Fernaig Bheag, "Fudanamine" and "Acheache"; two of Acha-na-Connlaich and Braintrath; two of "Culthnok," Ach-na-cloich, Blar-garbh, and Acheae; and two merklands of Avernish and Wochterory [? Auchtertyre] in Lochalsh. These—fourteen merklands in all—were confirmed to him by James IV. in 1495. In 1528, they were resigned by Ewen Alanson, and "for his good service" they were erected by the king into a portion of the Barony of Lochiel. These Lochalsh lands were included in the resignation of 1539, and in the regrant to Ewen and his grandson in the same year. A portion of Ewen's possessions in Lochalsh were afterwards, in 1548, granted by Queen Mary to John Grant of Culcabock, near Inverness, they having been apprised in his favour for the sum of £758 12s. 1d., as satisfaction for a "spulzie" committed on his lands by Ewen Cameron and others. The lands thus apprised included Achandarrach and Lundie, Fernaig-mhor, Fernaig-bheag, Fynnyman, and Achacroy, making in all five merks out of the fourteen. The remaining nine merks were similarly apprised to John Grant of Freuchie, with other twelve merks in the vicinity, the property of Alastair MacIan MacAlastair of Glengarry; as also twelve merks, being the hereditary fee of his son, Angus, all of which had been apprised for the sum of £10,770 13s. 4d. Scots. for satisfaction of a "spulzie" committed by Glengarry, his son, and their accomplices.* These lands do not appear to have returned to the Camerons, but were afterwards held for a time by Glengarry, in right of his wife, Margaret *de Insulis*, daughter of Alexander, Lord of Lochalsh.

In 1496, Ewen Cameron of Lochiel, Hector Maclean of Duart, John Macian of Ardnamurchan, Allan MacRuari of Moydart, and Donald Angusson of Keppoch, appeared before the Lords of Council, and bound themselves, "by the extension of their hands," to the Earl of Argyll, on behalf of the king, to abstain from mutual injuries and molestations, under a penalty of £500.†

Ewen of Lochiel, Macleod of Dunvegan, and Maclean of Duart, were the first Highland chiefs to join Donald Dubh of the Isles in his attempt to gain the Island Lordship; and for his share in this rebellion Lochiel was, in 1504, forfeited as a traitor, but he seems soon after to have again got into favour at court.

* Reg. Mag. Sig.
† Acts of the Lord of Council, quoted by Gregory.

In 1514, an Act of Council was passed, appointing persons of influence in the Highlands to take charge of particular divisions of the northern counties as Lieutenants. Ewen Cameron of Lochiel and William Mackintosh were appointed guardians in this capacity in Lochaber.

About 1524, Sir John Campbell of Calder, whose patrimony lay in Lorn, acquired, from Maclean of Lochbuy, certain claims, which that gentleman had hitherto made without effect to the lands of Lochiel, Duror, and Glencoe. Sir John made good use of the position and opportunities which possession of these claims had secured to him. At first he was violently resisted by the Camerons and Stewarts, the occupants of the lands in question, and suffered many injuries from them in the course of this dispute. But, by transferring his title to these lands to his brother Argyll, and employing the influence of that nobleman, Calder succeeded in establishing a certain degree of authority over the unruly inhabitants, in a mode then of very frequent occurrence. Ewen Allanson of Lochiel, and Allan Stewart of Duror, were, by the arbitration of friends, ordered to pay to Calder a large sum of damages, and, likewise, to give him for themselves, their children, kin, and friends, their bond of manrent and service against all manner of men, except the king and the Earl of Argyll. In consideration of these bonds of service, three-fourths of the damages awarded were remitted by Calder, who became bound also to give his bond of maintenance in return. Finally, if the said Ewen and Allan should do good service to Sir John in helping him to obtain and enjoy certain other lands and possessions, they were to be rewarded by him therefor, at the discretion of the arbiters.*

According to the family Seannachaidh, Ewen invaded the country of the Mackays in the far north. "What the quarrel was," he says, "I know not, but it drew on an invasion from the Camerons, and an engagement wherein the Mackays were defeated, and the Laird of Foulis, chief of the Monroes, who assisted them, killed on the spot." The

* Gregory, pp. 126, 127.

same writer continues—" Hitherto Lochiel had success in all his attempts. The vigour of his genius and courage bore him through all his difficulties. He had a flourishing family and an opulent fortune, but the death of his eldest son, Donald, which happened about this time, plunged him into so deep a melancholy that he, on a sudden, resolved to give up the world, and apply himself to the works of religion and peace. To expiate for his former crimes he set out on a pilgrimage to Rome, but, arriving in Holland, he found himself unable to bear up against the fatigue of so long a journey, and, therefore, he sent one Macphail, a priest, who was his chaplain and confessor, to do that job for him with the Pope. One part of the penance enjoined upon him by his Holiness was to build six chapels to as many saints, which he performed. Some of them are still extant, and the ruins of the rest are yet to be seen in Lochaber and the bordering countries. He also built a castle on the banks of the River Lochy, called Tor Castle, from the rock on which it was situated. Mackintosh afterwards designated himself by this castle, because it was built upon the grounds in dispute. However, it became the seat of the family of Lochiel, till it was demolished by Sir Ewen Cameron, with the view of building a more convenient house." Ewen's eldest son and heir, Donald, appears to have been a man of great promise. His father gave him, what was considered, in those days, a very liberal education, and he " soon came to have a relish for the elegancies and politenesses of society. His father's estate was such as enabled him to live in a rank equal to any of the young chiefs, his contemporaries, and his own behaviour soon got him a character among the courtiers. But the person with whom he contracted the most intimate friendship was George, fourth Earl of Huntly. This Lord was then a young man, in so great a reputation at court, that his Majesty honoured him with the government of the kingdom, during a voyage of gallantry that he made to the Court of France, in August 1535, in order to marry Magdalen, the eldest daughter of France, to whom he had been formerly betrothed. So much was Donald in favour with that earl that he complimented him with a valuable estate conterminous with his own, and lying eastward of the lake and river of Lochy. The charter is given by George, Earl of Huntly, to the Honourable Donald Cameron, *alias* Allanson, or MacAllan, of Lochiel, of the lands of Letterfinlay, Stronabaw, and Lyndaly, lying within the lordship of Lochaber, and sheriffdom of Inverness. The holding is blench, and bears date, at Edinburgh, 16th February, 1534."

Ewen, at the head of his followers, fought with John Moydartach of Clanranald, in 1544, against the Frasers, at the bartle of Kin-Loch-Lochy, better known as "Blar-nan-Leine," the history of which is already well known,* and for this he got into disfavour with Huntly, then Lieutenant of the North. Lochiel, also, in 1546, gave countenance to the rebellion of the Earl of Lennox, he having, among other things, written in that year to the Lord-Deputy of Ireland, promising his services to the English king, and saying that he had marched to the Lowlands, and taken a prey both from Huntly and Argyll. He also asked support for, and recommended, James Macdonald of Dunyveg —who had for a short time assumed the title of Lord of the Isles, and whom Ewen styles in his letter, as the "narrest of Ayr to the hous of the Yllis," and as a brave young man, "with great strength of kinsmen". Through the instrumentality of William Mackintosh of Mackintosh, his brother-in-law, who joined Huntly with a large force, to subdue the rebels and lay the country waste, Ewen Cameron, and Ranald, son of Donald Glas of Keppoch, were, with several others, apprehended; imprisoned for a short time in the Castle of Ruthven; afterwards tried, at Elgin, by a jury of landed gentlemen, for high treason, for the part they had taken at Blar-nan-Leine, and in the rebellion of the Earl of Lennox. They were both found guilty, and beheaded, and their heads were exposed over the gates

---

* Full details are given in the author's *History of the Macdonalds and Lords of the Isles*, pp. 381 to 395.

of the town, while several of their followers, who had been captured along with them, were hanged.

In addition to the Constabulary of Strome Castle, previously granted to Alan, Ewen's father, in 1472—with the twelve merklands of Kishorn, for the maintenance and faithful keeping of the Castle already possessed by him— Alexander of Lochalsh, in 1492, granted to " Ewin, the son of Alan, Captain of Clancamroun," 20s. of Strome Carranach, 20s. of Slumbay, 10s. of the quarter of " Doune," and 30s. of the three quarters of Achintee, in the Lordship of Lochcarron. These were confirmed to Ewen, along with his other lands, in 1495; and, in 1528, they were included in the new grant erecting all his lands into the Barony of Lochiel.

On the 6th of March, 1539, the Castle of Strome, with the lands attached to it, were granted by James IV. to Alexander of Glengarry and Margaret of the Isles, his wife, on her resignation of them. On the 11th of April, in the same year, Ewen Cameron resigned these with other lands. Strome and Kishorn, with others, were, in 1546, forfeited for the crime of treason and lese majesty, and they never after formed any portion of the possessions of Lochiel. They soon after passed to the Macdonalds of Glengarry, and ultimately to the Mackenzies of Kintail and Seaforth.

The charter of 1472, by Alexander of Lochalsh, is apparently the first charter of any lands possessed by the Camerons of Lochiel. The author of the "Memoirs," briefly referring to the grants of 1472, admits that, "the family I am writing of can produce none older than those I have mentioned, whereby it is now impossible to discover what the extent of their estate formerly was".

In 1528, James V. granted Ewen "for his good service, and for a certain pecuniary composition," the 40 merklands of Glenlui and Locharkaig, with half of the bailiary of Lochaber, "which were formerly possessed by his father, Alan, Donald's son, of the king's predecessors, and were in the king's hands by reason of Alan's death".* These were again confirmed, in 1539, to himself in life-rent and to his grandson, Ewen Beag, in heritage. In 1544, a previous grant of them, in 1505, is confirmed by Queen Mary to William Mackintosh of Dunachton, but, in 1552, these lands and others are granted to Alexander, Lord Gordon, they having in the meantime been forfeited by William Mackintosh for the crimes of treason and lese majesty. They subsequently changed hands repeatedly, until they finally became the undisputed and undisturbed possession of the Camerons of Lochiel.†

Referring to the acquisitions of this chief, Skene says that, "he appears, in consequence of his feudal claims, to have acquired almost the whole estates which belonged to the chief of Clanranald, and to have so effectually crushed that family that their chiefship was soon after usurped by a branch of the family. It was during the life of Ewen that the last Lord of the Isles was forfeited, and as the crown readily gave charters to all the independent clans of the lands in their possession, Ewen Cameron easily obtained a feudal title to the whole of his possessions, as well those which he inherited from his father as well those which he wrested from the neighbouring clans; and at this period may be dated the establishment of the Camerons in that station of importance and consideration which they have ever since maintained."‡

When the Highland chiefs were called upon to take out charters for their lands after the forfeiture of the last Lord

---

* *Origines Parochiales Scotiae.* A previous charter, dated 9th of January, 1527, was granted by James to Ewen MacAllan, including the lands of Glenlui and Locharkaig, so long in dispute between Lochiel and Mackintosh. It is given at length in the notes to the *Memoirs of Sir Ewen Cameron*, from Reg. Mag. Sig. Lib. XXII., R. 51.

† Referring to the acquisition of Locharkaig and Lochiel by the Camerons, first by Allan MacDhomh'uill Duibh, Skene says :—" This property had formed part of the possessions of the Clan Ranald, and had been held by them of Godfrey of the Isles, and his son, Alexander, the eldest branch of the family. After the death of Alexander, the Camerons appear to have acquired a feudal title to these lands, while the chief of Clan Ranald claimed them as male heir."—*Highlanders of Scotland*, Vol. II., pp. 196, 197.

‡ *Highlanders of Scotland*, Vol. II., pp. 197, 198.

of the Isles, Ewen set out for Edinburgh, and procured from James IV. a confirmation of his previous charters from Alexander of Lochalsh, "in presence," the author of the "Memoirs" informs us, "of all the great officers of the crown, and of many other noble lords, spiritual and temporal, who are all designed witnesses to it". He remained some time at court, and got into favour with the king, whom he afterwards loyally supported in all his wars, including the disastrous battle of Flodden, from which Ewen was fortunate enough to escape with his life.

During the minority of James V., Lochiel faithfully adhered to the fortunes of John, Duke of Albany, then governor of the kingdom. When he took charge of the Government he had no more faithful subject than Cameron of Lochiel, who aided him in all his wars, became a great favourite at court, for which he was fully rewarded by the charter granted to him by the king in 1528, erecting all his lands into the Barony of Lochiel, already referred to, and that in which the Captain of Clan Cameron is for the first time designed "of Lochiel". In the same year a Royal mandate was issued to the Earls of Sutherland and Caithness, Lord Forbes and Fraser of Lovat, and the Captain of the Camerons for the extermination of the Clan Chattan "and invaid thame to thair vter destructioun, be slauchtir, byrning, drouning, and vther wayis: and leif na creatur levand of that clann, except preistis, wemen, and barnis". The women and bairns were to be transported by ship to Norway. The commission was, however, never executed, from an unwillingness on the part of those in whose favour it was granted to carry out its terms against the Mackintoshes and their friends.* In 1531, he obtained a charter to the lands of Inverlochy, Torlundy, and others in the lordship of Lochaber, extending to thirteen merk-lands of old extent, "which belonged to the king in property, but were never in his rental, and were occupied by the inhabitants of the Isles and others, who had no

* *Chiefs of Grant*, Vol. I., p. 101.

right to them," for a payment of 40 merks yearly. At the same time, and for a similar amount per annum, the lands of Invergarry, Kilinane, Laggan, and Achindrom, of the old extent of twelve merks, all of which also belonged to the king in property, but never were in his rental, and were also occupied by the inhabitants of the Isles and others, who had no right to them. In 1536, the same king granted to "Donald Camroun, the son and heir of Ewin Allanson, Captain of Clancamroun, the non-entry and other dues of various lands, including the £6 land of Sleisgarrow in Glengarry". This grant was repeated in the following year. He also, in 1536, received a charter, dated the 8th of November, granting him the lands of Knoydart, Glen Nevis, and others in Inverness-shire.

It appears that, in 1492, Ewen had granted a bond of manrent to Farquhar (whose cousin he afterwards married), apparent heir to his father, Duncan Mackintosh of Mackintosh, in which he bound himself to assist and defend him against all men, even his own superior, Alexander Macdonald of Lochalsh, in case the latter, in the event of a dispute with Mackintosh, should refuse to arrange terms. In 1497, however, after Farquhar's imprisonment in the Castle of Dunbar, and immediately on the death of his father, Duncan Mackintosh, the Camerons broke through their engagement, refused to make any acknowledgment to Mackintosh for the lands they occupied in Lochaber, and then invaded the Braes of Badenoch and Strathnairn, plundering all the Mackintosh lands in those districts.

Farquhar's cousin, William Mackintosh, son of Lachlan Badenoch, led the clan in the absence of the chief, and after punishing the Macgregors of Rannoch and Appin, and the Clan Ian of Glencoe, who accompanied the invaders, he turned his attention to the Camerons. "His cousin, Dougal Mor MacGhillichallum, offered to 'daunton the Camerons for some time' if he were allowed thirty fighting men, and the use of the lands of Borlum for a year. His offer being accepted, he set about carrying out his plan, which was to sail up Loch Ness in the night-time and surprise and lay waste some part of the Cameron lands, returning to his head-quarters before the invaded country could be raised against him. He was completely successful, making several of these inroads at unexpected times to the no small disquiet of the Lochabrians." This version is quoted from the historian of Cameron's enemy.*

Gregory says that, about the year 1500, the feud which had so long subsisted between the Camerons and the Macleans, regarding the lands of Lochiel, broke out into renewed violence. The Macleans carried of a large number of cattle from Lochaber, an injury which was soon after fully revenged by the Camerons. These broils were stopped for a time through the influence of Argyll, when the Macleans, who appear on this occasion to have been the aggressors, received a temporary respite under the Privy Seal. A few years later, however, the old quarrel was revived, and another feud was carried on for some time with great bitterness. Traces are found of similar quarrels during the greater part of the reign of James V., who died in 1542.

In October, 1544, and April, 1545, Ewen Cameron, with MacDonald of Glengarry, made expeditions to Grant's lands of Glenmoriston and Glenurquhart, still spoken of as the "Raid of Urquhart". For this summonses were issued, under the royal signet, dated the third of August, 1546, against Lochiel and his coadjutors. The summonses are preserved at Castle Grant, and from them it is found that Ewen Allanson was accompanied by his grandson and heir, Ewen—son of his eldest son Donald, who had died a few years before, and of Agnes or Anne, daughter of Sir James Grant, then Laird of Urquhart. The spoil taken was a rich one. Among the goods, cattle and horses taken from the laird's home farm were two hundred bolls of oats, with the fodder; one hundred bolls of bere; one hundred cows; one hundred calves; forty young cows; ten one-year-old stirks; eight horses and four mares; four young horses; one hundred and forty ewes; sixty gimmers and

---

* Alexander Mackintosh-Shaw's *History of Clan Chattan.*

dinmonts; one hundred lambs. From the Castle they carried away, twelve feather beds, with bolsters, blankets, and sheets; five pots, six pans, one basket, and one chest containing three hundred pounds in money; two brewing cauldrons; twenty pieces of artillery; ten stands of harness; and several other articles named, of considerable value, including doors, bedsteads, chairs, forms, and three large boats. The tenants were similarly treated, according to the value of their possessions; goats, kids, wedders, swine, and cloth, being mentioned among the spoil taken from them. In two cases, sixty ells of linen, and sixty ells of woollen cloth, were carried away, in addition to the household furniture belonging to the owners.* The number of cattle and sheep, and the quantity of corn and other goods taken was very large, and shows that the people of Glenurquhart were very well-to-do in those days. No doubt this raid was an element in securing Ewen's conviction and execution in the following year, though the principal charge against him was his share in the battle of Blar-nan-leine, and his support of the Earl of Lennox.

Such is a sketch of the career of the greatest chief the Clan Cameron had yet produced, and, if we accept the authority of the family historian, "a chief of the greatest abilities of any of his time. He is still famous," he says, "in these parts for his courage and military conduct, for the greatest part of his life was employed in warlike adventures, either in the service of the crown, or his own private quarrels. However, he was so far from neglecting the government and policy of his [own] country that his people increased in numbers and riches, as his estate did in value and extent. In a word, he omitted no opportunity of serving the interest of his family; and in this was much wiser than any of his predecessors that he was careful to secure his large and extensive possessions to his posterity by authentic charters," a few only of which he refers to as being then extant.

Ewen married, first, a daughter of Celestine of Loch-

* *Chiefs of Grant*, Vol. I., pp. 111-113.

alsh,* brother of John, last Earl of Ross and Lord of the Isles, with issue—

1. Donald, his heir, who, in 1520, married Agnes or Anne, daughter of Sir James Grant of Grant,† with issue— (1) Ewen Beag, who succeeded his grandfather (Ewen Alanson); (2) Donald, who succeeded his brother, Ewen; and (3) John the Black, or "Ian Dubh," who married a daughter of Mackintosh, with issue—twin brothers, born after their father's death, the eldest of whom, Allan, succeeded to the chiefship as Allan Cameron MacIan Duibh. (4) John, Minister of Dunoon, from whom John, the famous Principal of the University of Glasgow; the Camerons of Worcester, and others. Donald, Ewen's eldest son and heir, died long before his father—between the years 1536 and 1539.

He married, secondly, Marjory, daughter of Lachlan, "Badenoch," second son of Malcolm Mackintosh X. of Mackintosh,‡ and sister of William XIII., and of Lachlan Beag XIV. of Mackintosh. By this lady, he had issue—

* Hugh Macdonald, the Sleat Seannachie, in the Collectanea de Rebus Albanicis, p. 320. This alliance will account for the Constableship of Strome Castle having been conferred upon Ewen Alanson, and upon his eldest son, by the Lords of Lochalsh, in succession, as well for the lands bestowed upon them by each of these lords in Lochaber, Lochcarron, and Lochalsh.

† An indenture is entered into at Urquhart, between John Grant of Freuchie and Ewen Allanson, chief of the Camerons, on the 22nd of October, 1520, in which they bind themselves and their apparent heirs—James Grant and Donald Cameron— and their heirs for ever, to defend each other in their persons, goods, lands, possessions, kin, friends, party, rights, actions, and quarrels, against all-comers, with the usual exceptions in favour of the sovereign, and their own superiors—the Earls of Moray and Argyll. And all this "for the mair securitie, God villing, the said Donald Ewin Allansone sone shall haif to spous and . . . band of matrimonie in faice of haly kirk, Agnes Grant, dochtir to the said Johne the Grant". A papal dispensation was necessary to admit of the marriage, but in the event of its not being forthcoming between the date of the indenture and fifteen days after the immediately following Martinmas, John Grant is taken "bundin and oblist to caus thame be handfast and put togiddir . . . for mariage to be completit". Both parties gave their "bodyly ayth" and touched the "haly evanglist". Thomas, Lord Fraser of Lovat; Alexander Cumming, son and apparent heir to Alexander Cumming of Altyre; and Patrick Grant in Ballindalloch, were sureties for the implement of the contract, under a penalty of 1000 merks—*Chiefs of Grant*, Vol. III., pp. 64, 65.

‡ *History of the Mackintoshes and Clan Chattan*, p. 186. The authors of the "Baronage," and of the "Memoirs," both of whom make her the daughter of *Duncan* Mackintosh, are in error.

2. Ewen, afterwards one of Allan Cameron's tutors, and progenitor of the family of Erracht, known in the district in Gaelic as "Sliochd Eoghainn 'ic Eoghainn". He was assassinated at a meeting of the clan held at Inverlochy Castle.

3. John, another of the tutors, progenitor of the Camerons of Kin-Lochiel. He was beheaded at the Castle of Dunstaffnage.

Ewen, as already noticed, was executed, in 1547, at Elgin, for high treason, when he was succeeded by his grandson,

XIV. EWEN CAMERON,

Generally called "Eoghainn· Beag" to distinguish him from his grandfather, Eoghainn MacAilein, who, as we have just seen, outlived Donald, his eldest son, for many years. Eoghainn Beag, in consequence, succeeded his grand-father as fourteenth chief of the clan, when quite young, but nothing is known of his short and apparently uneventful career, except the way in which he met his death in early life. When quite a young man he became acquainted with a daughter of Macdougall of Lorne, by whom he had a natural son, "Domhnull Mac-Eoghainn Bhig," better known as "Taillear Dubh na Tuaighe," afterwards one of the most celebrated warriors of the clan.

On the tenth of October, 1548, Ewen entered into a contract with James Grant of Freuchie, concerning certain lands which had changed hands in the time of his predecessor, after the raid of Urquhart, and of which Ewen was now to have the profits and duties. The lands were to "be in pand to the said Ewen," in all time coming, subject to his good behaviour towards Grant, and in no case were they to be alienated from him except by the advice and consideration of John Mackenzie of Kintail ; Kenneth his son and heir ; John Grant of Mulben, son and heir to Grant himself ; John Grant of Culcabock ; and others.*

* For the complete document see the *Chiefs of Grant*, Vol. III., pp. 102, 103.

The cause and manner of the violent death of Eoghainn Beag is thus described:—"Being in his younger years much enamoured of a daughter of the laird of Macdougall, he found the lady so 'complaisant' that she fell with child to him. Her father dissembled his resentment and artfully drew Lochiel to a communing in Island-na-Cloiche, where, having previously concealed a party of men, he made him his prisoner upon his refusing to marry her, and shut him up in the Castle of Inch-Connel, in Lochow, a fresh-water lake, at a good distance from Lochaber, to which his friends could not have easy access, on account of the difficulty of providing themselves with boats. As soon as the news came to Lochaber, his clan resolved to hazard all for his relief, and, having made the necessary preparations, his foster-father, Martin MacDhonnachaidh of Letter-Finlay, chief of the MacMartins, an ancient and numerous tribe of the Camerons, put himself at the head of a large party, and soon made himself master of the castle. Lochiel was then playing cards with his keeper or governor, named MacArthur, and was so overjoyed at his approaching delivery, that, observing him much alarmed at the noise made by the assailants, he over-hastily discovered the design for which he paid dear. For the villain (MacArthur), to satisfy his own and his master's resentment, immediately extinguished the lights, and thrusting his dirk or poniard below the table, which stood between them, wounded him in the belly. His deliverers, in the meantime, rushing into his apartment, carried him to their boats, where, the night being cold, he called for an oar to heat himself with exercise, but, upon stretching his body, he became first sensible of his wound, which soon after proved mortal. His party having landed and put him to bed returned to the castle, and, in revenge of his death, dispatched MacArthur and all the men that were with him." *

Donald, the natural son of Ewen Beag, by the daughter of Macdougall, was, from his infancy, in the charge of his father, who sent him secretly to be nursed by a tailor's wife, in

* *Memoirs of Lochiel*, pp. 33, 34.

Blar-nan-Cleireach, or Lundavra, from which circumstance he was afterwards called "An Taillear Dubh". This will be as suitable a place as any to give an account of his remarkable career. He was named Donald, probably after his grandfather. Tradition has it that he was afterwards brought up by MacLachlan of Coruanan, hereditary standard-bearer to Lochiel. In due time, he grew up a brave and prudent man, famous for his sarcasm and ready wit, but even more so for the skill with which he wielded his battle-axe, the favourite weapon of the Camerons of Lochaber. From this came his sobriquet of "Taillear Dubh na Tuaighe," by which designation he has ever since been known in the Highlands.

The mother of Allan MacIan Duibh, the young chief of Lochiel, was a Mackintosh, and she hated her husband's clan with a fierce hatred. As the mother of the chief she lived in one of the family residences, "Eilean na'n Craobh," a picturesque island, near the shore, in Lochiel,—almost opposite the Church of Kilmallie,—with still a few trees on it, and it is there that we find Donald, or Taillear Dubh na Tuaighe, first appearing prominently in the traditional history of Lochaber. He hated the Mackintoshes quite as much as the mother of his young chief hated the Camerons; and nothing pleased him better than to wield his irresistible "tuagh," or axe against them on the battle-field. In return he was hated by them, especially by Ian Dubh's widow, by John of Kinlochiel, and Ewen of Erracht, the sons of Marjory Mackintosh, daughter of Lachlan Badenoch, second wife of Ewen Allanson.

On the first occasion on which the Taillear Dubh comes on the scene as a hero he was quite a young man. A skirmish had been fought between the Camerons and the Mackintoshes, in which many of the latter were slain. Donald was deputed to carry the tidings to the chief's widow at Eilean na'n Craobh, a task which many would shrink from, knowing her strong will and Mackintosh proclivities. He, however, boldly went, and walked straight into her presence, battle-axe in hand. On seeing him outside she cried out sternly, "Thig a nuas, a Thaillear, ach fag do thuagh shios," "Come in, tailor, but leave your axe without"; to which he responded, "Far am bi mi fhein bi' mo thuagh," "Where I will be, my axe will be". "Ciamar a chaidh an latha?" "How did the day go?" she asked. "Oh!" he answered, "Gheibheadh tu bian cait air da pheighinn, agus rogha is tagha air planc," "You could get a cat's skin for twopence, and pick and choice for a plack". On hearing this contemptuous reference to her clan's defeat, she became so enraged that she threw the infant chief, some say, into the fire, others, into the ashes, when, in a moment, Donald raised his battle-axe above her head, exclaiming sternly, "A bhean a rug an leanabh tog an leanabh," "Woman, who gave birth to the child, lift (? or rear) the child;" which command she deemed prudent instantly to obey.

The news having at once spread abroad, a meeting of the leaders of the clan was held as to what should be done with the unnatural mother of the young chief, when it was decided not to leave him any longer in the hands of one who had proved herself so unworthy of her position and trust. It was also decided to send her back to her own people—she having forfeited any right to be considered a member of the Clan Cameron—and it was done in this way. She was mounted on horseback with her face to the animal's tail, and driven in that position to within the boundary line of the Mackintosh country, accompanied by a few Mackenzies who had come from Brahan to assist the Camerons in the recent battle; and for which they were afterwards rewarded by grants of land on the estate of Lochiel. Their descendants are in North Ballachulish to this day. The Camerons at the same time resolved not to leave their infant chief any longer to the guardianship of his grand-uncles of Kinlochiel and Erracht, and they sent him to Mull, to the widow of his uncle Donald Dubh, a lady of the family of Duart. Donald MacEoghain Bhig in the meantime went to reside with his grandmother, Lady Grant of Grant, from which place he was soon called by a party of his clan to protect them from the oppression of Kinlochiel and Erracht, who were acting in the most despotic and selfish manner towards them.

Donald, the Taillear Dubh, again became the leader of the Camerons, and in every field in which he led them they are said to have been victorious. So successful was he that some of the people began to suspect him of a fairy origin, and that a special charm was upon him. He was not only famous for his use of the Lochaber axe, but was fleet-footed as the mountain deer, which stood him in good stead on one occasion. While out hunting one day, he accidentally fell into the hands of the Mackintoshes, who were quite jubilant over their prize, and longing to see him slain. " Had I fallen into your hands like this, what would you do with me ? " asked Mackintosh of his captive. " I would at least give you a chance of escaping with your life ; and if you could get free I would let you," replied the Taillear. " Then I shall do the same with you ; you will not have to say that you outstrip Mackintosh in generosity," replied the chief; who thereupon formed his men into a ring, with Donald in the centre, giving the order, " Men, present your arms, and if he rushes upon you it will but make an end of him all the quicker ". Donald, after committing himself to God in prayer, exercised his battle-axe, as if with the intention to attempt an opening by which he could effect an escape, threatening to break the circle at various points, saying " Na'n deanainn mar b'aill leam, chuirinn cleith as a, ghàradh," "If I but could do as I would wish, I would put a stake out the wall, (or paling) ". After various evolutions and frantic rushes towards different points of the circle—always stopping short, until he convinced them that he thought his efforts were hopeless, and thus threw them off their guard—he at last, after one of those attempts, and while near one side of the ring made a sudden spring, this time in earnest, and in the act slipped his hand along the haft of his axe to its extreme end, which the rope attached to his wrist enabled him to do, and so getting a longer reach, the deadly weapon lighted like a flash on the head of one of his captors. A stake did disappear from the wall, and Donald was free from what seemed the arms of death. He then fled as fast as his feet could carry him, pursued by his enraged enemies, the foremost among them being the chief himself, who, according to some versions of the tradition, is said to have been on horseback. At last Donald came to a wide ditch which he leapt lightly, and got safe across. Mackintosh leaping after him, fell into the mire. The Taillear Dubh, raising his axe above the head of his pursuer, addressed the floundering chief— " Dh fhaodainn, ach cha dean " " I might, but I will not ". Mackintosh, naturally grateful for the generosity of his foe, waved back his men from the pursuit, when Donald extended to him his hand and pulled him out of the ditch.

The spot where he made this leap is near the banks of the Caledonian Canal, at Gairlochy, and is to this day called " Leum an Taillear " ; while the ditch, though now filled in, still bears the name of " Lochan Mhic-an Toisich ".

Various rumours were current about Donald's final disappearance from Lochaber. Some said that he was murdered by command of the young chief, Ailean MacIan Duibh, who had now returned home, Donald's enemies having induced him to believe that he was ambitious to be chief himself; that he was securing the hearts of the people with that intention ; and that he asserted himself to be the offspring of a lawful marriage, and therefore legitimate chief of the clan. Allan, it has been said, believed these tales, and consented to his cousin's death. When he disappeared there was therefore great indignation among the majority of the clan, who believed that he had been murdered. Others alleged that, being tired of fighting, he had retired to some monastery, and that he was seen in the district of Cowal.

The indignation of those who believed that the young chief agreed to have Donald put to death, waxed so hot that Allan had again to leave Lochaber. He did not feel safe at home, the majority of the clan entertaining this belief, and he prudently retired from the district until their fury abated.

The fate of this celebrated warrior had been enveloped in uncertainty for centuries, but it is now accounted for. There is no doubt that he actually did seek safety in Cowal, where he married and left issue; one of his descendants, at the present day, being the Rev. Dr. Malcolm Campbell Taylor, Professor of Church History in the University of Edinburgh. The name Taylor, in this case at anyrate, came from the "Taillear"—whose descendants are known as "Cloinn an Taillear" or the Children of the Tailor, Domhnull MacEoghainn Bhig.*

Though unaware that any tradition existed in Lochaber concerning him, the Taylors of Stratheachaig knew that their progenitor was called "Taillear Dubh na Tuaighe," but that his real name was Donald Dubh, and that he was the offspring of one of the chiefs of Lochiel. On one of the oldest tombstones of the family the tuagh or battle-axe is carved—not the modern, long-handled, prettily designed, Lochaber axe, but the old, deadly-looking weapon, having a short handle, with a rope attached, which was the one always used in battle by the leaders of the clan.

The MacLachlans of Strath-Lachlan are said to be descended from the Camerons, and related to the MacLachlans of Coruanan; and that may have been the link that led Donald to that district for safety; or his maternal grandfather may have induced the Earl of Argyll to give him a holding in Cowal.

The Taillear Dubh was in special danger from the families of Erracht and Kinlochiel, as, in defence of the absent chief, he had been the cause of the death of these plotting relatives, who were always playing into the hands of their kinsmen, the Mackintoshes. When Allan again

---

* For the best version of this tradition we are indebted to Mrs. Mary Mackellar, the well-known poet—one of the "Sliochd Ian Duibh" Camerons of Lochaber, who for many generations occupied and were known as the Camerons of "Druim-na-Saille".

returned to take the lead into his own hands, he was told that his relative, Domhnull MacEoghainn Bhig, *alias* Taillear Dubh na Tuaighe, had always been his best friend. He was informed of how he had saved him from his heartless mother, and how he watched over his interests during the years of his absence from Lochaber. He regretted having blamed him wrongfully; and to make amends, as well as to please his offended clan, he is alleged to have paid him the compliment of placing his effigy in the family coat of arms as supporters, with his battle-axe conspicuously held up. There he remains; his name lives in the songs, proverbs, and traditions of his native land; and next, perhaps, to the great Sir Ewen himself, he is the ideal warrior and hero of his clan. His name rouses their pride and affection; and as long as there is a clansman in Lochaber, or Gaelic spoken, the name of Taillear Dubh na Tuaighe will be remembered among his countrymen.

In 1576-77, we find "Allaster Dow McAllane McEwin of Camroun, and John Cam, his brother of surnawm," applying to the Lord Regent and the Lords of the Secret Council to be set at liberty by the Earl of Athole, who had some months before apprehended them by force, and imprisoned them at Blair Athole. They were represented before the Council by "Ewin McAne, Capitane of Inverlochy, their fader brother". The Earl of Athole alleged in defence, that his prisoners had been denounced rebels and put to the horn, and were so when he apprehended them, and continued so then, for having committed diverse slaughters, heirschips, and oppressions upon certain of his own tenants and servants and others of the king's lieges, for which they were fugitives from the law. They were ordered to be brought before the Council on the 25th of February, in that year, with the letters of horning and other evidences of their guilt, failing which the usual penalties would follow against Athole. On the 26th of February, Mr. Andro Abircromby, servitor of John, Earl of Athole, presented, in his master's name, "Allister Dow McAllan VcEwin Cameroun and John Cam, his brother, and also produced letters raised by the brothers and other friends of the late Donald Dow MacKewin, by which the said Allister and Johnne were denounced for the slaughter of the late Donald ". Allister Dow is found in ward in Edinburgh, under date, 1st March, 1576. On the 1st of January, 1577-78, it is recorded that Colin, Earl of Argyll, and John Campbell of Caddell, who had become sureties to enter and present before the Privy Council, Allister Dow McAllane VcEwin Camroun, and John Cam, his brother, when required, under a penalty of £1000, having failed, though repeatedly called upon, to do so, it was agreed to enforce the penalty against him, and letters were ordained to be sent to the officers of the army and the sheriffs in those parts, charging them to pass, arrest, apprise, compel, poind, and destrain the said earl's readiest lands, goods, and gear ; and failing his moveable goods, to apprise his lands, conform to the Act of Parliament, to the avail and quantity of the said sum of £1000.

It is believed that this entry is the only foundation for Gregory's assertion that one of the Cameron chiefs was murdered at this date, and also for the statement, by the author of the "Memoirs" of Sir Ewen Cameron, that Taillear Dubh na Tuaighe was put to death by order of his chief. There was no chief named Donald Dow MacEwen at this period, and it is pretty clear that Donald Dubh MacEoghainn Bhig lived for many years after 1577.

Since the foregoing was written we have received a few interesting notes from Professor Taylor, Edinburgh, already mentioned, a descendant of the famous warrior. He enters into an able and minute argument to show that Donald MacEoghainn Bhig, and Taillear Dubh na Tuaighe were one and the same. The fact will be admitted by all who have given the question any consideration, and it is therefore unnecessary here to discuss it. It may be well, however, to give Professor Taylor's reasons for the conclusion that his warlike ancestor has long out-lived the date at which he is said to have been assassinated, as well as other

interesting reminiscences of the celebrated Taillear Dubh, which he supplies. We have already stated that, at one period of his life, Donald MacEoghainn Bhig went to reside for a time in the country of the Grants. In connection with this incident in Donald's career, Professor Taylor says, that in the united parishes of Abernethy and Kincardine, in the very home of the Grants, there are at the present time a considerable body of Camerons, only second to the Grants themselves in point of numbers, and second to none in respect of industry, probity, and independence. They are known to this day as "Sliochd nan Gillean Maola Dubh," and their account of themselves is, that they are descended from twelve young men who, according to the custom of the times, accompanied a daughter of the house of Lochiel on the occasion of her marriage to one of the Stewarts of Kincardine—the date of which event is placed in the first half of the 16th century. The strangers have fairly prospered, with one notable exception; for the family of the "Ceann Tighe" has decayed. The tradition among these Camerons is, that the leader of the Gillean Maola was Taillear Dubh na Tuaighe, and there is still living, near the Manse of Abernethy, an old woman, Anne Cameron, the last of her family, whose father was acknowledged by all the Camerons in the district to be their Ceann Tighe, or head; but, according to her account and theirs, her father was not of the "Sliochd nan Gillean Maola Dubh," but a descendant of "Taillear Dubh na Tuaighe, 'chuir an ruaig air Macintoisich," as she described him. He was the head or leader of the original twelve, and his representatives were considered the leaders of their descendants. The Strathspey tradition agrees with that of Lochaber in that the Taillear Dubh was the son of a former chief of the Camerons, and the champion of their independence in his day. Professor Taylor proceeds:—
"The only other district which has had a steadfast tradition, connecting the Taillear Dubh with it, is in Cowal, where a group of families, MacIntaylor—later, Taylor—by name, have always regarded themselves as his

descendants. It adds weight to their tradition that *one link* suffices to connect the oldest survivors of the sept with their progenitor of 200 years ago. Their grandfather, who fought at Culloden in 1746, died in 1817, at the great age of 96, had the family account from his grandfather, regarding whom there is unimpeachable evidence, of date 1685-6. It is also noteworthy that their tradition carries them up by name, to about 1580, when the first of them is said to descend from the Taillear Dubh. Regarding its general drift no more need be said than that it corresponds, in all the main particulars, with that of Lochaber. Where it differs, as in certain minor and unimportant details, the difference, from a critical point of view, is in favour of the Cowal version, as being the simpler, and therefore, presumably, the older form. These Cowal people were wont to regard themselves as Camerons of the Camerons and to designate themselves, down to the closing years of last century, as 'Clann an Taillear Dhuibh Chamronaich'. It would appear to have depended entirely on the scribes of the day, the notaries and clerks of various kinds, whether their names should be written in English, and transmitted to their posterity as MacIntaylor or as Camerons—a fact illustrated by numerous other instances in the Highlands." After further detailed criticism on various points, the Professor continues:—"The same passage in the *Records* [and already quoted by us, p. 55] which misled Gregory, seems also to have misled the author of the Introduction to Lochiel's 'Memoirs'; for whereas the former found in it the murder of a chief, which probably never happened, the latter evidently found in it, and with greater excuse and a greater show of probability, the assassination of Donald MacEwen Beg, for which also there seems to be no foundation, except this error. Closely scanned, the passage itself shows that it does not record the death of Donald MacDonald MacEwen, the chief; so neither does it register the fate of Donald MacEwen Beg; for it speaks of the brothers of the dead man—a phrase which cannot apply to Donald MacEwen Beg, who had no brothers." Dr. Taylor then points out that the perpetrators of the murder were befriended by Argyll, and were partisans of Donald MacEoghainn Bhig, and that the murder referred to in the *Records* took place when Allan of Lochiel was only 10 years old; whereas he did not return to Lochaber—after which event he is said to have agreed to the murder of Donald—until he was seventeen years old. The Professor then concludes:—"This point, however, does not depend on minute criticism. Allan MacIanduy had, in the meantime, been confided to the care of his relative, Mr. John Cameron, minister of Dunoon and Kilmun, in Cowal. Thither, also, we find Donald MacEwen Beg following him about this time—a fact which was unknown to the author of the 'Memoirs'. The Earls of Argyll and Athole having made up their feud, bonds of assurance and friendship were signed in favour of each other by these lords, at Dunoon and Dunkeld respectively. That which was subscribed by Argyll bears date 'at Dunoon, the xx. day of Julii, the year of God, 1576 years,' and is attested '*before thir witnesses, Donald McEwan VcOneill, in Lochaber*, and others'." He mentions another document as having been witnessed by the same person, under the designation of "Donald Cameron of Lochaber," on the 16th of May, 1577, and urges that this Donald is no other person than Taillear Dubh na Tuaighe, whose memory, under the latter designation, "has been cherished by his descendants in Cowal, down to the present generation". They have preserved a persistent claim of descent from him, and we have no hesitation in expressing the opinion that they are perfectly justified in doing so.

Ewen Beag and his followers refused to attend a Royal Court, held at Inverness, in 1552, when a commission was granted to the Earls of Huntly and Argyll against the Camerons and the Macdonalds of Clanranald, who proceeded to Lochaber to punish them, but the result is involved in obscurity. Ewen died about this time; but whether he was captured and executed under Huntly's commission has not been ascertained. It is, however, placed beyond dispute that he must have died before 1554, for in that year Queen Mary granted to George, Earl of Huntly and Murray, the nonentry dues of all the lands belonging to "the *deceased* Ewin Camroun, *alias* Littil Ewin, Captain of the Clancamroun, and also the marriage of his brother and heir, Donald Dow, or other lawful heir ".*

Leaving no legitimate issue, Ewen was succeeded by his brother,

XV. DONALD CAMERON,

Commonly known as "Domhnull Dubh Mac Domhnuill," who is found on record in the year 1564, when Queen Mary granted to "Donald Cameroun, the son and heir of the deceased Donald Cameroun or Alansoun of Locheill, the five pennylands called Lettirfinlay, of the old extent of 40s.; the five pennylands, called Stronnabaw, of the same old extent ; and the five pennylands of Lindalie, of the old extent of 50s., all of which were formerly held by them of the deceased George, Earl of Huntlie, by whom the lands were forfeited ".† The Earl of Huntly had been convicted and forfeited for high treason in the previous year for his opposition to the Queen, during her visit to Inverness. On that occasion, Donald Cameron of Lochiel joined her Majesty against the forces of the rebellious Earl, arriving too late to meet her at Inverness, but just in time to take part, with his followers, in the battle of Corrichy, fought on the 28th of October, 1562. His lands had been previously forfeited with those of the Earl of Huntly, who was Lochiel's superior, but on application they were restored as a reward for his personal loyalty on this occasion, and the faithful services previously rendered by him since he had assumed the chiefship of the clan. The charter differed from the previous one, insomuch that it was changed from a blench feu into a ward, but, according to the family chronicler, ennobled with all the immunities

---

* *Origines Parochiales Scotiae.*
† *Origines Parochiales Scotiae,* Vol. II., Part II., p. 177.

and privileges that the Earl and his predecessors formerly enjoyed.

In 1564 Grant of Freuchie became cautioner for Donald Cameron of Lochiel. Certain parties, of whom the Earl of Athole was the principal, became bound that Donald should remain in ward in Edinburgh under a penalty of 2000 merks, until Grant should come forward as his security. Donald at the same time came under a formal obligation to keep good rule in his own territorry, and in no way to trouble his neighbours. If he failed in this, he offered Grant as security that he should appear before the Council to answer for his conduct, under a penalty of 2000 merks. Donald executed a bond to this effect at Edinburgh, on the 3rd of November. On the 10th, his cautioner, Grant, executed the same at Freuchie, and it was finally recorded before the Privy Council on the 27th of the same month. Lochiel gave Grant a bond of relief, dated the 20th of November, he being in ward at the time, and by an act of the Privy Council, dated the 29th of June, 1565, at Dunkeld, Grant was discharged from all his obligations under the bond.*

Donald Dubh, according to the Memoirs, married a daughter of the Laird of MacLean,† without issue, and according to all the authorities, as well as the current traditions of the country, was succeeded as chief by his infant nephew—son of Ian Dubh, or Black John, third son of Donald, eldest son of Ewen Allanson, thirteenth chief, by Agnes or Anne Grant of Grant.—

XVI. ALLAN CAMERON,

Generally described in contemporary records as "Alein Mac Ian Duibh," but sometimes as "Alein Mac Dhomhnuill Duibh," the latter designation being applied to him, as the patronymic of the clan. This will account for the

* Lochiel's Bond, and Grant's Discharge are given in full at pp. 130, 132, Vol. III., *Chiefs of Grant*.

† According to Douglas's *Baronage*, Hector Mor Maclean of Duart who has a charter in 1539, 1542, 1548, and 1553, had three daughters, one of whom was "married to Donald, Captain of Clancameron".

error into which the author of the "Memoirs" has fallen in calling him the son of Donald Dubh, his predecessor in the chiefship, while in point of fact he was Donald's nephew. His grand-uncles, Erracht and Kinlochiel, took possession of the estate, on the pretence that they were acting as Allan's guardians, but it was feared by the more immediate friends of the young chief that his life was not safe from these grasping relatives, if he should continue to reside in Lochaber. They, therefore, removed him to Mull, to be brought up, as has been said, under the charge of the Macleans of Duart. The clan was governed in his absence by his grand-uncles, and Gregory informs us that, they made themselves so obnoxious by their insolence and tyranny, that Donald Mac Eoghainn Bhig, "the bastard son of a former chief," was brought forward by a party in the clan to oppose them. The laird of Mackintosh, taking advantage of these dissensions, invaded the Cameron territory, and forced the chief's uncles and guardians, Erracht and Kinlochiel, to enter into a treaty regarding the disputed lands of Glenlui and Locharkaig which was considered so disadvantageous to the Camerons that the feeling displayed by the clan when the terms of it became known was so strong that the Guardians were obliged to repudiate it and prepare for an immediate attack on the Mackintoshes. To strengthen themselves in their expedition against Clan Chattan, they attempted a reconciliation with Donald Mac Eoghainn Bhig— Taillear Dubh na Tuaighe, and arranged a meeting with himself and some of his followers at the Castle of Inverlochy, on which occasion, Ewen of Erracht was murdered by some of Donald's followers, and John of Kinlochiel was compelled to leave the district; but the latter was soon after apprehended by the Earl of Argyll, at the instance of Donald MacEoghainn, and executed at the Castle of Dunstaffnage. Young Allan of Lochiel was then called home, but he was soon after obliged to leave Lochaber again and keep away for a time, until, while resident in Appin, he nearly lost his life in a local broil, when his followers invited him home; and, about 1585, he again assumed command of his clan.

When he first returned to Lochaber he was about seventeen years old. The broil in Appin is thus described:—
"The laird of Glenurchy, predecessor to the Earl of Breadalbane, chosing to hold a Baron court in that neighbourhood, Lochiel went thither to divert himself, and there, accidentally meeting with one Macdougall of Fairlochine, a near relation of the Bastard, he challenged him upon some unmannerly expressions which he had formerly dropped against him with relation to that gentleman's [supposed] death. But Macdougall, instead of excusing himself, gave such a rude answer as provoked Lochiel to make a blow at him with his sword, and some of the bye-standers, willing to prevent the consequences, seized and held him [Lochiel] fast. While he made a most violent struggle to get loose, one of his servants, happening to come up at the time, fancied that he was apprehended by Glenurchy's orders, whom he foolishly suspected to have designs upon his life. This put the fellow into such a rage that he had not patience to examine into the matter; but encountering with Archibald, Glenurchy's eldest son, whom the noise of the bustle had drawn thither in that unlucky juncture, he barbarously plunged his dagger into his heart. The multitude, upon this, turned their swords against the unlucky fellow, but he, with his dirk in the one hand, and his sword in the other, defended himself with such incredible valour, that it is likely he would have escaped by the favour of approaching night, if he had not, as he retreated backwards, stumbled upon a plough that took him behind and brought him to the ground, where he was cut to pieces. No sooner had the enraged multitude dispatched the servant than they furiously rushed upon the master, who, though he received several wounds, had the good fortune, after a vigorous and gallant defence, to make his escape, wherein he was much assisted by the darkness of the night, which covered his retreat. The news of this, and several other adventures, made his clan impatient to have him among

them. All their divisions were now at an end, and their chief was of sufficient age and capacity to manage his own affairs, so that he was welcomed to Lochaber with universal joy," openly expressed by a united people.

Allan was a brave chief. He made several raids into the Mackintosh country, carrying away large booties on each occasion. In the quarrels which then raged so hotly between the Earls of Moray and Huntly, he joined the latter, and guarded the Castle of Ruthven for Huntly, while he attempted unsuccessfully to repair it. This involved Lochiel in constant feuds and sanguinary conflicts with the Mackintoshes, but he generally succeeded in getting the best of them, and was often able to carry a rich spoil from the enemy's country to his own.

In a letter by Robert Bowes to Lord Burleigh, dated the 23rd of September, 1591, describing what the king, then at Perth, was doing, he mentions, among other things, his Majesty's attempt to appease the quarrels and slaughters which then daily occurred between the Earl of Huntly and the lairds of Grant and Mackintosh, with others, in which the lairds of Lochaber and Cameron had "killed XLI. of Macintoyshes men, and XXIII. tennants of Grant, and hurt the Larde of Balendalough". Soon after this Lochiel again defeated the Mackintoshes on their own lands of Badenoch, with a loss of fifty men.

On the 14th of March, 1586, Lachlan Mackintosh bound himself to preserve and guard the lands of Urquhart, Glenmoriston, and all others belonging to the Grants against the incursions of the Camerons, Macdonalds, and their neighbours. In return, Grant and his curators bound themselves to invest Mackintosh in certain lands in Lochalsh and Kishorn, and in the castle of Strome, Lochcarron, with the office of Constable of the latter, all as formerly held by Cameron of Lochiel, but which had been forfeited by Ewen Allanson, and conveyed to James Grant of Freuchie, after the Raid of Urquhart, as compensation for the spoil carried away, on that occasion, by Lochiel and his companions.*

* *Chiefs of Grant*, Vol. I., pp. 112, 113.

On the 27th of March, 1588, a bond of mutual assistance, entered into a short time previously, between Mackintosh and Grant of Freuchie, was supplemented by a Royal Commission issued in their favour, and the Earl of Huntly, by which they were empowered to proceed against Allan, who, with a large following, had, during several months of the year 1584, made a descent upon the Mackintosh lands in Lochaber, and committed several depredations upon the inhabitants. On the 30th of June, 1589, we find Allan and Grant entering into a bond of mutual friendship, directed specially against the Macdonalds of Glencoe. In 1590, the two are again opposed to each other, under the leadership, respectively, of the Earls of Huntly and Murray.

An indenture is recorded between Huntly and Allan Cameron of Lochiel, dated 6th of March, 1590-1, by which the latter became bound to assist Huntly against all his enemies, particularly the Mackintoshes and Grants; while the earl, on the other hand, engaged to reward Allan to his entire satisfaction, and promised him that he should enter into no agreement with his own opponents which did not also include Lochiel. In terms of this treaty, Allan Cameron fought with Huntly at the battle of Glenlivet, in 1594, where, at the head of a few of his clan, he performed signal service against his old enemies, the Mackintoshes, whom "he defeated, and pursued with great eagerness, and did Huntly such services as merited a different reward" from that which he afterwards received.

There is a complaint brought before the Privy Council on the 7th of December, 1598, at the instance of John Dunbar of Moyness, George Dunbar in Clune, and William Falconer in Lethinbar, several gentlemen of the name of Rose, including Kilravock; Holme, Cantray, and several Camerons, for a raid upon the complainers, accompanied by very heartless conduct towards the female members of their families. The charge is for convocation of the lieges to the number of 200 "brokin hieland men and sorneris, all bodin in fear of weir, with bowis, darlochis and tua handit swordis, steilbonnettis, haberschonis, hacquebutis and pistolettes," who came, on the 8th of the preceding October, under cloud and silence of night by way of brigandage, to the said George Dunbar's dwelling house in Clune, pertaining heritably to the said George Dunbar of Moyness, and there treasonably raised fire in the said house, and in another cottar house of the said George Dunbar, burnt and destroyed the same, put violent hands on Marjory Dunbar, spouse of the said George Dunbar, and on Isabel Dunbar, spouse to the said William Falconer, tore their clothes of them and shot them naked furth of their houses, the said Isabel Dunbar being then lying bedfast in great "disease and dolour," she being but twelve days before delivered of a bairn; which bairn they most barbarously, without pity or compassion, threw out of her arms and cast forth on the midden. And not satisfied therewith they at the same time reft and away-took from the said George, furth of his house, his whole "insicht," plenishing, moveables, goods, and gear, together with three score [and] ten horses and nolt; and as many of the said nolt as would not drive, to the number of eighteen, they barbarously houghed and slew; committing here-through open and manifest treason, convocation of his Majesty's lieges, etc., etc. The charges to appear and answer had been successfully served upon several of the party, whose names are given in the Privy Council Record, but upon none of the Camerons present. The only one described by the family name is the chief, who is designated as "Allane Camroun of Locheldy," but the following whose names appear, seem to be all Camerons, though none of them are so named in the Record:—

"Allaster McAllaster Vc Coneill of Glenneves, Ewne McConeill VcEwne VcConeill of Blarmayselach, Johnne Badach Mc VcEwne of Errach, his brother Ewne, Duncan McMertine of Letterfindlay, his brother Donald McMertine, Ewne MacMartine, Donald McAneduy VcEwne, Allane McAne of Innerloch, Johnne Moir McAllane VcAne of Callardy, Allaster Dow McAllane VcEane of Culchinny, Johnne Oig McAllane VcEane, Ewne Mc-

Condoquhy, Dougall Oig McConeill VcCondoquhy Roy, Ewne McEane Tuich, Johnne McEan Tuich, Angus Oig McInnes VcMertine VcEane, Donald Dow McConeill VcEane VcMartyne, Dougall McAllaster VcConeill, Allaster McConeill, Williame McConduquhy Ban Millygane, Ewne McConduquhy VcEwne of Auchnesune, Johnne McEwne VcAllaster Roy, Duncan McAngus VcEane VcMartine, Donald Roy McAngus VcEane VcMartine, Donald Our VcInnes VcEane VcMartine," with about two hundred others, all of whom, not appearing, were denounced rebels by the Privy Council.*

Allan's reign was one of the most cloudy and disastrous in the history of the clan, though he was one of its bravest and most distinguished chiefs. His constant feuds with the Mackintoshes and with the Earls of Huntly and Argyll kept him constantly in hot water, and in the end he lost the greater portion of the lands which had been acquired by his predecessors; while he was, for a time at least, compelled to acknowledge Argyll as his superior, and to hold the remaining portion of his lands as that nobleman's vassal. The family Seannachaidh gives an interesting narrative of these and the other local feuds which occurred during Allan's rule. He describes how Mackintosh resolved to be revenged upon Lochiel for past raids into the Mackintosh country, and how for that purpose he prevailed upon the Earl of Argyll, whose sister he had married, to invade Lochaber from the West, while, with all the forces he could raise, he himself attacked him from the North, expecting that he would thus compel the Camerons to submit to such terms as he would be pleased to offer them. Lochiel, though he knew nothing of this confederacy, was so much on his guard, that Mackintosh found him quite prepared to stop his passage across the Lochy. Both parties continued inactive for several days. But provisions at last failing him, Mackintosh was reduced to great straits; Lochiel's party increased daily; and there was no appear-

* Register of the Privy Council.

ance of the expected assistance to his opponent from Argyll; so that Mackintosh was ultimately obliged to take advantage of the night to beat a retreat. Lochiel, suspecting that a stratagem was intended by his opponent, pursued him with great caution, until convinced that he had really retired. He would have been glad to have overtaken him and given him battle, but Mackintosh was soon out of reach.*

No sooner had Allan returned to the Isle of Lochiel, where he then lived, than he was informed of the arrival of another body of the enemy from the West, which not a little surprised him; for he had no expectations of any invasion from that quarter. This force was commanded by Campbell of Ardkinglas, who drew up his men, about 800 strong, at Achinloinbeg, opposite the island; but on being informed that the Mackintoshes had left, he retired to Inchdoricher, where he was well sheltered, and resolved to remain there for the night.

Lochiel, who had that morning dispersed his followers, immediately issued orders to have them again convened with all haste, and with his ordinary personal servants, eleven in number, he succeeded in finding his way, by private paths, where the Campbells encamped, and having carefully viewed them, he resolved to attempt to frighten them away with the few followers he had. He thought the effort might be made without much danger, for they were surrounded by lofty hills and dense woods on every side. With this object he placed his men at suitable distances from each other, and instructed them to fire, all at once, upon a given signal, and then to fall upon their faces on the ground. This performance was repeatedly gone through, and the enemy, several of whom were killed, became much alarmed. Thinking they had been surrounded on all sides, and afraid to advance or retreat, they continued where they were until morning, when they hurriedly retired and returned home.

But the severe laws that were put in force at the time, for

* *History of the Mackintoshes*, pp. 298, 99.

reducing the Highlands and for settling the peace of the country, gave Allan much more uneasiness than all the power of his enemies, and in the end did him greater injury. The Ministers of State, observing that the public were defrauded of the Crown rents and revenues in many places, procured an Act of Parliament commanding all chiefs and proprietors of estates in the Highlands and Islands holding of the Crown to appear personally, in the Court of Exchequer, before the 15th day of May, 1597, under pain of forfeiture, and not only to exhibit all their charters and writs, but also to find bail and security to pay the Crown revenues ; to make redress to all parties injured by losses and damages previously sustained; and to live peaceably in all time coming.*

This was a terrible blow to Lochiel, for he could not appear in consequence of the sentence of forfeiture and proscription previously passed against him, and as yet unremoved, "whereby he lost one of the best estates in the Highlands ". All this was owing to his hereditary enemy, Mackintosh, who engaged him in the fatal league with the Earl of Huntly, and who not only neglected Allan, contrary to express stipulation when he made his peace with the king, but, with the greatest ingratitude, took advantage of his misfortunes.

Lochiel took every means in his power to procure a remission so as to enable him to obey the Act of Parliament. But the time was so short, and the avarice of the courtiers so great (for they made a good profit of these forfeitures), that he did not succeed, and the Act was vigorously enforced. Finding himself thus in great danger of losing his whole estate, and foreseeing that he would soon be surrounded by a number of new enemies, as it would be the interest of all who shared in it to reduce his power and keep him down, he resolved to arrange his differences with Mackintosh, who was willing to accept any terms which admitted his right of property to the lands in

* *History of the Macdonalds and Lords of the Isles*, by the same author, pp. 199, 200, and 201, where the substance of this harsh act is fully set forth.

dispute, in the form of a regular treaty. Meantime Mackintosh, immediately after his return from Edinburgh, where he had gone to Court to obtain new charters to his estate, on conforming to the requirements of the new Act, invaded Lochaber at the head of a large force. He was, however, met by Lochiel, quite prepared to give him a warm reception. Friends on either side interposed and, in 1598, brought about an arrangement by which both parties agreed to the following terms :—

"Mackintosh mortgaged to Lochiel and his heirs one half of the lands in dispute for the sum of 6000 merks, and gave him the other half for the service of the men living upon them for 19 years; Lochiel's former title was reserved entire, but forfeitable, with the money, in case he should occasion a rupture of the friendship and amity then brought about between them, by any subsequent invasion or act of hostility, and Mackintosh became bound to preserve the same, under very severe penalties."

While Lochiel was busy arranging means for saving or recovering other parts of his property, an incident occurred that disconcerted all his measures, and drew new enemies upon him. John Og-Mac-Ian of Ardnamurchan, who had been betrothed to one of Allan's daughters, was basely murdered by his own uncle, while providing himself with a suitable equipage for the wedding, which, according to the custom of the times, was to have been celebrated with great magnificence. The murderer, commonly known as Mac Mhic Eoin, was a man of gigantic size and strength, and possessed the district of Suinart on lease from his nephew, MacIan, whom he had assassinated; not, it is said, in resentment of any injury done to him, but with the view of succeeding him in his estate and command of the clan as the next heir. For MacIan, Lochiel had the highest esteem, on account of his many excellent qualities; and he no sooner heard of his death than he determined to avenge it. The murderer, in dread of Allan's resentment, fled with all his goods and cattle to the Island of Mull, and placed himself under the protection of Lauchlan Mor Maclean, of Duart, a near relation, on his mother's side. Lochiel, getting information of his precipitate flight, pursued him with the few men he had about him, not exceeding sixty, and captured his goods, but notwithstanding the haste he had made, Mac Mhic Eoin managed to escape across the sound of Mull. Maclean, seeing all that passed, from the opposite shore, dispatched his eldest son, Hector, with 220 men, with Mac Mhic Eoin at their head, to recover the spoil. Lochiel, now finding himself obliged to fight, posted his men in an advantageous position, which largely made up for his deficiency of numbers. Mac Mhic Eoin, armed cap-a-pie, advanced with an air which indicated the highest contempt for his enemy; but feeling warm under the weight of his armour, he raised his helmet to admit fresh air, when one of Lochiel's archers at once observed this, and, taking aim, pierced him in the fore-head with an arrow, and mortally wounded him.

The following traditionary account of this episode, from two modern writers, will be found interesting. The first says:—The death of this ferocious warrior, as related by tradition, was characteristic. As he lay dying, he requested Lochiel to receive his sword, being unwilling to yield it to one of inferior station. As Lochiel approached, he made a blow at him with such force as to cut several ant-hills in its sweep, but it missed Lochiel. The armour in which he died was long retained at Acharn in Morven. His shield is still preserved at Laudal in that district. An old man in Ardnamurchan, still alive, though approaching 100 years, has often seen and put on his mail shirt.* The other, a fine Highlander, only recently gone from us, says:— The tomb of the renowned Mac-Mhic-Ian is still pointed out. The death of this celebrated personage, more famed for personal prowess than for more estimable qualities, is recorded in history as having taken place in Morvern in 1625, in a skirmish with the Camerons, to which clan, as the murderer of his uncle, John Og-Mac-Ian, the betrothed husband of Lochiel's daughter, he had become very obnoxious. In the traditionary narrative of the event, it is said that the Camerons and the followers of Mac-Mhic-Ian were drawn out and about to engage. One of the Clan

---

* *New Stat. Account for the Parish of Ardnamurchan*, written by the Rev. Archibald Clerk, LL.D., of Kilmallie.

Cameron, not the most powerful of them, observed Mac-Mhic-Ian uplifting his enormous helmet, upon which, drawing an arrow from his quiver, he remarked to a clansman, "though mighty this will do for him". "It is not," was the reply, "by the hand of the feeble, that he will fall." The bow was instantly bent; the swift arrow winged its unerring course; and the hand of the warrior, which at that moment was passing over his forehead, was pinioned to his skull. He fell; but, for a moment regaining his strength, he arose, and expressed a desire, it is feared a treacherous one, to deliver his sword to Lochiel. But the last spark of life was fast expiring. He clenched the huge weapon, and in the ire of death, transfixed it to the hilt in an opposite bank, and fell on it to rise no more. On his tomb there is the fitting representation of a mailed warrior, with a ponderous broadsword, and his bossy shield remains still in the possession of a gentleman residing in the immediate neighbourhood of Leac-nan-Saighid, or *the Ledge of arrows*, where the tragical event took place.*

The death of Mac-Mhic-Eoin so dispirited his followers that Lochiel secured an easy victory. Hector Maclean and twenty of his party were taken prisoners, but Lochiel immediately released them without any ransom. Lachlan Mor himself crossed the Sound of Mull during the action, and pursued Lochiel with a much larger force than his own, but he managed to escape without much loss.

Maclean was at the time engaged in a feud with the Macdonalds of Islay, in which he was soon after mortally wounded, when he expressed his grief that he had recently so much offended his relative, Lochiel; "for," says he, "he is the only chief in the Highlands of sufficient courage, conduct, and power to revenge my death, and I am confident that, if I had not injured and provoked him in the manner I have done, he would not have allowed himself much rest till he had effected it." Lochiel was no sooner informed of these remarks and of the death of Maclean

---

* *New Stat. Account for Morvern*, written by the late Dr. John Macleod, Minister of the Parish.

than he resolved to be avenged. He marched against the Macdonalds of Islay at the head of his clan, defeated them in a sanguinary battle, took Hector Maclean of Lochbuy, who aided the Macdonalds against his own chief, and several of his followers, prisoners of war, and detained them in chains for six months. Lochbuy, however, soon after had ample opportunity of being even with the Camerons.

This adventure gave Lochiel's enemies great advantage over him at court, where his son John, a young man of great ability, was busily engaged negotiating a settlement, and was in a fair way of succeeding. But those who expected to get possession of the portions of his lands contiguous to their own, exaggerated everything against him so much, that in the end they prevailed. "The Lord Kintail, predecessor to the Earl of Seaforth, got the estates of Lochalsh, Lochcarron, and Strome, from Sir Alexander Hay, the Secretary of State, who was the king's donatory to these and all the other forfeitures. The lands of Laggan, and Achadrome, Invergarry, Balnane and others, were obtained by the Laird of Glengarry and the Baron of Lovat, and his several estates in Lochaber fell to the share of others. In a word, he was stripped of the whole, except the disputed lands of Glenlui and Locharkike, which he still peaceably enjoyed by virtue of his late treaty with Mackintosh," entered into in 1598.

In this unfortunate position, Lochiel found it prudent to arrange matters with those who had obtained rights to his northern estates, as they lay so far away, and were not inhabited by his own clansmen. But his Lochaber lands he resolved to retain possession of at all hazards.

At Balmacan, Glenurquhart, the residence of Grant of Freuchie, Allan Cameron, on the 23rd of July, 1606, entered into a bond of mutual assistance and defence with Ranald MacAllan of Lundie and Allan Macdonald, his son, of Cillechriost infamy, the latter binding themselves to serve and assist Lochiel, subject only to the advice and consent of Grant.

The estate of Lochiel was purchased from the Secretary,

by Hector Maclean of Lochbuy, for a very small sum. But that gentleman finding, after several fruitless attempts, that he could not obtain possession, made it over, in 1609, to the Earl of Argyll, for the sum of 400 merks, the same amount that he had himself paid for it. Argyll's design in this purchase was probably not to keep the estate for himself, but seems rather to have been with the view of augmenting his influence, by forcing Lochiel to hold it direct from himself before he would consent to restore it. Several meetings took place between them, but they were unable to agree upon terms. The whole question was then submitted to his Majesty; and Clanranald—who had married one of Lochiel's daughters—was employed to negotiate for him at court.

The king succeeded to the English crown in 1603, and though he was "naturally merciful and just, yet he was somewhat too credulous, and very apt to take impressions from such as were about him, whereby he was often exposed to the artifice of subtile and designing politicians; many innocent persons suffered by this foible; but especially, after his going to England, where, being at a distance, he had not the opportunity to examine matters as he ought, and probably would have done, had he been nearer. Of this the unfortunate Clan Macgregor afford us a melancholy instance." The king was so prejudiced against this brave race that he resolved to get them utterly extirpated, and not only did he give the Earl of Argyll a commission to carry out his purpose, but wrote to all the chiefs and others of power in the Highlands to assist him vigorously—promising high rewards to such as should contribute most to the destruction of the Macgregors. Lochiel "was often solicited to join in that cruel confederacy, but he was too well acquainted with their story to comply, until the necessity of his own affairs obliged him; for his Majesty would hear of nothing in his justification upon any other terms, so that he was in the end forced to enter into indentures with the Earl of Argyll, as his Majesty's Lieutenant, and the Earl of Dunbar, Lord Treasurer, whereby the king became obliged not only to restore him to his estate, holding of the crown, but likewise to receive him as his tenant and vassal for the lands of Glenlui and Locharkaig ; and, in a word, to free him from all dependence and vassalage of any sort. The contract contains several other conditions in favour of Lochiel, who, though he never designed to injure the proscribed Macgregors, his faithful friends, yet thought there was no crime in embracing that opportunity to recover his estate, and ingratiate himself with his Majesty. Clanranald was also a party to all these contracts, in behalf of his father-in-law, whom he served with uncommon zeal. He was a youth of extraordinary qualities, a polite courtier, and very adroit in the management of business. He had formerly, in name of Lochiel, agreed with the Earl of Argyll respecting the Barony of Lochiel, the terms of which were submitted to the king. With these two contracts he set out, and upon his arrival at Salisbury, where the court then resided, he found a ready compliance from the king to all his demands ; for his indignation against the Macgregors was as strong as ever." This appears from his letter to Lochiel, wherein, after reciting Clanranald's negotiations, with the conditions of the two indentures, his Majesty is pleased to ratify them in the most ample manner, and assures him that, upon performance of the services thereby stipulated, they should be executed and fulfilled, and the charters and rights to his estate expedited, according to law. "Your neighbour," continues his Majesty, "hath likeways shown unto us the articles set down and agreed upon betwixt the Earl of Argyll and him, concerning the prosecution of our said service, whereby the earl hath submitted unto us his right and title acclaimed by him to your lands of Lochiel, and hath promitted to underly, and perform what we shall decern thereanent. You may be very glad that the earl hath taken this course, for we shall so determine in that matter for your welfare and security, as in reason, equity, and justice we ought to do ; and if your right to these lands be not good, we will be a means that the earl shall make the same better ; and, therefore, we will desire you, as you would have us blot out of our memory your former life, and to esteem and protect you, as our own vassal, tenant, and good subject, that you go on faithfully and carefully in this service, and prosecute the same to the final end thereof, in such form as you shall receive directions from the Earl of Argyll, our Lieutenant; and, in the meantime, that you seek all good occasions whereby you may do some service by yourself, and how soon the same is ended, you shall do well to repair to us that you may receive your promised reward, and understand our further pleasure concerning such other services as we shall employ you in." His Majesty also promised to cause the Marquis of Huntly to do Lochiel justice respecting a difference which had long existed between the two.

Allan refused to attack the Macgregors. They had often aided him in his wars, and he was too well acquainted with their story to act the barbarous part that was assigned to him by the Commission. Rather than be concerned in such horrid barbarities he preferred to treat with Argyll direct, with the view to recover a legal title to the estate of Lochiel; and, for this purpose he submitted in the end to terms which he had often previously refused. He agreed to renounce his former title, and to take a charter from Argyll in favour of his son John, holding the estate of him and his heirs taxed-ward, and paying yearly the sum of 100 merks Scots feu-duty. This bargain was concluded on the 22nd of August, 1612, the sum which he paid to Argyll, as the price of the lands, being the same as his lordship had previously paid Lochbuy for it.

Allan seems to have had his estates first forfeited about 1596, and ever after he is in constant trouble with his neighbours and with the crown. In the summer of 1605 he is summoned, with many others of the Western chiefs, to appear personally at Lochkilkerran (now Campbellton) to meet Lord Scone, Comptroller of the Kingdom, on the 20th of July, and to give security for the regular payment of his Majesty's rents and duties, and to bring with him and exhibit the title-deeds to all lands claimed by him. It was intimated that if any of the chiefs should fail to obey this proclamation, their title-deeds were at once to be declared null and void, and power was given to the Comptroller to pursue them with fire and sword, as rebels. That this might not be considered merely as an empty threat, the fighting men of the Western shires and burghs were summoned to attend at Lochkilkerran, well armed, and with forty days' provisions, to support the authority of the Comptroller. Robert Hepburn, lieutenant of the king's guard, was sent to the Isles to receive from their respective owners the Castles of Dunyveg, in Isla, and Duart, in Mull; and to prevent the escape of the islanders, the inhabitants of Kintyre and the Western Isles were ordered, by proclamation, to deliver up all their boats to this officer, being at the same time prohibited from using any boats whatever without his special licence.*

Allan Cameron, by a bond, dated at the Island of Lochiel, on the 8th of September, 1607, binds and obliges himself, his heirs and successors, to exoner, relieve, and skaithless keep, at the hands of the Lords of the Exchequer, Simon Lord Fraser of Lovat, Sheriff of Inverness, his deputies and clerks, of the sum of £710 Scots, contained in a precept of Chancery, on the lands of Knoydart, together with all duties, costs, and damage, that may follow on the obligation given.

We find Allan among six Highland chiefs who assemble in Edinburgh on the 28th of June, 1610, to hear his Majesty's pleasure declared to them. Gregory informs us that Maclean of Dowart, Macdonald of Sleat, Macdonald of Dunyveg, Macleod of Harris, the Captain of Clanranald, and Mackinnon of Strathordell, on that occasion presented themselves before the Council; and that to them was joined Cameron of Lochiel, "or, as he is styled in the record, Allan Cameron *MacIanduy* of Lochaber". The first step taken by the Government was to compel them to give sureties to a large amount for their re-appearance before the Council in May, 1611. The next was to oblige them

* Gregory's *Western Highlands and Islands*, pp. 306, 7.

to give a solemn promise that they should concur with and assist the king's Lieutenants, Justices, and Commissioners, in all matters connected with their several districts; that they should all live together afterwards in peace, love, and amity; and that they should agree to settle any questions of dispute arising between them according to the ordinary course of law and justice in the land. At the same time and place a particular feud between the Captain of Clanranald and Lochiel was arranged, by these chiefs "heartily embracing one another, and chopping hands together," in the presence of the Council, and promising to submit their disputes to the decision of the law.[*]

On the 9th of December, 1613, those who had charge of John, Allan's son and heir, were charged by the Privy Council to produce him to them, that they might take order regarding his education and the peace of the country. For their justification in so doing the Lords of Council say that Lochiel, "of his own natural disposition, being always inclined to murder, treason, and rebellion, it is very likely that he shall train up his eldest son, in that same wicked course of life, and now in his young age instruct him in all his policies, insolencies, and misdemeanours, wherewith he himself during the whole progress of his bi-past life has been exercised".

Shortly after this, Allan found himself face to face with a new and altogether unexpected complication with the Earl of Argyll, who, examining his charter chest, about the year 1608, accidentally discovered the title-deeds, which, in the reign of James V., Colin, third Earl of Arygll, had acquired to the lands of Lochiel. The successors of the third earl had hitherto allowed this claim to lie dormant; it had, indeed, been forgotten. The seventh Earl of Argyll, eager to extend the influence of his family, especially at the expense of his rival the Marquis of Huntly—to whose party the Camerons were attached—proceeded to avail himself of his recently discovered claim to the superiority of the lands of Lochiel. Having, to obviate any difficulties that might

---

[*] *Western Highlands and Islands*, pp. 339, 40.

arise, procured from Hector Maclean of Lochbuy, for a small sum, a surrender of any title which that chief might have to the lands, Argyll easily succeeded in obtaining a new charter from the king in his own favour.* He then instituted the usual legal process for removing Allan Cameron of Lochiel and his clan from that part of their possessions in question, much to the astonishment of Allan, who never knew that there was any defect in the title-deeds by which he and his immediate predecessors held their lands. Hastening to Edinburgh to take advice, Lochiel there met the earl, who prevailed on him to submit the question to the decision of their law-agents. The result was in favour of Argyll, from whom, by agreement, Lochiel took a charter of the lands, to be held by him as the earl's vassal, paying him a feu-duty of 100 merks, as already stated. The Marquis of Huntly, then superior of a great part of Lochaber, and from whom Lochiel held Mamore and other lands, was highly offended that Argyll should have been allowed so easily to obtain a footing in that district; and he endeavoured to prevail on Lochiel to violate his recent agreement with Argyll. To this demand Cameron would not consent; qualifying his refusal, however, by protestations that, although he now held one portion of his estates from the Earl of Argyll, yet that his so doing would not affect his obedience and service to the Marquis of Huntly, but that he should continue as loyal to that nobleman as he and his predecessors had always been in the past. This answer did not satisfy the Marquis, who secretly resolved upon Lochiel's ruin; and, as the easiest way to accomplish it, he sought to renew the dissensions which had, during the minority of Allan, caused so much bloodshed in the clan. The Camerons of Erracht, Kin-Lochiel, and Glen Nevis were easily induced to embrace an offer from the Marquis to become his immediate vassals in the lands which Lochiel hitherto held from Huntly. Accordingly, the Marquis's eldest son, the Earl of Enzie, proceeding to Lochaber with a body of his vassals, put

* Reg. of Privy Seal, lxxvii., fo. 65.

his adherents among the Camerons in possession of the lands of which, by the mere will of the marquis, Lochiel was now deprived. On the departure of Enzie, Lochiel appointed a meeting with his hostile kinsmen, at which he pretended being perfectly well aware that they had been compelled, by force, to enter into the plans of Huntly; and he, therefore, requested them to restore the lands to him, when he doubted not he would be able to satisfy the Marquis. At first, they made a verbal promise to do as he requested; but, when he desired them to subscribe a document to that effect, they declined, and pressed him to go with them to the marquis, with whom they engaged to reconcile him; after which they were to restore his lands. "Lochiel," says our authority, "like ane auld subtile fox, perceiving their drift, and being as careful to preserve his head as they were to twine (separate) him from it," promised to take the matter into consideration, and parted from his refractory clansmen on apparently good terms. He then made another journey to Edinburgh to consult his legal advisers as to the best course to pursue for the recovery of his lands. While there, he received intelligence that his enemies in the clan had appointed a meeting to consider the best means to kill him, and thus secure themselves in their new possessions. Upon this he hastened to Lochaber, sending private notice to such of the clan as still adhered to him, to meet him at a certain place, on the day appointed for the meeting of the opposite faction, and within a short distance of the spot selected by the enemy. The chief supporters of Lochiel, on this occasion, seem to have been the Camerons of Callart, Strone, and Letterfinlay. Placing most of his followers in ambush, Allan approached the rendezvous of his opponents with only six attendants, and sent to demand a conference with a like number of the enemy. His enemies, seeing him with such a small force, and thinking he had only just arrived in the country, and that he had no time to collect his adherents, thought this a favourable opportunity for getting rid of him, and, accordingly, made towards him and his attendants, resolving to kill the whole party. The wary Lochiel retreated, so as to lead his pursuers past the wood where his own men lay in ambush, and then, on a given signal, the foe were attacked in front and rear, and routed, with the loss of twenty of their principal men killed (of whom Alastair Cameron of Glennevis was one), and eight taken prisoners. The rest were allowed to escape; and Lochiel then replaced himself in possession of the disputed lands, teaching, as our authority quaintly observes, "ane lessone to the rest of his kin that are alyve, in what forme they shall carrye themselves to their chief hereafter".* On the news of this proceeding reaching the Privy Council, Lochiel and his followers were proclaimed rebels; a price was set upon the heads of the leaders; and a commission of fire and sword was given to the Marquis of Huntly and the Gordons for their pursuit and apprehension.† The clan, or at least that division of it which had followed Lochiel in the recent quarrel, continued for several years in a state of outlawry.‡

The following account of the difficulty with Huntly is thus given in the family Manuscript:—Lochiel having, in order to save the rest of his estates in Lochaber, employed the Marquis's eldest son, the Earl of Enzie, in whom he had absolute confidence, to put in for the gift of them from the king's donator, at such prices as could be agreed upon. His Lordship accepted the service, and made the purchases accordingly; but, as he had only acted in this affair as Lochiel's trustee, it was never doubted that he would resign them in favour of Lochiel's son, John, as soon as this should be demanded. But the earl acted upon more interested motives than was supposed, for he resolved either to keep the estates to himself, or, if he did restore them, it would be

* Original State Paper in Gen. Reg. House, entitled, "James Primrois' Information anent the Ilis and Hielandis, Sept. 1613". (Primrose was then Clerk to the Privy Council.) Record of Privy Council, December, 1613; July, 1617. Reg. of Privy Seal, lxxxii., fol. 285.
† Record of Privy Council, December, 1613; and Denmylne MS., Advocate's Library, *ad tempus*.
‡ *Western Highlands and Isles*, pp. 342-346.

upon such conditions of dependence and servitude as he knew perfectly well Lochiel would not consent to; nor could all the importunities of Allan and his friends prevail upon Lord Enzie to do him justice. These lands were then wholly possessed and occupied by Camerons; and Lochiel, knowing that no others dare inhabit them without his consent, resolved to keep possession of the lands, believing, in the circumstances, that it would be no easy matter to dispossess him.

Thus were affairs situated when Clanranald was commissioned to negotiate for him at Court; and his Majesty was so bent upon the extirpation of the Macgregors, that, in order to engage Allan in that service, he not only, as already stated, consented to all his demands, but also compelled Huntly to restore the lands which he had recently taken from Lochiel. Allan disliked the service required of him, but he thought it no crime to defend his own, and the better to enable him to do so, he secured the assistance of several of his neighbours, particularly that of Glengarry, to whom he gave one of his daughters in marriage, and, as her portion, the lands of Knoidart, reserving a small annuity and the superiority to himself; also the lands of Laggan and Achadrome, Invergarry, and Balnane, of which last Glengarry had formerly procured a gift from Sir Alexander Hay. Huntly was fully aware of the extreme difficulty of securing possession of the lands in question by force, and he made no attempt in that direction. He, however, adopted what he thought more effectual means, by bribing several of Lochiel's nearest relations, the sons of the late tutors, and others of that faction, whom, by under-hand negotiations, he carried over so entirely to his own interest, that they accepted leases of these lands from him, and engaged themselves not only to make good their possessions, but also to renounce any dependence upon Lochiel as their chief; and so absolutely to become Huntly's creatures as to agree to fight for him to the last drop of their blood against all comers.

When Lochiel discovered this treasonable plot, which

had all along been arranged with the greatest secrecy, he was much surprised and concerned as to what was best to be done. If the plot was allowed to mature, he saw that his ruin was complete, for, as his rebellious relatives had already gained over many members of the clan to their side, he knew that they would day by day increase in strength and numbers, and that his authority and reputation would be lost, and his family reduced to extremities. The conspirators, besides, to cover their crimes, added new guilt to their perfidy by patching up a title, and giving out that the head of their faction was the true heir of Ewen MacAllan, and that, consequently, he had a just claim to the estate and the chiefship of the clan. "What kind of logic they made use of to set aside the posterity of the elder brother I know not," says our authority, "but it is certain that they had a powerful faction in the clan, which abetted their interest at first; but the greatest part of them, being made sensible of their error, were easily reclaimed, and not only returned to the obedience of the chief, but assisted him in destroying their leaders, who continued obstinate to the last; for he commanded sixteen of them to be put to the sword, and by that terrible and exemplary punishment pulled up a faction by the root, that began at his very birth, and continued till that time. The news of this slaughter, which must be allowed to have been more necessary than justifiable, soon reaching the Marquis and his son, the Earl of Enzie, they resolved not to put up with the affront, and threatened to have him and his clan treated in the very same manner as their friends the Macgregors. They made hideous representation of matters at Court, and, having obtained a new sentence of outlawry and proscription against them, they applied to all the chiefs in the North for their assistance in executing it. However, they were all heard, and even Mackintosh, who thought with the rest that Lochiel had done nothing wrong, was so generous as to refuse his concurrence, alleging in excuse that by his treaty with Lochiel he could not attack him without incurring the penalty, which, as he then pretended, was the loss of the lands in dispute. That gentleman, having by this drawn the Marquis's indignation upon him, was some time thereafter, by his interest, arrested and confined in the Castle of Edinburgh upon this pretext, that he had not found surety for the peaceable behaviour of his clan, as he was by law obliged. But this friendship between him and Lochiel did not long subsist, for having marched into Lochaber in July, 1616, at the head of his clan, in order, as he gave out, to hold courts as heritable steward of that lordship, Lochiel, upon his approach, guarded all the fords of Lochiel, and opposed his crossing the river.* This, Mackintosh interpreted as a breach of the fore-mentioned treaty, which expired that year; and he applied to the Lords of the Privy Council, who, by their decree, found that Lochiel was liable in the mulct or penalty, and not only decreed and ordained him to remove, but also granted in July, 1618, letters of intercommuning or outlawry against all the inhabitants of the disputed lands. This brought on several invasions from Mackintosh, who gained nothing by them, but forced Lochiel, who was unable to grapple with so many enemies, to the cruel necessity of giving ear to some proposals of agreement offered by the Marquis of Huntly and his son, who now began to prefer their interest to their resentment. Several persons of the highest quality acted as mediators between the parties, and bestirred them-

---

* It is recorded in the Register of the Privy Council, under date, 10th June, 1617, that Lachlan Mackintosh of Dunachton, in the previous July, repaired and went to his "awan" (abhuinn, river) of Keppoch upon the water of Spean, where having staid and remained until the day appointed for holding the said courts, expecting nothing less than that any person or persons dared to have presumed to have interrupted or staid the holding of said courts. Then it was that "Allan Camroun of Lochzell, accompanied and assisted be Duncan Camroun, *alias* M'Martain; Dowgaill Camroun; Dowgall Camroun, *alias* M'Martain; Ewine Camroun, *alias* M'Martain M'Condochie M'Ewine" and others, with convocation of his Majesty's lieges to the number of two hundred men, all "bodin in feir of weir with bowis, dorlochais, durkis, Lochaber axis" and other weapons, stopped his passage, resolving by open violence to withstand the holding of said courts. Endeavouring to cross the usual ford, the Mackintoshes were fired upon by the Camerons, and Lachlan was "violentlie stayit" from crossing and from holding his pretended court. It appears that Mackintosh, after several attempts to punish the Camerons, succeeded in getting Allan's son, John, confined for some time in the Tolbooth of Edinburgh.

selves so effectually that they in the end brought them to submit to the following articles :—

1st. That there should be friendship and amity between them, and that Lochiel should renounce all his former rights to the several estates in dispute.

2nd. That the Marquis and his son should, in lieu of his claim, give Lochiel's son, John, a charter of the lands of Mammore, held of themselves and their heirs, for payment of 20 merks Scots yearly of feu-duty, and the service of the men living upon them, as often as it should be required.

3rd. That the said Marquis and his son and their heirs should not dispossess the present tenants of the estates that were by this bargain adjudged to them, but continue the said tenants in their several possessions for the same rents that they formerly paid to Lochiel. And

4th. To prevent future quarrels, it was stipulated that all differences that should thereafter happen to arise between the parties contracting should be referred to the decision of Alexander, Earl of Dunfermline, Lord Chancellor; John, Earl of Perth; Thomas, Lord Binny; and several others named in the indenture, who were the persons that acted as mediators; and, in default of them, to the sentence and decree of the Lords of Justiciary.

In terms of this treaty a charter was given to John, Lochiel's eldest son, by George, Earl of Enzie, with consent of his father, bearing date, 24th of March, 1618. By one of the articles it was agreed that the Marquis and his son should grant separate charters to the Camerons of Letterfinlay, Glenevis, Balanit, and others of Lochiel's friends and dependents, and of the several lands they had hitherto possessed as his tenants and vassals; and thus Allan was obliged to give up nearly two-thirds of his estate lying to the east and south of the Loch and River of Lochy. "Such was the reward he received for all the blood, trouble, and lands which he lost" in the service of the Marquis of Huntly, who, however, now engaged to assist him against his old enemy, Mackintosh—an engagement which his Lordship performed to the utmost of his power; for, personally, he hated Mackintosh, and was only too glad to do everything in his power to vex and trouble him.

Mackintosh finding it impossible to carry out his purpose against Lochiel, now supported by Huntly, resolved upon the expedient of misrepresenting and undermining him at Court, whither he proceeded. He found the king inclined to favour him, in consequence of the part he took in prosecuting the unfortunate Macgregors. These services Huntly magnified to the utmost, while he described Lochiel as a person "who contemned the royal authority, and who scorned to live by any other laws than his own—a common robber, destitute of all humanity; and filled the king's ears with such horrid notions of his barbarity and cruelty," that he obtained from his Majesty a letter to the Privy Council, at the same time conferring upon himself the honour of knighthood, "which show," says our author, "how easy it is for designing people to ruin the most innocent at the Courts of Princes, when there are none to vindicate them". This is the letter:—

> James R——Right Trusty and Right Well-beloved Cousins and Councillors, and Right Trusty Councillors, we greet you well,—Whereas, Allan MacCoilduy, in contempt of us and our government, standeth out in his rebellion, oppressing his neighbours, and behaving himself as if there were neither king nor law in that our kingdom: it is our pleasure that ye ratify what Acts ye have heretofore made against him; and further that ye expede a commission in due form to Sir Lachlan Mackintosh, the Lord Kintail, the Laird of Grant, and such others as the said Sir Lachlan may nominate, to prosecute the said Allan with fire and sword, till they apprehend him, or at least make him answerable to our laws; and that ye direct strict charges to all these of the Clan Chattan, wheresoever inhabiting, to follow the said Sir Lachlan in that service; also that ye charge the Marquis of Huntly and the Lord Gordon as Sheriff of Inverness, to be aiding and assisting to our said Commissioners: Moreover, that charges be directed to the friends of the Earl of Argyll, and all others next adjacent to the said Allan, in noways to assist him; with certification that whosoever shall aid, assist, relieve, or intercommune with him shall be accounted partakers of his rebellion, and be punished accordingly, with rigour: And the premises commending to your special care, as ye will do us acceptable service, we bid you farewell. Given at our Palace of Whitehall, the 6th day of May, 1622.

On the 18th of June, Mackintosh obtained a commission, in terms of this letter, addressed to himself and twenty-two other chiefs and gentlemen in the Highlands, but it was never, for various reasons, enforced. Mackintosh died suddenly four days after, on the 22nd June, at Gartenbeg, in Strathspey, on his way home from Edinburgh; and by the interest of friends an arrangement was soon after arrived at between the parties.

In the commission, Allan is described as the "one 'lymmair' that lies out and refuses to give his obedience, who being unworthy of our favour formerly shown unto him, when he stood in danger of our laws, and having made shipwreck of his faith and promised obedience, and shaking off all fear of God, reverence of us and our authority, and regard of justice, and being diverse times rebel and at our horn for cruel and detestable murders and other insolencies committed by him, he now has associated unto himself a number of other thieves, traitors, and 'lymmaris,' by whom he intends to entertain an open rebellion and to disturb and disquiet our peace in the Highlands, which we with so great pains, travels, and expenses, have settled in obedience; and whereas it is a matter touching us very highly in honour that such an unworthy caitiff shall so long stand out, as if he were neither subject to king, law, nor justice;" after which follows the names of the Commissioners and the usual powers.

Lord Mackenzie of Kintail, with whom, in the meantime, Lochiel settled an old dispute regarding his Lochalsh lands, declined to accept the commission against him. The Laird of Grant, though he was a son-in-law of Mackintosh, rendered Allan important services, instead of acting against him on this occasion in terms of the commission. Lord Lovat, another of those to whom it was addressed, was an old and hereditary friend of the family; while the Marquis of Huntly and his son, the Earl of Enzie, were, at the time, on bad terms with Mackintosh. The others named in the commission were equally unwilling to help Mackintosh, the result being that he was "at last obliged once more to try his fortune at the head of his own clan". Lochiel was prepared for him, and his men were keen "to measure the justice of their cause by the length of their swords; but he himself being unwilling to oppose the Royal commission, a treaty was artfully set on foot, and the parties agreed to submit all their differences to the Earl of Argyll, the Laird of Grant, and other arbitrators. Lochiel, by this, designed no more than to get rid of his present difficulties; and, though there was a decree pronounced, adjudging the estate to Mackintosh, who, in lieu thereof, was thereby ordained to pay Lochiel certain sums of money, yet he cunningly shifted the ratification, and continued in possession till his title became legal once more"; and the matter was left pretty much in this position until the rights of the family were finally secured by his famous grandson, Sir Ewen Dubh, of Killiecrankie renown.

This is fully corroborated by the public Records, from which the following additional particulars are given:— After the death of Sir Lachlan Mackintosh, Sir John Grant, as trustee for William Mackintosh, then a minor, obtained a licence for himself and others, dated 17th December, 1622, to intercommune with Lochiel, on condition that he would first treat with him to get him to return to his allegiance to the Crown, and only after that as to his difference with Mackintosh. The licence was afterwards continued to the end of July, 1623. After some correspondence, a conference was arranged which took place at Abertarff, on the 11th of July, 1623, Lochiel having on the 13th of June previously granted a safe-conduct, "under the pane of perjurie, infamie, and defamation for ever," to Grant and his companions. The question of allegiance was settled, without any apparent difficulty, and an agreement was entered into at Kilmichael, Glassary, on the 21st of September, 1623, that Allan should obtain a lease of the lands of Glenlui and Locharkaig during the minority of William Mackintosh, for ten years, at an annual rent of 1200 merks, half of which was to be remitted as the interest of a wadset, of half of the lands, made, in 1598, by Sir Lachlan Mackintosh to Lochiel, for 6000 merks. Mackintosh on attaining his majority was to be entitled to redeem the lands within the next four years. All the woods were reserved by Grant for Mackintosh, in whose interest they were to be sold, Lochiel getting ten per cent. of the price realized, on giving security that the purchasers and the workmen should be respected and protected while engaged in cutting the forest. By the contract, as finally agreed upon, Sir John Grant undertook to procure a complete remission for Allan for all his past misdeeds— "faultis, wrangis, injuries, and oppressionis, both criminall and civill"—and to get his son John released from the Tolbooth of Edinburgh, where he was then confined. Lochiel was to appear before the Privy Council on the 10th of July, 1624, and to give security for his good behaviour in future. On his having signed the agreement, Sir John Grant at once secured the release of young Lochiel, which with his other actions on this occasion made a deep impression on Allan, and filled him with warm sentiments of gratitude towards Sir John, as will be abundantly seen from the following letter addressed to him by Lochiel on the 18th of May, 1623 :—

> Having knowledge of the great trouble that your worship has taken and sustained now and from the beginning, for the relief of my son, your worship's carnal friend, from his long ward, until finally your worship has accomplished your worship's promise thereof; this is to thank your worship duly for the same, and promising, as I am bound by nature, to honour your worship's house, that I shall endeavour, myself and my whole power, to serve and pleasure your worship, during my life, all that I can. My son has visited your worship, even as he ought, and as I advised him to do; for I am glad he be with your worship while your worship pleases. Therefore let your worship take your time of him while your worship likes, and when your worship's will shall be that he comes here, where he has not been this large while byegone, let your worship advertise me aforehand, that I may send some servants to convoy him home, and then henceforth let himself acknowledge his duty towards your worship as he is adebted to do. For me, I will remain a fervent belover of my own, your worship's, blood, in the old form unto my death, etc., etc.

In a postscript he asks that Sir John Grant should send him the remission, which reaches him on the 31st of May. This appears from a letter, dated at Lochiel, the 2nd of June, in which he acknowledges its receipt, but complains that the writer of it "has not caused to be inserted any of the crimes contained in the Letters of horning and commission, raised at the instance of the late Mackintosh, his friends against me and my friends, which should be the special and first crimes that should be in my remission, seeing that the Clan Chattan, being my enemies of old, they are of all parties and competitors most ready to pursue me. Your worship will remember the promise made at our meeting that these Letters of horning and commission should be produced, and that the crimes contained therein should be first inserted in my remission; and likewise James promised to relax me and my friends from all these hornings. Therefore your worship shall write over to James Gibson to mend this fault, as I have written to him myself, and to get my remission passed anew, to the effect that these crimes may be inserted in it, otherwise I think my remission avails me little, since the wrongs done against my principal parties are omitted. For, as to the rest of my parties, although I had made no mention of them, I am assured never to be pursued by one of them that are my own friends, and I am fully reconciled to them." The original of the bond of caution granted by Allan is dated the 21st of September, 1623, and is preserved in the General Register House, Edinburgh, and the completed remission thereon was finally issued in his favour on the 28th of June, 1624. From the date of this submission and pardon, Allan and the Camerons were at peace—and consequently prospered, during the remainder of his reign—with the exception of a few unimportant local quarrels.

The most important of these, of which we have any account is the Raid of Moyness, which occurred in October, 1645. The Camerons proceeded to Morayshire, and carried away a large number of cattle from the lands of Moyness. Next day they were overtaken by the Grants in the Braes of Strathdearn, when Grant of Lurg, who commanded his clansmen, sent forward a powerful man, named Lawson, requesting the Camerons to leave the cattle, to avoid the shedding of blood. On his way back with the answer, one of the Camerons let fly an arrow, shooting him dead on the spot; upon which a sanguinary conflict immediately followed. The Lochaber men were defeated, nineteen "of one branch of the Clan Cameron" being left dead on the field, and all the cattle taken from the party. A great many of their men were also seriously wounded. Sir James Grant at once complained to Lochiel, who replied in the following terms :—

GLENLOCHARKEG, *18th October, 1645.*

Right Honourable and Loving Cousin,—My hearty commendations being remembered to your worship. I have received your worship's letter concerning this misfortune, an accident that never fell out betwixt our houses the like before in no man's days; but praised be God I am innocent of the same and my friends both in respect that they got within your worship's bounds, but to Morayland where all men take their prey, nor knew not that Moyness was one Grant, but thought that he was one Moray man, and if they knew him they would not stir his land more than the rest of your worship's bounds in Strathspey. And, sir, I have gotten such a loss of my friends which I hope your worship shall consider, for I have eight dead already, and I have twelve or thirteen under cure, which I know not who shall die or who shall live of the same. So, sir, whosoever has gotten the greatest loss I am content that the same be repaired to the sight of friends that loveth us both alike; and there is such a trouble here amongst us that we cannot look to the same for the present time, until I wit who shall live of my men that is under cure. So not further troubling your worship at this time, for your worship shall not be offended at my friends' innocency.

A week after he wrote as follows to the Earl of Seaforth, who had in the meantime complained of his conduct :—

LOCHAIRKEAG, *27th October, 1645.*

Right Honourable Lord,—I have received your lordship's letter concerning the unhappy accident that is fallen betwixt the laird of Grant's men and my kinsmen, which came to our loss both unknown to me, because I was in Argyll in the meantime; for the laird of Grant was the only man I love best in the north, because I came lately out of his house, and it came no ill betwixt us since then, till this unhappiness came lately; therefore I am willing to refer it to friends that will wise our weal both sides, and specially your lordship be the principal friend there; but my poor friends had nothing but the defenders' parts because they were in force to fight or die—not to trouble your lordship with many words to further occasion, commits your lordship to God's protection.*

The family historian concludes a sketch of Allan in the following terms :—" In all his troubles, he was vigorously supported by the Earls of Argyll and Perth, and the Lord Madderty, who espoused his interest with a zeal that seemed to be inspired with the truest affection and friendship. The Marquis of Huntly and the Earl of Enzie, his son, likeways showed him great favour after the reconcilement I have mentioned, nor were the lairds of Glengarry and Clanranald, his sons-in-law, the lairds of Grant, and others of his neighbours, less active in promoting his interest. Many of the letters that passed between him and

---

* These letters are printed in *The Chiefs of Grant*, Vol. II., pp. 76-76. At p. 529, the following story is related in connection with this raid :—

The Strathspey men on their way after the Camerons, and as they passed Kylachie, Mr. Mackintosh of Kylachie made offer of himself and his people to accompany them, but they declined his assistance, excepting one man of the name of Grant he had, who was a famous bowman. He went with them and acted valiantly. One of the Strathspey men there was one Grant of the old Ballindalloch family, who in that affair behaved most cowardly. As a punishment for his conduct, he was obliged every Sunday after sermon at Inverallon, during a year, to stand up, and say, in face and hearing of the congregation, " I am the man who behaved most cowardly on such an occasion"; and opposite to him, the other Grant, who had gone along with them from Kylachie, stood up and said, " I am the man who behaved valiantly on that occasion ".

these noble persons are still extant.* They were collected by his grandson; and as they generally relate to the passages I have pointed out, so the most important transactions of his life may be collected from them, and some other writs that are still to be found in the family. By this it appears that the Lord Madderty, brother to the Earl of Perth, was surety for him in all his transactions in the Low Country, and that he had the custody of his charters and such other papers as it was thought could not be safely kept at home, in these troublesome times. He had the good fortune to be reconciled with his majesty before his death. This favour he owed chiefly to the friendship of the Earls of Argyll and Perth, who represented matters in such a light that the king gave him a full remission for all the illegal and irregular steps of his life, which are therein recited. It is dated the 28th June, 1624, which was the last year of that king's life. His majesty was likewise pleased to write to his Council to receive him and his clan as his most loyal and dutiful subjects; and because he would be obliged, in obedience to the laws, to go in person to Edinburgh, in order to find surety for his clan, the king further commanded them to issue forth Letters of Protection, discharging the Lords of Session and Justiciary, and all other judges to sustain process against him and his clan for years, for any cause, civil or criminal, preceding that date. The only person that now gave him trouble was the laird of Mackintosh; but he had too much cunning and mettle for him." The recital of the adventures that befel him in his frequent journeys to Drummond Castle, the principal seat of the family of Perth, his address and cunning in eluding the stratagems made use of by Mackintosh to secure his person, while he was an outlaw, would no doubt prove entertaining, but our authority's "intended brevity" did not admit of his recording them.

Allan outlived the battle of Inverlochy, fought in 1645, and sent 300 of his name to join Montrose, though

---

* Supposed to have been written about 1733.

himself so old and infirm as to be unable to do anything but look on as a mere observer. He is alleged by some authorities to have sent the messenger, "Ian Lom Macdonald," the famous Gaelic bard of Keppoch, who induced Montrose to return to Lochaber and fight the battle of Inverlochy, where he gained such a glorious victory over the Earl of Argyll, who, at the time, had Allan's grandson, Ewen, the youthful heir of Lochiel, under his charge.

Allan married a daughter of Stewart of Appin, described as "a handsome young lady," who "so absolutely gained upon his affections by an excess of beauty, wit, and good nature, that he continued fond of her while she lived". By her he had issue—

1. John, who appears repeatedly on record during the life of his father. He is described as "a gentleman of exquisite judgment, who had a genius happily turned for the management of civil affairs".. He married, in October, 1626, Lady Margaret, daughter of Robert Campbell of Glenfalloch—who, in 1640, succeeded his brother, Sir Colin, in the estates and Baronetcy of Glenorchy, and became father of the first Earl of Breadalbane—with issue—(1) Ewen, afterwards the famous Sir Ewen Dubh, who succeeded Allan as seventeenth chief, and of whom presently; (2) Allan, who married in August, 1666, Jean, sister of James Macgregor of Macgregor. Allan was a gentleman of great parts, but he died in early life; (3) a daughter, who, as his second wife, married John Campbell, second of Barcaldine, son of Sir Duncan Campbell of Lochnell, with issue—a son, progenitor of the Campbells of Balliveolain.

2. Donald, progenitor of the Camerons of Glendesseray and Dungallon, and Tutor to his celebrated nephew, Sir Ewen, in which capacity he "acquitted himself with singular probity and honour".

3. Jean, who married "Alastair Dearg," eldest son of Donald Macdonald, VIII. of Glengarry, who died before his father, but whose son, Eneas, by Jean Cameron, succeeded as IX. of Glengarry, and was subsequently, in

1660, created a Peer of Scotland, as Lord Macdonell and Arros.*

According to the author of the "Memoirs," others were married respectively to Glengarry, Clanranald, the laird of Appin, Maclean of Ardgour, Macdonald of Keppoch, and "the rest to other gentlemen of that neighbourhood, whose names did not then occur" to him.

Allan died, far advanced in years, about 1647, when (his eldest son having predeceased him), he was succeeded by his grandson, the famous

XVII. SIR EWEN CAMERON,

Generally known among the Highlanders as "Sir Eoghainn Dubh," who, as already stated, was a minor when his grandfather died. Allan, the fifteenth chief, having died before his father, Ewen succeeded as his grandfather's heir. He was born in February, 1629, in the Castle of Kilchurn, the residence of his mother's family, the Campbells of Glenorchy, immediate ancestors of the Earls of Breadalbane. For the first seven years of his life Ewen was brought up, according to the custom of the times, in the house of his foster-father, "an antient gentleman, and Captain of a numerous tribe of the Clan Cameron, called by his patronimick, the tribe of Mackmartins," after which his care and education devolved upon his uncle, Donald, who, as his guardian, by skill and industry, preserved to him the remaining portion of the estate, most of which was lost during Allan's later years, when from old age and infirmities, he was unable to look after his affairs.

The Earl of Argyll, whose interest in Lochiel and his property had become more marked in recent years, feared that the youth's education might be neglected in Lochaber, and he strongly urged that for a time he should be handed over to his lordship's care. After considerable difficulty and hesitation on the part of the clan this was agreed to, and Ewen, when twelve years of age, proceeded to Inveraray, where, in 1641, he was placed under the charge of a special teacher.

* Mackenzie's *History of the Macdonalds and Lords of the Isles*, pp. 303, 304.

This, as is well-known, was an important period in the history of Scotland. Argyll and Montrose were soon to lead two opposing armies—the one for the Covenant and the other for the king. Argyll ravaged, burnt, and plundered the lands of Montrose, and Montrose retaliated by returning the compliment ten-fold, carrying the war into the county of Argyll, even to Inveraray. Soon after, on the 2nd of February, 1645, the battle of Inverlochy was fought, on which occasion three hundred Camerons joined Montrose, although their young chief was still under Argyll's charge. The result of this battle is too well known to need recapitulation here.

It is stated that Old Allan, who was then alive, though too frail to lead his men, looked on from a distance, and, immediately after the battle, congratulated Montrose on his great victory, and entertained him for four days in Lochaber. It will appear strange that Argyll still continued favourable to the Camerons and their young chief, and carefully attended to his education; but he had hopes, no doubt, of instilling his views into the mind of his youthful charge, and, through him, ultimately secure the clan in support of his own grasping policy. In this, however, he was completely disappointed. Our hero had already begun to give evidence of the qualities which he exhibited in so remarkable a degree during his long and glorious career as a Highland chief. Pennant says that Argyll, intending to bring him up "in the principles of the Covenanters, sent him to school at Inverara, under the inspection of a gentleman of his own appointment. But young Lochiel preferred the sports of the field to the labours of the school." Argyll, observing this, brought him back to himself, and kept a watchful eye over him, carrying him along with him wherever he went." This is corroborated by the author of the "Memoirs," who says that "His lordship had omitted nothing that he thought could contribute to the improvement of the fine qualities which he daily found increasing in his young ward". When about fourteen years of age, he was "of a good growth, healthful, vigorous, and sprightly. Though he had a good genius for letters, and a quick conception, yet his excessive fondness for hunting, shooting, fencing, and such exercises so carried his mind that he showed no inclination for his book, which obliged his preceptor often to execute his authority." Argyll, after the battle of Inverlochy, went south on some State business, taking his ward along with him, with the view of entering him at Oxford to complete his education. Passing through Stirling, on his way, he halted, that his companions and followers might obtain refreshments, but the pestilence, which at that time prevailed throughout the kingdom, raged to such an extent in the town, that Argyll deemed it prudent not to leave his carriage. Lochiel, however, stole away unperceived, and wandered through the town without any idea or concern as to the risk he was incurring. A search was made for him, when he was found in a house where the whole family was infected with the plague, but he escaped the contagion, to the great gratification of Argyll and his friends.

On the way south they remained a few days in Edinburgh, and afterwards at Berwick, where Lochiel often ran "the risk of getting his brains dashed out in quarrels, which he was daily engaged in with the youth of that town; so soon did he begin to act the patriot, and to employ his courage in vindication of the honour of his country". Argyll found it necessary not to permit him to go out of doors without a guard of two or three men to keep him out of mischief, if any one reflected in the slightest degree upon his Highland countrymen.

On another occasion, when Montrose attacked Castle Campbell, a stronghold on the borders of Fifeshire, then in possession of Argyll, a party of the Macleans, who were out with Montrose, marched up to the very walls of the castle. Though the garrison was six times the number of the Islanders, the inmates of the castle "had not the courage so much as to fire a gun, or even to look them in the face". Young Lochiel, who was present, was so disgusted with the cowardly conduct of the governor of the castle that he upbraided and told him to his face that he and every one of his garrison ought to be hanged; and then, turning to Argyll, exclaimed, "For what purpose, my lord, are these people kept here? Your lordship sees the country destroyed; and that they may be easily cut to pieces, one by one, without their being capable to unite and help one another; but your fellows are so unfit for the business for which they were brought here, that they have not courage so much as to look over the walls." Argyll made scarcely any answer at the time, but he soon after dismissed the governor, making him the scapegoat for what had actually occurred before his own eyes, while he was present in the castle, and when he could have assumed the command himself.

After the battle of Philipshaugh, which had proved so disastrous to Montrose, a Parliament was held by the Covenanters at St. Andrews, and several of the leading prisoners were taken thither to receive their doom. Among those condemned to death, on that occasion, were the Earl of Hartfell, Lord Ogilvy, and Sir Robert Spotiswood. Argyll took Lochiel along with him to that "bloody assembly"; and though "too young to make any solid reflections on the conduct of his guardian, yet he soon discovered an aversion to the cruelty of that barbarous faction". He was in the habit of visiting the prisoners personally in their dungeons as he travelled from place to place; but not knowing the reasons of their confinement, he is said to have had no other object in view than to satisfy his curiosity.

Lord Ogilvy, one of those condemned to die, had cleverly managed to effect his escape the night before the morning appointed for his execution. Another, the Earl of Hartfell, was saved through the influence of Argyll, "out of mere spite" to the Hamiltons, "whose blood [Hartfell's] they thirsted for". In consequence of Lord Ogilvy's escape, Sir Robert Spotiswood, and the others under sentence, were so strictly guarded that their nearest friends and relatives were denied access to them. Lochiel, however, determined to see the unfortunate men before their execution, and the difficulty of effecting his purpose only increased his curiosity and resolution to carry it into effect. He chose his opportunity when Argyll was otherwise busily engaged, and finding his way alone to the stronghold in which the doomed Royalists were confined, he called for the Captain of the Guard, and boldly demanded admittance. The officer, hesitating as to what he should do, excused himself by the strictness of his orders. Lochiel, nothing daunted or anywise put about, answered, "What! I thought you had known me better than to fancy that I was included in these orders! In plain terms, I am resolved not only to see these gentlemen, but expect you will convey me to their apartments." This was spoken with such an assurance that the Captain of the Guard, fearing the frowns of the Marquis if he disobliged his favourite, ordered the doors to be opened, personally showed Lochiel into Sir Robert Spotiswood's room, made excuse that he could not stay, and then retired, leaving the two alone together.

This interview was the turning point in Lochiel's long and remarkable career; and what took place is so interesting and so eloquently told by the author of the "Memoirs," that we give it almost in his own words, merely modernising the spelling. He says:—That venerable person [Sir Robert Spotiswood] appeared no way dejected, but received his visitant with as much cheerfulness, as if he had enjoyed full liberty. He viewed him attentively all over, and, having informed himself as to who he was, and of the occasion of his being in that place, said, "Are you the son of John Cameron, my late worthy friend and acquaintance, and the grandchild of the loyal Allan MacCoilduy, who was not only instrumental in procuring that great victory to the gallant Marquis of Montrose, which he lately obtained at Inverlochy, but likewise assistant to him in the brave actions that followed, by the stout party of able men that he sent along with him?" and then, embracing the youth with great tenderness, he asked him how he came to be put in the hands of Argyll. Lochiel having satisfied him on this point, Spotiswood continued, " It is surprising to me that your friends, who are loyal men, should have entrusted the care of your education to a person so opposite to them in principles, as well with respect to the Church as to the State! Can they expect you will learn anything at that school but treachery, ingratitude, enthusiasm, cruelty, treason, disloyalty, and avarice." Ewen excused his friends, and answered that Argyll was as civil to and careful of him as his father could possibly be, and he wished to know why he charged him with such vices. Sir Robert answered, that he was sorry he had so much reason ; and that, though the civility and kindness he spoke of were dangerous snares for one of his years, yet he hoped, from his own good disposition, and the loyalty and good principles of his relations, that he would imitate the example of his predecessors, and not of his patron. Sir Robert then proceeded to explain the history of the Rebellion from its beginning, the different factions that had conspired against the Crown, the nature of the constitution, insisting much on " the piety, innocence, and integrity of the king". He omitted no circumstance which he thought necessary to give Lochiel a clear conception of the state of affairs. The youth was amazed at the narrative, to which he listened with great attention. It affected him greatly, and "he felt such a strange variety of emotions in his breast, and conceived such a hatred and antipathy against the perfidious authors of these calamities, that the impression continued with him " for the remainder of his life.

Sir Robert Spotiswood was much pleased that his remarks had produced the desired effect. He urged upon his young friend to leave Argyll as soon as he possibly could, and exhorted him, "as he valued his honour and prosperity in this life, and his immortal happiness in the next, not to allow himself to be seduced by the artful insinuations of subtle rebels, who never wanted plausible pretexts to cover their treasons; nor to be ensnared by the hypocritical sanctity of distracted enthusiasts; and observed that the present saints and apostles, who arrogantly assumed to themselves a title to reform the Church, and to compel mankind to believe their impious, wild, and indigested notions as so many articles of faith, were either excessively ignorant or stupid, or monstrously selfish, perverse, and wicked. Judge always of mankind, by their actions; there is no knowing the heart. Religion and virtue are inseparable, and are the only sure and infallible guides to pleasure and happiness. As they teach us our several duties to God, to our neighbour, to ourselves, and to our king and country, so it is impossible that a person can be imbued with either, who is deficient in any of these indispensable duties, whatever he may pretend. Remember, young man, that you hear this from one who is to die to-morrow, for endeavouring to perform these sacred obligations, and who can have no interest in what he says, but a real concern for your prosperity, happiness, and honour."

Several hours elapsed, while he listened to the eloquent and doomed Royalist, before Lochiel became aware that he had remained so long. "He took leave with tears in his eyes, and a heart bursting with a swell of passions, which he had not formerly felt." He next visited the apartments of Colonel Nathaniel Gordon and William Murray, brother of the Earl of Tullibardine, both under sentence of death. Murray "was a youth of uncommon vigour and vivacity, and, though only in his nineteenth year, he bore his misfortune with such a heroic spirit as greatly impressed Lochiel, to whom the doomed youth stated that he was not afraid to die, since he was to die for the performance of his duty, and was assured of a happy immortality for his reward." Next day these unfortunate men were executed in presence of the young and generous Lochiel.

The effect of Sir Robert Spotiswood's eloquence on the scaffold was so much dreaded by the dominant faction that his mouth was actually stopped by the gag, while he was at the same time tormented with the canting exhortations and rhapsodies of the officiating ministers of the Kirk.

Lochiel occupied a window, with Argyll and other leaders, directly opposite the scaffold, and the horrid proceedings carried out before his eyes, in the name of religion, so impressed his young, heroic spirit, that he gave open expression to his excessive grief. It is recorded, that the exemplary fortitude and resignation of the noble sufferers drew tears from the eyes of most of the spectators, though they had all been prepossessed against the victims, by the clergy and other fanatics, as accursed wretches, guilty of the most enormous crimes, and "indicted by God himself, whose Providence had retaliated upon themselves the mischiefs they had so often done to His servants". When the bloody work was over, Lochiel, who still maintained complete secrecy regarding his visit to the doomed Royalists on the previous evening, asked, "What were their crimes? for nothing of the criminal," he remarked, "appeared in their behaviour; they had the face and courage of gentlemen, and they died with the meekness and resignation of men that were not conscious of guilt. I expected to have heard an open confession of their crimes from their own mouths; but they were not allowed to speak, though I am informed that the most wicked robbers and murderers are never debarred that freedom." Argyll was much surprised and not a little startled upon hearing these observations from so young and inexperienced a man, and he used all his arts and eloquence to remove the impressions which he found had been made on the generous mind of his ward. He justified the conduct of his own party, and painted the actions of his opponents in the most odious colours, saying, "that the behaviour of the sufferers did not proceed from their innocence, but from certain confirmed opinions and principles which were very mischievous to the public, and had produced very fatal effects; that the crimes of robbery, murder, theft, and the like were commonly committed by mean people, and were too glaring, ugly, and odious in their nature to bear any justification, and that, therefore, it was for the benefit of mankind that the criminals should be allowed to recite them in public; because the design was not to make converts, but to strike the audience with horror; that the Provost did wisely in not allowing the criminals to speak, and especially Sir Robert Spotiswood, for he was a man of very pernicious principles, a great Statesman, a subtle lawyer, and very learned and eloquent, and, therefore, the more capable to deduce his wicked maxims and dangerous principles in such an artful and insinuating manner as would be apt to fix the attention of the people, and to impose upon their understanding. There is such a sympathy in human nature, and the mind is so naturally moved by a melancholy object, that whatever horror we may have at the crime, yet we immediately forget it, and pity the criminal when he comes to suffer; the mind is then so softened, that it is very apt to take such impressions as an artful speaker is inclined to impress upon it; the misery of his condition is an advocate for his sincerity; and we never suspect being imposed upon by a person who is so soon to die, and who can have no interest in what he endeavours to convince us of; and yet experience shows us great numbers who die in the most palpable and pernicious errors, which they are as anxious to propagate even at the point of death as they were formerly when their passions were most high." His Lordship then proceeded to explain the causes of the war, and accused the king and the Ministers of being its sole authors. He alleged that the massacre of the Protestants in Ireland was by his Majesty's warrant; that all the oppressions in England, the open encroachments upon the civil and ecclesiastical liberties of Scotland, and all their other grievances, were the effect of the king's assuming an absolute and tyrannical authority over the lives, liberties, and properties of his subjects; he inveighed against Montrose and his followers, not only as the abettors of slavery and tyranny, but as common robbers, and as the public enemies of mankind. He said that the malefactors who had been executed were guilty of the same crimes, and that they justly suffered for murder, robbery, sacrilege, and rebellion. In a word, he pled his cause with such persuasive eloquence, and with such seeming force of argument and reason, that his address would doubtless have made dangerous impressions upon the mind of his young pupil, had he not been wholly prepossessed by the more solid reasonings of Sir Robert Spotiswood. That great man had fully informed him of all that was necessary to prevent his being thereafter imposed upon; and there is such a beautiful uniformity in truth that it seldom misses to prevail with the generous and unprejudiced.

Lochiel did not then think it prudent to answer Argyll at any length, or to reveal his real sentiments. All he said was that he was told that Montrose was a very brave man, and that, though he had killed many in battle, he had never heard of any whom he had put to death in cold blood; that he wondered that so good a man as the king was said to be could be guilty of so much wickedness; and that he believed the charge either to be the misrepresentations of his enemies, or that such things were the doings of those who managed for him; that he was himself perhaps too young to judge, but he thought it hard that any man should suffer for what he believed to be true; and that, if the gentlemen whom he saw that day meeting death with so much courage were guilty of no other crimes than fighting for the king—whom they owned as their master—and differing in points of religion, he thought that the laws were far too severe.*

He was so horrified at the number of executions, the injustice, in his opinion, done to the king, and the aversion which he had conceived to his Majesty's enemies, that he resolved upon leaving Argyll, and returning to Lochaber on the first opportunity that presented itself, fully determined to join Montrose. Meanwhile, the Battle of Preston had been fought and lost by the Royalists; Cromwell was supreme in the South. He had been invited to Scotland by Argyll and his adherents. Berwick and Carlisle had

---

* *Memoirs of Lochiel*, pp. 76-82.

been delivered up to him by their orders, and, soon after, the king himself was brought to trial and executed. Argyll had meantime returned to Inveraray. More sanguinary work followed. Argyll and Mr. John Newry, "a bloody preacher," induced David Leslie, who commanded the Covenanting troops, to break his word of honour; and after disarming the country people—who surrendered on condition that they would be granted their lives and liberty—were mercilessly put to the sword and massacred in cold blood. Leslie was so horrified at the barbarous slaughter of the disarmed and helpless people that he turned round to Newry—who gloated over the atrocious work as only a religious fanatic could, and who was at the time walking with Argyll, ankle deep in human blood—and asked him, "Now, Mess John, have you not, for once, gotten your fill of human blood?" These words had the effect of saving eighteen persons, who, however, were immediately carried prisoners to Inveraray, where they would have been allowed to die from starvation were it not for the humane and generous action of Lochiel, who secretly visited them every day, and directed food to be conveyed to them, unknown to their enemies, by his own body-servants, or others in whom he placed confidence.

These inhuman proceedings made Lochiel still more anxious to return home, but as Argyll still continued personally very kind and agreeable to him, he was unwilling or afraid to intimate his wishes to him. He, however, privately wrote to his uncle, in Lochaber, asking him to demand his return home, for some important purpose, and promising to send him back to Inveraray whenever Argyll should require him to do so. On receipt of this communication from his nephew, the Tutor convened a meeting of the leading men of the clan, and, soon after, Argyll was addressed by the Camerons in a body, while his Lordship was in Moidart to reduce Castletirrim, the stronghold of Clanranald, and the last which held out for the Royal cause in those parts of the Highlands. His Lordship, we are told, the more easily complied with the demand of the Camerons "that he foresaw he would quickly have business enough on his hands in settling the State, which then changed as often as the moon ".* Lochiel, soon after, in his eighteenth year, returned to Lochaber, amid the plaudits of his retainers, who received him with great pomp, and came a day's journey to meet him.

He was received by his clansmen with the greatest enthusiasm. They were gratified to see that he even exceeded the flattering accounts which had reached them regarding him, and they were still more delighted to find that, notwithstanding his upbringing and education under Argyll's influence, he still adhered to the political and patriotic principles of his ancestors.

His biographer informs us that, at this time, he was "healthful and full of spirits, and grown up to the height of man, though somewhat slender. Though he had made no progress in letters, yet his natural quickness, and the polite company among whom he had the good fortune to be bred so formed his behaviour and polished his conversation, that he seemed to anticipate several years of his age. The truth is, the want of an academical education was an advantage to him, whatever losses he might afterwards sustain by that defect ; and the reason is obvious, for the time employed on words and terms is of no further advantage than as it lays a foundation for the nobler acquisition of substantial knowledge, and before youth advance to any tolerable reflection they commonly exceed that age, and in place of a just and solid reasoning they acquire crude and undigested notions which render them disagreeably conceited and self-sufficient." He then proceeds to reason that, as teachers generally are more conversant with books than with men, it is no wonder if they are somewhat stiff and pedantic in their manners and conversation ; and that it is natural to those brought up under such influences to imitate, in these respects, those by whom, in their youth, they are taught ; and experience shows that several years must pass before they can entirely lay aside

* *Memoirs of Lochiel*, pp. 76-82.

the habits contracted under such influences in early life ; "but as Lochiel had the misfortune not to be troubled with books, by the iniquity of the times, so his early introduction with good company gave him this advantage above those of his years, that he was sooner ripe for company and action, and more adroit in the exercises befitting a gentleman, wherein the Marquis was very careful to have him trained by expert masters ;" which was very much to his credit, when we consider the circumstances of the times.

Lochiel's principal amusement was hunting, of which he was passionately fond. He destroyed all the wolves which then largely infested his own district, and he is said to have killed, with his own hand, the last wolf seen in the Highlands of Scotland. In pursuit of his favourite amusement he exposed himself to continual hardships and fatigue, which only made him the more vigorous and robust, acquiring strength and experience which well-fitted his naturally robust constitution of body and mind for the many difficulties and dangers which he had to go through during his long and remarkable career. He kept Colonel Cameron, who commanded those of the clan who joined Montrose, constantly about him. This officer, who had secured for himself a high reputation for gallantry, and had been repeatedly wounded in the late war, related to his young chief the leading events and incidents of the campaign. These Lochiel listened to with great interest, and he was so charmed with the story and with the valour and general conduct of his clansmen, exhibited during the war, that he succeeded in procuring a life-pension for their commander from Charles II. On hearing the Colonel's relation of the distinguished gallantry of Montrose, Lochiel keenly bewailed his own misfortune for having missed the opportunity of serving under such a commander, and being trained in such a noble school ; and he often expressed the hope that the illustrious hero would soon again lead his countrymen in the cause of the king, in which event the young chief declared his resolve to join him at the head of his clansmen.

The first opportunity which he had of leading them in the field was in a raid against Macdonald of Keppoch, who, despising our hero on account of his youth, and the indifference of his uncle, still his guardian, refused to pay an annuity due by him on a mortgage which Lochiel held over Glen-Roy. Preparations were made by the Camerons to enforce payment. Lochiel gathered his men, placed himself at their head, and invaded the Keppoch country with several hundred resolute followers. Macdonald, though he at first determined, and made preparations, to oppose the invaders, finding them resolute and well led, deemed it prudent to arrange terms, and Lochiel's claims were promptly admitted and satisfied. A similar dispute arose between him and Glengarry, who refused to pay a feu of superiority due by him to the head of the House of Lochiel for the lands of Knoydart. This claim was also amicably arranged, and a treaty entered into which Glengarry subsequently carried out in every particular. These incidents establish the fact that Lochiel's great qualities as a soldier and a leader of men were recognized by his turbulent neighbours even at this early age.

For a considerable time after this period nothing remarkable seems to have occurred either in his own history or in that of his people. The author of the " Memoirs " states that " Lochiel had, all this time, the pleasure to see his people happy in a profound peace, while the rest of the kingdom groaned under the most cruel tyranny that ever scourged the afflicted sons of men. The jails were crammed full of innocent people, in order to furnish our governors with blood-sacrifices wherewith to feast their eyes ; the scaffolds daily smoked with the blood of our best patriots ; anarchy swayed with an uncontroverted authority ; and avarice, cruelty, and revenge seemed to be Ministers of State. The bones of the dead were digged out of their graves, and their living friends were compelled to ransom them at exorbitant sums. Every parish had a tyrant, who made the greatest lord in his district stoop to his authority. The Kirk was the place where he kept his court; the pulpit his throne, or tribunal, from whence he issued out his terrible decrees; and twelve or fourteen sour, ignorant enthusiasts, under the title of elders, composed his councils. If any, of what quality soever, had the assurance to disobey his edicts, the dreadful sentence of excommunication was immediately thundered against him, his goods and chattels confiscated and seized, and he himself being looked upon as actually in possession of the devil, and irretrievably doomed to perdition, all that conversed with him were in no better esteem." The history of those times is already too well known to need recapitulation here. Fearful excesses were resorted to on both sides. We shall not attempt to show in whose favour the balance turned. The subject is not pleasant, but we confess a preference for the patriots of those days than for the Kirk. The former were honest, though, no doubt, mistaken in supporting a worthless king. The Kirk was dishonest, hypocritical, and intolerant, but the nation ultimately benefitted by it, in spite of its godless cant and cruel persecution of far better men than those of whom its leaders were then generally composed.

It is unnecessary to discuss the mean conduct of the clergy in their dealings with, perhaps, their equally mean and worthless king. The particulars of the second expedition of Montrose, his capture, and execution, are well known; but it may be stated that, when his sentence was read to him, he declared that, so far from being troubled at his head being ordered to be hung on the Tolbooth of Edinburgh, and his limbs in conspicuous places in four of the principal cities of the kingdom, "he heartily wished that he had flesh enough to be sent to every city in Christendom as a testimony of the cause for which he suffered". Such heroism and nobility of spirit had no counterpart among his enemies.

The king was now in the power of the Kirk. In 1650 he sent the following letter, directed on the back :—

"*To our Right Trusty, and Right Well-beloved Ewen Cameron of Lochiel, and to the rest of the Gentlemen and Friends of the Name of Cameron.*

"CHARLES R.

"Right Trusty and Well-beloved Cousin, and Trusty and Well-beloved, wee greet you well. The condition and calamity of this Kingdom cannot but be too well known unto you. Ane insolent enemy having gott so great ane advantage against the forces that were raised for the defence of it, and having overrun the parts upon the South sides of the Forth and the Clyde, and having of late also gotten into their hands the Castle of Edinburgh, by the treachery of those that commanded in it; which city they before desolated, ruined the church, and maliciously and insolently burnt our Palace there. These injureys, and the maney other grevious pressures lying upon our good subjects in the South, East, and Western Shyrs, cry alowd for relief, assistance, and revenge. Therefore wee have, with the Estates of our Parliament, been consulting and adviseing for remedys; and have emited the act of levey which comes to your Shyrs, and which wee thought fitt to accompany with our oun letter: Conjureing and desireing you, by all the bands of your duty to God, love to your country, and respect to our person, that you will speedily and effectwally rise and putt yourselves in arms for the relief of your distressed brethren, and to revenge their bloodshed by the sword in diverse corners of the countrey; besides the multitudes starved to death in prissons, and famished and dying every day for want of bread in each town and village. These things, wee know well, exceedingly affect you; therefore wee will not lay any thing more before you but our own resolutions, which is, either, by the blessing and assistance of God, to remedy and recover these evils and losses, revenge what these insolent enemys have crewelly and wickedly done, vindicate this hitherto unconquered Nation from the ignominy and reproach it lyes under; or to lay down our life in the undertaking, and not to survive the ruine of our people, for whose protection and defence we would give, if we had them, as many lives as wee have subjects. And wee are assured and perswaded you will not be wanting in your duties, but will chearfully come to offer your lives for the defence of your Religion, your Countrey, your King, your own honours, your wives, your children, your liberty, and will be worthy your forefathers and predecessors, and like them in their virtue, and brave defending their countrey. We will, therefore, in assurance you will strive who shall be soonest in sight of the enemy, march with the present forces wee have towards Stirling (where the nixt assault will certainly be), and either make good that place till you come to us, or die upon the place; and if the handfull we carry with us shall be overborn by greater numbers throwgh your slackness in comeing to our assistance, you will have the shame that yow have not already come upon the call of a redoubled defeat given to your naturall and covenanted brethren, and that yow have not now used extraordinary dilligence, being so earnestly prest by your king on his part. But wee confidently expect from you all imaginable expressions and effects of duty, dilligence, loyalty, and courage. And so wee bid yow heartily fairwell. Given att our Court att Perth, the 24th of December, 1650, and in the second year of our reign."

In response to this Royal message Lochiel declared his intention of joining the king, with a body of his clansmen, early in the following spring, but finding much difficulty in raising them, in consequence of many of his name living on the lands of others, he applied to Argyll, through whom he obtained a warrant, from the Committee of Estates, empowering him to raise the Camerons wherever he could find them. Meanwhile the Scottish army, of which the king was nominal Commander, was defeated by Cromwell at Inverkeithing, and a report of that disaster was communicated to Lochiel as he was on his march to join the Royal Standard, at the head of a thousand of his clansmen.

In the spring of 1652, he was the first of the Highland chiefs who joined the Earl of Glencairn, with a body of seven hundred brave followers, afterwards considerably augmented by fresh arrivals from Lochaber. Having received a Colonelcy in this army he soon had an opportunity of displaying his metal, and of giving the first example of his bravery and courage in the field. "He was always the first that offered himself in any dangerous piece of service, and, in all that he undertook, acquitted himself with such conduct and valour that he gained great glory and reputation." Soon after joining Glencairn, he found himself and his men in a position where they narrowly escaped from the imminent danger of being cut to pieces by the enemy, under Colonel Lilburn, then newly appointed Commander, in succession to Monk and Colonel Dean. He was at this date, 1652, a youth only twenty years old.

Glencairn having encamped with his army at Tullich, in Braemar, Lochiel and his men were posted at a pass, which lay at some distance, to prevent the Earl being surprised by the enemy, possessed of a garrison within a few miles of him. Lochiel placed guards and sentries in suitable places, often visiting them in person; and, notwithstanding his youth, acted the part of a vigilant and prudent officer. Early the following morning, as he sent for orders from the General, his scouts hastily returned, informing him that the enemy were advancing at a smart pace, but they could not tell him their exact number. Having ordered his men to their several posts, he ascended a hill near, where he had a full view of the foe. Lilburn, who commanded in person, with his whole army, having made a halt to form, gave Lochiel sufficient time to enable him to advise Glencairn of the position. The latter at once retreated to a morass two miles distant, where he secured himself from the enemy's horse, about which he was most concerned, but in the confusion he forgot to send Cameron orders to retire.

Finding himself in this position, Lochiel smartly posted his men so advantageously that he was not only able to sustain the attack of the enemy, who charged him with great fury, but to drive them back several times with considerable loss. Half of his followers were armed with bows; and these he posted against the enemy's horse. They were excellent archers, and seldom missed their aim, galling the foe with their unerring arrows. The ground was rugged and uneven, and covered with much snow, which not only rendered the cavalry of the enemy comparatively useless, but made the position much more difficult for the foot. Further, he could only be attacked in one place, posted, as he was, in a narrow pass between two high mountains. These disadvantages abated much the fury of the English; and Lochiel, concluding that in spite of their superiority of numbers, they were not invincible, drew out two hundred of his men, whom, in the situation in which they were at the time placed, he could not otherwise employ—and having ordered a competent officer to maintain the pass with the remainder of his force, he, at the head of this band, charged a body of the enemy, separated from the main army by a hill, quickly broke them, and threw them into confusion; but having no force to support him, and afraid of being surrounded, he considered it prudent not to pursue his advantage too far.

The English General, perceiving that he could not force the pass so gallantly defended by Lochiel, and angry at the loss of so many of his men, whom the Highlanders killed without much danger to themselves, he drew off about half his troops, and, conducted by guides, whom he brought with him, took a round of the hills, and succeeded in getting between our hero and the main army under Glencairn; but by this time, Lochiel's quarter-master, whom he had sent to Glencairn for orders, returned, intimating that his lordship was in complete security, and that the Camerons were ordered to retreat as best they could; whereupon Lochiel retired gradually up the hill, facing the enemy—who dared not pursue him, on account of the roughness of the ground and the snow that covered it—on both sides. The pass being thus opened as Lochiel retired, Lilburn drew his men together and marched in the direction of the Highland army; but finding that he could not force an engagement as they were then posted, and the season of the year not admitting of his continuing in the field, he fell back and returned to Inverness, where he had his head-quarters. On his way thither he placed strong garrisons in the Castles of Ruthven and others in which he deemed this precaution necessary. Lochiel followed him for several miles, and whenever he found the ground favourable, harrassed him and killed several of his men and horse. Having finally seen the English fairly out of the district, he returned in triumph to Glencairn, who received him with open arms, and congratulated him as the Deliverer of the Highland Army.

The conflict in the pass lasted for several hours, and though Lochiel had a few of his men killed and several wounded, the enemy lost six times as many men, and several of their horses. In the following spring, Glencairn again took the field, but his army soon melted away. The leaders became divided among themselves as to the mode of carrying on the war, and there was consequently little chance of success against the enemy; but though he dared not engage Lilburn in a general battle, he constantly harrassed him, repelling his attacks, beating up his quarters, burning and destroying several of his garrisons.

Lochiel, determining to keep clear of any faction at head-quarters, to enable him to do so, always chose the most distant posts, where he had the additional advantage and pleasure of being more frequently engaged against the enemy than anyone else; and the invariable success of his arms on these occasions made the General in command most willing to employ him and give him the opportunities, which he so much desired, of measuring swords with the English. That his services were appreciated and acknowledged in high quarters will be seen from the following letter sent him by the king :—

"*To our Trusty and Well-beloved the Laird of Lochiell.*

"CHARLES R.

"Trusty and Well-beloved, wee greet yow well. Wee are informed by the Earl of Glencairn with what notable courage and affection to us yow have behaved yourself at this time of tryall, when our interest, and the honour and liberty of your countrey, is at stake ; and, therefore, wee cannot but express our hearty sense of such your good courage, and return yow our princely thanks for the same. And wee hope all honest men, who are lovers of us or their countrey, will follow your example, and that yow will unite together in the wayes wee have directed ; and under that authority wee have appointed to conduct yow, for the prosecution of so good a work. So wee doe assure yow wee shall be ready, as soon as wee are able, signally to reward your service, and to repair the losses yow shall undergoe for our service ; and so wee bid yow fairwell. Given att Chantilly, the 3rd day of November, 1653, in the fifth year of our reign."

Information having reached him that his own country was about to be invaded by the English from Inverness, Lochiel was soon after obliged to return home to defend it.

On his arrival in Lochaber he found Macdonald of Glengarry, and Keppoch willing to join him in the common defence of their respective properties ; and with this object they met at Glenturrit, agreeing to raise their men and meet afterwards on a moor above Aberchalder, a few miles from Fort-Augustus, whenever they should hear of the enemy's advance. Lochiel, in the meantime, allowed most of his men to separate and retire to their homes, but hearing of the approach of the English sooner than he anticipated, he resolved to march to the place of rendezvous with only some four hundred of his followers, whom he had still about him, thinking that, by the assistance of Glengarry and Keppoch, he would be able to engage the enemy successfully. On his arrival he was disappointed only to find Keppoch there in terms of their previous agreement, and that Glengarry was "walking and discoursing with the English Commander in the very centre of his troops," numbering 1500 men and several troops of horse, encamped on the plain below. Lochiel becoming exasperated, openly expressed his suspicions, even of Keppoch's fidelity, which the latter resented by leaving the field and marching his men home.

The English soon after raised their camp and marched to a wood at the end of the Pass of Clunes, where they halted, and from whence their commander, Colonel Brayn, sent a messenger to Lochiel requesting permission to march peaceably through the Cameron country, assuring him that he had no design of injuring either himself or his people; provided he was not provoked by their conduct to attack them. Lochiel was personally in favour of measuring swords with the English in the pass, where he would have great advantages over them, and could keep them until more of his followers could arrive from their homes. His leading men strongly advised him against this course, and they were supported by General Drummond, who accompanied Lochiel, with the view, it is said, of taking the command of the confederated clans, to prevent disputes among themselves; and Lochiel, unwillingly, gave way to the counsel of his friends. He, however, closely watched the movements of the enemy, who, after encamping for a night at Inverlochy, commenced a return march to Inverness, neither inflicting nor receiving any injury in Lochaber during his long march there and back.

In consequence of Glengarry's defection on this occasion, Lochiel was never fully reconciled to him after, though, when the estate of Glengarry was subsequently forfeited and Argyll got a gift of it, and afterwards gave it to Lochiel, he, notwithstanding the old difference, regranted it entire to its original owner.* After this Lochiel joined Glencairn, and took part in several lively skirmishes fought between the Earl and the English, in which the young chief and his followers displayed their usual gallantry, but nothing remarkable is recorded of him at this period.

In 1654, General Middleton arrived from Holland, and

---

* The author of *Lochiel's Memoirs* says, "Argyll's disposition of it to Lochiel is still extant, and is to be seen in the hands of M'Kenzie of Rose-End".

succeeded Glencairn in the command of the king's troops; whereupon he at once wrote Lochiel as follows :—

"Honoured Sir,—The King is very sensible of your affection to him, and I am confident how soone he is in a capacity, will liberally reward your services. I doe not at all doubt of your constant resolution to prosecute that service vigorously with all your power for the King's interest and your country's honour, and I doe assure you that no man shall be more ready to assist you in anything than, etc.
(Signed) "JOHN MIDDLETONE.
"TOUNG, March, 1654.

"P.S.—I expect that you, with your friends, will not faill to come considerably, to join me, as soon as you are advertized by the Earl of Glencairn of his march towards me."

Lochiel soon after joined him "with a full regiment of good men," whom he almost immediately led into action, when they maintained their previous renown for intrepidity and courage.

By General Monk's tactics, who arrived in the North in April, 1654, Middleton was reduced to severe straits, being hemmed in on all sides, without provisions for his troops, and having no garrison or safe place of retreat. He was thus constantly obliged to fight and defend himself in the open country, occasioning many severe conflicts between his forces and the English. On these occasions Lochiel was always to the front, and often signally distinguished himself. "His men seemed to be spirited by his example, and in the end became so hardy and resolute that they despised all danger while he was at their head. There was little blood drawn during that campaign where he was not present, for he chose to be in that part of the army that opposed General Morgan, who, being an active and brave officer, seldom allowed rest to his enemies." Lochiel thus gained in reputation every day, and became almost adored by his trusting followers.

Monk used every means in his power—terrorism or conciliation, as best suited the circumstances—to divide the Highland army, and, having succeeded with many of the other chiefs, he was naturally more anxious to secure Lochiel, the most distinguished for bravery and courage of them all. He spared no temptation to bribe him into submission, and made him so many insinuating offers and proposals "that several of his best friends were surprised that he so much as hesitated to accept them. Among others, he offered to buy the estate of Glenlui and Locharkaig for him; to pay all his debts; and to give him whatever post in the army he pleased." The proferred bribes proved ineffectual, and Monk determined to place a strong garrison at Inverlochy, in the very heart of the Cameron country, and thus, as he thought, place Lochiel's estate entirely at his mercy, or force him and his men home to defend it. He succeeded in the latter; for Lochiel, learning Monk's intention, marched straight into Lochaber, raised additional men, and determined to fight the enemy on their way from Inverness, whence, he was informed, they were coming, across the hills. Meanwhile, however, the English, on the advice of Argyll, who supplied them with men to pilot them, came round by sea, in five ships, and landed safely at Inverlochy in their own boats, with a year's provision, and ample materials to construct a fort. Colonel Bryan, who had led the English through the same country the year before, was appointed governor of the garrison, which consisted of 2000 effective troops, commanded by the most skilful and resolute officers in Monk's army, and attended by a large following of workmen, servants, their wives and children.

The extensive woods then abounding in the district furnished the governor with such plentiful material that, in less than twenty-four hours after landing, he had his troops fully secured against all danger from attack. Lochiel arrived in the neighbourhood the following morning, and, having personally reconnoitred the situation from a neighbouring eminence, satisfied himself of the impossibility of successful attack, and resolved to retire to the woods of Achadalew, three miles westward from the garrison, on the northern shore of Lochiel. Having taken counsel here with his friends, he dismissed his men for a few days, that they might remove their cattle further away from the enemy, and obtain provisions for themselves, which, in consequence of their long absence from home, was quite exhausted. He only kept thirty-two young gentlemen and his own personal servants along with him as a body-guard, in all numbering thirty-five, or, as another authority has it, thirty-eight persons. He could not have fixed on a more suitable place to await the return of his men, not only having, where he halted, means of safe retreat into the wood, in case of a sudden surprise, but having the English garrison so well in view that the smallest party could not be sent out of it without his having timely notice of its proceedings. At the same time, he artfully got spies, who kept him fully informed of everything that took place, admitted into the garrison, and who, in consequence of their cunning familiarity with the soldiers, and their frank offers of service in any capacity in which they could be of use, were never in the least suspected.

Lochiel, through these emissaries, received private intimation that the governor, encouraged by the dismissal of the Camerons, was that same day, the fifth after his arrival, to send out a detachment of 300 men, attended by several workmen, to bring in fresh provisions, and to cut some fine old oak trees, which, he was informed, were to be found in great numbers on both sides of Lochiel. The chief was much annoyed at himself for having dismissed so many of his men. He ascended an eminence, from whence he had a full view of all the enemy's proceedings, and soon discovered two ships, full of soldiers, sailing towards the wood, where he and his men were concealed. One of them anchored on his, and the other on the opposite, shore of the Loch. Resolving to have a nearer view, he, under cover of the wood, posted himself so near the spot where they landed, that he was able to count them as they drew up, their number being about 140 men, besides officers, and workmen with axes and other instruments. Having thus fully satisfied himself, he returned to his friends, and asked their opinion as to what was best to be done, "now that such a party of the enemy had offered their throats to be cut," as he expressed himself. The majority of his party were young men, fiery, hot-headed, full of vigour and courage, courting every opportunity of pleasing their chief, whom they almost worshipped. These youthful spirits discovering his inclinations, were anxious to attack the English right off, at all hazards; but the few older and more experienced amongst them attempted to dissuade him by all the arguments they could suggest. They urged that the great inequality of their number rendered the attempt mad and ridiculous; that, supposing the enemy were mere cowards, yet they were strangers, and the very despair of the impossibility of escaping by flight in a strange country would impel them to fight desperately for their lives; and, being more than four to one, they would surround their assailants and cut them to pieces; but in this case the combat would be still more hazardous and desperate, for the enemy instead of being cowards, were choice old troops, hardened and inspirited by long practice and success in war, and commanded by experienced officers, who knew well how to use such advantages; that it would be quite a sufficient proof of their own courage to fight such an enemy upon equal terms; and that, upon the whole, the best thing to do, in the circumstances, was immediately to dispatch such persons as their chief should chose, to call in more men, and, on the arrival of these, to fight, when they would have a reasonable chance of success, on something like equal terms.

Among those present were a few who had served under Montrose, and Lochiel asked their opinion separately. They declared that they never knew even Montrose to engage under such great disadvantages as to numbers; besides, they looked upon the present enemy as far superior to any troops that he ever had occasion to fight; for, though he seldom fought but where there were some regiments of old soldiers against him, yet the greater portion of them were generally such as enlisted not out of zeal for the Covenant, but were otherwise forced, and, therefore, not to be compared with veteran troops.

Notwithstanding these views, Lochiel was determined, and would not be dissuaded from the hazardous attempt.

" Whether impelled by an excess of courage, or by a youthful spirit of emulation (for he had Montrose always in his mouth), it is certain that he never appeared absolutely inexorable but on this occasion." He upbraided his friends as enemies to his and their own glory, in magnifying danger, where, he said, there was so little reason ; alleging that he had allowed the same enemy to escape on a previous occasion, at the Pass of Clunes, by their advice, when he had an opportunity of cutting them to pieces ; and that, had they been then treated as they ought to have been, and as they deserved, they would neither have had the boldness to fix themselves in the heart of his country, nor the insolence to cut down his woods without his leave ; but they should not again have a tree of his without paying for it with their blood ; that if they were not chastised, the Camerons, who were now the only free people within the three kingdoms, would soon find themselves in miserable servitude, at the mercy of blood-thirsty enthusiasts, who had enslaved their country and imbrued their impious hands in the blood of their sovereign, and still thirsted for that of his few remaining subjects ; that however they magnified the enemy's courage, yet it might be remembered by several of those present, that they had oftener than once held their own with success in conflicts more hazardous ; and, particularly, at Braemar, where he himself defended a pass with a handful against an army of English. He further pleaded, that the enemy, being in absolute security, would be so confounded and stupified by a bold, sudden, and unexpected attack, that they would imagine every tree in the wood was a Highlander holding a broadsword in his hand, and cutting their throats ; that the enemy had no other arms but their heavy muskets, which would be useless after their first fire ; and that it would be their own faults if they allowed the English time to fire a second volley ; that supposing he and his party should be obliged to retreat, which was really the worst that could happen to them, it would be quite easy for them to retire, right into the wood, through which the enemy dare not follow them for fear of ambush ;

and even though they should do so, the Highlanders, who were much nimbler, had the neighbouring mountains for security; that, as to the proposal of sending for more men, they knew that to be impracticable, for those living in the neighbourhood were now in the more remote mountains with their cattle, and the rest lived at too great a distance to afford assistance on such short notice; he truly believed there was no need of their aid, for if every one there would undertake to kill his man, which he expected each would do with his first shot, he would personally answer for the rest!

Lochiel delivered this oration in such a manner that not one of his men opposed his wish any further. They declared in one voice that they were ready to march whenever he should command them, though it were to certain destruction, on condition that he and his younger brother Allan, yet a mere stripling, would agree to absent themselves from danger, as all the hopes of the clan depended on their safety. They entreated him to be prevailed upon in what they strongly urged was so reasonable a request. Lochiel would not listen to the proposal respecting himself, but commanded that his brother Allan, who would not otherwise keep out of the fray, should be bound to a tree; and that, since he could not spare any of his men, a little boy, who came to them accidentally, should be left in charge of him.

In the meantime Lochiel's scouts brought in word that the enemy, having continued for a short time where they landed, marched slowly along the shore about half-a-mile in a westward direction, and were now at the village of Achadelew, pillaging the houses and capturing the poultry. Lochiel, judging that this, while they were in disorder, was the proper moment for attacking them, drew up his men in an extended line, one deep, and desired them to march slowly, so as not to get disordered while entangled among the trees, till they came in view of the enemy, and not to fire a shot until they touched the very breasts of the enemy with the muzzles of their guns. About half the brave band carried bows, and were excellent archers. To these he gave similar orders, mixing them with the musketeers. But the men were too young and too forward to observe the first part of his orders with sufficient exactness. They marched so quick, or rather ran at such a pace, that Lochiel, who, by some accident or other, was obliged to fall a little behind, ran a great risk, before he could overtake them, of being shot from a bush, where one of the enemy lurked ; but his brother Allan, who had forced the boy in charge of him to unloose him, luckily came up at that very moment, and shot the fellow dead, with his gun to his eye, and levelled at Lochiel, who had never observed him.

The English, it seems, were warned in time by some of their own stragglers, and were in good order when the Camerons came in view, but they received them, too rashly, with a general discharge of their muskets, at such a distance that the volley did no harm, and the Highlanders were up with them before they were able to load a second time, firing into their very bosoms, and killing more than thirty of them on the spot. They then fell upon them with a deadly onslaught, plying their broadswords with terrible fury.

This manner of fighting was new to the English. At first they acted entirely on the defensive, and, by holding their muskets before their foreheads, endeavoured to defend themselves from the terrible blows of the broadsword. But the Highlanders striking them below, they were soon obliged to change that defence. Some of them used their swords, and struck at their enemies with strength and fury, but their blows were mostly ineffectual. The Highlanders received them on their shields, and the mettle and temper of the enemy's blades were so bad that they bent in their hands and became useless, thus exposing them to certain death. Others of them fixed their bayonets in the muzzles of their pieces, as the custom then was, but they were equally unsuccessful, for the more violently they pushed the more firmly their weapons entered and stuck in the leathern targets of the Highlanders, leaving their owners naked and defenceless. Those who clubbed their muskets did more mischief, but fared little better in the end, for, though they made some sure strokes, the firelocks were at that time so clumsy and heavy that they could seldom recover them for a second blow; besides, the Highlanders, covering themselves with their targets, generally broke the force of the weapon, but their superior numbers gave the enemy such an advantage as to keep the conflict a long time in suspense, and though their ranks were often pierced, disordered, and broken, yet they as often rallied and returned to the charge, which exceedingly surprised the Highlanders, who were not accustomed to such long and doubtful actions; and it is more than probable that, had the English weapons been equal to the courage of those who wielded them, the Camerons would have paid dearly for their rashness.

The numbers of the enemy at last diminishing by the slaughter of their best men, they gradually gave ground, but not to run, for, with their faces to the Highlanders, they still kept retreating in a body, though in disorder, fighting with invincible obstinacy and resolution. But Lochiel, to prevent escape to their vessel, fell upon the following stratagem:—He commanded two or three of his men to run in advance of the retreating enemy, and from a bush to call out, so as to make them imagine that another body of mountaineers was intercepting their retreat. This manœuvre, however, had the opposite effect intended by it. They stopped, and animated by rage, madness, and despair, renewed the fight with greater fury than ever. They were still superior in numbers to the Camerons by more than one half, and wanted nothing but good weapons to make Lochiel repent that he had intercepted their escape. They no longer had any regard for their own safety, and with their clubbed muskets delivered such strokes as would have brought their enemies to the ground, if they had been aimed with as much discretion as they were forcibly applied. But this served only to hasten their destruction, for, exerting all their strength in giving these ineffectual blows, the sway of their heavy muskets, which generally struck the ground, rendered them unable quickly to recover themselves. The Highlanders made use of this advantage, and stabbed them with their dirks or poniards, while they were thus bent and defenceless; whereby their numbers were quickly diminished, and they forced them again to flee as best they could.

Being thus broken and dispersed, "they fled as fear or chance directed them. The Highlanders pursued with as little judgment. In one place you might have seen five Highlanders engaged with double that number of Englishmen; and in another, two or three Englishmen defending themselves against twice as many of their enemies." But the greater number made for the shore, where we shall for a little leave them and follow the brave Lochiel, who in the meantime had a miraculous escape.

He had followed alone a few of the enemy, who fled into the wood, where he killed two or three of them with his own hand. The officer in command of the invaders also flew in the same direction; and, concealing himself in a bush, Lochiel did not notice him, but the Englishman, observing that the other was alone, started suddenly out of his lurking-place, attacked Lochiel as he passed, threatening, as he rushed furiously upon him, sword in hand, to revenge the slaughter of his countrymen by his instant death. Lochiel, sword in hand, received him with equal resolution. "The combat was long and doubtful; both fought for their lives, and as they were both animated by the same fury and courage, so they seemed to manage their swords with the same dexterity. The English gentleman had by far the advantage in strength and size; but Lochiel, exceeding him in nimbleness and agility, in the end tripped the sword out of his hand. But he was not allowed to make use of this advantage, for his antagonist, flying upon him with incredible quickness, they closed and wrestled till both fell to the ground in each other's arms. In this posture they struggled and tumbled up and down till they fixed in the channel of a brook, between two straight, steep banks, which then, by the drought of summer, happened to be dry. Here Lochiel was in a most desperate situation, for, being undermost, he was not only crushed under the weight of his antagonist (who was a very big man), but also badly hurt and bruised by the sharp stones in the bed of the rivulet. Their strength was so far spent that neither of them could stir a limb"; the Englishman, being uppermost, at last recovered the use of his right hand, seized a dagger that hung at his belt, and made several attempts to stab Lochiel, who all the time held him fast; but the narrowness of the place where they where, and the posture they were in, rendered this very difficult, almost impossible, while he was so tightly embraced by his antagonist. The Englishman, however, made a violent effort to disengage himself, and in the act raised his head, stretched and exposed his neck, when Lochiel—who by this time had his arms at liberty—with his left hand suddenly seized his opponent by the right, and with the other by the collar. He then jumped at the Englishman's extended throat, which, he used to say, God had put in his mouth, biting it right through, and keeping such a hold that he brought away the mouthful! "This," he said, "was the sweetest bite I ever had in my life!" His face was covered all over with the gush of warm blood that flowed from the wound, but he soon had an opportunity of washing it, for, hastening to the shore, he found his men chin-deep in the sea, doing their best to destroy the remainder of the enemy, while attempting to recover their vessel, at anchor near the shore; and, wishing to save the few remaining, after such a splendid victory, Lochiel, with great difficulty, staid the fury of his men, and offered quarters, when all, about thirty-five in number, submitted. The first that delivered up his arms was an Irishman, who, having offered Lochiel his hand, bade him adieu, and ran away with such speed that, though hotly pursued, he effected his escape, after crossing the river, to Inverlochy. It is reported of this man that ever after, when saying his prayers, "which every soldier in those religious times was obliged to do," he put up the special petition—"That God, in his mercy, would be pleased to keep him out of the hands of Lochiel and his bloody crew for the rest of his life!"

Before the others laid down their arms one of them attempted to shoot Lochiel, who, however, observed him while he had his gun to his eye, and plunged himself into the sea at the moment that the ungrateful rascal drew his trigger. This he the more easily effected, as he was already chin-deep in the water; but his escape was so narrow that a part of the hair from the back of his head was shot away, and the skin a little ruffled by the ball.

The Camerons showed no more mercy. They flew upon their enemies like tigers, cutting them to pieces wherever they got at them. In vain did Lochiel interpose his authority; his followers were deaf to everything but the dictates of fury and revenge. Nor did the English, after their violation of the laws of war, seem to expect anything else, for one of them, whom the Camerons supposed from his dress to be an officer, having got on board his ship, resolved to do what one of his men had failed in, and that he might take surer aim, he rested his gun upon the side of the vessel. Lochiel noticed him pointing his gun, and, judging that he had no chance of escape "but by ducking, as he did before, kept his eye fixed upon the finger that he had at the trigger. But his foster-brother, who was close by, happening at the same time to notice the danger his chief was in, and preferring his safety to his own, immediately threw himself before him, and received the shot in his mouth and breast. This is perhaps one of the most astonishing instances of affection and love that any age can produce. If fortitude and courage are qualities of so heroic and sublime a nature, what name shall we invent for so noble a contempt of life, generously thrown away in preservation of one of much greater value?" Lochiel immediately revenged the death of the brave youth with his own hand, and, after the utter destruction of the enemy, he carried his body three miles on his back, and interred him in the burial-place of his own family, in the most honourable way which, in the circumstances, he could contrive. The Camerons lost only four men, in addition to Lochiel's devoted foster-brother, who so nobly sacrificed his life to save his chief, during this remarkable conflict.

Having thus disposed of the enemy, they proceeded to count the number of them slain, when it was found that not less than one hundred and thirty-eight lay dead on the field, not a soul having escaped, but the Irishman already mentioned, and another, who subsequently became Lochiel's cook, and acted in that capacity for him as long as he lived. Having lodged the night after the battle in the house of a woman on Lochiel-side, whose son was among the few of his followers slain, Lochiel took his prisoner with him, when the woman—taking into her head that the stranger who accompanied him was he who had killed her son—immediately attacked him, and would have strangled him, had not Lochiel interposed, separated them, and sent his prisoner, under guard, to another house, for the night. He ever after found him most zealous and trustworthy, ready to do anything required of him, often at the risk of his own life.

The author of the "Memoirs" relates two stories which well illustrate the difference between the ideas and tempers of the two classes of men—the Highlanders and their English enemies. The courage of the Southrons, he says, was merely mechanical, flowing from discipline and habit, and serving simply for their bread, while that of the Highlanders was "from the notions they have of honour and loyalty, and of the services which they think they owe to their chief, as the root of the family, and the common father and protector of the name. As this has something of greatness and generosity in the principle, so the actions flowing from it participate of the same spirit. Of this we have already had an illustrious example [in the case of Lochiel's foster-brother]; and, indeed, the almost unparalleled bravery of the Camerons, during the terrible and extraordinary skirmish described, exemplify the same in a number of persons. Nor did it less appear in the generous emulation that inspirited them to exert the utmost efforts of their strength and courage before their young chief. One of them having shot an arrow at too great a distance, and Lochiel, observing that it did not pierce deep enough to kill the man, cried out that 'it came from a weak arm,' at which the Highlander thought himself so much offended that, despising all danger, he rushed among the thick of the enemy, and recovering his own arrow, plunged it into the man's body to the feathers." This action would have cost him his life, had not Lochiel quickly dispatched a party to his relief.

The character of the English soldiery our author illustrates thus :—" After their defeat, being hard put to it by the pursuing enemy, they plunged into the sea in hopes of recovering their ships. One of them, observing that a piece of beef and some small biscuits had dropped out of his pockets by the floating of the laps of his coat, he, preferring the recovery of his provisions to the safety of his life, fell a-fishing for them, and had his head divided into two parts by the blow of a broadsword as he was putting the first morsel of it into his mouth." Not one, however, called for quarter, and in the confusion of retreat, no one parted with his arms, but with his life. "They were pitied more than blamed. They did all that men could do in the circumstances they were in. Not a single man of them betrayed the least cowardice, but fought it out with invincible obstinacy while any of them remained to make opposition, and their frequent attempts on the chief's life, even after quarters were offered, show that their fortitude and courage remained so firm to the last, that they disdained to be survivors of a defeat which they looked upon as shameful and ignominious. In short, they were not conquered, but destroyed." From this it is clear that the Highlanders had a very sturdy enemy to deal with, apart altogether from their great inequality of numbers.

Colonel Bryan, Governor of Inverlochy, was quite ignorant of what had taken place within so short a distance of his garrison, until a few of his workmen, who had fled from

Achadalew, as soon as the fight commenced, had reached the fort; but before the garrison was able to turn out, the Irishman, already referred to, arrived, and informed the garrison that every man of his party had been cut to pieces.

The men in the other ship—which, during the engagement, had been on the opposite shore, a little to the westward of Achadalew—discovered that their friends were engaged with the Camerons, and they at once sailed in the direction of the scene of carnage, but did not disembark until Lochiel had retired with his men, when they landed, "and beheld the dismal fate of their countrymen, whose bodies they put on board the other empty vessel, which they hauled along with them to Inverlochy," where, on their arrival, they were met by the governor and his officers, whose astonishment, upon seeing the dead bodies of their friends, was intense. "The deep wounds and terrible slashes that appeared on these mangled carcases seemed to be above the strength of man. Some had their heads cut down a good way into the neck; others had them divided across by the mouth and nose; many, who were struck upon the collar-bone, showed an orifice or gash much wider than that made by the blow of the heaviest hatchet; and often the shearing blade, where the blow was full, and met with no ordinary obstruction, penetrated so deep as to discover part of the entrails. There were some that had their bellies laid open, and others with their arms, thighs, and legs lopped off in an amazing manner. Several bayonets were cut quite through, and muskets were pierced deeper than can be well imagined. The governer and many of his officers had formerly occasion to see the Highlanders of several clans and countries, but they appeared to be no extraordinary men, neither in size nor strength. The Camerons they had observed to be of a piece with the rest, and they wondered where Lochiel could find a sufficient body of men of strength and brawn to give such an odd variety of surprising wounds. But they did not know that there was as much art as strength in fetching these strokes, for, where a Highlander lays it on full, he draws it with great address the whole length of the blade, whereas an unskilful person takes in no more of it than the breadth of the place where he hits. He is likewise taught to wound with the point, or to fetch a backstroke as occasion offers, and as in all these he knows how to exert his whole vigour and strength, so his blade is of such excellent temper and form as to answer all his purposes." Thus the terrible nature of the wounds were accounted for. When the actual facts and exploits of this sanguinary conflict became known, the courage and conduct of the Highlanders at once became the subject of admiration throughout the whole kingdom. "Lochiel was by all parties extolled to the skies as a young hero of boundless courage and extraordinary conduct. His presence of mind in delivering himself from his terrible English antagonist, who had so much the advantage of him in everything but vigour and courage, by biting out his throat, was in every person's mouth." The devoted self-sacrifice of his young foster-brother, to save his chief, also became the theme of admiration and astonishment among those who were unacquainted with the affection and devotion of the Highlanders, in those days, to their chiefs.

Mrs Mary Mackellar, the well-known Gaelic poet, who is so well acquainted with the history and traditions of her native district of Lochaber, relates the following curious incident in this connection:—Sir Ewen used to say that the only time he ever felt the sensation of fear was on the occasion of an incident which occurred, in which the biting out the Englishman's throat at Achadalew, was referred to in an awkward moment. When attending Court in London, many years after the event, he went into a barber's shop to get his hair and beard dressed, and, when the razor was passing over his throat, the chatty barber observed—" You are from the North, sir". "Yes," said Sir Ewen, "I am; do *you* know people from the North?" "No," replied the irate barber, " nor do I wish to; they are savages there. Would you believe it, sir; one of them tore the throat out of my father with his teeth, and I only wish I had the fellow's throat as near me as I have yours just now." Sir Ewen's feelings may be more easily imagined than described as he heard these words and felt the edge of the steel gliding over the vital part so particularly threatened. He never after entered a barber's shop.*

Almost immediately after the Achadalew affair, Lochiel resolved to join General Middleton, requesting those of his people who lived near Inverlochy to make their peace with the Governor, who demanded no other terms than that they should live peaceably towards himself and his garrison. This was soon arranged, and the people secured from ruin during their leader's absence from the district. The Governor being thus put off his guard, sent out parties to bring in wood and other materials to strengthen his fortifications. Lochiel, however, was kept well informed of what he was doing, and, returning to the district, he immediately posted a body of his most resolute followers in a secure place, less than half-a-mile westward of the fort. The same morning a body of two hundred men came out from the garrison marching in Lochiel's direction. Observing them, he detached twenty of his band to a secret place to the rear of the enemy—between them and the garrison—with orders to rush out and intercept them, in case they retreated, as they naturally would, in that direction, when attacked in front by the Camerons. They marched in good order until they arrived at the village of Achintore, where Sir Ewen and his band, who furiously rushed forward, scattering them in all directions, lay concealed. The memory of Achadalew struck terror into their hearts, when they found themselves so suddenly and unexpectedly attacked by a force the strength of which they did not know, and could not ascertain. The men in ambush rushed forth to intercept them in their flight, gave them a full charge of their firelocks in front, and then charged with their broadswords, killing more than half their number. Those who

* *Guide to Fort-William, Glencoe, and Lochaber*, p. 54.

escaped were pursued to the walls of the fort, but many of them were taken prisoners and distributed among such of the Camerons as lived a good distance from the garrison.

Lochiel, with his devoted and gallant band, now returned to General Middleton, by whom they were received with great demonstrations of triumph. Nothing of special importance took place for some time after this, but Lochiel was kept constantly in action, daily becoming a greater terror to the enemy. Middleton was anxious to force on a battle, but his principal officers openly opposed him, and in consequence of these divisions his army soon after almost melted away.

Meanwhile Lochiel received information that the Governor of Inverlochy, taking advantage of his absence, was cutting down large quantities of his woods at Lochaber for the purpose of providing the garrison with an ample supply of fuel during the incoming winter. Annoyed at this, he asked and received permission from Middleton to return home, with about a hundred and fifty men—leaving the main body of his followers at headquarters—to punish the Governor for stealing his wood. He marched at night, going by the most unfrequented paths through the mountains, and soon arrived in the vicinity of the garrison, undiscovered by the enemy, when he was informed by his friends of circumstances which enabled him to execute his designs of revenge almost immediately.

The woods on which the English were employed occupied the shoulder of Ben Nevis, about a mile eastward from the garrison. Lochiel marched to this point, called Strone-Nevis, early on the following morning after his arrival, carefully posted his men, and gave them the necessary instructions. He kept sixty, under his own immediate command, in a tuft of wood at a point opposite where the soldiers sent out from the garrison, with the hewers of the wood, always took up their position. Two other bodies of thirty men each were told off to his right and left, respectively, where they were concealed, commanding them all to rush forth as soon as the concerted signal was given, which was to be a great shout of "Advance, Advance!" as if the wood was full of men. The remainder of his men he placed in a pass between the wood and the garrison, to lie in ambush, and not to move out of that, unless they found that the enemy were making a successful resistance when attacked by the Highlanders in front; but if they noticed them running away, in retreat, they were to rush forward in advance of them, place them between two fires by giving them a volley in front, then attack them with their broad-swords, and kill as many as they could. They were, however, specially ordered to give quarter to any who offered to lay down his arms and surrender.

About four hundred marched out from the garrison, taking their usual position, quite innocent of the fate which immediately awaited them. Everything turned out as Lochiel anticipated; a general slaughter at once ensued; the Highlanders, issuing forth from their places of concealment, made a great noise, loudly echoed by the surrounding mountains. This, accompanied by the simultaneous sounds of several bagpipes, frightened the enemy, who, in consequence, made no resistance; for they believed themselves surrounded by large bodies of Highlanders pouring in upon them from all sides, and they immediately fled at their highest speed. More than a hundred of the English were killed on the spot, and the remainder having been attacked unexpectedly by those in ambush, between them and the garrison, a second slaughter took place. Not more than a third of the four hundred escaped. These were pursued to the walls of the fort, and the whole thing was over so quickly that it became a matter of history before the Governor actually knew that his men had even been attacked. Not a single English officer escaped, they being the only men among the garrison troops who had the courage to offer any resistance to the Highlanders. Among them was a young gentleman, a great favourite with the Governor, who, exasperated at the loss of his friend and that of his men, became furious, and swore immediate revenge upon Lochiel and his whole clan.

For this purpose he next morning ordered out the whole garrison—about fifteen hundred men. Lochiel, as usual, obtained timely notice of his enemy's movements, and, betaking himself to stronger and higher ground, kept in view of his opponents, as he himself marched round the mountains, with pipes playing and colours flying. He made every effort to induce the English commander to follow him, and so get him entangled in the woods, narrow paths, and other obstructions abounding in the neighbourhood, where he could be successfully attacked, but the Governor was too wary to fall into the trap prepared for him. After traversing many difficult and rugged paths he turned right about, and by the help of good guides, found his way to the garrison, heartily fatigued and disgusted with his fruitless expedition. The Camerons, following closely on their heels, repeatedly insulted him and his followers, and whenever the nature of the ground favoured, and they came to close quarters, they invited the English to advance, for that their chief was there, ready to receive their Governor, if he wished to speak to him; besides other very tantalising and insulting remarks.

Lochiel's name had now become such a terror that the English were careful to give him as few opportunities as possible of annoying them, though he occasionally managed to capture or kill small parties from the garrison. Many curious adventures in which he took the leading part are still the subject of talk in Lochaber. The following, recorded by his biographer, is a good specimen :—"A good part of the revenue of his estate being paid in cattle, and commonly sold to drovers, who disposed of them to others in Lowland markets, he employed a subtile fellow, who haunted the garrison, to whisper it adroitly among the soldiers, that a drove belonging to him was on a certain day to pass that way, and that, Lochiel himself being now returned to General Middleton, it might easily be made a prize of. The fellow managed it so that it came to the Governor's ears, who gave private orders to seize the cattle. Against the day prefixed, Lochiel ordered some cows with their calves to be driven, with seeming caution and privacy, to a place at a proper distance from Inverlochy; but before they came there, the calves were taken from their mothers, and driven separately a short way before them, though always in their sight. This, as it gave from a distance the appearance of two droves, occasioned a reciprocal lowing and bellowing, which, being reverberated by the adjacent hills and rocks, made a very great noise. The soldiers were quickly alarmed, and ran, without observing much order, as to a certain prey; but Lochiel, who lurked with his party in a bush of wood near by, rushing suddenly upon them, with loud cries, had the killing of them all the way to the garrison." The Governor was so enraged at such tricks, so frequently played upon him and his men, that he set so close a watch upon Lochiel that he narrowly escaped with his life on repeated occasions.

Shortly after the incident described, our hero received a message from General Middleton that he had just been defeated by General Morgan at Lochgarry, who had suddenly surprised him, and killed many of his men, when he thought himself quite free from any danger. In consequence of this defeat, Middleton,—who had previously invited the king to come over from France in the following spring, promising him that the country as one man would rise to support him, gave up all hopes of Loyalist success,— sent express instructions to Lochiel to come to him, not so much with the intention of continuing the war, as with the view of concerting means of giving it up on the best and most honourable terms which, in all the circumstances, they could secure.

Lochiel proceeded on this journey, accompanied by three hundred of his followers, by the most secret and inaccessible mountain-paths; but the Governor of Inverlochy, hearing of his movements, advised General Morgan of his departure, pointing out the great service that he would render to the State if he succeeded in capturing Lochiel dead or alive. The chief, however, soon managed to reach Braemar. Here he took up his quarters for the night in a small shealing, where, greatly fatigued, he slept soundly in his plaid, on a bed of heather. He was disturbed early in the morning by a remarkable dream, which, according to his biographer, was the means of saving his life. He saw a grizzly-bearded man, of disordered countenance and low stature, who, coming where he was, and, striking him smartly on the breast, exclaimed, in a loud voice, " Lochiel, get up, for the Borrowing days will soon be upon you ".* Being no believer in dreams, he immediately fell asleep ; the grizzly little man repeated his first performance, calling out louder than before. Lochiel thought it was merely a trick played upon him by one of his own retinue, who slept with him in the shealing, and, after chiding him for his interference, and getting a denial, he again fell asleep ; but no sooner had he done so than the little man again appeared, doubling the force of his blow, and crying aloud, as if in terror, " Arise quickly, Lochiel, arise, for the Borrowing days are already upon you ". He immediately started from his bed, and before he was able to pull on his hose, he was informed that the ground outside was literally covered with horse and foot, and that some of them were already almost at his bothy's door. He instantly fled to the top of the nearest hill, whence, looking behind him for the first time, he beheld a whole regiment of dragoons, and several companies of foot, sent from the Castle of Kildrummie by General Morgan, to capture our hero, on receipt of the message from Inverlochy that he had started on his way to meet General Middleton, promising the officer commanding a rich reward if he brought him in dead or alive.

The Camerons felt themselves in perfect security, and were completely off their guard. They lost all their baggage, among which were many valuable articles, including " a quantity of unset diamonds, besides a dozen of silver spoons curiously wrought, and on which the whole decalogue was engraved with great art ". All these fell into the

* These are the last three days of March, which, being generally tempestuous, often prove fatal to sheep, lambs, and cattle, weakened, when badly fed, by the severity of the preceding winter. The three days are said to be borrowed from April, whence they are called the " Borrowing days ".

hands of the enemy. Next night, Lochiel slept on the top of a mountain where no horse, and scarcely any foot, could reach him. During the following day he arrived safely at General Middleton's headquarters. Here he remained for a few days, taking part in a council, at which it was resolved to discontinue the war, and to have the army broken up, each shifting for himself as best he could, the season being so far advanced that they could no longer keep in the open field. Middleton, with a few of his officers, resolved upon retiring to the Western Isles, while others accompanied Lochiel to Lochaber, whither they secretly found their way. Cromwell,—finding that he required now to direct his attention more to his English subjects, was anxious to arrange terms with the Scottish Loyalists,—intimated to the Highland chiefs, through secret agents, that he would accept their submission, and that, upon laying down their arms and returning to their homes, they would be restored to their fortunes and estates; and this, in the unpromising nature of their prospects, naturally induced several of them to accept the terms offered, and give up the war, at least until there should appear a better prospect of carrying it on more successfully.

During the winter Lochiel and his guests visited General Middleton at Dunvegan Castle, in the Isle of Skye, where the General and many of his officers found shelter. Several other chiefs also attended, and after much deliberation it was resolved that they should all submit, before they were completely ruined, finding the king quite unable to support them with men, money, or arms. Middleton escaped to France. A few days before he left he handed Lochiel a document, in which was recounted his services on behalf of the king, specially referring to his never having submitted to the enemy, and his having given frequent proofs of his fidelity, courage, and conduct, and standing out to the very last, notwithstanding every difficulty, concluding thus :—
"And withal, I do hereby allow and desire him to take such speedy course for his safety, by capitulation, as he shall see fit, seeing inevitable and invincible necessity has

forced us to lay aside this war, and that I can do nothing else for his advantage". The document is dated "At Dunvegan, the last day of March, 1665," sealed, and signed "Middletone". Thus, for a time, ended the war.

We shall now accompany our hero into the more peaceful paths of diplomacy, a field in which he seems to have been as distinguished as in that of war. During his absence in the Isle of Skye, the officers at Inverlochy arranged several hunting parties, accompanied by considerable bodies of troops, at first keeping well together when out in the forest, but as they became better acquainted with the ground, and more assured of their safety in Lochiel's absence, they became bolder, and hunted separately. On one occasion many of the principal officers from the fort were out for a grand match, each having a small party of soldiers in attendance. They agreed to meet at night, at a spot near the garrison, and march in together. Lochiel was kept well informed of their movements from day to day; he determined to punish them, and for that purpose divided his men into small parties, with instructions to follow each of the garrison parties at a suitable distance, until they found a good opportunity of attacking them with success; with the result that most of the English officers were killed, and the rest taken prisoners. Such an unexpected loss of his principal officers and men filled the Governor with sorrow and feelings of revenge. The hunting matches were stopped, and he at once arranged means for obtaining intelligence of Lochiel's movements through "men of desperate circumstances, whom the hope of gain, and the security of living safe from the prosecutions of their defrauded creditors, allured from all parts of the kingdom," and formed the nucleus of the village of Fort-William, which, our author says, "would have soon increased into a tolerable market town in those remote parts, if the restoration of the Royal Family had not put a stop to it. It was no great difficulty for the Governor to find, among such a confluence of desperadoes, many bold, cunning fellows, proper enough for spies and intelligencers. Lochiel no sooner met with them, as he often did, but he commanded them to be hanged without delay,"* but he was so sharply looked after that he found it dangerous to remain longer near the garrison, though he had arranged a set of spies of his own, through whose information he repeatedly escaped capture.

Soon after this he called together the principal gentlemen of the clan, and told them of his intention to give up the war, as every chance of success had entirely vanished, and his present mode of life, wandering in the hills, had become well-nigh intolerable. He was now determined to secure honourable terms of peace for himself and them, and had formed his plans accordingly, but he expressed a desire that they should trust him with the details without in the meantime disclosing them. Such was their confidence, that they agreed to leave everything in his hands; asked him only to command them, and that they would do his bidding and execute his orders. He picked out about a hundred from amongst them, telling these to be in readiness to join him at any moment.

He had just received a communication from the laird of MacNaughten, in Cowal—a near relative of his own, and a Loyalist, who had in consequence to live in the hills to escape Argyll—that three English and one Scotch Colonel were surveying the district by order of General Monk, and that if he came with a few brave followers these might easily be captured and kept as hostages until he could secure favourable terms of surrender. Lochiel was delighted on receiving this intelligence, and he proceeded with his band of brave followers, keeping the high ground night and day, so as to avoid detection on his march. At the appointed place he met MacNaughten, who informed him of the whereabouts of the Colonels. The best plan by which to secure them having been arranged, Lochiel marched alone at the head of his men, during the night, to a village within four miles of Inveraray, where he arrived about one o'clock in the morning. It was only then that

* *Lochiel's Memoirs*, p. 139.

he told his followers the object of his visit, and directed them how to proceed. He informed them that at a small inn close bye the Colonels lay asleep, without any apprehension of danger. "It is probable they may have a sentry at the door, and some officers and servants lodged with them in the house, and, therefore, to prevent resistance, I have contrived the following stratagem, which may be executed quickly, easily, and without danger of alarming their guards. The house, being built of lime and stone, it will be no easy matter to break through the wall or to force open the door; we must, therefore, steal softly to it, and after seizing the sentry, if there be any, we must each of us take hold of the timber or kebbers that support the roof at the back side of it, and, pulling all at once, there will be an opening large enough for us all to jump in at the same time, and to make every person in the house our prisoners, without distinction. If we fail in this we must put fire to the thatch of the roof by which we will either destroy them or become masters of their persons. If their guards are alarmed, which is the worst that can happen, I expect that you will behave after your ordinary manner; but be sure to make as many prisoners as you possibly can, that being the chief thing I presently aim at." The plan was successfully carried out, and the four Colonels were taken alive. Among them was Lieutenant-Colonel Campbell, a Highlander, with whom Lochiel had previously been well acquainted. They were hurried away in a boat, provided and kept in readiness by MacNaughten, ferried across to the other side, and then marched, without halt, until Lochiel had them in a place of security on his own property. They were greatly horrified on finding themselves in the power of one whom they had learned to look upon as a savage and blood-thirsty barbarian, but his considerate and civil treatment soon induced them to look upon him in a very different light. Though their lodgings were not of the best, they were otherwise well provided for and entertained. Their military rank was respectfully acknowledged, and the only substantial cause of complaint they had was loss of their personal liberty. They were confined on an island in Locharkaig, where they were always provided with an ample supply of delicate fish. "At the head of it is a large forest of red deer, where there is, besides, great abundance of other game. Lochiel, who omitted no civility that he thought would add to the pleasure of his guests, carried them to the head of the loch in a boat, where he was met by some hundreds of his men, whom he had ordered to be convened for that purpose. These people, stretching themselves in a line along the hills, soon enclosed great numbers of deer, which, having driven to a place appointed, they guarded them so closely, within the circle which they formed round them, that the gentlemen had the pleasure of killing them by their broadswords, which was a diversion new and uncommon to them." They spent several days in this way, regaling themselves with every variety of venison and wild fowl. "They were much diverted with the activity and address of the Highlanders in all their exercises, and, instead of the barbarians they were represented to be, they found them a quick and ingenious people, of great vigour and hardiness." They were even more pleased with Lochiel himself. His politeness, good sense, modesty, and wit; his vivacity and cheerfulness, his constant anxiety to entertain them, deeply impressed them. They strongly urged upon him the propriety of coming to terms with the government, now that he was the only chief in the Highlands that held out, urging that he had already gained glory enough in the field, as well as for his devotion to the exiled dynasty.

This was the very thing Lochiel desired. He, however, wanted to be advised and courted into it, but pretended that nothing was farther from his intentions, saying that no wise man would trust himself in the hands of their Protector, "whose whole life was one continued scene of rebellion, ambition, hypocrisy, avarice, and cruelty". He charged him with all the blood spilt during the late Civil Wars, the murder of the king, and with numberless other crimes. He would have no dealings with such a man; for "it was still in his power to preserve his conscience and honour unstained, and to continue in that innocence, loyalty, and integrity of character" which was ever the duty of an honest man and a good subject. He, however, in time began to give way, especially to the reasoning of his old friend Colonel Campell, and ultimately acknowledged that it might possibly be for his interest and that of his people to submit, "provided they could procure such articles as would suit with their honour and the advantage of their country; but that for his own part, before he would consent to the disarming of himself and his people, and to involve them in the horrid guilt of perjury, by abjuring the king, his master, and taking oaths to the usurper, that he was resolved to live as an outlaw, a fugitive, and a vagabond, without regard to the consequences". To this Colonel Campbell replied that, if he expressed an inclination to submit, no oath would be required from him or from his followers; that he should virtually get terms of his own making; and that he himself would undertake to see the conditions performed; concluding his appeal with the remark, that the most powerful of the European monarchs "do not think it below their dignity to court our friendship, and yet the chief of a Highland clan thinks it a stain upon his honour to embrace the peace and friendship that is offered upon terms of his own making". Lochiel at last promised to consult his friends, and submit a copy of his terms next day. This he did, and appointed Colonel Campbell to carry his proposals to General Monk, as soon as they were finally adjusted. They met as agreed; Lochiel produced his proposals, Colonel Campbell proceeded to the headquarters of General Monk, and in due time returned with a letter, dated "Dalkeith, 19th May, 1665," in which the General says: "I have this day agreed upon such articles as I shall grant for the coming in of yourself and party, upon the powers you gave to Lieutenant-Colonel Duncan Campbell to treat for you. . . . In case you shall declare your approbation of these articles within fourteen days of the date hereof, I am content they shall stand good, and be performed to you; otherwise not." Scarcely any alteration was made on the articles submitted by Lochiel.

The full details of this remarkable treaty cannot now be given, the document itself having been burnt, in 1746, with many other valuable records, in Lochiel's house; but its most important conditions may be gathered from General Monk's letters.

<blockquote>
1st. Lochiel, for himself and in name of his whole clan, was to submit and to live in peace on condition that his Excellency demanded no oaths or other assurances but Lochiel's word of honour.

2nd. That the chief and all his friends and followers of the Clan Cameron should be allowed to carry and use their arms the same as before the war broke out, they behaving themselves peacefully, subject to these two conditions—1st, That Lochiel's train, when he travelled out of the Highlands, should not exceed twelve or fourteen armed men, besides his body servants, without a premit from the General, or from his successor in that office; and 2nd, That the gentlemen of the clan should not travel anywhere out of their own country with more than a certain number of armed men, to which they were limited, and they were not to go from home, armed in company, above a restricted number.

3rd. Lochiel and his clan were to lay down their arms, in the name of Charles II., to the Governor of Inverlochy, and take them up again immediately in name of the States, without any reference to Cromwell.

4th. Lochiel bound himself to pay the public burdens, suppress tumults, thefts and depredations, from and after the date of the treaty.
</blockquote>

It was agreed that he should receive full compensation for any wood destroyed and used by the Governor of Inverlochy after the date of the agreement. He was also granted a free and full indemnity for all riots, depredations, crimes, and everything of the like nature, committed by him or by his men during the late wars, and preceding the treaty. It was also agreed that reparation should be made to such of his clan and following as had suffered anything at the hands of the soldiers in garrison; and he and his tenants were discharged of all the cess, tithes, and public burdens, which they had left unpaid since the war began, but they were to pay them in all time coming. The eleventh article provided "that the said General Monk shall keep the Laird of Lochiel free from any bygone duties to William Macintosh of Torcastle, out of the lands pertaining to him in Lochaber (not exceeding the sum of five hundred pounds sterling), the said Laird of Lochiel submitting to the determination of General Monk, the Marquis of Argyll, and Colonel William Bryan, or any two of them, what satisfaction he shall give to Macintosh for the aforesaid lands in time coming ". There were several other articles, all favourable to Lochiel.

The next step was to carry out this highly honourable agreement within the specified period. Lochiel, determined to carry out his share of it, immediately set his prisoners free, at the same time asking them the favour of accompanying him to Inverlochy that they might see and testify to his ready and free compliance with at least one of the principal clauses of the treaty, in laying down his arms. This, in the most agreeable manner, they at once consented to do. Lochiel, having convened all the members of his clan that lived within a reasonable distance of the garrison, placed himself at their head, and marched to Inverlochy, accompanied by his late prisoners. His men, dressed in their usual warlike array, were told off in companies under command of the chieftains or Captains of their respective tribes, whose place it was to lead them in war, all armed, as if marching to battle, with pipes playing, and colours flying. The Governor marched out all his troops to the plain, in front of the garrison, to meet them, where they were placed in proper order. The Camerons drew up in two lines in front of the garrison troops. The Governor and Lochiel saluted one another ; the manner of the ceremony was agreed upon ; the treaty was read amid loud huzzas, with every appearance of satisfaction and demonstrations of joy on both sides. Lochiel and his men formally laid down their arms in name of the king, and immediately took them up in name of the States ; a magnificent entertainment was provided for the chief and his principal officers ; while his men were supplied with an excellent dinner on the plain on which they stood.

He would not allow his followers to mix with the English for fear that they might quarrel and produce fresh disturbance. One of his officers, however, had a dispute over their wine with a Lieutenant-Colonel Allan, which was afterwards amicably settled by the intervention of the Governor. With this single exception, the whole proceedings passed off in the most satisfactory manner. Lochiel wrote the same day to General Monk intimating his compliance so far with the conditions of the treaty. The general sent for him to Dalkeith, whither he started next morning. On his arrival Monk expressed his great pleasure at the manner in which he executed his part of the arrangements, and gave him a letter to that effect, dated Dalkeith, 5th June, 1655. Thus, a treaty was arranged and carried out between the powerful government of Oliver Cromwell and a Highland chief, upon terms so highly honourable to the latter as to appear in the present day scarcely credible.

Almost immediately after these arrangements had been completed, endless prosecutions were raised against the Camerons for offences committed so far back as the wars of Montrose. Monk however, continued Lochiel's friend, and he wrote to the Judges desiring them not to move in any actions raised for crimes committed prior to his capitulation. Soon, however, an action was raised against him before the Sheriff of Inverness; and on this occasion Monk procured an order from the Privy Council "discharging that judge to sustain process for any crime committed preceding the first of June, 1655". After this the Camerons were allowed for many years to live in peace. Lochiel received many favours from the government. Among other privileges he secured the management of the public revenues of his own district.*

* "1st, Lochiel (after he had closed his capitulation with the usurpers) entered into so strict a league and friendship with them, that for this cause they divided Lochaber and the places adjacent from the Shires of Inverness and Perth, and made the said Lochiel both Sheriff, Commissary, Commissioner, and Justice of the Peace of these places, who thereby not only enriched himself, but also did the usurpers several good offices, by helping to reduce the Highlanders under their obedience: 2nd, He was assisted in all lawsuits against Mackintosh by the usurpers. So as Mackintosh and his whole kin and friends were forced to deliver their arms to the garrison at Inverness, but Lochiel and the whole name of Clan Cameron were tolerated to bear arms in any part within the kingdom, except only within the garrisons."—*The True Information of the Respective Deportments of the Lairds of Makintoshe, and of Evan Cameron of Lochzield, in Reference to the Late Unnaturall Warrs.*

About this time he turned young MacMartin of Letterfinlay out of his property and forced him to leave the country. Old MacMartin and his people sided with the Camerons. Monk intervened; Lochiel arranged with the heir of Letterfinlay, whom he ultimately restored to his rights; and the General was so satisfied with his conduct that he continued a friendly correspondence with him until the Restoration.

It seems that Lochiel had no great faith in the Presbyterian clergy of his day, for, though he was anxious to have a minister placed among his people, that he "might be of service in reclaiming them," yet "the turbulent tempers of the clergymen of these times, joined with their stupidity and ignorance, their avarice, pride, and cruelty," gave him so bad an opinion of them that he was afraid to admit any of them into his country. Ultimately, however, he agreed to admit the clergy into Lochaber, the Council providing him with a stipend of eighty pounds yearly for each of two ministers.

Lochiel, now able to live at home in peace, married a young lady, to whom he had been for some time engaged, Mary, daughter of Sir Donald Macdonald, eighth Baron and first Baronet of Sleat. The wedding is said to have been memorable for its magnificence, and, on his return to Lochaber, he was entertained and "complimented by his clan with a sum equal at least to all the charges of that expensive wedding". His biographer records an incident, which occurred on the occasion, of so interesting a nature that we shall reproduce it in his own words:—" At this meeting he was agreeably entertained by a Highland bard, who sung or recited his verses after the manner of the ancients, and who inherited no small portion of their spirit and simplicity. He laboured under the common misfortune of the brotherhood of Parnassus, and came all the way from Braemar, or thereabout, to petition for three cows that had been taken from him in the late wars. He artfully introduced himself by a panegyric on the chief; and while he magnified his power, he ingeniously complimented his clan, whose friendship and protection he begged. He made frequent mention of those qualities that were most favourable for his purpose, with cunning enough; for as pity, generosity, and compassion are virtues inseparable from great souls, so they answered his aim in opening the hearts of those whom he petitioned. The poem is written in a strong, nervous, and masculine style, abounding with thoughts and images drawn from such simple objects as he had either seen or occasionally heard of, but expressed in a manner peculiar to the emphasis and genius of the Gaelic, for he understood no other language. Here is no ostentation of learning, no allusions to ancient fable or mythology, no far-fetched similes, nor dazzling metaphors brought from imaginary or unknown objects. These are the affected ornaments of modern poetry, and are more properly the issue of art and study, than of nature and genius. But the beauty of this consists in that agreeable simplicity, in that glow of imagination and noble flame of fancy, which give life and energy to such compositions." Our author gives an English translation of the poem, which, he says, no more resembles the original "than the naked and disfigured carcase of a murdered hero does a living one in full vigour and spirit; for the Gaelic has all the advantages of an original language. It is concise, copious, and pathetic; and as one word of it expresses more than three of ours, so it is well-known how impossible it is to preserve the full force and energy of a thought or image in a tedious circumlocution." The English version extends to no less than seventy-six lines, and if the Gaelic original was so far superior to it as our authority would have us to believe, it must have been a highly successful effort.*

* The following is the English version of this poem, as given in *The Memoirs of Sir Ewen Cameron* :—

> To Abrian shores I wing my willing flight,
> To see with wondering eyes the matchless knight,
> The generous chief, who the brave clan commands,
> And waves his bloody banner o'er the lands.
> The hero, to whom all that's great belongs:
> The glorious theme of our sublimest songs,
> Whose manly sport the savage is to trace,
> Inured to toil, and hardened in the chase.

SIR EWEN CAMERON, SEVENTEENTH OF LOCHIEL.

Macaulay, in his *History of England*, refers to this poem, and the occasion of it. Of the poem, and of Lochiel—whom he describes as the "Ulysses of the Highlands"—he says: "As a patron of literature, he ranks with the magnificent Dorset. If Dorset, out of his own purse, allowed Dryden a pension equal to the profits of the Laureateship, Lochiel is said to have bestowed on a celebrated bard, who had been plundered by marauders, and who implored alms in a

> Strong as an eagle, with resistless blows
> He falls impetuous on his fiercest foes.
> His fiercest foes beneath his arm must die,
> Or quick as birds before the falcon fly,
> Keen to attack, the approach of danger fires;
> A mighty foe, still mightier force inspires;
> His courage swells the more that dangers grow,
> And still the hero rises with the foe.
>
> Oft I, young chief, have heard thine actions told,
> Thy person praised, thy generous name extolled;
> Now to my eyes, these graces stand confessed,
> With which kind fame my ravished ears possessed.
> See! his fresh looks with manly beauties glow,
> His brawn and air, his strength and vigour show,
> In just proportion every feature shines,
> And goodness softens the majestic lines;
> The charms of modesty through all we trace,
> And winning sweetness smiles in every grace.
>
> What numerous tribes thy loved commands obey!
> In shining helms, and polished armour gay:
> Brave champions all, whose brawny arms do wield
> The offensive broad-sword and defensive shield.
> Ah! many a foe has then laid victims been,
> And hapless widows mourn their edge too keen.
>
> Immortal chief! with early triumphs crowned,
> Thy conduct guides, thy courage gives the wound,
> Matchless the guns, the bows well-backed and long,
> Pointed the shafts, the sounding quivers strong;
> Dreadful the swords, and vigorous the hands
> Of our well-bodied, fierce, and numerous bands—
> Bands, whose resistless fury scours the fields,
> Greedy of slaughter, and unknown to yield!
>
> Hence your fierce Camerons (for that name they bear),
> As masters rule, and lord it everywhere;
> Even of such power might sceptred monarchs boast!
> Happy when guarded by so brave an host:
> An host, whose matches no one chief can tell,
> In arms to equal, or in strength excel.

pathetic Gaelic ode, three cows and the almost incredible sum of fifteen pounds sterling."

Lochiel and his clan lived in peace during the whole of the year 1659, though considerable commotion went on at headquarters. When his friend, General Monk, resolved upon supporting the Scottish Parliament against the English generals, Lochiel determined to act with him, and accompanied him in his famous expedition to England which resulted in the Restoration of Charles II. in 1660. His reputation preceded Lochiel in the south, and he was treated with the greatest consideration by the English people, wherever he went. They came in crowds to meet the Scottish army, expecting deliverance at their hands, praying for their success, and petitioning for a

> O let me, sir, their loved protection gain,
> For this I came, nor did I come in vain!
> Great as their courage is, their generous mind,
> To want still liberal, and to suffering kind!
> But first to thee, great chief, I make my moan;
> Heroic Ewen! True son of prudent John,
> Illustrious Allan's heir, with beauty crowned,
> And as a lion bold, when foes surround.
>
> If, or your judgment does approve my song,
> Or, if my sufferings claim redress of wrong—
> Three cows well-fed (no more, alas! had I),
> With drink and food sustained my poverty;
> These I demand; oh! they the victims are
> Of lawless ravage, and destructive war.
>
> Nor I to those with doubtful hopes complain,
> Whose liberal hands did former wants sustain,
> My losses, now repeated, aids demand,
> Since I no milk, nor other cow command.
> Else I all summer must on herbage dine,
> And in the cold of shivering winter pine!
>
> Brave Callart, with the shining armour shone,
> I next address: To thee I make my moan,
> You to the field the embattled warriors lead,
> And hear with pity when poor sufferers plead;
>
> Your natural goodness does my hopes secure,
> Nor need I tell you more, but that I'm poor!
> With thee I join brave Dougal's worthy heir,
> And Martin's son, who all the virtues share.
> Witness, O Heavens! how I esteem the three,
> So much ennobled by their ancestry!

free parliament in England. Lochiel, as the guest of Monk during the celebrated march to London, was carefully provided for in suitable quarters on his arrival. The general had him in his own company on all occasions where there was opportunity of doing him honour, and when the king made his triumphant entry to the city, "the general desired Lochiel to keep all the way as near to him as he possibly could; and when his Majesty alighted, it was his own fault, but he held the king's stirrup, as he had an inviting opportunity. The effect of his modesty, or rather bashfulness, he had some reason to repent of, for another, who had more assurance, got before him and performed that office, for which he was royally rewarded." He was, however, afterwards introduced to kiss the king's hands, when he was received very graciously, the general having previously made known who Lochiel was, and the nature of his merit and services to the crown. He was also introduced to the Dukes of York and Gloucester. General Middleton had already made the former fully acquainted with his position and history, especially as to the biting out the Englishman's throat at Achadalew, which had become a leading subject of conversation in court circles. The Duke of York especially received him most graciously, with marks of esteem and favour, and on several occasions he took pleasure in chaffing him about the famous bite, and other incidents of his early life.

The garrison at Inverlochy was ordered south, and by an order of General Monk to Colonel Hill, then governor, the houses and all the material which could not be shipped were presented to Lochiel; while, at the same time, the key of the fortress itself was given up to him. The order is dated 18th of June, 1660, at Cockpitt, where Monk then resided. But while Lochiel was thus in favour at Court, he was not yet destined to be free from trouble in his own country, though, for a time at least, his quarrels were not of a sanguinary character.

Argyll having been brought to trial before the Scottish Parliament and condemned, and executed, in 1661, proved most unfortunate for the Camerons. Lochiel's uncle, Donald Cameron, one of his tutors during his minority, and two others of his relations, having advanced to Argyll, between 1650 and 1660, the sum of 16,345 merks, obtained a mortgage from him upon a certain property which had been forfeited by the Marquis of Huntly and granted to Argyll, and as an additional security, he gave them a warranty over the estates of Suinart and Ardnamurchan, then Argyll's property. Having been duly infefted in these lands, his relatives made them over to Lochiel. On the execution of Argyll, his estates were regranted to Huntly free of all the debts, and Lochiel was thus left with nothing but his claim upon Suinart and Ardnamurchan. Parliament acknowledged this claim, and recommended that a charter of the lands should be granted to him, "suitable to the extent of the sum" advanced by his relatives, but in consequence of the crafty and able tactics of his enemy, the Duke of Lauderdale, he was unsuccessful, though Monk, now Duke of Albemarle, Middleton, and the crown were all in his favour. "The king, being perpetually dunned by the continued application of the greatest men of his Court, at last ordered Lauderdale to present the signature or grant of these lands to be superscribed by his Majesty, according to the usual form ; and this being part of his office, as principal Secretary of State, he was obliged after repeated orders to comply. But when the grant came to be laid before the king, he took care that there should not be as much ink in the pen as would suffice to write the superscription, so that when his Majesty had wrote the word 'Charles' he wanted ink to add 'Rex,' and though the king often called for more," not another drop could be procured at the time, and the matter was left in that incomplete state, while Lauderdale induced several of Lochiel's enemies to raise action against him for old scores, thus for the time skilfully diverting his attention from his claims on the lands in question.

The Earl of Callander succeeded in getting Parliament to grant him a claim against Lochiel for acts committed before the Restoration, but he was afterwards acquitted, the Earl being unable to substantiate the details of his claim before a Commission appointed for the purpose.

About the same time Mackintosh began again to press his ancient claim to the lands of Glenlui and Locharkaig. With the nature of this claim the reader is already acquainted. On the advice of Lauderdale, Mackintosh, in 1661, petitioned Parliament, and ultimately obtained a decree adjudging him the lands, and ordering Lochiel not only to divest himself of the property, but to find security that neither he nor his clan should for the future molest Mackintosh nor his tenants in the peaceable possession thereof, under a penalty of 20,000 merks. This happened in Lochiel's absence, he being at the time at Court in London, pushing his claims to the lands of Suinart and Ardnamurchan, and to a pension of £300 sterling per annum which the king agreed to grant him, but never effectually carried out. The action of Parliament in this matter the Court of Session held to be an encroachment upon its privileges.

The Act and Decree granted on this occasion, at the instance of Lachlan Mackintosh, against Sir Ewen Cameron of Lochiel, gives such an interesting narrative of the various other acts and decrees issued against the Camerons, during the preceding half-century, that we are induced to reproduce it, notwithstanding its length. It is taken from the Appendix to *Dunachton, Past and Present*, a very rare work, by Charles Fraser-Mackintosh, M.P., published in 1866. The document is dated the 5th of July, 1661, and is as follows :—

Anent the supplication given in to the Honourable Commissioners appointed for Bills, by Lachlan Mackintosh of Torcastle, against Ewen Cameron, now of Lochiel, showing that the said supplicant and his predecessors, Lairds of Mackintosh, being for many ages heritable proprietors of the lands of Glenlui and Loch Arkaig in Lochaber, continually troubled in their possession thereof by the Clan Cameron, who are notoriously known to have been from the beginning, and continues still, a most rebellious and lawless people, given to depredations, thefts, and oppressions ; for remeid whereof, the deceased Sir Lachlan Mackintosh, goodsir to the supplicant (being heritable Steward and Bailie of the Lordship of Lochaber), went in anno 1616 to Lochaber to hold Courts, and in an hostile manner was resisted and pursued for his life by Allan Cameron of Lochiel

(chieftain of the said clan), so that the Lords of Secret Council, knowing the
barbarity and lawlessness of that people, after that matter was sufficiently proven
and cleared before them, and decreet given thereanent, they issued letters charging
the said Allan to enter his person in ward, and thereafter, upon his contempt,
issued letters of inter-communing, with an ample commission of fire and sword,
against the said Allan and his clan, as the same at length bears; and at last John
Cameron, son to the said Allan, was apprehended and put in ward in the Tolbooth
of Edinburgh until he should find sufficient caution to keep the Laird of Mackintosh and his tenants harmless and skaithless in the peaceable possession of the said
lands of Glenlui and Loch Arkaig, where he remained for the space of three years,
until the said Sir Lachlan, the supplicant's goodsir, died, and then was released by
the Laird of Grant, who pretended to be the supplicant's father's tutor; and the
said John Cameron, resolving to keep the Laird of Mackintosh in continual trouble
and vexation, did take assignation to a right of wadset of the said lands from the
Laird of Grant in the year 1635, and in the year 1637, the said supplicant's
deceased father having consigned in the hand of the Provost of Inverness the sum
specified in the said wadset, did in the year 1639 obtain a declarator of redemption against the said Ewen Cameron, now of Lochiel, *in foro contradictorio*, and
the money of the wadset was given up and delivered by the said Provost of
Inverness to Donald Cameron, tutor of Lochiel (as his discharge thereof bears);
and therefore the said supplicant, his said father, obtained a decreet of renewing
before the Lords of Council and Session against the said Ewen and his tenants,
possessors of the said lands, and thereupon caused charge denounce them to the
horn (whereat as yet they lie unrelaxed), and in the year 1648, having meaned himself to the Parliament, they for his furtherance to the possession of the said lands,
appointed him, by act of Parliament, Governor of Inverlochie, which act was
thereafter rescinded in the year 1649, so that the said Ewen Cameron and his kin
and followers, taking advantage of the times, have since Whitsunday, 1637,
masterfully, in high contempt of his Majesty's laws, kept the possession of the said
lands, and resolved never to quit the same, unless authority and force compel him;
whereby his Majesty and Estates of Parliament might evidently perceive that the
said Ewen Cameron and his predecessors and followers have been always a lawless
and rebellious people, and that they most unjustly have wronged and oppressed
the supplicant's predecessors, and specially his said deceased father, who during
the space of twenty-four years now byepast, has lain out of the profit of his money
and possession of his lands. And thereby his said father, in his own time, and now
the said supplicant and remanent children are reduced to a very hard condition,
having little or nothing to live upon, the rest of his lands being life-rented by his
mother. And therefore craving that warrant might be granted for warning of the
said Ewen Cameron to compear before his Majesty's Commissioners, Grace, and
Estates of Parliament, at a certain day, to hear and see him decerned to put the
said Lachlan Mackintosh's supplicant in the peaceable, actual, and corporal
possession of the foresaid lands of Glenlui and Loch Arkaig, and to denude himself *omni habili modo*, and to find sufficient caution that the said supplicant, his
tenants and servants, shall be harmless and skaithless, in the peaceable possession
of the said lands in time coming, under such pains as our said Sovereign Lords
Commissioner, his Grace, and Estates of Parliament, should ordain, as at more
length is contained in the said supplication—which supplication being read in
presence of the Commissioners of Parliament appointed for Bills, the said Lachlan
Mackintosh, supplicant, compearing personally, with Mr. George Mackenzie,
advocate, his procurator, who, for verifying of the said petition or libel, produced in
their presence an instrument of sasine of the date the 9th day of March, 1621, proceeding upon a precept directed furth of the Chancery, of the date the 6th day of February, 1621, bearing Anna Grant, spouse to the said deceased Sir Lachlan Mackintosh
of Torcastle, to be infefted in life-rent during all the days of her lifetime, and

William Mackintosh, his son, in all and haill the town and lands of Glenlui and Loch Arkaig, and certain other lands therein specified, which sasine is under the sign and subscription of John Grant, notary public, and registered in the Register of Sasines for Inverness, the 13th of April, 1621 years, by William Lauder, the keeper of the said Register, with a decreet obtained before the Lords of Secret Council, at the instance of Sir William Oliphant of Newton, knight, his Majesty's advocate, for his Highness's interests, and Lachlan Mackintosh of Dunachton, Heritable Bailie and Steward of the Lordship and Stewartrie of Lochaber, against the said deceased Allan Cameron of Lochiel, and certain other persons therein specified, of the date the 10th day of June, 1617 years; whereby the Lords of Secret Council found that, in the month of July, 1616, the said Allan Cameron and certain other persons, his accomplices, convocated and assembled together the number of two hundred men, boden in fear of war with unlawful weapons to stop and impede the said Lachlan Mackintosh of Dunachton from holding of Courts within the said Lordship of Lochaber, and that they shot a number of muskets and hagbuts at the said Lachlan and his company, and stayed him from holding of the said Courts; and that thereby they committed a very great insolency and contempt to the breach of his Majesty's peace, and violated his Highness's laws and acts of Parliament, made against the convocation of his Majesty's lieges, and their wearing of hagbuts and pistols; and therefore ordained letters to be directed, charging the said Allan Cameron of Lochiel and remanent other persons, defenders, to pass and enter their persons within the Tolbooth of Edinburgh, therein to remain upon their own expenses, ay and until order were taken with them for the said insolence as accords, within fifteen days next after the charge to be given to them, under the pain of rebellion and putting them to the horn, which letters of horning, raised upon the said decreet and executions of horning, and denunciation following thereupon, registered in the books of the General Register of Hornings and Inhibitions upon the penult day of July, 1617 years; together with a commission granted by our late Sovereign Lord, King James VI., of blessed memory, to Archibald, Earl of Argyll, William, Earl of Tullibardine, Colin, Lord Kintail, and certain other persons, to convocate his Majesty's lieges in arms for taking and apprehending of the said Allan Cameron of Lochiel and other persons contained in the said decreet, at the instance of the said Lachlan Mackintosh of Dunachton, and putting them in sure firmance and captivity, aye and until order were taken with them, which commission is dated 27th June, 1617. Item—A decreet of removing obtained before the Lords of Council and Session at the instance of the said Lachlan Mackintosh of Dunachton, against the said Allan Cameron and certain other persons therein contained, of the date the 27th of November, 1616, decerning and ordaining the said Allan Cameron of Lochiel to flit and remove himself, his wife, bairns, servants, family, sub-tenants, cottars, goods and gear, furth and from the town and lands of Glenlui and Loch Arkaig, with parts, pendicles, and pertinents, lying within the Lordship of Lochaber and Sheriffdom of Inverness, and to desist and cease therefrom, and leave the same void and redd, to the effect the said Lachlan Mackintosh, supplicant, his men, tenants, and servants, might enter thereto, peaceably brook, enjoy, occupy, labour, manure, set, use, and dispose thereof as his heritage at his pleasure; with letters of horning raised thereupon, and executions of the same following thereupon, registered in the Sheriff Court books of Inverness upon the 1st day of March, 1617 years, with other letters of horning, raised upon the said horning, at the instance of the said Lachlan Mackintosh, designed therein Sir Lachlan Mackintosh of Torcastle, Knight, for charging the Sheriff of Inverness and his deputes, within whose bounds and jurisdiction the said lands of Glenlui and Loch Arkaig lie, for ejecting and outputting of the said Allan Cameron of Lochiel and remanent other persons contained in the said decreet of removing furth of the said lands, houses, biggings, yards, etc., so far as they occupy thereof, and to hold him furth thereof, and to enter the said Sir Lachlan Mackintosh to the peaceable possession thereof, keep, maintain, and defend him therein, which letters of horning are dated the 2nd day of August, 1617 years. Item—Letters of publication and proclamation at the instance of the said Sir William Oliphant of Newton, Knight, and Lachlan Mackintosh, commanding, charging, and inhibiting all and sundry the lieges and subjects of this realm, that none of them presume or take upon hand, and reset, supply, or intercommune with the said Allan Cameron of Lochiel and remanent other persons, contained in the said decreet, obtained at the instance of the said Lachlan Mackintosh, before the Lords of Secret Council, their wives, nor bairns, furnish them meat, drink, house, harbour, nor no other thing comfortable or necessary to them, have intelligence with them privately or publicly, directly nor indirectly, by word, writ, nor message, nor furnish nor sell to them any kind of victual, arms, powder, or ball, nor take their goods or gear in keeping, which letters of publication are under the signet of the Secret Council, and dated the last day of July, 1617 years. Item—Decreet of Declarator of Redemption obtained at the instance of William Mackintosh of Torcastle, against Ewen Cameron, son and apparent heir to the deceased John Cameron of Lochiel, and Donald Cameron, his tutor, James Grant, now of Freuchie, son and heir to Sir John Grant of Freuchie, before the Lords of Council and Session, upon the 5th day of March, 1639 years, decerning and ordaining the towns and lands of Glenlui, Loch Arkaig, and others contained in the said decreet, which was wadset to the said Laird of Freuchie, to be duly, lawfully, and orderly loosed, out-quit, and redeemed from Ewen Cameron, son and apparent heir of the deceased John Cameron, fiar of Lochiel, and that it should be leisome to the said William Mackintosh, his heirs and assignees, to have full and free regress, access, and ingress again to the said lands, and he to renounce and overgive the same, with all right, title, interest, claim, kindness, property, and possession, he has or may pretend thereto, in favour of the said William Mackintosh, and that in respect of the said William Mackintosh his consignation of the sum of 18,000 merks in the hands of James Cuthbert of Drakies, then Provost of Inverness, conform to a contract of wadset, passed betwixt the deceased John Grant of Freuchie and Sir Lachlan Mackintosh of Torcastle, Knight, on the one and other parts, dated the 12th day of January, 1621 years. Item—An order of redemption used by the said William Mackintosh of the said lands, with letters of horning raised upon the said decreet of declarator and executions thereof, registered in the Sheriff Court books of Inverness, upon the 22nd day of November, 1639 years. Item—The extract of the tutory of Donald Cameron, lawful brother to the deceased John Cameron, fiar of Lochiel, bearing him to be served tutor to Ewen Cameron, son lawful to the said deceased John Cameron, before the Sheriff of Inverness, dated the 14th day of March, 1637 years. Item—The extract of the discharge granted by Donald Cameron, tutor of law served to Ewen Cameron, son lawful and apparent heir to the deceased John Cameron, fiar of Lochiel, and James Cuthbert of Drakies, of the said sum of 18,000 merks, which was condated at Inverarny, the 6th day of February, 1640 years, and registered in the books of Council and Session upon the 9th day of May the same year, under the sign and subscription of Sir Archibald Primrose, Clerk of Register, then Clerk of the Secret Council. Item—A decreet of removing obtained before the Lords of Council and Session, at the instance of the said William Mackintosh of Torcastle, against the said Ewen Cameron of Lochiel, Donald Cameron, tutor of Lochiel, and certain other persons therein contained, of the date the 27th day of July, 1647 years, decerning and ordaining them to remove from the lands of Tharoch, Mufrolich, and certain other lands specified in the said decreet, lying within the Lordship of Lochaber and Sheriffdom of Inverness, to the effect the said William Mackintosh might enter thereto, with letters of horning raised upon the said decreet in anno 1647 years, and thereafter new letters raised on the same, which were executed against the said Ewen Cameron and Donald Cameron, his tutor, and remanent tenants, and is registered at Inverness, the 20th day of February, 1655. And the said Ewen Cameron, now of Lochiel, defender, compearing also personally, with Messrs William Maxwell and James Chalmers, advocates, his procurators, who produced the extract of a decree obtained at the instance of the said William Mackintosh of Torcastle, against the said Ewen Cameron of Lochiel, Donald Cameron, tutor of Lochiel, and certain other persons, before the Sheriff of Inverness and his deputes, of the date the 5th day of June, 1655 years, decerning them to make payment to the said William of the haill maills, farms, kains, customs, casualties, and other duties of the lands forsaids, and other particularly expressed in the said decreet yearly, the years therein mentioned, and which decreet is given in absence. Item —A summons of reduction raised at the instance of the said Ewen Cameron against William Mackintosh, for reducing of the foresaid decree for maills and duties, and other decreets obtained before the said Lords of Council and Session, with the executions of the said summons and with a suspension of the foresaid decreet obtained for maills and duties before the Sheriff of Inverness, and executions of the said suspension ;—which petitions above mentioned, with the foresaid sasine, decreets, commission, letters, and other writs foresaid, produced for the part of the said supplicant for instructing thereof, and decreet, summons of reduction, and letters of suspension, also above mentioned, produced for the part of the said Ewen Cameron, defender, together with the report of the said Commissioners of Parliament appointed for Bills, and with the defences, answers, duply and triply aftermentioned proponed and given in by either of the said parties *hinc inde* against others, being all heard, seen, and considered by the said Estates of Parliament, and they therewith being well and ripely advised ;— his Majesty, with advice and consent of the said Estates of Parliament, decerns and ordains the said Ewen Cameron, defender, to repossess the said Lachlan Mackintosh, supplicant, in the foresaid lands of Glenlui and Lock Arkaig, and pertinents thereof; and for that effect to put him in the peaceable, actual, and corporal possession of the same, and to denude himself thereof *omni habili modo* in favours of the said Lachlan Mackintosh, supplicant ; and also the said Ewen Cameron, defender, to find presently sufficient caution to the Clerk of Register or his deputes that he shall noways trouble or molest the said Lachlan Mackintosh or his tenants in the possession of the foresaid lands, and that under the pain of twenty thousand merks, etc., etc.

The Chancellor, Lord Glencairn, had written a letter to the Lord President and Lords of Session, at the time sitting at Edinburgh, dated London, 7th June, 1661, to the following effect :—

"Since I came to this place, I understand his Majesty has taken such notice of the Laird of Lochiell, his faithful service done to him, that he has proposed a way for composing the difference betwixt Mackintosh and him, which will shortly come to your hands : I shall desire you, therefore, if Mackintosh offer to take advantage of Lochiell, his absence, or to prevent his Majesty's commands by insisting in action before you against Lochiell, now in his absence, that you continue the action until you know his Majesty's further pleasure, which will be signified to you by my return."

The Lords of Session at once intimated the receipt of this letter to Parliament and to the Privy Council, with the result that nothing was done until July, 1662, when Mackintosh obtained a decree of removal against Lochiel and his clan from the lands in question, based on the sentence of Parliament of the previous year. The question was debated before the Lords of Session by the ablest men at the bar, and reasons were given on both sides, for which much could be said; but legally, Lochiel had the worst of it, and decree went against him. He had, however, great influence at Court, and he determined to use it in this emergency. He at once petitioned the king, who gave him a private audience, and listened patiently to all he had to say. Lochiel urged upon his Majesty to interpose his authority, to compel Mackintosh to accept a sum of money in lieu of his claim for restitution of the lands, pointing out that, as the Camerons were in possession, and had been, for centuries, they would never give up the lands and their dwellings without great bloodshed. He predicted the consequences of attempting to remove them by force, and he had good reasons to come to the conclusion that this would be the last occasion on which he would have the honour of seeing the king. "He had," he said, "been a great part of his youth a fugitive and outlaw for his attempting to serve his Majesty; but that gave him no great pain, because he suffered in a glorious cause, and only shared in the common calamities of his country, but henceforth he must resolve to live among hills and deserts, a fugitive and vagabond, merely because he was the chief of a clan for whom, though he was bound by the law, he was sure he could not answer when they came to be dispossessed by the ancient enemy of his family." To this his Majesty replied—"Lochiel, I know that you were a faithful servant to the crown, and that you have often, with great bravery, hazarded your life and fortune in that cause; fear not that you shall be long an outlaw, whatever shall happen in that quarrel, while I have the power of granting a remission; but as to the affairs of law and private right, I will not meddle with it, but shall write to my council to endeavour to compromise matters, so as to prevent public disturbance. In the meantime, I think it your interest to hinder Mackintosh's attaining to possession; and I assure you that neither life nor estate shall be in danger while I can save them." Lochiel naturally felt much cheered by the reception he had received, and by the encouragement given him by the king. He at once informed the Duke of Albemarle of what passed between him and the king, and urged upon him to do all in his power to keep Mackintosh from again getting into favour at Court. His Grace promised every assistance. The Duke of York, to whom Lochiel was previously known, also used his influence with the king in his behalf. His Royal Highness at the same time recommended him to the Earl of Clarendon, then Prime Minister, and to several others of the leading men at Court, but Lauderdale still continued his implacable enemy, even going the length of opposing the king in writing to his commissioners for Scotland in favour of Lochiel, as long as he could; but his Majesty having determined that his wishes in this should be at once carried out, a letter in the following terms was addressed, "To our Right Trusty and Right Well-beloved Cousin and Counsellor, the Earl of Middleton, our Commissioner to our Parliament in Scotland":—

"CHARLES REX.
"Right Trusty and Well-beloved Cousine and Counsellor, we greet you well.—We haveing formerly written to our Privy Councill about the dicrence likely to arise betwixt the Lairds of Macintosh and Locheill, we are still of the same opinion that though we will not meddle in the point of law or right, which (we are informed) is already determined, yet we have thought fit to recommend to your care, to endeavour so to settle and agree them as the peace of those parts be not disturbed. Given att Hampton Court, the 30th May, 1662, and of our reign the 14th year."

Lochiel left London, and arrived in Edinburgh about the same time as this letter, when he found that during his absence a warrant for his seizure and imprisonment had been obtained by Mackintosh. He at once petitioned the Privy Council for protection, and his request was granted, but the order was only available up to the 24th of June following. During this interval he married his second wife, a daughter of Sir Lachlan Maclean of Duart; and having done all he could to secure the active interest of his friends in Parliament and in the Privy Council, he left Edinburgh before his order of protection had expired, and in due time arrived with his young wife safely in Lochaber, to the great delight and gratification of his devoted clansmen.

Through Lauderdale's influence in the Privy Council, the king's letter was not read until the 4th of September following, and in the interval Mackintosh petitioned for a commission of fire and sword against Lochiel and his friends. Through the influence of the Commissioner and Chancellor, Mackintosh, on this occasion, failed in his object; but in 1663 he obtained a warrant charging Lochiel to appear before the Council within fifteen days, upon certification that, if he did not, their Lordships would issue a commission of fire and sword against him. Sir Ewen received information of what had occurred through his friend the Chancellor, but resolved not to appear, and the commission against him was issued on the 25th of August. Among those authorised to execute it were the Marquis of Montrose, the Earls of Caithness, Moray, Athole, Errol, Marischal, Mar, Dundee, Airlie, Aboyne, and several more of the leading men both in the Lowlands and in the Highlands. Letters of concurrence and intercommuning, or outlawry, were issued against him and the whole Clan Cameron; while all the men between sixteen and sixty years of age in the counties of Inverness, Ross, Nairn, and Perth, were ordered to convene in arms, and to put the law in execution against "these rebels and outlaws," whenever Mackintosh should consider it fit to call them together for that purpose. On his return to Dunachton, Mackintosh wrote to each of those named in the commission, and afterwards visited them in person, urging upon them the necessity of preparing to carry out the Privy Council's commands, but only four out of the four counties named would move, namely, John Grant of Rothiemurchus, and William Forbes of Skellater, married to two daughters of Kyllachie, and David Ross of Urchany, and John Campbell of Auchindown, both related to Mackintosh himself on the mother's side. On the contrary, they strongly opposed the action which he proposed, and urged him to accept the money payment which Lochiel was willing to give in satisfaction of his claim. In these circumstances, Mackintosh resolved to punish the Camerons by his own clan and any of the neighbours which he could induce to join him. In this he also failed, and Lochiel, in the meantime, to show his determination and ability to fight, sent several parties to the enemy's country, with instructions to carry away the cattle of such of the Mackintoshes as were still willing to follow their chief on the proposed expedition to Lochaber. Mackintosh at once showed fight, and sent a party of "twenty vigorous youths" on a similar expedition to Lochaber, especially to capture some of the principal persons named in his commission, expecting to force Lochiel to comply with his demands by detaining these persons, when caught, in captivity "and threatening their lives"; but this party only succeeded in "killing two cow-herds whom they met by accident". He ultimately arranged with his followers by granting them several demands which he had previously refused them, and so induced them to agree to follow him—going the length, in the case of the Macphersons, of granting "a renunciation of any title or pretence he had to the chiefship, and a premium of £100 sterling" for their services on this occasion. *

* Mr. Mackintosh-Shaw says, that Mackintosh's "prime difficulty was with Andrew Macpherson of Cluny, who at length offered to accompany him on three conditions—that the heads of the Macphersons should always hold the next place in the clan to the chiefs of Mackintosh; that all lands then in possession of the Mackintoshes which had at any time been held by the Macphersons should be restored to them; and that Mackintosh should give a written acknowledgment that the assistance he received from Cluny was not of the nature of service which he had a right to demand, but simply of goodwill, and what one neighbour might render another." Alexander Mackintosh of Connage; William Mackintosh of Kyllachie; and Donald Macqueen of Corriebrough, raised other difficulties, more or less important. These are fully set forth by the same writer, who, after describing what had taken place in the meantime, informs us that, on the 21st of August, 1665, before leaving Badenoch, where he had a meeting with the Earl of Moray, "Mackintosh was induced by some of his advisers to consent to an arrangement with Cluny, under which Cluny was to go with him to Lochaber in consideration of a hundred pounds

Lochiel kept himself fully informed of his enemy's proceedings, and being so much in favour with the principal Lords of Parliament and of the Privy Council, he succeeded in January, 1665, in procuring an order, signed by the Earl of Rothes, the king's Commissioner to Parliament, commanding Mackintosh to appear in Edinburgh within a certain number of days, and forbidding him to put his commission of fire and sword in force until the pleasure of the Privy Council was made further known to him. Mackintosh reluctantly obeyed, but he complained bitterly of these new proceedings against him. The reply received to his complaint was a peremptory command to remain in the city until Lochiel, who had also been sent for, should arrive. On the appointed day a meeting of the Privy Council was held, at which the Commissioner, Chancellor, all the principal Officers of State, and others in authority, were present. Both Lochiel and Mackintosh put in an appearance, and the king's letter was read in their hearing. The Chancellor stated that his Majesty's zeal for the welfare and happiness of his people, and the particular commands which he had in consequence laid upon his Parliament and Council to endeavour to bring about a reconciliation between the parties by way of compromise, could not but have its due influence, and dispose them "to agree to such measures as should be agreeable to justice and the wisdom of his Majesty's Council". In answer to the questions put, both answered that they were willing to submit the dispute between them to the arbitration of the Privy Council. Two days after they were again called before the Council, when it was intimated to them that the Council had satisfied themselves as to the

sterling, Mackintosh at the same time agreeing to accept the aid of the Macphersons as that of friends and neighbours." The £100 was paid to Cluny, on the 12th of September, at Kiltyre, on the march to Lochaber. In the bond given to him by Mackintosh it is declared that the services of Cluny and his clan are "out of their meer goodwill and pleasure," and Mackintosh binds and obliges himself, in addition to the payment of the money, "to assist, fortify, and join with Cluny and his friends in all their necessary adoes".—*History of the Mackintoshes and Clan Chattan.*

value of the lands in question, and as to the nature of all the questions in dispute. After a long argument, the Chancellor recommended that they should, by the aid of friends, agree upon a price to be paid by Lochiel, at the same time stating that, failing this, the Council would proceed to settle the question. Lochiel and Mackintosh, with the aid of powerful friends and lawyers on both sides, tried to come to terms, but they still differed so much that there was not the least probability of any agreement being arrived at. Within eight days they were recalled before the Council, when it was declared, through the Chancellor, as the unanimous decision of their lordships, that a sum of 72,000 merks paid by Lochiel to Mackintosh would be a just sum between the demands of the one and the offer of the other, and the Council decreed accordingly.

Mackintosh would not listen to this proposal, and he resolved to leave the city privately, without coming to any final agreement. His intentions were, however, discovered, and, just as he was leaving, he was arrested by order of the Council, and detained in captivity until he found security that he, his clan, and followers should keep the peace. He then offered voluntarily to delay the execution of his commission against Lochiel for a year longer, on condition that the Council would agree to dispense with his finding caution for any but his own tenants. Lochiel and the Council agreed, and Mackintosh was permitted to return home. He, however, no sooner reached his destination than he invited all the leaders of his clan to an entertainment, with their friends and followers, at his house, and by granting them such demands as they had been for some time making upon him, induced them to subscribe a bond, agreeing to follow him in an expedition to Lochaber whenever he might call upon them to do so.

.Lochiel, who was kept fully informed of what Mackintosh was doing, wrote to his friend, the Earl of Moray, then Sheriff of Inverness-shire, asking his lordship to hold his usual Circuit Courts in Badenoch, Strathspey, and neighbouring districts—where the Macphersons, and others, who usually followed Mackintosh, resided—and as his vassals were bound to attend the Earl on such occasions, they would not be able to follow Mackintosh. This plan was at once adopted by Moray, after which he marched to Inverness, for the purpose of settling disputes which had arisen there between the town and the Macdonalds. Mackintosh came to Stratherrick, at the request of the Earl. On the 30th of August, he arrived at Dalchaple, with banners displayed, and next day he had a visit from his principal leaders—Kyllachie, Connage, Aberarder, and Corriebrough—who, after pointing out the danger and disadvantages of the step he was about to take, and the advantages of disposing of the lands in dispute, in a peaceable manner and on good terms, made him an offer of a hundred thousand merks for the lands of Glenlui and Locharkaig on behalf of the Earl of Moray. "On finding that he had been brought to Stratherrick only to hear this, Mackintosh flew into a violent passion, declaring that he had no intention whatever of alienating his inheritance, and that even were such an act necessary he would never accept so despicable a consideration."* It is supposed that this offer was made on behalf of the Earl of Argyll, who was proposed as security for the payment of the price offered, while the Mackintosh leaders were accompanied on the occasion of their making the offer by a prominent member of the Campbell clan. Mackintosh would listen to nothing but the carrying out of his own views; and he finally marched, on the 11th of September, at the head of a body of 1500 men, to Lochaber.

In connection with this expedition, it is recorded that, "Lochiel, having heard that Mackintosh was on his march, thought it full time to provide for his defence, and in a few days he got together his whole clan; who, having been prepared beforehand, and willing for the service, were sooner with him than he expected. He was likewise joined by a small party of the MacIans of Glencoe,

* *History of the Mackintoshes and Clan Chattan*, pp. 375, 376.

and another of the Macgregors, who offered their services as volunteers; and found, upon the muster, that he had got 900 armed with guns, broadswords, and targes, and 300 more who had bows in place of guns; and it is remarkable that these were the last considerable company of bowmen that appeared in the Highlands. With these he marched straight to Achnacarry, and encamped on the bank of the River Arkaig," on its east side, thus securing the only ford on the river. Here both remained facing each other for two days, after which Mackintosh moved his men two miles further west along the side of Locharkaig. Lochiel, after throwing up an embankment at the Ford, left it in charge of fifty doughty clansmen, moved his main body westward, and took up his position opposite the Mackintoshes. Here he called a council of war, and informed his friends of his full determination to settle the long-standing feud now, once and for all, by the sword. He expressed full confidence in his men, and told them that as he had the king's promise of a remission, he had no apprehensions as to the result; concluding by informing them "that if any of them wanted inclination to engage, and had not put on a fixed resolution to die or conquer, he begged of them to retire, and he would afford them such opportunities as would save their honour". Any such cowardly action was spurned by every one present, whereupon Lochiel determined to execute his plans that very night.

In the meantime, on the 12th of September, John Campbell, younger of Glenorchy, afterwards in 1681, first Earl of Breadalbane, who had been sent by Argyll, presented himself to Mackintosh with proposals of peace. This is the same gentleman described at a later period of his life, in Mackay's *Memoirs* as, "of fair complexion, having the gravity of a Spaniard, being as cunning as a fox, wise as a serpent, and slippery as an eel". A preliminary conference was at once arranged. The first day's deliberations produced no result, except a short truce to the 16th, during which the Mackintoshes took up their position and encamped at Clunes, immediately facing the Camerons. At a second meeting on the 16th, certain proposals were made to which the friends of both parties agreed, but Mackintosh rejected them, declaring that he would rather hazard his whole fortune than consent to such terms. His leading followers rebelled, refused to fight under existing conditions—"would never draw sword in the quarrel"—but Mackintosh was unbending. Next morning, however, his friends found him more willing to listen to them. They offered to make up the amount of the £1,760 difference in the money offered among themselves, and finally succeeded in inducing him to consent to an absolute sale of the lands to Lochiel on the terms previously offered, and now repeated by him, namely, 72,500 merks, or only 500 merks—which scarcely represented the interest of the portion of the money to be paid later on—more than the sum actually named as a fair compromise between the parties by the Privy Council a few years previously.

Mr. Mackintosh-Shaw describes the final settlement in the following terms, quite consistently with the more detailed account given of them in Lochiel's *Memoirs*:—While Mackintosh was undergoing the persuasive attempts of his friends, young Glenorchy had arrived at the Clan Chattan camp, and had shown additional reasons why those attempts ought to succeed, in a force of 300 men which accompanied him, and in a written order from the Earl of Argyll to employ all the power of the latter, if necessary, to bring the dispute to an end. Campbell's arrival, and Mackintosh's assent, seem to have taken place at an opportune moment, as Lochiel has concocted one of the surprises for which he was famed, and in which he was generally successful. On the preceding night he had dispatched Cameron of Erracht, with a body of picked men by boats, to the northern side of Locharkaig, there to remain concealed until an opportunity should present itself of taking the enemy by surprise. He himself was, in the meantime, to make his way with the main body by the head of the loch to the same place, a distance of some eighteen English miles. He had not advanced far on his march when he was met by young Glenorchy, bringing back with him Erracht and his party. It was only by advancing the same cogent reasons which he had already urged upon Mackintosh that Glenorchy could prevail on Lochiel to give up his intention of fighting, and to consent to the agreement into which his opponent was now willing to enter. On the following day (Monday, 18th September), a formal contract was drawn up and signed, on the one hand binding Mackintosh to sell Glenlui and Locharkaig to Lochiel, or any person he might nominate, and on the other binding Lochiel and six others to pay to Mackintosh 12,500 merks of the price in the town of Perth on the 12th of January, 1666, and at the same time to give sufficient security for the payment of the remainder of the price at the Martinmas terms of 1666 and 1667. On the 20th, Lochiel crossed the Arkaig, and met his late enemy at the house of Clunes. Both were attended by their principal friends and clansmen. They "saluted each other," says the Kinrara MS., "drank together in token of perfect reconciliation, and exchanged swords, rejoicing at the extinction of the ancient feud". The feud had raged for three centuries and a-half, during which time, says tradition, with its usual looseness of expression, a Mackintosh and a Cameron had never even *spoken* together.*

The author of the "Memoirs" gives the additional information that "Lochiel, though much fretted at the disconcerting of his measures, was still resolved to fight the enemy the very next day [after his arrival], and to continue his march, but Breadalbane [Glenorchy] told him roundly that he was equally allied to them both; that he came there to act the part of a mediator; and whoever of them proved refractory, he would not only join with the other against him, but also would bring all the power that Argyll was master of, with his own, into the quarrel; and he thereupon showed a communication he had from the Earl of Argyll to that purpose. Lochiel found himself under the

* *History of the Mackintoshes and Clan Chattan*, pp. 381, 382

necessity of consenting ; and his firm resolution of fighting had this good effect, that it hastened on the agreement, and in a manner compelled Mackintosh, who was pushed on by his people, to consent to these very proposals that had been formerly made by the Privy Council and afterwards by the Earl of Murray," on Lochiel's behalf. This agreement was completed in legal form on the 20th of September, 1665, about 360 years after the commencement of the quarrel, one of the longest duration, perhaps, mentioned in history, and, considering the strength of the parties, as bloody as any local feud of which there is any record. Though Mackintosh gained nothing, the Camerons lost largely by it in men and property, and the final settlement was considered as favourable to them as they could possibly expect in existing circumstances, though during the long period of the dispute, they, in defence of their claim and position, "gave away or abandoned their original inheritance, which was four times above this in value, as their original charters from the Lords of the Isles, all confirmed by King James IV., with the charters granted by succeeding Princes, erecting the whole into a free barony, with many powers and privileges, testify to this day ; and all this, besides the loss of the pension of three hundred pounds sterling per annum," already mentioned, and of Suinart and Ardnamurchan, which now belonged to the Earl of Argyll, with the rest of his father's forfeiture, by a grant from the Crown.

Lochiel's settlement with Mackintosh was for him, in the circumstances, a most favourable one ; for not only did the yearly rents of the lands far exceed the interest of the money paid to Mackintosh, but there were oak and fir woods on both sides of Loch-Arkaig, and on other parts of the lands in question, worth more than four times the sum paid for the whole. Lochiel, however, overlooked to make provision in the agreement for the arrears of rent due since the mortgage on the estate was redeemed in 1639, and this cost him, later on, in 1688, no end of trouble and annoyance. He entertained the leading men of the two clans— his own and the Mackintoshes—in his house for days after the agreement was finally completed, when they parted all fully satisfied with the terms arranged.*

The Marquis of Athole had offered Lochiel the money to pay the sum awarded to Mackintosh. Argyll offered it on somewhat easier conditions, but still conditions which, in future, secured—and which no doubt it was intended to secure—to him the superiority of the lands. There was to be no interest payable for the money itself, but Lochiel consented to hold the lands from Argyll as his superior, to pay him a feu-duty of one hundred pounds Scots per annum, and to grant him the service of one hundred men-in-arms whenever he should require them. These conditions landed Lochiel later on in a very difficult position, in connection with a dispute which had arisen between Argyll and the Macleans of Duart, with whom Sir Ewen was connected by marriage and consanguinity. Lochiel joined the Macleans in that quarrel, having, after visiting Argyll at Inveraray, and leaving him without notice, hastened back to Lochaber, where, being joined by the Macdonalds of Glengarry, Keppoch, Glencoe, and others, he marched into Mull, and prevented the intended invasion by Argyll for that year.

To have men in arms without authority was then, as at all times, an offence of a grave character, and, to punish Sir Ewen, Argyll applied to the Privy Council, who, on the

---

* The Camerons had other troubles at this period, and Lochiel seems to have been quite ready, immediately on being relieved from his ancient difference with Mackintosh, to settle scores, according to the old plan, elsewhere. "'There was an old feud,' we are told, "between the Camerons in Lochaber and Struan Robertson, in the upper part of Perthshire, and on the 14th of August, 1666, the renowned Chief Ewen, or Evan, Cameron came, with about eighty followers, including several duniwassals (gentlemen), to Struan's lands of Kinloch—quartered there for a night upon the tenants, beat and threatened them, broke into and searched houses, all for the purpose of laying hold of their enemy, who, however, was out of the way. Disappointed of their primary object, the Camerons took twenty-six head of cattle, and made off with them to their own country. The misdeed being fully proven in November (following) against Ewen Cameron of Lochiel, Sorlie Cameron, John Oig Cameron, and John and Duncan McEwen Cameron, the Lords of the Privy Council ordained the first-named (who did not appear) to pay Struan a fine of a thousand merks, and the others, who had been confined for some time in Tolbooth of Edinburgh, to restore to Struan the twenty-six stolen cattle."—*Domestic Annals of Scotland*, Vol. II., pp. 308, 309.

29th of July, 1669, issued a proclamation, wherein, among others, Lochiel, Maclean, and several chiefs, including Argyll himself, are ordered to find annual caution to keep the peace. He had himself previously, however, secured legal authority for punishing the Macleans, and, consequently, the proclamation only affected his opponents, impartial though it at first appeared by the inclusion of his own name. At this time, Argyll had also a warrant out against Lochiel for money due. Sir Ewen, however, started for Edinburgh, in the most secret manner, and, notwithstanding Argyll's opposition, who was there before him, and was himself a member of the Privy Council, their Lordships, on the 28th October, granted Lochiel a personal protection. He remained in Edinburgh most of the following winter ; and he is said to have been so exasperated at Argyll's conduct to himself and his friends the Macleans, that he would have shot his Lordship on a certain day, as he was stepping into his carriage, to attend a meeting of the Privy Council, had not his servant, who stood at his back, wrested the pistol out of his raised hand, as he was about to shoot Argyll.

Lochiel resided in Mull during summer, for the next few years, and Argyll remained at home. In the spring of 1674, he was taken seriously ill with a "bloody-flux"—the only illness he had all his life—occasioned by cold and fatigue endured in supporting the Macleans. His complaint, so severe that his physicians despaired of his life, lasted for a whole year, but even when so ill, he was still able to render great service to his friends, by his counsel. Ultimately, however, Argyll succeeded in bringing about an arrangement, in terms of which Lochiel agreed to visit him at Dunstaffnage Castle, whither he set out in June, 1675. Mutual explanations were given, during which Argyll fully satisfied Lochiel that he was prepared to arrange the matter in dispute with the Macleans on favourable terms, provided that Cameron should accompany him to Mull with fifty men, so that the whole question might be submitted to mutual friends for their decision and award. This was agreed to, and ratified by contract, dated the 5th of June, 1675.

The long-vexed question between Lochiel and Argyll having thus been settled, the latter invited the former to spend a few days with him at Inveraray. Lochiel at once accepted. Shortly after his arrival, Argyll suggested that his guest should be shaved by his Lordship's valet, a Frenchman, who, he said, was a great adept at his art. Lochiel agreed. While the operation was proceeding, two stalwart Camerons of the chief's retinue, who were in the room, were seen standing close together, their backs pressed firmly against the inside of the door, one having his eyes fixed on Argyll, the other on the valet. Some chaffing remarks having passed between the chiefs as to the suspicious action of the men, Lochiel requested the Earl to ask themselves to explain their conduct. One of them at once answered, " That knowing well there had been a difference between his Lordship and their chief, on account of the assistance he had given to the Macleans, they suspected, when the valet was called for, that there might be a design of murdering their chief under cover of that service, seeing that he had a servant of his own who used to perform it, and that, therefore, they were determined, if their suspicion proved true, first to despatch his Lordship, and then the valet". Being asked, "What they thought would have come of themselves in such an event as that?" they coolly replied, "We did not think about that, but we were resolved to revenge the murder of our chief". Argyll praised them highly, and gave them some money, at the same time telling Lochiel that he believed no prince in the world had more faithful and loving subjects than he had.

Shortly after this, Lochiel had occasion to visit Edinburgh, when he had the good fortune to meet his Royal Highness the Duke of York, afterwards James II. The Prince not only received him with every mark of attention, but, in a full Court, honoured him specially by his conversation, questioning him in the most agreeable manner about the adventures of his youth. He openly congratulated him upon having arranged a settlement of the long dispute between himself and Mackintosh, and upon its happy issue ; stating, at the same time, that even if his brother, the king, had gone the length of purchasing these lands for him, since they were so long in his family, and so conveniently situated for his clan, it would be but small reward for the great services which he had rendered to the Royal house. The Prince, at the close of this address, asked Lochiel for his sword, which he at once handed to him, but the Duke could not draw it from the scabbard ; for the weapon, it seems, "was somewhat rusty, and but little used, as being a walking sword, which the Highlanders never make use of in their own country. The Duke, after a second attempt, gave it back to Lochiel, with the compliment that his sword never used to be so uneasy to draw when the Crown wanted his services. Lochiel, who was modest even to excess, was so confounded that he could make no return to so high a compliment ; and knowing nothing of the Duke's intention, he drew the sword, and returned it to his Royal Highness, who, addressing those about him, said smiling—'You see, my lords, Lochiel's sword gives obedience to no hand but his own,' and thereupon he was pleased to knight him." * These expressions of favour from the Prince were soon imitated by his courtiers, and Lochiel was highly complimented by them all on his past exploits and his loyalty to the Crown.

* The version in the text is that given by the author of the *Memoirs of Sir Ewen Cameron*, who knew Lochiel personally. Sir Walter Scott "improves" it by transforming the duke into the king, and other embellishments, as follows :—After the accession of James II., Lochiel came to Court to obtain pardon for one of his clan, who, being in command of a party of Camerons, had fired by mistake on a body of Athole men, and killed several. He was received with the most honourable distinction, and his request granted. The king, desiring to make him a knight, asked the chieftain for his own sword, in order to render the ceremony still more peculiar. Lochiel had ridden up from Scotland, being then the only mode of travelling, and a constant rain had so rusted his trusty broadsword that, at the moment, no man could have unsheathed it. Lochiel, affronted at the idea which the courtiers might conceive from his not being able to draw his own sword, burst into tears. "Do not regard it, my faithful friend," said king James, with ready courtesy, "your sword would have left the scabbard of itself, had the royal cause required it." With that, he bestowed the intended honour with his own sword, which he presented to the new knight as soon as the ceremony was performed.—*Tales of a Grandfather.*

His visit to Edinburgh on this occasion was in connection with the case of two soldiers killed in Lochaber by some of his men. There was no word about their trial while the royal Duke remained; but as soon as he left, proceedings were commenced. Lochiel, however, was again successful. He told off some of his friends to get at the prosecution witnesses, with orders to fill them with drink ; the result being that they were all sound asleep in an obscure out-of-the-way house, when they should have been ready to be sworn and examined as witnesses in the case, and Lochiel's friends were dismissed, in the absence of any evidence against them, to the great regret and disappointment of his enemies.

The following extracts from Fountainhall's *Decisions* evidently refers to, and further explains, this incident :— " November 14th, 1682.—Complaints being exhibited against Cameron of Lochiell and some of his clan for sorning, robbing, deforcing, and doing violence and affronts to a party of the king's forces, who came their to uplift the cess and taxation : The Lords ordained them to be presently disarmed of their swords, pistols, and skiendurks, and to be securely imprisoned." " November 30th, 1682.—At Privy Council, Cameron of Lochiell, mentioned 14th November, 1682, is fined, as the head of that clan, in £100 sterling, for the deforcement and violence offered by his men to the king's forces, when they came there to exact the taxations, and three of them are referred to the Criminal Court to be pursued for their lives, as guilty of treason, for opposing the king's authority ; the Clerk-Register became cautioner for Lochiel. This was done, as was thought, to cause him give way to Huntly's getting a footing in Lochaber."

In August of this year, a Commission under the Great Seal was issued, renewed, by Proclamation from the Council, in 1685, to the Sheriff of Inverness-shire, to hold Circuit Courts throughout the Highlands for the trial of various offences. Among other places the Sheriff visited Lochaber, where his presence, it can be easily understood, was anything but agreeable to Sir Ewen, who had arranged, and carried out pretty successfully, a plan of his own for punishing offences among his people. The Sheriff having arrived in the district, with a following of seven hundred men to protect him on his journey, not only proceeded to try and punish offences covered by his Commission, but also crimes and delinquencies committed during the late civil wars. Even Sir Ewen was summoned to the Court, when he presented himself before the Sheriff with a following of four hundred men, on the pretence of guarding his Lordship, but really with the object of saving his own people from what he considered the exercise of severe oppression and injustice. "He foresaw that the Sheriff's haughty and tyrannic procedure would be attended with trouble; and to prevent it he could fall upon no method so effectual as that of dismissing the Court by some political contrivance or other. He singled out three or four of the most cunning or sagacious, but withal the most mischievous and turbulent, among his followers. Under pretence of enquiring into their conduct, with these he walked a short way from the place where the Court was sitting, and, pretending to be very thoughtful and serious, he dropped these words in their hearing, as if he had been meditating and speaking to himself: 'Well, this Judge will ruin us all! He must be sent home! I wish I could do it! Is there none of my lads so clever as to raise a rabble and tumult among them, and set them together by the ears? It would send him a-packing. I have seen them raise mischief when there was not so much need of it!' The fellows I have mentioned caught at those expressions with great greediness. They quickly mixed among the Sheriff's train, and in three moments thereafter, Lochiel had the pleasure of seeing that vast crowd of people in an uproar. The cries of murder and slaughter resounded from all quarters. Several thousands of swords and dirks were drawn, and yet none knew the quarrel, and such a dreadful noise and confusion of tongues ensued, with the rattle of swords and other weapons striking against one another, that the meeting resembled a company of Bedlamites broke lose from their cells, with their chains rattling about them." The Sheriff and the members of his Court got into a state of great terror, and seeing Lochiel coming in their direction, at the head of his men, with drawn swords, they ran to meet him, craving his protection. This Lochiel at once granted, and afterwards convoyed the Sheriff and his whole retinue, at their own request, safely out of his country, a service for which his Lordship subsequently procured for him the thanks of the Privy Council! After all the noise and uproar, only two men were killed, and a few wounded. The Sheriff was never able to discover how the row began, or who was responsible for it; for the fellows who started it stole quietly away, and rejoined Lochiel and a body of his followers at a distance, whenever they saw the sparks taking effect, and that the desired blaze was sure to follow. The Sheriff never after held a Court in Lochaber, and Lochiel, as usual, succeeded most effectually in gaining his object by clever strategy.

To add to the general confusion, not only in the Highlands, but throughout the kingdom, the Earl of Argyll landed with an expedition from Holland, in May, 1685. The king immediately sent for Lochiel, and had a long conference with him on the subject, in his private Cabinet. The Committee in Edinburgh advised his Majesty to send Lochiel north to assist in suppressing the rebellion. The brave chief at once expressed his willingness to do anything in his power, and offered with the assistance only of his own friends, the Macleans, to be alone responsible for Argyll and his rebellion. The king answered that the chief command had been already entrusted to the Marquis of Athole, by the Privy Council. Lochiel returned to Scotland, and received his Commission from the Council on the 20th of May. He was soon with Athole, in Argyllshire, at the head of 300 of his followers, while as many more were commanded to follow him to Inveraray as soon as they could get ready. There were, however, more men already in the field than were actually required—for Argyll had only about 1500 followers altogether—and Lochiel sent some of his men home. His offer to attack the enemy, with the Macleans alone, offended the Marquis of Athole, and brought about so much friction and made such a noise in the camp, that the latter intimated to the Privy Council his suspicion of Lochiel's loyalty, who, he said, he feared was in concert with Argyll.

Unfortunately an incident followed which for a time gave apparent strength to this unfounded charge. Lochiel was ordered out at night to reconnoitre, without having been informed as to others who had been sent out before him. He mistook one of these parties for the enemy, one of whom rushed forward towards them and fired his pistol, wounding one of the Camerons. Lochiel's followers thereupon fell upon the whole party, and would have cut them all to pieces, had not Cameron of Callart recognised a Mr. Linton of Pendrich lying on his back, defending himself by his blunderbus from the broad-sword of one of the Camerons. This discovery saved the remainder, but four or five of the other party were killed, and several wounded, before Callart came up. Lochiel was extremely sorry for the accident; and he soon had reason to regret it very seriously.

The Marquis called a council of war to consider his conduct, and to decide upon the proper action respecting it. "This accident," says our authority, "joined with the malicious report already stated, so far confirmed many in their suspicions of treachery, that some had the rashness to propose the ordering out of a strong detachment of the troops, and to make Lochiel and his men all prisoners; and the Lord Murray, the Marquis's eldest son, offered to perform that service, but Mr. Murray of Struan being present in the council, opposed the motion, as not only dangerous, but destructive of the king's interest; 'for,' said he, 'such a man as Lochiel, at the head of such a body of men, will not be easily made a prisoner by force. The Macleans and Macdonalds will probably join him; whereby the king will not only be deprived of the services of his best troops, but a division made in the army, of which the common enemy will, no doubt, take the advantage. Besides, it would not only be unjust, but even barbarous, to condemn so many people, who came there to serve their prince, without being heard ; and it is more than probable, that when the matter comes to be discovered, it will come out to be wholly an accident occasioned by some mistake or other.' This opinion prevailed, and the council broke up without coming to any violent resolution. Lochiel, all this while, kept his men aside, and was joined by the Macleans. After the first emotions of his passions were over, he began to deliberate on what he should do, and soon determined that he would not be made prisoner. If he was to suffer, he resolved that it should be by the sentence of his master and Sovereign, who had hitherto honoured him with his Royal favour. The Macleans encouraged him in this resolution, and generously offered to stand by him in all fortunes. He advanced near to the camp, that he might the more easily inform himself of what passed, and drew up his men in two lines, with orders to the left to wheel about in case of being attacked, in order that, being thus joined back to back, they might make two fronts. In this posture they stood all that night and for most of the following day, and towards the evening they had orders to join the army, with a full assurance of safety ; for by this time the Marquis had informed himself fully of the matter, which he owned to Lochiel to be a mere accident, for which he was not to be blamed, and signified as much in a letter he wrote on that subject to my Lord Tarbat, who intimated it to the Council." Lochiel after this brought in a few prisoners.

Argyll was shortly after captured near Glasgow, sent on to Edinburgh, where he was, on the 30th of June, 1685, beheaded, without trial, on his old sentence, for high treason.

The army was disbanded on the 21st of June, and Lochiel, with the other leaders, received a communication, conveying to them the thanks of the Privy Council for their hearty concurrence in the king's service, and authorising them to disband their forces.

The execution of Archibald, Earl of Argyll, proved afterwards most unfortunate for Lochiel. The Duke of Gordon obtained a gift of the superiority of that portion of Lochiel's lands which the latter held as the vassal of Argyll, and Gordon had himself duly infefted in it. The Duke of York having previously expressed himself in his favour, Lochiel proceeded to Court, with a view of securing the superiority for himself, which was not only promised to him, but, with it, the lands of Suinart and Ardnamurchan, as soon as the necessary documents could be completed. But, through an error of his own agent, in drawing out the deeds, and in consequence of the king's death on the 6th of February, 1685, before new ones could be completed, Lochiel was again disappointed.

Great honours were conferred on the marquis of Athole on his return south. He was admitted a Member of the Privy Council, made Keeper of the Great Seal, and appointed to several other important offices. Though he, at the time, professed himself quite satisfied as to Lochiel's innocence of the unfounded charges of disloyalty made against him at Inveraray, no sooner did he get into power than he brought him to trial for his alleged misconduct; and by transmitting most unfavourable misrepresentations to the new king, he secured a warrant for his apprehension. For this purpose, he dispatched Captain Mackenzie of Suddie to Lochaber, on the pretence of putting down some local squabbles in the district, but with private orders to seize Lochiel, and bring him to Edinburgh. This, as usual, was easier said than done. His eldest daughter, Margaret, was at the time in Edinburgh; and she, obtaining secret information of Athole's designs upon her father, at once dispatched a soldier of the name of Cameron, in the City Guards, to apprise him of his danger. Lochiel removed meanwhile out of the way, and, on the arrival of Captain Mackenzie in Lochaber, he set out for Edinburgh, consulted his friends there, posted to London, and arrived there before his enemies were actually aware that he had left home. On his arrival, he found that the grossest misrepresentations had been sent in advance of him, and his old friends became so convinced of their truth, that not one of them could be induced to introduce him to the king, who, they anticipated, would leave him to be dealt with, for his alleged crimes, according to law ; and this notwithstanding that Robert Barclay of Ury, the famous Quaker, and great favourite of the king, wrote several letters to the English nobility in his favour. Ultimately, however, Viscount Strathallan undertook to inform the king that Lochiel was in the city. He kept his promise, adding that he had been in town for several days, and that all his own friends refused to introduce him. The king sent word to Lochiel, commanding him to see him next morning in the Royal dressing-room, at the same time requesting Lord Strathallan to tell him that "he needed no one to introduce him to us, and that we expected the first visit". Sir Ewen was naturally much pleased on receiving the Royal message. He punctually obeyed the king's commands, and on his arrival threw himself at his Majesty's feet, saying, "that he came there as a criminal with a rope about his neck, to put himself and all he possessed in his Royal mercy". The king extended to him his hand to kiss, and, commanding him to rise, told him that he had heard of his misfortune, at the same time adding, "that accidents of that nature had often fallen out among the best disciplined troops," and that nothing but actual rebellion would ever convince him that he could be disloyal. Sir Ewen expressed his intense gratitude for the Royal favour, in the most modest manner, carefully avoiding to make any disparaging reflection on his bitterest enemies.

A most curious incident in connection with this interview was yet to come. The king, having completed his toilet, commanded Lochiel to follow him closely behind, when, followed by Sir Ewen, he walked right into the middle of the Chamber of Presence, crowded by a very splendid and numerous Court, whom his Majesty humorously addressed thus :—" My lords and gentlemen, I advise you to have a care of your purses, for the king of the thieves is at my back " ; and then, turning to Lochiel, he informed him, in the hearing of all present, that he would be glad to see him often, during his stay in town, at the same time thanking him, before the whole Court, in audible terms, for his services during the late rebellion. "Never," says Drummond, "was there a brighter example of the servile complaisance of courtiers than Lochiel had on this occasion; for he now had them all about him, congratulating him upon his Majesty's favour, and offering him their services, though, the very day before, he could find but one among them that would serve him so far as barely to mention his name to his Majesty. The king, on his part, let slip no opportunity of testifying his esteem. Sir Ewen never appeared in Court during this visit to London but his Majesty spoke two or three words to him; and if he chanced to meet with him elsewhere, he had always the goodness to inquire about his health, and now and then to put some jocose question to him, such as, "If he was contriving how to steal any of the fine horses he had seen in his Majesty's stables, or in those of his courtiers?"

The Duke of Gordon, during Lochiel's absence in London, raised an action against him in the Court of Session, to get his rights and titles to the whole of the Cameron estates annulled in virtue of the Duke's titles to the superiority of the Mamore portion, and his having obtained, as he alleged, the superiority of the other portion on the forfeiture of Argyll. To both these the Duke had secured grants at different periods from kings Charles and James; that from the latter being dated the 29th of January, 1686. James knew nothing of Lochiel's interest in these superiorities, and expressed himself highly indignant when he discovered that he had been imposed upon by the Duke of Gordon, when he came to know the facts. Lochiel complained bitterly of the manner in which he was treated, and forcibly argued that, if the Duke could prevail against him in such an action, he would be worse punished for his loyalty than the leaders on the other side had been for their rebellion. The king having promised him full reparation, sent for the Duke of Gordon, and severely reprimanded him for making him the author of such a barbarous injustice, by the surreptitious grants he had obtained from him of Lochiel's estates, and he insisted upon the whole question being left to his own disposal as sole arbitrator. To this peremptory demand the Duke felt bound, though most reluctantly, to consent, and he signed articles accordingly. Gordon had also taken proceedings against Lochiel, in conjunction with a Mr. Seaton, for a debt due to the forfeited Earl of Arygll. The king opposed this claim also, and the result was in both cases communicated to the Commissioners of the Treasury, in a letter dated the 21st of May 1688, in which the king intimated— " His Royal will and pleasure, that Sir Ewen Cameron of Lochiel should have new rights and charters of the property of his lands, formerly held by him of the late Earl of Argyll, and fallen into our hands by reason of his forfeiture, renewed and given by George Duke of Gordon, our donatory in the superiority thereof, for a small and easy feu-duty, not exceeding four merks for every 1000 merks of free rent". In reference to the debt, the letter concludes with a command, that Lochiel "be fully exonered and discharged for the same at all hands, and in all time coming, notwithstanding of any procedure that may have already, or hereafter may be made against him at the instance of any person whatever". In addition, the king subsequently declared "that he would not have Lochiel nor any of his people liable to the Duke's courts, for he would have Lochiel master of his own clan, and only accountable to him or his Council, and to have no further to do with his Grace than to pay him his feu-duty". A formal deed embodying these conditions was drawn up, but the Duke still attempted to avoid signing the necessary charter, and in fact refused to do so, until compelled by the king himself, two days after, when he was commanded to sign it in his Majesty's presence; and Lochiel was then, for the first time, legally the absolute and independent master of his own clan.

Shortly after this, however, he is again in difficulties.

Mackintosh, armed with a commission of fire and sword, determined to invade the lands of Keppoch, in Lochaber, to eject the Macdonalds for non-payment of rents which Mackintosh claimed from them as legal superior of their lands. Lochiel attempted to arrange matters between them, but failing in doing so, he immediately afterwards proceeded to Edinburgh. In his absence, the Macmartin Camerons, who were closely related to the Macdonalds of Keppoch by frequent intermarriages, as well as being otherwise on friendly terms with them, finding that Lochiel had left home without expressing any views on the question, or leaving any instructions as to what his followers were to do, offered their services to Keppoch. Mackintosh marched to Lochaber with about a thousand of his own men, and a company of the king's troops, under Captain Mackenzie of Suddie, by order of the Privy Council. Keppoch, on the 4th of August, 1688, with about half the number of the invaders, easily defeated the Mackintoshes and took their chief prisoner, while many of his followers, including four of the leaders, were slain, as well as Captain Mackenzie of Suddie, who was mortally wounded.* Great numbers were taken prisoners; the loss was altogether very severe, and the victory most decided in favour of the Macdonalds. Before releasing his prisoner, Keppoch compelled him to renounce his claims and titles to the lands in dispute. Lochiel was held responsible by the Privy Council for the conduct of his vassals on this occasion. He, however, managed in a very clever manner to escape. Viscount Tarbat, a member of the Council, was a relative and a good

---

* Scott gives the following account of Captain Mackenzie's death:—"He was brave, and well-armed with carabine, pistols, and a halbert or half-pike. This officer came in front of a cadet of Keppoch, called Macdonald of Tullich, and by a shot aimed at him, killed one of his brothers, and then rushed on with his pike. Notwithstanding his deep provocation, Tullich, sensible of the pretext which the death of a Captain under Government would give against his clan, called out more than once, 'Avoid me, avoid me'. 'The Macdonald was never born that I would shun,' replied Mackenzie, pressing on with his pike; on which Tullich hurled at his head a pistol, which he had before discharged. The blow took effect, the skull was fractured, and Mackenzie died shortly after, as his soldiers were carrying him to Inverness."—*Tales of a Grandfather.* This battle is known as the "Battle of Mulroy". It was the last clan battle fought in the Highlands.

friend of Lochiel, and he agreed, if the Council should decide against him, to make a certain signal to Sir Ewen from the window of the Council Chamber. Lochiel was accused, not only as accessory to Keppoch's conduct, but as principal author of the bloodshed, "in so far that it was notorious that Keppoch durst not have attacked Mackintosh with his own followers without the assistance of the Camerons, for whose crimes Lochiel was obliged to answer". It was carried by a majority of their Lordships, that he should be at once arrested and committed to prison for further trial, and a warrant was issued for his apprehension forthwith.

Lochiel was quite prepared. Lord Tarbat made the preconcerted signal; and, after some difficulty as to where he would hide himself, the happy thought occurred to him of retiring into the city prison, under pretence of visiting one of the prisoners. No one, he correctly conceived, would ever dream of his having gone to such a place to conceal himself, and he knew that a clansman of his own, on whom he could rely, held a position of trust in the prison. This man, James Cameron, who was jail clerk, favoured his designs; and, remaining in the prison until after dark, Sir Ewen stole out of the city as privately as he could, and, with his usual good fortune, soon arrived safely among his friends in Lochaber.

Shortly after, in the month of October, he received intimation from the Chancellor that the Prince of Orange was preparing to invade the kingdom with a great fleet, and requesting him to march into Argyllshire, with as many men as he could get together on such short notice. This message was confirmed by the Privy Council in a second order, dated the 4th of the same month, and it was at once obeyed. Lochiel and Sir John Drummond, with a force of 1200 men, kept that county from rising, until they received intimation from the Chancellor that the king had been betrayed, deserted on all hands by his friends, and that he had fled to France. While on this service Lochiel was put in possession of Suinart and Ardnamurchan by the Lord Lieutenant, in terms of a warrant from the Earl of Balcarres, dated the 3rd of October 1688. He received a new grant of these lands from the king himself, on his arrival in Ireland, soon after; and no more is heard of the action raised against him by the Privy Council in connection with the battle of Mulroy, fought between the Mackintoshes and the Macdonalds of Keppoch.

Lochiel spent the winter projecting measures for a Confederation of the Clans, in the interest of James, from whom he received a letter, dated the 29th of March, 1689, after his Majesty had arrived in Ireland, requesting him, his friends, and followers, to be ready to take the field, at a place to be appointed, whenever called upon to do so. The king also gave strong assurances in this letter of his devotion to the Protestant Religion, stating that he would respect the liberty and property of the subject; that he would re-imburse any outlays to which Lochiel might be put; and send him at the proper time commissions, signed, with power to him to fill them in, and to name his own officers. On receipt of the document, Sir Ewen visited all the chiefs that lived near him, and wrote to those at a distance, seeking their co-operation; and he found them all heartily willing to join in any efforts to restore the king. They subsequently convened, in general meeting, and agreed so completely among themselves as to what they would do, that they arranged for a rendezvous on the 13th of May following, at Dalmucomer, near Lochiel's residence, and communicated their resolution to the king, requesting him to send over a suitable person to lead them, and promising to hazard, if necessary, life and fortune in his cause. Matters, however, soon took another turn.

The Privy Council, unanimous in favour of James, made preparations for war, and expressed their gratitude for the services offered by his friends, but, when William of Orange arrived in London, the Council for a time hesitated, and ultimately it was resolved to offer him the Crown of Scotland through Viscount Dundee. Sir George Mackenzie of Rosehaugh, and a few others, opposed this proposal with great power and eloquence. The important events which followed are so well known to the ordinary student of Scottish history that they shall here be passed over, except where Lochiel and the Camerons come prominently on the scene. Viscount Dundee, who had left the Convention, sent an express to Sir Ewen Cameron for information as to the state of feeling in the North. This was at once intimated to the other chiefs in Lochiel's neighbourhood, and they agreed without delay to dispatch eight hundred men under Macdonald of Keppoch to convey Dundee to Lochaber; but his lordship meantime made a detour into the Highlands, on the way getting many promises from the people to join him, immediately they were called upon to serve their king. He received a most favourable communication from Lochiel, for himself and for the other chiefs, informing him of their having sent Keppoch to meet him on the borders of the Highlands. Anxious to meet his friends in the North as soon as possible, Dundee changed his course, and marched for Inverness, where he found Keppoch, who, instead of executing his commission, laid siege to the town, arrested the magistrates and many of the most wealthy citizens, insisting upon their paying a heavy ransom before he would set them at liberty. Dundee rebuked him so severely for his conduct, that he at once retired to his own country, instead of conducting Dundee, in terms of his commission, to the other chiefs. This was a bad beginning, for Dundee had to return to the South, where he found letters awaiting him from the king, and a commission appointing him Commander of his Majesty's forces in Scotland. He also received letters and commissions for the Highland chiefs, which he at once dispatched to them. He was strongly urged, in letters from Lochiel, to visit Lochaber, and this he finally decided to do, marching thither straight through Rannoch. When he arrived he received from Sir Ewen and his people every possible honour and consideration, and was furnished with a residence about a mile distant from Lochiel's own house. Having been fully assured by the other chiefs of their readiness to join him at the appointed place of rendezvous, he wrote intimating this to the king, then in Ireland, praying him to come over and command the Highlanders in person, promising that he would have the support of the people generally in his efforts to regain the throne of his ancestors.

General Mackay, who commanded for William, made many attempts to induce Lochiel to join him, offering him a large sum of money, the government of Inverlochy, and the command of a regiment, with whatever titles of honour and dignities he might choose, assuring him that these offers were made with William's full consent and authority. Lochiel, in characteristic fashion, handed the letters unopened to Dundee, requesting that his lordship would be good enough to dictate the proper answers.

Dundee soon found himself at the head of a following of 1800 horse and foot, "whereof one-half belonged to Lochiel," and with these he marched to meet Colonel Ramsay, one of Mackay's lieutenants, on his way from Athole to Inverness, who, hearing of Dundee's advance, blew up his ammunition, and marched at his best speed night and day, until he was clear out of the country. In May, 1689, Dundee marched back to Lochaber, when Lochiel invited him to reside in his old quarters at Strone, his lordship having deemed it prudent to dismiss his men, in consequence of the scarcity of provisions, on condition that they would return, on a day's notice, to join his standard.

While here, Macdonald of the Isles arrived with about seven hundred men, and Dundee being thus strengthened, proposed to a council of war, that they should employ their time until the arrival of the other clans in drilling and otherwise disciplining their troops. The younger chiefs and the Lowland officers at once approved of the proposal, but Lochiel, now an experienced officer, in the sixtieth year of his age, was of a different opinion, and expressed himself to the council in the following eloquent and forcible terms:—" That, as from his youth he had been bred among the Highlanders, so he had made many observations upon the natural temper of the people and their method of fighting; and to pretend to alter anything in their old customs, of which they were most tenacious, would entirely ruin them, and make them not better than newly-raised troops; whereas, he was firmly of opinion that, with their own chiefs and natural captains at their head, under the command of such a General as Viscount Dundee, they were equal to a similar number of the best disciplined veteran troops in the kingdom; that they had given repeated proofs of this during the wars and victories of Montrose: and that in the skirmishes wherein he himself had been engaged, he had invariably the good fortune to rout the enemy, though always superior to him in numbers. Besides, in all his conflicts with Cromwell's troops, he had to do with old soldiers whose courage had been fatal to the king and kingdom." Having given an instance of the bravery and success of the Macleans against the enemy in a recent skirmish, he continued:—" That since his lordship, and, perhaps, few of the Low-country gentlemen and officers in the council never had an opportunity of being present at a Highland engagement, it would not be amiss to give them a general hint of their manner of fighting. It was the same as that of the ancient Gauls, their predecessors, who had made such a great figure in Roman history. He believed all the ancients had used the broadsword and targe in the same manner as the Highlanders did then, though the Romans and Grecians taught their troops a certain kind of discipline to inure them to obedience. The Scots, in general, had never made such a figure in the field since they gave up these weapons. The Highlanders were the only body of men that retained the old method, excepting in so far as they had of late taken to the gun, instead of the bow, to introduce them into action; that so soon as they were led against the enemy, they came up within a few paces of them, and having discharged their pieces in their very breasts, they threw them down and drew their swords; the attack was then so furious that they commonly pierced the enemy's ranks, put them into disorder, and determined the fate of the day in a few moments. They loved always to be in action, and they had such confidence in their leaders that even the most daring and desperate attempt would not intimidate them if they had courage enough to lead them on, so that all the miscarriages of the Highlanders were to be charged to some defect of conduct in their officers, and not for want either of resolution or discipline on the part of the men. He further added, that as a body of Highlanders conducted by their own chiefs were commonly equal to any foot whatever, so when they came to be disciplined in the modern manner, and mixed with regular troops under strange officers, they were not one straw better than their neighbours; and the reason he assigned for this change, was that being turned out of their ordinary method, and not having the honour of their chief and clan to fight for, they lost their natural courage, when the causes that inspire it were removed. Besides, when by the harsh rules of discipline, and the savage severity of their officers in the execution of them, they came to be reduced to a state of servitude, their spirits sank, and they became mere formal machines, acting by the impulse of fear. However military discipline might do in standing armies, yet, since it was not proposed that theirs was to continue any longer than the then position of affairs rendered it necessary, they had no time to habituate the men to it, so as to make it easy and useful to them; and, therefore, it was his opinion that, in all events, it was better to allow them to follow the old habit in which they were bred, than to begin to teach them a new method which they had not the time to acquire." This was the address of a wise, experienced and far-seeing leader, founded on actual experience. "Lochiel's opinion determined the council; and my Lord Dundee, recollecting all that he had said, declared that as he was certain of victory from men of so much courage and ferocity, he would not have made the proposal had he been as well acquainted with them as Lochiel had now made him; and that, as everything he had advanced carried conviction along with it, and even though it had not, yet as there was no argument like matter of fact, he thought himself obliged to take them on the word of one who had so long and so happy an experience." The Highlanders were allowed to continue their ancient tactics.

While waiting for the return of those of his followers who had been permitted to go home, for want of provisions, as already stated, and for others who were to be with him by the date of the appointed rendezvous, an incident occurred which, but for Lochiel's prudence, might have terminated the campaign before the war had begun. A party of Camerons resolved to be avenged on the Grants, who had recently hanged two or three of their men on what was considered slight provocation. They were of opinion that neither Lochiel nor Dundee would be very much opposed to this expedition, especially if they succeeded in bringing in supplies for their half-starved followers. They would not, however, run the risk of the Commander's refusal, by asking permission to go into the enemy's country, but marched privately to Glen Urquhart, where they found the Grants fully armed, ready to oppose them. One of the Macdonalds of Glengarry, who lived in Urquhart, thought that his name and the clan to which he belonged was not only sufficient to secure him from personal attack, but that his intimate relationship to the chief was enough to protect the Grants, among whom he resided, from the revenge of the Camerons. Confident of this, he boldly marched out to meet them, and, intimating his name and genealogy, desired that, on his account, they would depart peaceably, without injuring the inhabitants, his neighbours, and friends. The intruders replied that, "if he was a true Macdonald, he ought to be with his chief in Dundee's army, in the service of his king and country; that they were at a loss to understand why they should, on his account, extend their friendship to a people who had, but a short time before, seized on several of their men, and hanged them without any other provocation than that they served king James, which was contrary to the laws of war as well as of common humanity; that as they esteemed him, both for the name he bore and the gentleman to whom he belonged, so they desired that he would instantly separate himself and his cattle from the rest of his companions, whom they were determined to chastise for their insolence; but Macdonald replied that he would run the same fate as his neighbours; and, daring them to do their worst, he departed in a huff." The Camerons, without further preliminaries, attacked the Grants, killed several of them, and dispersed the remainder. They then seized their cattle, and drove them to Lochaber in triumph. Dundee and Lochiel connived at their conduct, as they anticipated; but Glengarry became furious about the death of his clansman, who was slain among the Grants, and he demanded satisfaction from Lochiel and his clan.

Macaulay describes the result in the following terms:— "Though this Macdonald had been guilty of a high offence against the Gaelic code of honour and morality, his kinsmen remembered the sacred tie which he had forgotten. Good or bad, he was bone of their bone, he was flesh of their flesh; and he should have been reserved for their justice. The name which he bore, the blood of the Lords of the Isles, should have been his protection. Glengarry in a rage went to Dundee and demanded vengeance on Lochiel and the whole race of Cameron. Dundee replied that the unfortunate gentleman who had fallen was a traitor to the clan as well as the king. Was it ever heard of in war that the person of an enemy, a combatant in arms, was to be held inviolable on account of his name and descent? And, even if wrong had been done, how was it to be redressed. Half the army must slaughter the other half before a finger could be laid on Lochiel. Glengarry went away raving like a madman. Since his complaints were disregarded by those who ought to right them, he would right himself: he would draw out his men, and fall sword in hand on the murderers of his cousin. During some time he would listen to no expostulation. When he was reminded that Lochiel's followers were in number nearly double that of the Glengarry men, 'No matter,' he cried, 'one Macdonald is worth two Camerons'. Had Lochiel been equally irritable and boastful, it is probable that the Highland insurrection would have given little more trouble to the Government, and that all the rebels would have perished obscurely in the wilderness by one another's claymores. But nature had bestowed on him in large measure the qualities of a statesman, though fortune had placed those qualities in an obscure corner of the world. He saw that this was not a time for brawling : his own character for courage had been long established, and his temper was under strict government. The fury of Glengarry, not being inflamed by any fresh provocations, rapidly abated. Indeed, there were some who suspected that he had never been quite so pugnacious as he had affected to be, and that his bluster was meant only to keep up his own dignity in the eyes of his retainers. However this might be, the quarrel was composed ; the two chiefs met with the outward show of civility at the General's table," * and the parties were soon as good friends as ever. Macaulay, who adapts the story from Lochiel's Memoirs, does not state the fact that, when Glengarry declared that the courage of his men would make up for the disparagement of numbers between them and the Camerons, " Lochiel laughed at the remark, and said merrily that he hoped a few days would give Glengarry an opportunity of exerting that superiority of valour he boasted of so loudly against the common enemy ; and that he would be exceedingly well-pleased to be out-done in the generous emulation " on such an occasion. Nothing could better illustrate the peculiar character of the material of which Dundee's army was composed than this row between two of his bravest and most distinguished leaders.

This was how matters stood with the Jacobites about the middle of July, 1689. Mackay soon after marched north to Athole, and Dundee, at the head of about 1800 Highlanders, proceeded south to meet him, leaving orders for the others to follow as soon as they could be got together—though the day arranged for the general gathering of the clans had not yet arrived. Lochiel, at this time,

History of England, pp. 340-342, Vol. III., 1855.

had only his Lochaber men along with him, numbering about 240, but he dispatched his eldest son, John, and several others to Morvern, Suinart, Ardnamurchan, and the surrounding districts to bring in his adherents from these places with all speed. Dundee, however, was so anxious to have Sir Ewen along with him that he requested him to follow him with the small body he then had, leaving orders for his son to follow with the others as soon as possible. Lochiel with this small band overtook Dundee just before he entered Athole, where they were soon joined by about 300 Irish, under the command of Major-General Cannon. Proceeding on their way, they arrived at Blair Castle on the 27th of July, where they obtained intelligence that Mackay had just entered the Pass of Killiecrankie. Dundee at once called a council of war to consider whether they should stop where they were, or proceed to engage Mackay before he could extricate himself from the Pass. It was a serious question to decide, for his main body had not yet come up, the appointed day of rendezvous being still in the future. The old officers, who had been bred to the command of regular troops, were all in favour of waiting, as their force was only about half the number of the enemy, and the result of the campaign, they urged, might depend upon whether they should win or lose the first battle. The Highlanders, though hardy and brave, these young gentlemen alleged, were only raw and undisciplined troops, who had not seen blood, and that they were much fatigued by the want of food, and by their long and rapid march ; not having had even the common necessaries of life. These and various other reasons were urged for continuing on the defensive, where they were, for the present ; and they were stated with so much plausibility and apparent conclusiveness that they were silently, and very generally accepted, until Alexander Macdonald of Glengarry addressed the council, and declared that, though it was quite true that the Highlanders had suffered much on the march, as had been so eloquently described, yet that these hardships did not affect them as they would soldiers bred in an easier and more plentiful mode of life; they would be able and willing to engage the enemy at once, for nothing delighted them more than hardy and adventurous exploits. If they were kept back until they were attacked by the enemy they would lose that spirit and resolution which invariably characterised them when they were the aggressors. The other Highland chiefs, except Lochiel, generally expressed concurrence in Glengarry's remarks, but Dundee, observing that Sir Ewen still continued silent, withheld his opinion, until he should hear what the experienced chief of the Camerons had to say on the subject; "for," he said, "he has not only done great things himself, but had such great experience, that he cannot miss to make a right judgment of the matter, and, therefore, his views shall determine mine". Sir Ewen, in answer to this compliment, depreciated what he himself had done in the past, and modestly urged that no example could be taken from his experience. The reason why he had not spoken earlier in the discussion, was that he had already determined to submit to his lordship in all things, as his conduct was so well adapted to the genius of the Highlanders; but as he had commanded him to express his opinion, it was in one sentence, "Fight immediately; our men are in heart; they are so far from being afraid of their enemies, that they are eager and keen to engage them, lest they escape from their hands. Though we have few men, they are good, and I can assure your lordship that not one of them will fail you." He strongly urged the propriety of this course, even though he might only have one man to the enemy's three, and, again addressing Dundee, he said—" Be assured, my lord, that if once we are fairly engaged we will either lose our army or secure a complete victory. Our men love always to be in action. Your lordship never heard them complain of hunger or fatigue while they were in chase of their enemy, which at all times were equal to us in numbers. Employ them in hasty and desperate enterprises, and you will oblige them; and I have always observed that when I fought under the greatest disadvantages as to numbers, I had still the completest victory. Let us take this occasion to show our zeal and courage in the cause of our king and country, and that we dare attack an army of fanatics and rebels at the odds of nearly two to one. Their great superiority in numbers will give a necessary reputation to our victory, and not only frighten them from meddling with a people conducted by such a general, and animated by such a cause, but will encourage the whole kingdom to declare in our favour." This spirited and warlike oration naturally pleased Dundee, whose eyes brightened with satisfaction and delight during its delivery; and he pointed out to the other officers that the sentiments and arguments expressed by Lochiel were those of one who had formed his conclusions and judgments from the infallible test of long experience, and who had an intimate acquaintance with the people and the subject upon which he had so eloquently addressed them.

No further objections were offered to the course urged by the brave Sir Ewen, and it was unanimously agreed that they should fight at once, a resolution received with exclamations of joy by all the Highlanders, and which much gratified their general. Before, however, the council separated, Lochiel begged to be heard once more, while he addressed a few sentences to Dundee himself, to whom he said:—"My lord, I have just now declared, in presence of this honourable company, that I was resolved to give an implicit obedience to all your lordship's commands; but I humbly beg leave, in the name of these gentlemen, to give you the word of command for this once. It is the voice of your council; and their orders are that you do not engage personally. Your lordship's business is to have your eye on all parts, and issue your commands as you think proper; it is ours to execute them with promptitude and courage. On your lordship depends not only the fate of this brave little army, but also of our king and country. If your lordship denies us this reasonable demand, for my own part, I declare that neither I, nor any that I am concerned in, shall draw a sword on this important occasion, whatever construction may be put upon my conduct". In this appeal Lochiel was supported by the whole council, but Dundee asked a few words in reply. He said :—" Gentlemen, as I am absolutely convinced, and have had repeated proofs of your zeal for the king's service, and of your affection to me, as his general and your friend, so I am fully sensible that my engaging personally this day may be of some loss if I shall chance to be killed ; but I beg leave of you, however, to allow me to give one harvest-day to the king, my master, that I may have an opportunity of convincing the brave clans that I can hazard my life in that service as freely as the meanest of them. You know their temper, gentlemen, and if they do not think that I have enough personal courage, they will not esteem me hereafter, nor obey my commands with cheerfulness. Allow me this single favour, and I promise, upon my honour, never again to risk my person while I have the honour of commanding you." Finding him thus determined, the council gave way, and at once broke up to prepare for immediate action in the field.

Dundee having completed his arrangements marched forward at the head of his men, to meet the enemy, never halting until they were within a musket shot of Mackay's army, which numbered about 3500 foot, and two troops of horse. After a few preliminaries here—on the ground—necessary by the enemy's formation, his lordship, in a very short time, arranged his brave little army in order of battle.

Sir John Maclean, a youth only eighteen years old, at the head of his men, occupied the extreme right ; next to him, on the left, were the Irish, under Colonel Cannon ; on their left again was the Tutor of Clanranald, with his brave Macdonalds ; and next came Glengarry and his men. In the centre were stationed the few horses they had, including about forty of Dundee's old troops, in very poor condition. To the left of the horse, Lochiel at the head of the Camerons, took up his position ; while next to him, on the extreme left, was Sir Donald Macdonald, leading his Islesmen. "Though there were great intervals between the battalions, and a large void space left in the centre, yet Dundee could not possibly stretch his line so as to equal that of the enemy; and wanting men to fill up the void in the centre, Lochiel, who was posted next the horse, was not only obliged to fight Mackay's own regiment, which stood directly opposite to him, but also had his flank exposed to the fire of Leven's battalion, which he had not men to engage, whereby he thereafter greatly suffered. But what was hardest of all, he had only 240 of his clan with him, and even of these, sixty were sent as Dundee's advance guard, to take possession of a house from which he apprehended the enemy might gall them if they put men into it. But there was no helping the matter. Each clan, whether small or great, had a regiment assigned to it, and that, too, by Lochiel's advice, who attended the general while making his dispositions. His design was to keep up their spirit of emulation in point of bravery; for, as the Highlanders place the highest value upon the honour of their families or clans, and the renown or glory acquired by military actions, so the emulation between clan and clan inspires them with a certain generous contempt of danger, and gives vigour to their hands and keenness to their courage, a statement fully confirmed and exemplified on this occasion."

By the time Dundee got his army into order it was well on in the afternoon, and his men, aggravated by the fire of the enemy from the low ground, were anxious to be led into action; but as the sun was shining straight in their faces, they were held back until near sunset. During this interval Lochiel visited his Camerons and appealed personally to each of them, every one of whom declared in turn that they should conquer or die that day. He then told them to make a loud noise by shouting as much as they could. This they did with a good will. It was at once taken up by the whole Highland army to right and left of them, and faintly returned by the enemy. The noise of the cannon and muskets, "with the prodigious echoing of the adjacent hills and rocks in which there are several caverns and hollow places," made the Highlanders fancy that their shouts were much louder and more spirited than those of the foe, when Lochiel, taking advantage of this idea, exclaimed, "Gentlemen, take courage, the day is ours; I am the oldest commander in the army, and have always observed something ominous and fatal in such a dead, hollow, and feeble noise as the enemy made in their shouting. Ours was brisk, lively, and strong, and shows that we have courage, vigour, and strength. Theirs was low, lifeless, and dead, and prognosticates that they are all doomed to die by our hands this very night." These words went through the little army fast as lightning, and, such an opinion coming from Lochiel, greatly encouraged and animated both officers and men.

At seven o'clock Dundee gave the order to advance, commanding that as soon as the Macleans moved on the right, the whole body should instantly march forward and charge straight among the enemy. "It is incredible with what intrepidity the Highlanders endured the enemy's fire; and though it grew more terrible on their nearer approach, yet they, with a wonderful resolution, kept up their own, as they were commanded, till they came up to their very bosoms, and then pouring it in upon them all at once, like one great clap of thunder, they threw away their guns and fell in pell-mell among the thickest of them with their broadswords. After this the noise seemed hushed; and the fire ceasing on both sides, nothing was heard for some few moments but the sullen and hollow clashes of broadswords, with the dismal groans and cries of dying and wounded men." The brave Dundee fell mortally wounded by a shot about two handbreadths within his armour on the lower part of his left side. From this it was concluded that he must have received his wound "while he raised himself in his stirrups and stretched his body to hasten up his horse," at a point in the engagement, to turn his charger to the right to enable him to wave his hat for some of the men to come to the rescue of the Earl of Dunfermline and sixteen brave horsemen, who had succeeded in routing the enemy's cavalry by a very brilliant charge. The Highlanders, though they had to mourn the loss of about a third of their men, secured a complete victory, and few of the enemy escaped ; but having lost their brilliant commander, the result was dearly bought, and the war may be said to have been ended—before it was well commenced—by a Highland victory, perhaps the most brilliant on record.

Lochiel, after having ordered his men to advance, seems to have been much encumbered by the use of what Macaulay describes as "the only pair of shoes in his clan". Not being able to keep pace with his men, he commended them to the protection of God, sat down by the way, and deliberately pulling off the encumbrances that crippled him, had the agility to get up to his men as they were drawing their swords, in close quarters with the enemy.

Stewart of Garth informs us that Lochiel was attended on this occasion by the son of his foster-brother—who had saved him at Achadalew, by receiving the shot intended for his chief in his own mouth. " This faithful adherent followed him like his shadow, ready to assist him with his sword, or cover him from the shot of his enemy. Soon after the battle began, the chief missed his friend from his side, and, turning round to look what had become of him, saw him lying on his back, with his breast pierced by an arrow. He had hardly breath before he expired to tell Lochiel, that seeing an enemy, a Highlander in General Mackay's army, aiming at him with a bow and arrow from the rear, he sprung behind him, and thus sheltered him from instant death." *

Macaulay's description of the Highland charge and its results is so spirited that we shall give it, though it is entirely drawn, but slightly coloured, from the *Memoirs of Sir Ewen Cameron*, from which we have already given the details :—" It was past seven o'clock. Dundee gave the word. The Highlanders dropped their plaids. The few

* Stewart's *Sketches of the Highlanders*, Vol. I., p. 70

who were so luxurious as to wear rude socks of untanned hide spurned them away. It was long remembered in Lochaber that Lochiel took off what probably was the only pair of shoes in his clan, and charged barefoot at the head of his men. The whole line advanced firing. The enemy returned the fire, and did much execution. When only a small space was left between the armies, the Highlanders suddenly flung away their firelocks, drew their broadswords, and rushed forward with a fearful yell. The Lowlanders prepared to receive the shock; but this was then a long and awkward process, and the soldiers were still fumbling with the muzzles of their guns and the handles of their bayonets, when the whole flood of Macleans, Macdonalds, and Camerons came down. In two minutes the battle was lost and won. The ranks of Balfour's regiment broke. He was cloven down while struggling in the press. Ramsay's men turned their backs and dropped their arms. Mackay's own foot were swept away by the furious onset of the Camerons. His brother and nephew exerted themselves in vain to rally the men. The former was laid dead on the ground by the stroke of a claymore. The latter, with eight wounds in his body, made his way through the tumult and the carnage to his uncle's side. Even in that extremity Mackay retained all his self-possession. He had still one hope. A charge of horse might recover the day; for of horse the bravest Highlanders were supposed to stand in awe. But he called on the horse in vain. Belhaven, indeed, behaved like a gallant gentleman; but his troopers, appalled by the rout of the infantry, galloped off in disorder; Annandale's men followed; all was over, and the mingled torrents of red-coats and tartans went raving down the valley to the Gorge of Killiecrankie."* Mackay's whole army had vanished, all the men he could collect after the battle being a few hundreds.

Next morning the Highlanders, who had retired during the night, returned to the field of the recent carnage, where, Drummond informs us, the dreadful effects of the fury

* *History of England*, Vol. III., pp. 360-361.

appeared in many horrible figures. The enemy lay in heaps almost in the order in which they were posted, but so disfigured with wounds, and so hashed and mangled, that even the victors could not look upon the amazing proofs of their own agility and strength without surprise and horror. Many had their heads divided in two halves by one blow; others had their skulls cut off above their ears, by a back stroke, like a night-cap. Their thick buff belts were not sufficient to defend their shoulders from such deep gashes as almost disclosed their entrails; several pikes, small swords, and the like weapons, were cut quite through, and some that had skull-caps had them so beat into their brains, that they died upon the spot.* It was noticed that few, if any, of the Highlanders were killed after they drew their swords, and that the majority of those of them who fell were slain within a few paces of their enemies, before they fired their last volley and fled, as the Highlanders came to close quarters. Lochiel lost one-half of his entire force, mainly through a furious fire, directed on his flank as he charged, by Leven's battalion, which, as we have already seen, had no Highlanders against it in front.

In this connection, General Stewart records the following incident:—At the same time that Sir Ewen was distinguishing himself so brilliantly in the service of King James, his second son, Donald, was a captain in the 21st Scots Fusiliers, serving with Mackay in the army of King William.

* "An Officer of the army," present at Killiecrankie, in a rare pamphlet, entitled "Memoirs of the Lord Viscount Dundee," describes the terrible effects of the Highland claymore, in very similar language to the above. He says that before the battle "The Highlanders threw away their plaids, haversacks, and all other utensils, and marched resolutely and deliberately in their shirts and doublets, with their fusils, targets, and pistols ready, down the hill on the enemy, and received Mackay's third fire before they pierced his lines, in which many of the Highlanders fell, including Dundee, the terror of the Whigs, the supporter of King James, and the glory of his country. Then the Highlanders fired, threw down their fusils, rushed in upon the enemy, with sword, target, and pistol, who did not maintain their ground two minutes after the Highlanders were amongst them; and I dare be bold to say, there were scarce ever such strokes given in Europe as were given that day by the Highlanders. Many of General Mackay's officers and soldiers were cut down through the skull and neck to the very breasts; others had their skulls cut off above their ears like night-caps; some soldiers had both their bodies and cross-belts cut through at one blow; pikes and small swords were cut like willows."

As General Mackay observed the Highland army being drawn up on the face of the hill, to the westward of the Pass, he turned round to young Lochiel, who stood next to him, and, pointing to the Camerons, said—"There's your father, with his wild savages; how would you like to be with them?" "It signifies little," replied Captain Cameron, "what I would like ; but I recommend you to be prepared, or perhaps my father and his wild savages may be nearer to you before night than you would like." And so, indeed, they were.

Dundee had such confidence in the experience, judgment, and prudence of Sir Ewen, that he consulted him on every important occasion, and he openly expressed the opinion that "he was the fittest person in the kingdom" to command the Highland army.

Cannon, being the next highest officer in rank, on the fall of Dundee, assumed command. Having buried their great commander and the leading officers who fell at Killiecrankie, in the church of Blair-Athole, a large additional body of Highlanders joined them, just three days after the battle—the very day appointed, before Dundee left Lochaber, for the general rendezvous of the clan. Of this new body 500 were Camerons, under Lochiel's eldest son, John, and his cousin, Cameron of Glendesseray. It was, however, all too late. The war was already practically over. Cannon mismanaged everything. The chiefs had no confidence in him. He sent a party on an expedition to Perth, which were so badly led that Mackay easily overtook and defeated them. The Lowland officers and the Highland chiefs disagreed in council. Lochiel and the Highlanders proposed fighting Mackay at once. The Lowland officers, who had scarcely any personal following, opposed this as imprudent, though Lochiel declared that he was prepared to fight the enemy by his own clan, with the assistance only of three hundred horse that had just joined them. In spite of this and the urgent appeals of the other chiefs, the Lowland officers, who all had a vote in the council of war, carried the proposal, that the army should march into Aberdeenshire; the only reason given for this cowardly conduct being the expectation of increasing their forces by the accession of more of their northern friends. Lochiel was disgusted, and retired sullenly to Lochaber, leaving the command of his clan to his son John; but the Highlanders became so dispirited, and Cannon, the commander, got into such disrepute, that after a few skirmishes the army gradually melted away, and Cannon followed the Camerons to Lochaber, where he remained during the winter.

On the 1st of November, 1689, James wrote a letter to Lochiel, from Ireland, acknowledging his services and that of the other chiefs in his cause, promising to send over the Earl of Seaforth, then in Ireland, "to head his friends and followers," and at the same time to send the Duke of Berwick with considerable forces. These were never sent. The Earl of Seaforth arrived in the following spring, but brought nothing with him except letters and commissions for the chiefs. The one to Lochiel is dated "At our Court at Dublin," on the 31st of March, 1690. The usual liberal but empty promises were repeated by the king, but never redeemed; he never had the opportunity. A council of war was held on the arrival of General Buchan, who came over from Ireland, Cannon and other high officers being present, to decide as to their future movements. At this meeting several of the leaders proposed to make their submission to King William on such favourable terms as they then knew they would be sure to obtain. Cogent and many were the reasons urged for the adoption of this course, but, as usual, Lochiel was implacable. He was supported by Sir Donald Macdonald of Sleat, Sir John Maclean of Duart, and Clanranald, in his determination to hold out and fight for the ungrateful James, though it was admitted by all that he sent them nothing but empty promises; and some doubted his inclination to redeem them, even should he ever possess the power to do so.

Lochiel addressed them, concluding an eloquent and spirited appeal to their patriotism and loyalty in the following terms :—" For my own part, gentlemen," he said, " I am resolved to be in my duty while I am able : and though I am now an old man, weakened by fatigue, and worn out by continual trouble, yet I am determined to spend the remainder of my life after my old manner, among mountains and caves, rather than give up my conscience and honour by a submission, let the terms be never so inviting, until I have my master's permission to do it ; and no argument, or view of interest or safety, shall prevail with me to change this resolution, whatever may be the event ". On the conclusion of these remarks all opposition vanished, and it was agreed that General Buchan should in the meantime march south to the border of the Lowlands, with twelve hundred men, but that the Highlanders, except such as volunteered to join Buchan, should remain until they laid down their crops in the spring. Not one of the Highland chiefs joined him. He started about the middle of April towards Strathspey, and was defeated by Sir Thomas Livingstone, at Cromdale, early in May, with considerable loss.

On the 16th of June following, two of the less prominent leaders—Macdonald of Largo, and MacAlastair of Loup—made their submission, and the Government sent emissaries to the Highlands to sound the other chiefs as to whether they would submit on any reasonable terms. They, however, with one voice, refused to listen to any proposal, though they were all disposed for terms, without the full consent of James. But they agreed to meet the Earl of Breadalbane, who had been appointed by Government to negotiate with them, and consider terms of submission, in view of their obtaining the permission of James to give up the war. They had several meetings with the earl at Achallader, near his own property, where they agreed upon the following articles, as the only terms on which they would give up the struggle and lay down their arms :—

1st. As a preliminary article, they demanded full power and liberty to send such a person as they should choose to the Court of St. Germains upon the Government's charges, in order to lay the state of their affairs before King James, and to obtain his permission and warrant to enter into a treaty.

2nd. This article being granted, they next demanded the sum of £20,000 sterling to refund the great expenses and losses they had sustained by the war. In order to obtain this they represented that the people were so impoverished that it would be impossible to keep them from making depredations on their low-country neighbours, unless they were enabled to stay at home, and apply themselves to agriculture and the improvement of their country.

3rd. That King William should, at the public charge, free them from all manner of vassalage and dependence on the great men, their neighbours, as King James was to have done, for which they produced his letters; so that, being free from the tyranny and oppression of these superiors, they might have their sole dependence on the Crown, and be enabled effectually to suppress thieving, and employ their people in the service of their country.

4th. That King James's officers might have full liberty either to remain at home or to go into foreign service as they pleased, and that they, and all others engaged in his interest, should not only have passports for that purpose, but also be carried to the port of Havre de Grace at the expense of the Government.

5th. That they be all allowed to wear and use their arms as they were used to do; and that no other oaths should be put to them except that of simple allegiance; and that they should have full and free indemnity for all crimes whatever committed by them, or any of them, during the war; and that in the meantime there should be cessation of arms.

In the following September, before any effect could be given to the terms of this treaty, Argyll was ordered by the Council to join the Earl of Glencairn in the North, with orders to reduce the Highlanders. These noblemen, however, had little success. But the Government was determined; an act of sequestration was taken out against Lochiel and the other chiefs, and, to execute it, a commission was granted, in the month of November, to Colonel Hill, Governor of Fort-William, to collect Lochiel's rents. He was, however, as might be expected, quite unable to carry out his instructions, " but remained confined within the walls of his fort " until a treaty of peace was finally arranged.

King William ultimately agreed that Sir George Barclay and Major Duncan Menzies should visit James at the Court of St. Germains, to obtain the desired permission for the Highland chiefs to lay down their arms and come to terms with the Government; and, on the 27th of August, William wrote to the Privy Council, informing them of what he had agreed to, and intimating that, as the vassalage and dependence of some of the Highland chiefs upon others in their neighbourhood had occasioned many feuds and differences among them, which obliged them to neglect the improvement and cultivation of their lands, that he was graciously pleased now, not only to pardon, indemnify, and restore all who had been in arms, and who should take the oath of allegiance before the first of the following January, but that he had also resolved to pay the cost of the purchase of the lands and superiorities which were the subjects of those disputes and animosities, so that in future they would be entirely dependent, as its immediate vassals, on the Crown. He urged upon the Council the utmost application of the royal authority to carry this arrangement into effect, and at once to issue an indemnity such as he desired, without any limitation or restriction whatever, to all who agreed to take the oath of allegiance to him and Queen Mary, before the 1st of January, 1692, in presence of the Council, or before the Sheriffs or their Deputes in the respective shires wherein the chiefs resided. Any leaders who declined, or were obstinate, were ordered to be prosecuted with the utmost severity of the law.

Notwithstanding these offers, which must be considered liberal enough in the circumstances, not one of the Highland chiefs took advantage of the indemnity offered to them, until the return of their commissioners from St. Germains, a few days before the time stated therein expired. The letter from James granting the required permission is addressed "To our trusty and well-beloved general, Major Thomas Buchan, or to the officer commanding-in-chief our forces in our ancient kingdom of Scotland," and is in the following terms :—

"James R. Right trusty and well-beloved, we greet you well. We are informed of the state of our subjects in the Highlands, and of the condition that you and our other officers there are in, as well by our trusty and well-beloved Sir George Barclay, Brigadier of our forces, as by our trusty and well-beloved Major Duncan Menzies : And therefore we have thought fit hereby to authorise you to give leave to our said subjects and officers, who have hitherto behaved themselves so loyally in our cause, to do what may be most for their own and your safety ; and so we bid you farewell. St. Germains, this 12th day of December, 1691, and in the seventh year of our reign."

Lochiel did not get his copy of this letter from Buchan—who was at the time residing with Glengarry—until within thirty hours of the expiry of the period allowed him under the conditions of indemnity to submit to William's Government; but by a great effort he managed to arrive at Inveraray, where the Sheriff of the county resided, on the very day on which the period of the indemnity expired, with unfeigned reluctance made his submission, and saved himself from prosecution and possible ruin; but William took advantage of his delay in not coming forward until the last moment, "as a pretence to defraud him of his share of the £20,000 sterling, promised and due to him by the treaty, and of the superiority of his lands, which he stood engaged to purchase for him," as already stated.

In 1696, Sir Ewen, then sixty-seven years of age, made over the greater part of his estates to his eldest son, John, reserving the life-rent to himself.

John was a thorough Jacobite, and took part in all the political intrigues and other proceedings of the Highland chiefs, which culminated in the Rising of 1715, for the restoration of the exiled James. In 1706, a warrant was issued for his apprehension on the charge of high treason, but it does not appear that it was ever executed. About the same time John seems to have made over the estates to his eldest son, Donald, afterwards so distinguished as the "Gentle Lochiel" of the 'Forty-five. John Cameron of Lochiel, and his brother, Lieutenant Allan Cameron, are included in a summons issued against all the Highland chiefs, "and other suspected persons," early in September, 1715, to appear at Edinburgh, by a certain day, to find security for their good conduct. Sir Alexander Erskine and Patrick Murray of Auchtertyre were the only persons named who complied, and all the others, including the brothers Cameron, were denounced and declared rebels.

John is said "to have had a greater genius for civil than for military affairs," and we are informed that his leadership of the clan in 1715 "seems to have given but little satisfaction either to his father or the clan, and it is reported that they expressed an unwillingness again to serve under him ". On the 17th of September, he, with a party of Macdonalds, Macleans, his own clan, and a few others, attempted to surprise the garrison at Inverlochy, when, sword in hand, they took two redoubts in the vicinity of the garrison, capturing a lieutenant and twenty men in one, and a sergeant and five men in the other, after which they proceeded to Argyleshire. Having held out for a short time, the Camerons submitted to General Cadogan in 1716, and delivered up their arms. John, having been forfeited for his share in the Rising in 1715, escaped to France, and never after visited his native land.

Sir Ewen seems to have retired entirely into private life after his submission in 1692, his age and infirmities having rendered him quite unfit, even were he disposed, to take an active part in the Rising of 1715, or in the proccedings which led up to it. He is known to have owned a plantation in the West Indies for some years before he died, a remarkable fact in the history of such a man. This he made over to members of his family, with his landed property, several years before he died.

The following account of his latter years and of his death is abridged from a copy taken by Miss Cameron of Lochiel from one of the Balhaldy Papers, and reproduced in the Editor's Preface to the *Memoirs*, though it was not incorporated in any of the manuscripts to which he had access. It will be noticed that the writer of the original manuscript was personally acquainted with Sir Ewen, and, therefore, his description may safely be accepted as perfectly accurate :—"Sir Ewen's eyes retained their former vivacity, and his sight was so good in his ninetieth year that he could discern the most minute object and read the smallest print ; nor did he so much as want a tooth, which seemed as white and close as one would have imagined they were in the twentieth year of his age. In this state he was when I had the good fortune to see him in 1716, and so great was his strength at that time that he wrung some blood from the point of my fingers with a grasp of his hand. He was of the largest size, his bones big, his counténance fresh and smooth, and he had a certain air of greatness about him which struck the beholders with awe and respect. He enjoyed continued perfect health from the cradle to the grave, except the flux, by which he was laid up during the whole of the year 1674; and not a drop of his blood was ever drawn, except on one occasion when a knife had accidentally pierced his foot."

"The story which I am going to tell," the same writer continues, "would be absolutely incredible were it not vouched by a multitude of witnesses. Very early in the morning on which the Chevalier de St. George landed at Peterhead, attended only by Allan Cameron, one of the Gentlemen of his Bedchamber, Sir Ewen started, as it were, in a surprise from his sleep, and called out loudly to his lady—who lay near him in another bed—that his king was landed, that his king had arrived, and that his own son, Allan, was with him. She awoke, and, inquiring if he wanted anything, he repeated the same statement over and over again, and commanded that a large bonfire should be put on, and the best liquor be brought out to his lads (as he called his clansmen), that they might make merry and drink his king's health. The lady, who at first fancied he was raving, took little notice of him, but he was determined and positive, and gave his commands with such authority, that she was at last obliged to obey them. Not only his own grand-children and his domestics, but all the people in the neighbourhood, were convened to take part in this celebration, which they continued 'with uncommon festivity and mirth' until the next day was nearly spent. His lady was so curious that she noted down the words upon paper, with the date, which she, a few days after, found verified in every particular, to her very great surprise."

It will be remembered that he had a somewhat similar experience on the occasion of his visit to General Middleton at Lochgarry; and in the present case "his waking through his sleep, his expressing the words, and giving the orders here related, stand vouched not only by the lady and a servant that lay near him, but likewise by the multitude convened to the solemnity, who all came and kissed their chief's hand, and informed themselves of the truth of it. Besides, contrary to his usual custom, he talked of nothing else all the next day; gave orders from time to time to carry out more liquor to his lads, and said that he would see his son Allan, but should never have the honour of seeing his king." This landing of the Chevalier at Peterhead took place in December, 1715, three years and a few months before Lochiel's death.

Pennant says that Sir Ewen outlived himself, that he became a second child, and was even rocked in a cradle, so much were the faculties of his mind and the members of his body impaired. Tradition has it that he was even fed on woman's milk, and suckled as an infant before he died. The account quoted from Miss Cameron's copy of the Balhaldy Papers, written by one who was personally acquainted with him in his later years, appear sufficiently conclusive on the point. The fact of his mind continuing unimpaired until late in life, except during the high fever from which he died, is also corroborated in Patten's *History of the Rebellion*, published in 1717. When Sir Walter Scott published his *Tales of a Grandfather*, he made every inquiry to ascertain if any trustworthy tradition, or other account, existed of the cradle, and he found none; but he ascertained that it was a current tradition then that Lochiel had lost the use of his lower limbs, and that he turned himself about in bed by the assistance of a rope and pulley.*

Than Lord Macaulay's description of him nothing could be finer :—" Sir Ewen Cameron of Lochiel, surnamed the Black, was," he says, "in personal qualities unrivalled among the Celtic Princes. He was a gracious master, a

---

* Scott records the following characteristic anecdote of Sir Ewen :—Being benighted, on some party for the battle or the chase, Evan Dhu laid himself down with his followers to sleep in the snow. As he composed himself to rest, he observed that one of his sons, or nephews, had rolled together a great snow-ball, on which he deposited his head. Indignant at what he considered as a mark of effeminacy, he started up and kicked the snow-ball from under the sleeper's head, exclaiming—" Are you become so luxurious that you cannot sleep without a pillow ?"—*Tales of a Grandfather.*

trusty ally, a terrible enemy. His countenance and bearing were singularly noble. Some persons who had been at Versailles, and among them the shrewd and observant Simon Lord Lovat, said that there was in person and manner a most striking resemblance between Louis the Fourteenth and Lochiel, and whoever compares the portraits of the two will perceive that there really was some likeness. In stature the difference was great. Louis, in spite of high-heeled shoes and a towering wig, had hardly reached the middle size. Lochiel was tall and strongly built. In agility and skill at his weapons he had few equals among the inhabitants of the hills. He had been repeatedly victorious in single combat. He was a hunter of great fame. He made vigorous war on the wolves, which, down to his time, preyed on the red deer of the Grampians; and by his hand perished the last of the ferocious breed which is known to have wandered at large in our island. Nor was Lochiel less distinguished by intellectual than by bodily vigour. He might, indeed, have seemed ignorant to educated and travelled Englishmen, who had studied the Classics under Busby at Westminster, and under Aldrich at Oxford; who had learned something about the sciences among Fellows of the Royal Society, and something about the Fine Arts in the galleries of Florence and Rome. But though Lochiel had very little knowledge of books, he was eminently wise in council, eloquent in debate, ready in devising expedients, and skilful in managing the minds of men."* In another part of the same work, Macaulay says that he was especially renowned for physical prowess; that his clansmen looked big with pride when they related how he had broken hostile ranks and hewn down tall warriors; and that he owed quite as much of his influence to these achievements as to the qualities which, if fortune had placed him in Parliament or at the French Court, would have made him one of the foremost men of his age.

Sir Ewen was married three times: first to Mary,

* *History of England*, pp. 319, 320.

daughter of Sir Donald Macdonald, eighth Baron and first Baronet of Sleat, by Janet, daughter of Kenneth, first Lord Mackenzie of Kintail, without issue.

He married, secondly, in June, 1662, Isabel, eldest daughter of Sir Lachlan Maclean of Duart, first Baronet, and sister of Sir Hector and Sir Allan, second and third Baronets, by Mary, daughter of Sir Roderick Mòr Macleod of Macleod, with issue—

1. John, his heir.

2. Donald, a man "of great honour and merit," Major in the service of the States of Holland. He fought at Killiecrankie, with the rank of Captain, under General Mackay, against his father, Sir Ewen; but we can trace nothing further of his history except that he died, without issue, about the same time as his father, in 1719.

3. Allan, "a man of extraordinary parts and great integrity". He was a Gentleman of the Bedchamber to the Chevalier de St. George, and was one of the select few who landed with him at Peterhead, in December, 1715. After the Rising he was among those summoned to appear in Edinburgh. He did not, of course, obey, but returned with the Prince to France, where he remained for several years at his Court. In 1725 he came back to Scotland on a mission to the Highland chiefs, and was employed in correspondence and negotiation with them, on behalf of the Chevalier, until about 1729, when he appears to have again returned to France, where he lived with James for several years. He died before 1745. He married a daughter of Fraser of Lovat, with issue—three daughters, one of whom married Campbell of Lochdochart, by whom she had numerous issue. In a letter from the Chevalier, signed "James R.," to Donald Cameron, younger of Lochiel, addressed as "Mr. Johnstone, junior," and dated 11th April, 1727, he refers to his uncle thus— "Allan is now with me, and I am always glad to have some of my brave Highlanders about me, whom I value as they deserve".

4. Margaret, who married Alexander Drummond of Balhaldy, with issue.

5. Anne, who married Allan Máclean of Ardgour, with issue.

6. Catherine, who married William, Tutor of Macdonald, and brother-german of Sir Donald Macdonald, eleventh Baron and fourth Baronet of Sleat, with issue — Ewen (with several others), progenitor of the Macdonalds of Vallay.

7. Janet, who, about 1698, married John Grant of Glenmoriston, as his second wife, with issue—ten sons and five daughters. She died on the 9th of February, 1759, in the eightieth year of her age, when her descendants numbered over two hundred persons.

Sir Ewen married, thirdly, Jean, daughter of Colonel David Barclay, seventeenth of Urie, with issue—

8. Ludovick, who acted as Major for his nephew, the "Gentle Lochiel," in 1745-46. He was designed "of Torcastle," from his having his residence there. He married a daughter of Chisholm, "a cousin of his own," with issue —(1) Allan ; and (2) Catherine, who married, first, Maclachlan of Coruanan ; and secondly, Macdonald of Greenfield. He had also two other sons.

9. Christian, who married Allan Cameron of Glendessery, with issue—two sons and three daughters.

10. Jean, who married Lachlan Macpherson of Cluny, great-grandfather of the present chief, with issue—seven sons and four daughters. Three of the daughters married, respectively, William Mackintosh of Aberarder, Donald Macpherson of Breakachy, and Lewis Macpherson of Dalraddie.

11. Isabel, who married Archibald Cameron of Dungallon, with issue—three sons and three daughters.

12. Lucy, who married, in 1707, Patrick Campbell of Barcaldine, as his second wife, with issue—(1) Colin of Glenure, who married, on the 9th of May, 1749, Janet, daughter of Hugh Mackay of Bighouse, son of George, third Lord Reay, F.R.S. On the 14th of May, 1752, Colin

was murdered at Balachulish, leaving issue—three daughters, one of whom, Louisa, inherited Bighouse, in 1770, on the death of her grandfather. She married, on the 11th of June, 1768, George Mackay of Island-handa, with issue—nineteen children. (2) Donald, a surgeon in the Royal Navy; (3) Alexander, an officer in the army; (4) Duncan, who succeeded his father in the estates and carried on the succession, and whose daughter, Lucy, married Sir Ewen Cameron, Baronet of Fassiefern, and was the mother of the famous Colonel John Cameron, of the 92nd Gordon Highlanders, who fell at Quatre-Bras; (5) Archibald, an officer in the army; (6) Robert, a merchant; (7) Allan, a general officer; (8) Isabella, who married Campbell of Achallader; (9) Mary, who married Macdougall of Macdougall; (10) Annabella, who married Campbell of Melfort; and (11) Jane, who married Campbell of Edinchip.

13. Ket, who married John Campbell of Achallader, with issue—two sons and four daughters.

14. Una, who married her cousin, Robert Barclay, twentieth of Urie, with issue—Robert, his heir, now represented by Barclay-Allardice of Urie and Allardice; two other sons, Evan and Alexander, both of whom died without issue; and one daughter.

15. Marjory, who married Macdonald of Morar, with issue.

Sir Ewen died of a high fever, though it had left him a few hours before his death, when "his memory and judgment returned, and he discoursed as sensibly as ever he was known to do in his greater vigour. He called his sons, Majors Donald and Ludovick, and all his friends and domestics that chanced to be about him, to each of whom he spoke a word or two, and then recommended to them in general, religion, loyalty, patriotism, and the love of their friends. In a word, his exit was suitable to his life, and he left a memory behind him so glorious that his name shall be mentioned in these countries with the utmost veneration and respect."

About 1688, an engraving, from the only picture of him

in existence, was issued, having the following lines printed underneath :—

> "The honest man whom virtue sways,
> His God adores, his king obeys;
> Does factious men's rebellious pride,
> And threatening tyrant's rage, deride;
> Honour's his wealth, his rule, his aim,
> Unshaken, fixed, and still the same."

The Editor of *Lochiel's Memoirs*, the late James Macknight, W.S., says (p. lvi., Preface) that "the old impressions of this engraving are now very scarce," but that the illustration prefaced to that work, and which has been executed by direction of the late Donald Cameron of Lochiel, and by him presented to the publishers of the work, is a much more accurate copy of the original picture. We understand that a copy of the scarce original engraving, with the above lines underneath it, is in the possession of Dr. Archibald H. F. Cameron, Liverpool, and, until recently, of Lakefield, Inverness-shire.

Having completed his ninetieth year, Sir Ewen died in February, 1719, when he was succeeded by his eldest son,

XVIII. JOHN CAMERON,

Who, in 1706, made over the estates to his eldest son Donald. They had previously, in 1696, been assigned to himself by his father, Sir Ewen. We had thus Sir Ewen and his son John both living, while the actual proprietor of the estate was Donald, nineteenth chief of the clan, so prominently known in connection with the Rising of 1745, and of whom presently. It will be remembered that John commanded the clan after Killiecrankie, when his father, Sir Ewen, returned to Lochaber. For this act a warrant was, in 1706, issued for his apprehension, charging him with treason; but it does not appear to have been executed, though, no doubt, it was in consequence of this warrant that he, in the same year, transferred the estates to his eldest son.

He was involved in all the schemes for the restoration of the Stuart dynasty, but his forte seems to have lain more in the civil than the military groove. He took part, as we have seen, in the Rising of 1715. For this he was attainted and forfeited, after which he left Scotland, and spent the remainder of his life in France; while his son, Donald, took his place at the head of the clan in Lochaber. His personal attendant, Duncan Cameron, was one of those who accompanied Prince Charles to the Highlands in 1745, to pilot his ships and party to a suitable place of embarkation, which he was well-fitted to do, from his accurate knowledge of the West Coast of Scotland. Duncan wrote an account of the voyage, which has been preserved by Bishop Forbes, and printed by Chambers in the *Jacobite Memoirs*. If the military genius of the family seemed to have gone somewhat under a cloud in the person of John, it was only to shine more brilliantly in that of his immediate successor, and others of his descendants. It was even said that his conduct in 1715 gave but little satisfaction to his father or his clan, and that the latter expressed unwillingness again to serve under him. It would, however, in the nature of things, be difficult to satisfy those who had fought under such a successful and brilliant leader as Sir Ewen, and this will probably account for any feeling of dissatisfaction that may have existed.

He married Isabel, daughter of Alexander, sixth, and sister of Sir Duncan Campbell, seventh of Lochnell, with issue—

1. Donald, his heir and successor.

2. John of Fassiefern, who married Jean, daughter of John Campbell of Achallader, with issue—four sons and seven daughters. The eldest son became distinguished as Colonel John Cameron, of the 92nd Gordon Highlanders, who fell so gloriously at Quatre Bras, and of whom, at length, under " The Camerons of Fassiefern ".

3. Alexander, a priest, who suffered for his sympathies with the Rising of 1745. He was apprehended in Strathglass, and sent to the hulks on the Thames, where he died shortly after, on board a ship, on her way to Hanover carrying a batch of Jacobite prisoners. Among them was

an old and intimate friend of Cameron—Father John Farquharson, in whose arms he died. He had been removed from his own miserable quarters by order of the captain of the ship, through the influence of his old companion, in whose arms he breathed his last.*

4. Dr. Archibald, executed at Tyburn in 1753, for his share in the Rising of 1745, at the age of 46 years, and of whom, with his family and descendants, in the proper place.

5. Evan, who died a planter in Jamaica. †

6. Miss Peggy.

Two other sons died young.

Lochiel died in exile at Newport, in Flanders, in 1747, or early in 1748, at a very advanced age; when he was succeeded as chief of the clan by his eldest son,

XIX. Donald Cameron,

Of 1745 celebrity, known as "The Gentle Lochiel". Though considerably advanced into middle life, he was always called "Young Lochiel," as his father was still alive. For several years before the Rising, Donald was in correspondence with the Chevalier de St. George. One of the letters which he received is given in the Appendix to Home's "History of the Rebellion," dated 11th of April, 1727, in which, addressing him as "Mr. Johnstone, junior," the Chevalier writes:—

I am glad of this occasion to let you know how well pleased I am to hear of the care you take to follow your father's and uncle's example in their loyalty to me; and I doubt not of your endeavours to maintain the true spirit in the clan. Allan

---

* This incident, and the subsequent movements of Father Farquharson, are fully described by Mr. Colin Chisholm, Vol. VII., pp. 144-145, of the *Celtic Magazine*.

† "It appears that Sir Ewen of Lochiel obtained or purchased property in the West Indies. How it was managed, by him, or by his son, we know not; but we see from other documents that, in singular contrast to the contempt for commerce attributed to the Highland gentry of the day, two of his grandsons, Evan and Alexander, went to the West Indies to manage this property. Evan took with him in 1734 *a cargo of people* from Maryburgh, as Fort-William was then called, to carry to the West Indies, and it was believed in the country that he had made rich in Jamaica."—Dr. Clerk's *Life of Colonel John Cameron of Fassiefern*, p. 104. See also Editor's Preface to the *Memoirs of Sir Ewen Cameron of Lochiel*, p. 29.

is now with me, and I am always glad to have some of my brave Highlanders about me, whom I value as they deserve. You will deliver the enclosed to its address, and doubt not of my particular regard for you, which, I am persuaded, you will always deserve. (Signed) JAMES R.

On the 3rd of October, 1729, Allan Cameron, Donald's uncle, referred to in the Chevalier's letter just quoted, writes to young Lochiel, from Albano, as follows :—

Dear Nephew,—Yours, of September 11th, came to my hand in due time, which I took upon me to shew his Majesty, who not only was pleased to say that you wrote with a great deal of zeal and good sense, but was so gracious and good as to write you a letter with his own hand, herewith sent you, wherein he gives full and ample powers to treat with such of his friends in Scotland, as you think are safe to be trusted in what concerns his affairs, until an opportunity offers for executing any reasonable project towards a happy restoration, which they cannot expect to know until matters be entirely ripe for execution, and of which they will be acquainted directly from himself; and, therefore, whatever they have to say at any time, either by you, by the power given you by the King's letter, or by any other person, the account is to be sent to his Majesty directly, and not to any second hand, as the King has wrote to you in his letter. Dear nephew, now that his Majesty has honoured you with such a commission, and gracious letter, concerning himself and family, and that he has conceived so good an opinion of your good sense and prudence, I hope this your first appearance, by the King's authority, will answer the trust he has been pleased to put in your loyalty, zeal, and good conduct, of which I have no reason to fear or doubt, considering the step you have already made. By executing this commission with prudence and caution, depend on it you have an opportunity of serving the King to good purpose, which in time will redound to the prosperity of your friends and family. I need say no more on this head, since you will see by the King's letter fully the occasion you have of serving his Majesty, your country, and yourself. But as I am afraid you will have difficulty to read it, his hand not being easy to those who are not well acquainted with it; the substance of it is, that he would not let you go without shewing you how sensible he is of your good zeal and affection to his interest and service; that Scotland, in general, when it is in his power (hoping that happy time will one day come) shall reap the fruits of the constant loyalty of his friends there; that you represent to them to keep themselves in readiness, not knowing how soon there may be occasion for their service; but that they take special care not to give a handle to the present Government to ruin them, by exposing themselves to their fury by any unreasonable or imprudent action, for that they shall have his Majesty's orders directly, when it is proper; and recommends entire union among yourselves in general; and towards the end of the letter, he is pleased to make yourself and family particular promises of his favour, when it pleases God he is restored; and while he is abroad all that's in his power. I hope this hint of the meaning of the letter will enable you, by taking some pains, to read it through; it being wrote in the King's own hand, there was no occasion for signing it.

I think it proper you should write to the King, by the first post after you receive his letter. I need not advise you what to say in answer to such a gracious letter from your King, only let it not be very long; declare your duty and readiness to execute his Majesty's commands on all occasions, and of your sense of the honour he has been pleased to do you, in giving you such a commission. I am not to choose words for you, because I am sure you can express yourself in a dutiful and discreet manner without any help. You are to write, sir, on a large margin, and to end, your most faithful and obedient subject and servant, and to address it,

To the King, and no more; which enclose to me sealed. I pray send me the copy of it on a paper enclosed, with any other thing that you do not think fit or needful the King should see in your letter to me; because I will shew your letter in answer to this, wherein you may say that you will be mindful of all I wrote to you, and what else you think fit.

This letter is so long, that I must take the occasion of the next post to write you concerning my own family; but the King, as well as Mr. Hay, bid me assure you, that your father should never be in any more straits, as long as he, the King, lived; and that he would take care from time to time to remit him; so that I hope you may be pretty easy as to that point.

I must tell you, that what you touched on in your letter to me of the 14th August, concerning those you saw there live so well, beyond what they could have done at home, they must have been provided for some other way than out of the King's pocket; and, depend upon it, some others have thought themselves obliged to supply them.

You are to assure yourself and others, that the King has determined to make Scotland happy, and the clans in particular, when it pleases God to restore him; this is consistent with my certain knowledge. You are only to touch upon this in a discreet way, and to a very few discreet persons; but all these matters I leave to your own good sense and prudence, for you may be sure there are people who will give account of your behaviour after you return home; but I hope none will be able to do it to your disadvantage; keep always to the truth in what you inform the King and that will stand; though even on the truth itself, you are to put the handsomest gloss you can on some occasions.

You are to keep on good terms with Glengarry, and all other neighbours, and let bye-gones be bye-gones, as long as they continue firm to the King's interest; let no private animosity take place, but see to gain them with courtesy and good management, which I hope will give you an opportunity to make a figure amongst them, not but you are to tell the truth, if any of them fail in their duty to the King or country.

As to Lovat, pray, be always on your guard, but not so as to lose him; on the contrary, you may say that the King trusts a great deal to the resolution he has taken to serve him; and expects he will continue in that resolution. But, dear nephew, you know very well that he must give true and real proof of his sincerity, by performance, before he can be entirely reckoned on, after the part he has acted. This I say to yourself, and therefore you must deal with him very dexterously; and I must leave it to your own judgment what lengths to go with him, since you know he has always been a man whose chief view was his own interest. It is true he wishes our family well; and I doubt not he would wish the King restored, which is his interest, if he has the grace to have a hand in it, after what he has done. So, upon the whole, I know not what advice to give you, as to letting him know that the King wrote you such a letter as you have; but, in general, you are to make the best of him you can, but still be on your guard; for it is not good to put too much in his power before the time of executing a good design. The King knows very well how useful he can be if sincere, which I have represented as fully as was necessary.

This letter is of such bulk, that I have enclosed the King's letter under cover with another letter addressed for your father, as I will not take leave of you till next post. I add only that I am entirely yours, A. CAMERON.

The letter enclosed from the Chevalier has not been preserved, but we have the substance of it in Allan's letter. The reference to Simon Lord Lovat shows that his lordship's character had been correctly estimated long before 1745, and that it was placed at its proper value by the friends of the Stuarts. It is to be regretted that we do not know the exact nature of the promises made by Charles and his father to Lochiel, for himself and for his family. We are told in the *Jacobite Memoirs* that Donald, before agreeing to "come out," took full security from the Prince for the value of his estates, and that it was "to fulfil this engagement that Charles, after the unfortunate conclusion of the enterprise," obtained a French regiment for him. Chambers, who, in a foot-note, quotes this from Bishop Forbes, says, of this alleged security, "that it is scarcely necessary to remark, that the presence of generous feelings does not necessarily forbid that some attention should be paid to the dictates of prudence and caution. Lochiel might feel that he had a right to peril his life and connection with his country, but not the fortune on which the comfort of others besides himself depended, especially in an enterprise of which he had a bad opinion, and which he only acceded to from a romantic deference to the wishes of another person." In this view the majority of people will agree.

The Jacobites, not only in the Highlands but in the Lowlands, were acquainted with the contents of the letters which passed between the Chevalier, Prince Charles, and young Lochiel. In 1740 he was one of the seven Highland chiefs who signed articles of association for the restoration of the Stuart line, engaging to take up arms, for that purpose, provided sufficient assistance was sent from France. These articles were taken to the Chevalier at Rome by Drummond of Balhaldy.

A letter is printed among the Stuart papers, from Lochiel, signed "Dan," dated the 22nd of February, 1745, addressed to the Chevalier de St. George, in which he refers to another letter recently forwarded by him, and in which he assures his Royal Highness of his steady adherence to whatever may conduce to the interest of his family, urging that, as "the season is now fast advancing," and that, as they had as yet no return from their friends in England, "how far it is necessary that we be informed of what is expected from the French, and in how soon, that we may have it in our power to settle matters so as will enable us to make that assistance to your Highness our duty and inclination direct". Shortly after the date of this letter, Prince Charles Edward embarked for the Highlands of Scotland, and immediately on his arrival at Borrodale, he sent messengers to several of the most influential chiefs, and, among the rest of course, to his trusted friend Lochiel, who, when told that the Prince had landed without troops, arms, or ammunition, resolved to take no part in what seemed, in consequence, such a perfectly hopeless enterprise. At the same time he determined to visit his Royal Highness in person, first out of courtesy, but particularly to induce him, if possible, to wait for the promised assistance from France, failing which, to urge him to give up his intention, and return across the Channel as quietly as he could.

Home informs us that Lochiel left Lochaber on this visit quite determined not to take up arms, and that on his way to Borrodale, he called at the house of his brother, John Cameron of Fassiefern, who, surpised to see him at such an unusual hour, asked what had brought him there so early in the morning. When Lochiel explained the object of his journey, Fassiefern asked, "What troops had the Prince brought with him? What money? What arms?" Lochiel answered that he believed he had brought with him neither troops, money, nor arms; and, therefore, he was resolved not to be concerned in the affair, and would do his utmost to prevent Charles from making such a rash attempt. Fassiefern approved of his brother's sentiments, and applauded his resolution; advising him, at the same time, not to go any further on his way to Borrodale, but to come into the house, and impart his mind to the Prince by letter. "No," replied Lochiel, "I ought at least to wait upon him, and give my reasons in person for declining to join him, which admit of no reply." "Brother," said Fassiefern, "I know you better than you know yourself. If this Prince once sets his eyes on you, he will make you do whatever he pleases." This conversation, Home informs us, was repeated to him in 1781 by Fassiefern himself.

No sooner had Lochiel arrived at Borrodale than the Prince and he retired together, when, according to the same authority, a discussion to the following effect took place:—The Prince began the conversation by bitterly complaining of the treatment he had received from the French Ministers who had so long put him off with vain hopes and deceived him with false promises of active support; their coldness in the cause, he said, but ill agreed with the opinions he had of his own rights, and with that impatience to assert them with which the promises of his father's brave and faithful subjects had inflamed his mind. Lochiel acknowledged the engagements of the chiefs, but observed that they were nowise binding, as he had come over to the Highlands without the stipulated aid; and, therefore, as there was not the least prospect of success, he advised his Royal Highness to return to France and to reserve himself and his faithful friends for a more favourable opportunity. Charles refused to follow Lochiel's advice, affirming that a more favourable opportunity than the present would never come; that almost all the British troops were abroad, and kept at bay by Marshal Saxe, with a superior army; that in Scotland there were only a few newly-raised regiments, that had never seen any service, and could not stand before the Highlanders; that the very first advantage gained over the troops would encourage his father's friends at home to declare in his favour; that his friends abroad would not fail to give their assistance; and that he only wanted the Highlanders, in the meantime, to begin the war.

Lochiel still resisted, entreating him to be more temperate, and consent to remain in the meantime concealed where he was, till he and other friends should meet together, and arrange as to what was best to be done. Charles, whose whole mind was wound up to the utmost pitch of impatience, paid no regard to this proposal, but answered that he "was determined to put all to the hazard. In a few days, he said, with the few friends that I have, I will erect the Royal standard, and proclaim to the people of Britain that Charles Stuart is come over to claim the crown of his ancestors, to win it, or to perish in the attempt ; Lochiel, who, my father has often told me, was our firmest friend, may stay at home, and learn from the newspapers the fate of his Prince." "No," said Lochiel, "I'll share the fate of my Prince, and so shall every man over whom nature or fortune has given me any power." Such was the immediate effect of this singular conversation, on the result of which entirely depended whether it was to be peace or war ; for it is admitted on all hands, that if Lochiel had persisted in his refusal to take up arms, the other chiefs would not have joined the standard of the Prince without him, and the incipient spark of the proposed rising must have there and then expired.

Lochiel now returned home, and dispatched messengers to all his vassals able to bear arms, commanding them to get ready at once to join their chief, and march with him to Glenfinnan, where it had been resolved to raise the standard of the Prince. In the meantime, on the 16th of August, two companies of the 1st Regiment of Foot, under Captain Scott, which had been sent from Fort-Augustus to re-inforce Fort-William, were cleverly surrounded and taken prisoners, by a small body of Keppoch and Glengarry Macdonalds, at the end of Loch-Oich. Lochiel, to whom word had been sent to come to the assistance of the Macdonalds, arrived just as Captain Scott and his men surrendered, when Donald, with a body of Camerons, took charge of the prisoners, and marched them to his residence at Achnacarry.

On the 19th, at the head of between 700 and 800 of his followers, Lochiel marched to Glenfinnan, where the Prince was anxiously waiting for the clans that he expected would have met him there on his arrival, and where it had been appointed to unfurl the standard. "At length," says Chambers, "about an hour after noon, the sound of a pibroch was heard over the top of an opposite hill, and, immediately after, the adventurer was cheered by the sight of a large body of Highlanders in full march down the slope. It was the Camerons to the number of 700 or 800,

'All plaided and plumed in their tartan array,'

coming forward in two columns of three men abreast, to the spirit-stirring notes of the bagpipe, and enclosing the party of soldiers whom they had just taken prisoners. Elevated by the fine appearance of this clan, and by the auspicious result of the little action just described, Charles set about the business of declaring open war against the Elector of Hanover." The standard having been unfurled on the arrival of Lochiel, by the Marquis of Tullibardine, he carried it back to the quarters of the Prince, surrounded by a guard of fifty stalwart Camerons.

Some five hundred firelocks and a quantity of French broadswords having been landed from the "Doutelle" at Castle Tirrim, 250 of the Camerons were sent for them, and, with 300 of Clanranald's men, they met the clans, who had marched from Glenfinnan on the 21st, at the head of Loch Eil, on their way south. Here the Prince issued the famous proclamation offering £30,000 for the person of King William, "Given at our camp at Kinlochiel, August the 22nd," and on the following night, Friday, the 23rd, he slept at Fassiefern House, on Lochiel-side, the residence of John, Lochiel's eldest brother, from whence 200 Camerons were dispatched in advance, with the Prince's baggage, to Moy, in Lochaber.

The Highlanders continued their march southwards. At Corrieyarrack they were informed by a soldier named Cameron of Cope's march to Inverness. This man deserted from the army of King William for the express purpose of conveying this news to his friends, with whose movements he appears to have made himself fully acquainted. The intelligence was received with exultation, and the Highland army at once descended the southern steep of Corrieyarrack, on their way to the Scottish capital, leaving Sir John Cope unmolested on his march to the Highland capital. While bivouacked at Dalwhinnie, Dr. Archibald Cameron, who appears to have held the rank of captain in the Highland army, Macdonald of Lochgarry, and O'Sullivan were ordered on an expedition against a small Government fort at Ruthven, with instructions to take the barracks. They failed in this object, losing one man killed and two mortally wounded, but on their return they brought in Ewen Macpherson of Cluny, who had just the day before accepted a command under Government, and received orders from Sir John Cope to embody his clan, numbering about 300 able-bodied fighting men. Cluny, it may be assumed, was not altogether sorry for his capture, for he is found returning from Perth a few days after to raise his clan for the Prince, who treated him with every consideration during the short period of his imprisonment.

It is not intended here to give a continuous and connected account of the proceedings and movements of the Highland army. These are already well-known. We shall only deal with the various points in the narrative where the Camerons, or their leader, come prominently on the scene.

From Blair Castle, Lochiel, with Lord Nairne, and 400 men, went on in advance, entering and taking possession of Dunkeld on the morning of the 3rd of September. The same evening the City of Perth was occupied by the Camerons, and next morning, Prince Charles having arrived, attired in a superb Highland dress of Royal Stuart tartan, trimmed with gold, they immediately proceeded to the Cross of the Fair City, and proclaimed the Chevalier, amid the acclamations of the people. Lochiel was then appointed, accompanied by Macdonald of Keppoch, Stewart of Ardshiel, and Sullivan, to lead 900 men, comprising a large majority of Camerons, sent forward for the capture of Edinburgh, with instructions to blow up the gates of the city, if necessary, to attain their purpose.* They were

---

* It has been stated that immediately before leading on this band, Lochiel met with an accident, by a fall from his horse, in consequence of which he was unable to execute in person the commission entrusted to him, and that Cameron of Erracht took his place. We have not been able to procure conclusive evidence on this point.

soon in possession without spilling a single drop of blood. When the inhabitants awoke in the morning, they found the government of the Capital transferred from the Provost and Magistrates in name of King George, to the Highlanders in name of King James, and everything in the city was going on, to all outward appearance, as if nothing extraordinary had occurred, the one guard having relieved the other as quietly, according to Home, as one guard relieves another in the routine of duty on ordinary occasions.

At the battle of Preston, fought on the 21st of September, Lochiel, at the head of his followers, occupied the left wing of the army, whose "line was somewhat oblique, and the Camerons, who were nearest the king's army, came up directly opposite to the cannon, firing at the guard as they advanced. The people employed to work the cannon, who were not gunners or artillerymen, ' fled instantly. Colonel Whiteford fired five or six field pieces with his own hand, which killed one private man and wounded an officer in Lochiel's regiment." The Camerons carried everything before them; the enemy fled, dragoons and artillery, and the foot "were either killed or taken prisoners," except about two hundred, "who escaped by extraordinary swiftness or early flight". The cannon, tents, baggage, and military chest of the king's army fell into the hands of the Highlanders, whose total loss only amounted to four officers and thirty men killed, and about seventy wounded; while five of the king's officers were killed and eighty taken prisoners, many of the latter being wounded. Their loss in men has been estimated at from four to five hundred, with some seven hundred prisoners.

Chambers says that "the victory began, as the battle had done, among the Camerons. That spirited clan, notwithstanding their exposure to the cannon, and although received with a discharge of musketry by the artillery guard, ran on with undaunted speed, and were first up to the front of the enemy," who, with Colonel Gardener and his dragoons, immediately reeled, turned, and followed their companions. Lochiel ordered his men to strike at the noses of the horses, as the best means of getting the better of their masters; but they never found a single opportunity of practising the *ruse*, the men having chosen to retreat while they were yet some yards distant. Hamilton's dragoons, at the other extremity of the army, no sooner saw their fellows flying before the Camerons than they also turned about and fled, without having fired a carbine. The whole action only lasted about four minutes, ending in "a total overthrow, and the almost entire destruction of the Royal army," and Lochiel, with his trusty Camerons, had the principal share in securing this decisive result. Of the four officers killed in the action two were Camerons—Lieutenant Allan Cameron of Lundavra, and Ensign James Cameron, both of Lochiel's regiment.*

Having spent several days in Holyrood, where he daily consulted his council of war—Lochiel being, of course, one of the members—in the drawing-room, the Prince resolved to march into England at the head of an army numbering between five and six thousand troops, some artillery, and abundance of arms and ammunition. On the 8th of November, the first division passed the Border, when they raised a loud shout and unsheathed their claymores. Lochiel, in the act of drawing his weapon, accidentally cut his hand, which was considered such a bad omen, that many of those present grew pale when they were told of the mishap.

A curious incident which occurred to Lochiel on the march through the North of England is recorded. The English populace were in utter terror of the Highland soldiers, whom they were led to believe were inhuman

* Just as the army was marching to the attack the Chevalier appeared at their head, very alert, and ready to lead them to the onset. Lochiel, however, who had a great respect and esteem for him, earnestly entreated him to forbear exposing his person, and advised him to take his stand upon a rising ground, under the guard of a party, from whence he might send his orders to any part of the army during the engagement as he should see occasion; for if any misfortune should befall him they were all ruined to a man; and that too much depended on his safety to hazard his person without more apparent necessity than their was; which advice the Chevalier followed, and retired with a party to a high field to the south-west of Seaton.—*Life of Dr. Archibald Cameron.*

beyond conception; they were told that they were cannibals, and were particularly fond of feeding on young infants. Great surprise was experienced when it was found that, instead of these wild charges being true, the Highlanders actually paid for everything they required, and expressed great gratitude for any refreshments given to them or favours shown to them. Donald Cameron of Lochiel, on entering the lodgings which had been marked off for him, his hostess, a woman of years, fell at his feet, supplicating him, with hands joined, and with a flood of tears, to take away her life, but to spare her two children. He demanded of her if she was mad, and to explain herself. She replied that everyone said that the Highlanders ate children, and made them their ordinary food. Cameron having assured her that they would do no harm to her little ones, or to anybody, whoever they may be, she fixed her eyes for a moment upon him with an air of surprise, and at once opened quickly a closet, calling out with a loud voice, "Come out, my children, the gentleman will not eat you". The children came out immediately from the closet, where she had concealed them, and fell at his knees.*

Lochiel accompanied the army all the way to Derby, and on the return march to Scotland, he was present, and, with his men, took a prominent part and did excellent service in the left wing of the Highland army at the battle of Falkirk, where the Highlanders again routed the enemy, under General Hawley, mainly composed of tried soldiers who had fought at Dettingen and Fontenoy. Here Lochiel was slightly wounded in the heel, by a musket ball, during the heat of the action, which, being observed by his brother, the doctor, who always kept near his person, "he begged him to retire to have it dressed, which he accordingly did ; but as the doctor was lending him his assistance, he himself received a slight wound,"† a ball

* *Memoirs of the Chevalier de Johnstone*, translated from the original French, by Charles Winchester, Vol. I., p. 60.
† *Life of Dr. Archibald Cameron*. London, 1753.

having entered his body, where it remained during the remainder of his life. Shortly after the battle, Lochiel was able to lead a detachment into the town of Falkirk, finding nothing but a few straggling parties in the streets, whither he was followed by the Prince, who, with Cameron, took up his quarters in the town for the night.

Next day, during which the Highlanders remained in the town, an incident occurred, which Home, himself an eye-witness, thus describes:—" Lord Kilmarnock, in the morning of the 18th, came to Falkirk, which is within half-a-mile of his house at Callender (where he had passed the night), bringing with him a party of his men to guard some prisoners who had been taken in the retreat, and carried to Callender. Lord Kilmarnock left the prisoners and their guard standing in the street, just before the house where Charles lodged, and going up stairs, presented to Charles a list of his prisoners, who were the two officers and some private men of the company of volunteers mentioned in the account of the battle. Charles opened the window to look at the prisoners, and stood for some time with the list in his hand, asking questions (as they thought) about them of Lord Kilmarnock. Meanwhile, a soldier, in the uniform of one of the king's regiments, made his appearance in the street of Falkirk, which was full of Highlanders; he was armed with a musket and bayonet, and had a black cockade in his hat. When the volunteers saw a soldier with his firelock in his hand coming towards Charles, they were amazed, and fancied a thousand things; they expected every moment to hear a shot. Charles observing that the volunteers, who were within a few yards of him, looked all one way, turned his head that way too; he seemed surprised, and calling Lord Kilmarnock, pointed to the soldier. Lord Kilmarnock came downstairs immediately; when he got to the street, the soldier was just opposite to the window where Charles stood. Kilmarnock came up to the fellow, struck his hat off his head, and set his foot on the black cockade. At that instant a Highlander came running from the other side of the street, laid hands on Lord Kilmarnock, and pushed him back. Kilmarnock pulled out a pistol, and presented it at the Highlander's head; the Highlander then drew his dirk, and held it close to Kilmarnock's breast. In this posture they stood about half-a-minute, when a crowd of Highlanders rushed in, and drove away Lord Kilmarnock. The man with the dirk in his hand took up the hat, put it upon the soldier's head, and the Highlanders marched off with him in triumph. This piece of dumb show, of which they understood nothing, perplexed the volunteers. They expressed their astonishment to a Highland officer who stood near them; and entreated him to explain the meaning of what they had seen. He told them that the soldier in the uniform of the Royal was a Cameron. 'Yesterday,' said he, 'when your army was defeated, he joined his clan; the Camerons received him with great joy, and told him that he should wear his arms, his clothes, and everything else, till he was provided with other clothes and other arms. The Highlander who first interposed, and drew his dirk on Lord Kilmarnock, is the soldier's brother; the crowd who rushed in are the Camerons, many of them his near relations; and, in my opinion,' continued the officer, 'no colonel nor general in the Prince's army can take that cockade out of his hat, except Lochiel himself.'"* Nothing could better illustrate the ties of clanship which existed in those days!

The Prince returned to Bannockburn on the evening of the 18th, leaving a portion of his army and the Highland chiefs at Falkirk. While there a document was prepared and signed by Lord George Murray, Lochiel, Macdonald of Keppoch, Macdonald of Clanranald, Stewart of Ardshiel, Macdonald of Lochgarry, Macdonald of Scothouse, and Simon Fraser, Master of Lovat, "dated the 29th January, 1746," urging upon the Prince, in the strongest terms, to retire to the North. Charles at once dispatched Sir Thomas Sheridan to argue against the recommendations of the chiefs. They in turn sent Macdonald of Keppoch

* Home's *History of the Rebellion*, pp. 180-182.

to reason with the Prince, who, in the end, most reluctantly agreed to the proposed retreat to the Highlands. The address is in the following terms :—

We think it our duty, in this critical juncture, to lay our opinions in the most respectful manner before your Royal Highness.

We are certain that a vast number of the soldiers of your Royal Highness's army are gone home since the battle of Falkirk; and notwithstanding all the endeavours of the commanders of the different corps, they find that this evil is increasing hourly, and not in their power to prevent, and as we are afraid Stirling Castle cannot be taken so soon as was expected, if the enemy should march before it fall into your Royal Highness's hands, we can foresee nothing but utter destruction to the few that will remain, considering the inequality of our numbers to that of the enemy. For these reasons we are humbly of opinion that there is no way to extricate your Royal Highness and those who remain with you, out of the most imminent danger, but by retiring immediately to the Highlands, where we can be usefully employed the remainder of the winter, by taking and mastering the forts of the North; and we are morally sure we can keep as many men together as will answer that end, and hinder the enemy from following us in the mountains at this season of the year; and in spring, we doubt not but an army of 10,000 effective Highlanders can be brought together, and follow your Royal Highness wherever you think proper. This will certainly disconcert your enemies, and cannot but be approved of by your Royal Highness's friends both at home and abroad. If a landing should happen in the meantime, the Highlanders would immediately rise, either to join them, or to make a powerful diversion elsewhere.

The hard marches which your army has undergone, the winter season, and now the inclemency of the weather, cannot fail of making this measure approved of by your Royal Highness's allies abroad, as well as your faithful adherents at home. The greatest difficulty that occurs to us is the saving of the artillery, particularly the heavy cannon; but better some of those were thrown into the River Forth as that your Royal Highness, besides the danger of your own person, should risk the flower of your army, which we apprehend must inevitably be the case if this retreat be not agreed to, and gone about without the loss of one moment; and we think that it would be the greatest imprudence to risk the whole on so unequal a chance, when there are such hopes of succour from abroad, besides the resources your Royal Highness will have from your faithful and dutiful followers at home. It is but just now we are apprised of the numbers of our own people that are gone off, besides the many sick that are in no condition to fight. And we offer this our opinion with the more freedom that we are persuaded that your Royal Highness can never doubt of the uprightness of our intentions. Nobody is privy to this address to your Royal Highness except your subscribers; and we beg leave to assure your Royal Highness that it is with great concern and reluctance we find ourselves obliged to declare our sentiments, in so dangerous a situation, which nothing could have prevailed with us to have done, but the unhappy going off of so many men.

We next find Lochiel and his Camerons—after the march of the Highland army from the south—in the neighbourhood of Moy Hall, where they, about a mile distant, sheltered Prince Charles when he departed suddenly from "Colonel" Anne's hospitable roof, on hearing of

Lord Loudon's approach from Inverness, at the head of fifteen hundred men, with the object of making his Royal Highness prisoner. This occurred on the morning of Monday, the 18th of February, 1746. Next day the Highlanders took the town of Inverness, Loudon retiring across Kessock Ferry. Two days after, the Castle, then called Fort-George, was besieged, and fell into the hands of the Highlanders, with sixteen pieces of cannon and a hundred barrels of beef. The stronghold was immediately blown up.

Lochiel proceeded to Fort-William early in March, in command of the Camerons, Keppoch Macdonalds, and Stuarts of Appin, to besiege that fortress. They were joined by about 300 of the Irish pickets under Brigadier Stapleton, who had, on the previous 5th of March, compelled the surrender of Fort-Augustus. In consequence of the difficulty experienced in transporting the cannon, the siege of Fort-William was not commenced until the 20th of the month, and it finally proved unsuccessful, notwithstanding the most vigorous efforts by Lochiel and his friends. While here the following letter, written and signed by Lochiel and Keppoch, was sent to Stewart of Invernaheil :—

GLENEVIS, *March 20, 1746.*

Sir,
  Yesternight we received a letter from Cluny, giving an account of the success of the party sent by his Royal Highness, and the command of Lord George Murray, to Athol ; a copy of which letter we thought proper to send you enclosed. And as you happen, for the present, to be contiguous to the Campbells, it is our special desire, that you instantly communicate to Airds, the Sheriff, and other leading men among them, our sentiments (which, God willing, we are determined to execute), by transmitting this our letter, and the enclosed copy, to any the nearest to you.

  It is our opinion, that, of all men in Scotland, the Campbells had the least reason of any to engage in the present war against his Royal Highness's interest, considering that they have always appeared in opposition to the Royal family since the reign of K. James VI., and have been guilty of so many acts of rebellion and barbarity during that time, that no injured prince but would endeavour to resent it, when God was once pleased to put the power in his hands. Yet his present Majesty, and his Royal Highness the Prince Regent, were graciously pleased, by their respective declarations, to forgive all past miscarriages to the most violent and inveterate enemy, and even bury them in oblivion, provided they returned to their allegiance : and tho' they should not appear personally in arms in support of the Royal cause, yet their standing neuter would entitle them to the good graces of their injured sovereign. But, in both ankles. They that a prince could shew or promise, the was advancing, raised h with their wonted zeal for rebellion and we ever form a the their arms." Another writer, on or common sense, would use the — "Notwithstanding barbarity as they do; and of which we have daily proofs, by their burning of houses, stripping of women and children, and exposing them to the open fields and severity of the weather, burning of corn, houghing [ham-stringing] of cattle, and killing of horses: to enumerate the whole would be too tedious at this time. They must naturally reflect, that we cannot but look upon such cruelties with horror and detestation; and with hearts full of revenge, and certainly endeavour to make reprisals. And we are determined to apply to his Royal Highness for leave and an order to enter their country, with full power to act at discretion; and, if we are lucky enough to obtain it, we shall shew that we are not to make war against women, and the brute creatures, but against men; and as God was pleased to put so many of them in our hands, we hope to prevail with his Royal Highness to hang a Campbell for every house that shall hereafter be burnt by them.

Notwithstanding the many scandalous and malicious aspersions, industriously contrived by our enemies, they could never, since the commencement of the war, impeach us with any acts of hostility that had the least tendency to such cruelty as they exercise against us, tho' often we had it in our power, if barbarous enough to execute it.

When courage fails against men, it betrays cowardice to a great degree to vent spleen against brutes, houses, women, and children, who cannot resist. We are not ignorant of their villainous intentions, by the intercepted letters from the Sheriff Airds, etc., which plainly discover, that it was by their application, that their General, Cumberland, granted orders for burning, etc., which he could not be answerable for to the British parliament, it being most certain that such barbarity could never be countenanced by any Christian Senate.

(Signed) DONALD CAMERON, *of Lochiel.*
ALEX. M'DONALD, *of Keppoch.*

I cannot omit taking notice that my people have been the first who have felt the cowardly barbarity of my pretended Campbell friends. I shall only desire to live to have an opportunity of thanking them for it in the open field.—D. C.*

On the 3rd of April, Lochiel received instructions to raise the siege, and proceed to Inverness, where the main body of the Highland army was preparing to oppose the king's forces on their way north under the Duke of Cumberland.

Secretary Murray had written to Lochiel from Fort-Augustus on the 14th of March, where he was, on his way to Fort-William, urging him from the Prince "to hasten the siege as much as possible; and that over, he proposes your people, Keppoch's, Clanranald's, Glengarry's, and the Stuarts should march through Argyllshire, not only to correct that crew, but to give an opportunity to our friends to join, while he [the Prince] with the rest of the clans and

* *Scots Magazine,* Vol. VIII., 1746.

our Lo̴̴̴̴̴̴̴̴̴h by the Highland road to get to P̴̴̴̴̴̴̴̴ join with you at Menteith, or w̴̴̴̴̴̴̴̴̴̴̴ proper. This our scarcity of ....ry, as we have no prospect of getting any, unless in possession of the Low-country; and as Cumberland must of necessity follow us, the coast will be left clear to our friends to land." The order to return to Inverness upset this arrangement. After a long and difficult march, Lochiel joined the main army, which "lay upon the ground among the furze and trees of Culloden wood, on the evening of the 14th of April". The Prince and his principal officers had taken up their quarters in Culloden House.

At Culloden, the Camerons, who, with the Athole men, occupied the right wing, displayed their wonted gallantry, and though great praise was afterwards heaped upon Barrel's and Munro's regiments, who confronted them, for their fortitude in bearing the attack of the Lochaber men, and for killing so many of them, according to Chambers, "these battalions were in reality completely beat aside, and the whole front line shaken so much, that, had the Macdonald regiments made a simultaneous charge, the day might have had a very different issue". Of the five clan regiments that charged, sword in hand—the Camerons, Stuarts, Frasers, Mackintoshes, and MacLeans—almost all the leaders and front-rank men were killed. Lochiel, however, escaped, but he was so severely wounded in both ankles, as he was in the act of drawing his sword, that he had to be carried from the field by his two henchmen,* and afterwards led away on horseback by his faithful followers. Home's version is that "Cameron of Lochiel, advancing at the head of his regiment, was so near Barrel's, that he had fired his pistol, and was drawing his sword, when he fell,

* Nothing could excel the love of the Camerons for their Lochiel, unless it was that of the Macdonalds for their Keppoch; for, being wounded in the very height and fury of the battle, two of them took hold of his legs, a third supported his head, while the rest posted themselves round him as an impregnable bulwark, and in that manner carried him from the field, over the small river Nairn, to a place of safety.—*Life of Dr. Archibald Cameron.*

wounded with grape-shot brothers, between whom carried him off in the charge in the following terms. Stewarts dreadful carnage in their ranks, the Highlanders continued to advance, and, after giving their fire close to the English line, which, from the density of the smoke, was scarcely perceptible, even within pistol shot, the right wing, consisting of the Athole Highlanders and the Camerons, rushed in, sword in hand, and broke through Barrel's and Munro's regiments, which stood on the left of the first line. These regiments bravely defended themselves with their spontoons and bayonets; but such was the impetuosity of the onset, that they would have been entirely cut to pieces had they not been immediately supported by two regiments from the second line, on the approach of which they retired behind the regiments on their right, after sustaining a loss in killed and wounded of upwards of 200 men. After breaking through these two regiments, the Highlanders, passing by the two field-pieces which had annoyed them in front, hurried forward to attack the left of the second line. They were met by a tremendous fire of grape-shot from the three field-pieces on the left of the second line, and by a discharge of musketry from Bligh's and Sempill's regiments, which carried havoc through their ranks, and made them at first recoil; but, maddened by despair, and utterly regardless of their lives, they rushed upon an enemy whom they felt but could not see amid the cloud of smoke in which the assailants were buried."*

The Rev. Dr. Shaw, in his manuscript History of the Rebellion, says that the attack of the Camerons and Athole men " on the left wing of the royal army, was made with a view to break that wing, and then to communicate the disorder to the whole army. This could not easily be effected when a second and third line were ready to sustain the first. But it must be owned," he continues, " the attack

---

* *The Scottish Highlands, Highland Clans, and Highland Regiments,* Vol. II., pp. 663, 664.

was made with the greatest courage, order, and bravery, amidst the hottest fire of small arms, and continued fire of cannon with grape-shot, on their flanks, front, and rear. They ran in upon the points of the bayonets, hewed down the soldiers with their broadswords, drove them back, and possessed themselves of two pieces of cannon. The rebels' left wing did not sustain them in the attack, and four fresh regiments coming up from the Duke's second line, under General Huske, they could not stand under a continued fire both in front, in flank, and rear, and therefore they retired." This is all confirmed in the Lockhart Papers, where almost the same phraseology is used.

By the assistance of his friends, Lochiel soon found his way to Lochaber, where he was followed by Secretary Murray and a few others. For three weeks after the battle, no attempt was made to penetrate the central and western Highlands, whither most of the followers of the Prince ultimately retired. On the 8th of May, a meeting of several of the chiefs and other gentlemen was held at Muirlagan, in Lochaber, where they entered into a bond for their mutual defence, and agreed never to lay down their arms or enter into a general peace, without the consent of all and of each other. Among those present were Lochiel, Young Clanranald, Barrisdale, Dr. Archibald Cameron, John Roy Stuart, Gordon of Glenbucket, Cameron of Dungallon, Lord Lovat, Major Kennedy, and Secretary Murray. A few days before this meeting, £30,000, in six casks, of gold had been received from France, by two frigates, which arrived on the west coast.

It was resolved to raise as many men as possible, and at the same time agreed that the Camerons, Glengarry, Clanranald, Keppoch, and Barrisdale Macdonalds, the Stewarts of Appin, Mackinnons, and Macleans, should assemble on that day week, Thursday, the 15th of May, at Achnacarry; while arrangements were made for the other clans to meet at more convenient centres. Anyone making separate terms with Cumberland for himself was to be held as a traitor to the Prince, and to be treated by all the other leaders as their common enemy.* For various reasons no one attended on the appointed day. Meanwhile Lochiel wrote to Cluny Macpherson as follows :—

LOCHARKAIK, *May 13, 1746.*

Dear Sir,

I have nothing new to acquaint you of. We are preparing for a summer campaign, and hope soon to join all our forces. Mr. Murray desires, if any of the piquets, or the men of Lord John Drummond's regiment, or any other pretty fellows are straggling in your country, that you convene them, and

---

* The following are the Resolutions referred to in the text :—

AT MUIRLAGGAN, *the 8th of May, 1746.*

We, subscribers, heads of Clans, commanders and leaders, do hereby unanimously agree, and solemnly promise forthwith, with the utmost expedition, to raise in arms, for the interest of his Royal Highness, Charles, Prince of Wales, and in defence of our country, all the able-bodied men that all and every one of us can command or raise, within our respective interests or properties.

Item, We hereby promise and agree, that the following Clans, viz., Lochiel, Glengarry, Clanranald, Stewarts of Appin, Keppoch, Barrisdale, Mackinnon, and Macleods, shall rendezvous on Thursday next, the 15th instant, at Auchnacarry, in the braes of Lochaber.

Item, We also promise and agree, that neither of us shall discover or reveal, to any of our men or inferior officers, the resolutions of our present meeting; or the day and place appointed for our rendezvous, till such time as our respective corps are assembled.

Item, To facilitate the junction of our army with all possible speed, it is agreed, that the Frasers of Aird, and others our friends on the north side of the river Ness, shall join the people of Glenmoriston and Glengarry; and that the Frasers of Stratherrick, the Mackintoshes, and Macphersons, shall assemble and meet at the most convenient place in Badenoch, on Thursday the 15th current.

Item, The Macgregors, Menzies, and Glenlyon's people, shall march to Rannoch, and join the Rannoch and Athol men; and be ready to receive intelligence and orders to meet the main body in the braes of Mar, or any other place that shall be most convenient.

Item, It is agreed that Major-General Gordon of Glenbucket, and Colonel Roy Stuart, shall advertise Lord Lewis Gordon, Lord Ogilvie, Lord Pitsligo, the Farquharsons, and the other principal gentlemen of the North, with the resolutions taken at this meeting; and that they shall agree among themselves as to a place of rendezvous, so as to be able to join the army where it shall be judged most proper.

Item, That Clunie Macpherson, and Colonel Roy Stuart, shall advertise the principal gentlemen of the Mackintoshes of our resolutions.

Item, It is agreed, that there shall only be one captain, lieutenant and ensign, two sergeants, and two corporals to every company of forty men; and an adjutant, quarter-master, and surgeon, to every regiment.

Item, That every corps shall appoint an officer and a number of men, not exceeding twelve, to remain in the country; with ample powers to punish deserters, who, immediately at their first appearance in the country, are to be hanged; unless they can produce a pass or furlough from a general officer.

Lastly, We further promise and engage ourselves, each to the other, to stand and abide by these our resolutions, for the interest of his Royal Highness, and the good of our country, which we apprehend to be inseparable, to the last drop of our blood; and never to lay down our arms, or make a separate peace, without

keep them with yourself till we join you; and give them money if you have any to spare. If not, send a trusty person here, and what money will be necessary for them, or other emergencies, shall be remitted to you. I have scarcely a sufficiency of meal to serve myself and the gentlemen who are with me for four days, and can get none to purchase in this country; so I beg you will send by the bearer as much meal as the two horses I have sent will carry, and I shall pay, at meeting, whatever price you think proper for it, besides a thousand thanks for the favour. I have not yet heard of the man I sent from your house towards Inverness to get intelligence. You sent one of your men along with him. Let me know if you had any account of him, or of the woman sent to Edinburgh, with any news you have from the South or North. Mr. Murray sent an express to Mr. Seton, and to ————, desiring they should come to him without loss of time. He is surprised what detains them, and begs you will desire them to hasten.

Some of the men refused to follow their leaders, and others had, in the meantime, delivered up their arms. On the 21st and 22nd, Lochiel, with 300 men, and Barrisdale, with 150, met at the appointed place, but on the 23rd they were surprised by a force of 1500 Government troops, who succeeded in taking one of Lochiel's officers and two of his men prisoners. The chief, who escaped across the lake in a boat, seeing no further chance of resistance, wrote to his brother chiefs advising them to disperse in the meantime, but to preserve their arms as long as possible, as he still hoped for assistance from France.

The following is Lochiel's letter:—

May 26th, 1746.

Gentlemen,
I send you this, to acquaint you of the reasons of our not being in your country ere now, as I last wrote you. Our assembling was not so general nor hearty as was expected, for Clanranald's people would not leave their own country, and many of Glengarry's have delivered up their arms, so that but few came back with Lochgarry to Invermely on Tuesday last, where he staid but one night, and crossed Locharkaik with his men, promising to return with a greater

the general consent of the whole. And in case any one engaged in this association shall make separate terms for himself, he shall be looked upon as a traitor to his Prince, and treated by us as an enemy.

Mr. Home adds:—This copy of the resolutions to take arms, dated Muirlaggan, May 8th, is not signed; but it is evident from the names of the clans mentioned in that paper, and from the letters of Lochiel, Cluny, and Secretary Murray, which follow in the Appendix, that almost every chief and chieftain, who escaped from the battle of Culloden, had agreed to the resolutions; nor is it at all surprising that no signed copy of the resolutions has been found, for the houses of Lochiel, Cluny, and most of the rebel chiefs, were set on fire and destroyed by the King's troops, when they came from Inverness to Fort-Augustus; so that no papers were preserved, but those which, before the arrival of the troops, had been buried in places where the ground was very dry.

number in two days, and that he would guard the passes on that side; neither of which was done, nor have we had any return from the Master of Lovat; so that there was only a few men with Barrisdale, and what men I had on this side of Lochy, who marched Wednesday night to Auchnacarry, where, trusting to Lochgarry's information, we had almost been surprised on Friday morning, had we not learned by other look-outs, that the enemy was marching from Fort-Augustus towards us; upon which we advanced, thinking to make them halt; but their numbers were so much superior that it had no effect, and we were almost surrounded by a party that came by the moor on the side of Locharkaik, who actually took an officer and two men of mine, which made us retreat for twelve miles; and there, considering our situation, it was thought both prudent and proper to disperse, rather than carry the fire into your country without a sufficient number, as was expected. It is now the opinion of Mr. Murray, Major Kennedy, Barrisdale, and all present, that your people should separate, and keep themselves as safe as possible, and keep their arms, as we have great expectations of the French doing something for us, or until we have their final resolutions what they are to do. I think they have little encouragement from the Government, as they get no assurances of safety, but for six weeks. I beg you will acquaint all your neighbours of this, viz., the Mackintoshes, Macgregors, etc., for at present it is very inconvenient for me to acquaint them from this; and be so good as let us hear from you as oft as possible, and when there is anything extraordinary, you may expect to hear of it, and the particulars of the enemy's motions.

Let me hear from you by the bearer, who will find me; and when any of you write to me, please direct as the bearer shall inform you, and let him know how I shall address to you.

P.S.—As Cluny has an easier opportunity of sending to the Master of Lovat than I, it is begged of him to send a double of this to the Master, to let him know what is doing. The above is our present resolutions, and what I have advised all my people to do as the best and safest course, and the interest of the public; yet some of them have delivered up their arms without my knowledge; and I cannot take it upon me to direct in this particular, but to give my opinion, and let every one judge for himself.

While at Achnacarry, the first thing the Camerons did was to hide their effects in the neighbouring woods and caverns, and, expecting that Cumberland's troops would soon deprive them of their cattle, they killed as many of them as they could use, and lived plentifully while they remained. The Prince was hurriedly passing through the district at the time, and visited his friends at Lochiel's residence, where he was prevailed upon, though the king's troops were advancing, to sit down and partake of the repast at the time on the table, "which was plentifully spread with provisions of all sorts, and wine and other liquors, in abundance, which the Highlanders get at a very cheap rate from France; for there being no officers of excise in those parts, except at Fort-William, where there is a garrison, prodigious quantities of liquors are run upon that coast, in exchange for their cattle, which they slaughter and barrel up for that purpose". After some discussion as to whether they would turn out and give battle to the foe, Lochiel, who opposed this, said—" But since the enemy is so near us, let us live as well as possible in the meantime, lest those come to take up our goods who will give us little or no thanks for them. Meanwhile my clan may be driving their cattle to the securest places, and my servants concealing my most valuable effects." His plate was buried in the ground, and the best part of the furniture was put away in the neighbouring caves and recesses. The clan went into the district of Morvern, and the gentlemen soon after left the house, which, in a few days, was burnt to the ground.

Cumberland, who arrived at Fort-Augustus on the 24th of May, almost immediately sent out detachments, with orders to burn the seats of Lochiel, Glengarry, Kinlochmoidart, Keppoch, Cluny, Ardshiel, Glengyle, and others, which they did, and mercilessly plundered the inhabitants. The excesses committed on helpless men, women, and children, are universally admitted to be unparalleled in history. They have made the name of Cumberland and his villainous lieutenant, Major Lockhart, for ever hateful to the Highland race. The latter blasphemously declared, when remonstrated with for his atrocities, that "not even an order from Heaven should prevent him from executing his orders". One writer declares that, "not contented with destroying the country, these bloodhounds either shot the men upon the mountains, or murdered them in cold blood. The women, after witnessing their husbands, fathers, and brothers murdered before their eyes, were subjected to brutal violence, and then turned out naked, with their children, to starve on the barren heaths. A whole family was enclosed in a barn and consumed to ashes. So alert were these ministers of vengeance that in a few days, according to the testimony of a volunteer who served in the expedition, neither house, cottage, man, nor beast was to be seen within a compass of fifty miles ; all was ruin, silence, and desolation. Deprived of their cattle and their small stock of provisions by the rapacious soldiery, the hoary-headed matron and sire, the widowed mother and her helpless offspring, were to be seen dying of hunger, stretched upon the bare ground, and within view of the smoking ruins of their dwellings."* Chambers says that, in addition to the burning of the residences of the chiefs, they plundered and burned those of many inferior gentlemen, and that even the huts of the common people were similarly destroyed. "The cattle, sheep, and provisions of all kinds were carried off to Fort-Augustus. In many instances the women and children were stripped naked and left exposed; in some the females were subjected to even more horrible treatment. A great number of men, unarmed and inoffensive, including some aged beggars, were shot in the fields and on the mountain-side, rather in the spirit of wantonness than for any definite object. Many hapless people perished of cold and hunger amongst the hills. Others followed, in abject herds, their departing cattle, and at Fort-Augustus begged for the support of a wretched existence, to get the offal, or even to be allowed to lick up the blood of those which were killed for the use of the army. Before the 10th of June the task of desolation was complete throughout all the western parts of Inverness-shire; and the curse which had been denounced upon Scotland by the religious enthusiasts of the preceding century was at length so certainly fulfilled in this remote region that it would have been literally possible to travel for days through the depopulated glens without seeing a chimney smoke or hearing a cock crow."†

Some time after this, a party from Brigadier Houghton's regiment came to Achnacarry, and finding destruction and desolation reigning supreme, it occurred to them to make a search, expecting to find some of the valuables which were amissing when the castle was destroyed. At first not a soul was to be seen, but by-and-bye they found the gardener, who had been so anxious about his master's effects

* *History of the Highland Clans.* † *History of the Rebellion*, p. 278.

that he had remained lurking about the place. The poor fellow was soon secured, and severely cross-examined as to the whereabouts of the hidden treasure. He pretended entire ignorance and inability to give any information; whereupon they "tied him to two halberts and lashed him on the naked back with rods, till the smart forced him to discover the place of concealment, where they found the hidden treasure"; and then dismissed him, telling him to go and inform his master of what had occurred—what he saw and suffered.

Lochiel managed to elude those in search of him for about two months, among his people in Lochaber, after which he found it expedient to remove to the Braes of Rannoch. Here he had the professional attendance of Sir Stewart Thriepland, an eminent Edinburgh physician, for the cure of his wounds. On the 20th of June, they met with Macpherson of Cluny, who led them to a more secure retreat in Benalder, on his own property. In a miserable hut at Mellanuair, on the side of this mountain, Lochiel and Cluny lived for several weeks, accompanied by Macpherson of Breakachie, Allan Cameron of Callart, and two of Cluny's attendants. The Prince, who had meanwhile been wandering in the Long Island, and afterwards in Lochaber and elsewhere on the mainland, proceeded to visit his friends on Benalder, with Macdonald of Glengarry and Dr. Archibald Cameron as guides, with two servants. These visitors were all armed, and, at a distance, Lochiel mistook them for a party of militia, who, he thought, had been sent from a Government camp, a few miles distant, in search of him. From the state of his wounds he was unable to escape, and he decided that there was no alternative but to fight. In this there did not appear to be much danger, for his party was equal to the strangers in point of numbers, and they had the advantage that they could fire the first volley without being observed; and, as they had a good stock of fire-arms, they could reload their pieces, and fire the second round before the intruders could reply.

They at once prepared to defend themselves. Twelve firelocks and pistols were prepared; the chief and his four companions took up their positions, and levelled each his piece; all was ready for saluting the approaching party with a carefully aimed volley, when Lochiel recognised his friends. Then, hobbling out as well as he could, he received the Prince with an enthusiastic welcome, and attempted to pay him his respects on his knees. This ceremony Charles at once forbade, saying, " My dear Lochiel, you don't know who may be looking from the tops of yonder hills; if any be there, and if they see such motions, they will conclude that I am here, which may prove a bad consequence!" Lochiel at once ushered him into the hovel, which, though small, was well furnished with viands and liquors. Young Breakachie had previously provided his friends with a good supply of newly-killed mutton, some cured beef sausages, plenty of butter and cheese, a large well-cured bacon ham, and an anker of whisky. The Prince, upon his entry, at the request of his friends, took a hearty dram, which he pretty often called for afterwards, to drink his friends' health; and when some minced collops were dressed for him with butter, in a large sauce-pan that Lochiel and Cluny carried always about with them, and which was the only cooking utensil they had, he ate heartily, and said, with a very cheerful and lively countenance, " Now, gentleman, I live like a Prince," though he had to eat the collops out of the saucepan, but with a silver spoon. After dinner, he asked Lochiel if he had always lived, during his stay in that place, in such a good way; to which Lochiel answered, " Yes, sir, I have; for now near three months I have been here with my cousin Cluny and Breakachie, who have so provided for me that I had plenty of such as you see, and I thank heaven that your Royal Highness has come safe through so many dangers to take a part". From this bothy they removed, two days after, to another shieling, farther into the recesses of the mountain, called Uisge-chiobair, which turned out " superlatively bad and smoky". Remaining here for three days, they removed to the " Cage " at Leitir-na-lic, two miles distant, in a more inaccessible part of Benalder, where there was barely room for the seven persons, who now composed the party, "four of whom were frequently employed playing at cards, one idle looking on, one baking, and another firing bread and cooking". The history and structure of this remarkable habitation is too well known to require detail here. The party remained in it until about one o'clock on the morning of the 13th of September, when information reached them, by messengers sent from Lochaber by Dr. Archibald Cameron and Cluny, who had gone there a few days previously on some private business, that two vessels had arrived at Loch-nan-uagh to carry the Royal fugitive and his friends to France. They started immediately, and on the 16th arrived at Lochiel's seat at Achnacarry, where they remained until night. The accommodation was wretched in the extreme, the house having, as already stated, been burned to the ground by the Government troops. They left the same night, and, on the morning of the 17th, they picked up Dr. Archibald Cameron and Cluny, in a glen at the head of Locharkaig, who killed a cow, on which, with good oaten cakes, they feasted right royally. At daylight on the morning of the 18th, they proceeded on their way, and next day arrived at Loch-nan-uagh, where the Prince, Lochiel, Dr. Archibald Cameron, Young Clanranald, John Roy Stuart, Glenaladale, Lochgarry, Macdonald of Dalily, his two brothers, and several others, went aboard the "L'Hereux". In all, twenty-three gentlemen and a hundred and seven men of humbler rank sailed in the two frigates, and "were seen to weep" as they sailed, most of them for the last time, from their native shore.

Lochiel arrived safely on the coast of Brittany on the 30th of August, 1746, and shortly after obtained from the king the command of Albany's French regiment, with power to name his own officers. He was thus enabled, though his estate was forfeited, to live in the style of a gentleman of his position and rank, and at the same time to find suitable employment for many of his unfortunate friends, in a profession congenial to their tastes and recent experiences. His brother, Dr. Archibald, was appointed physician to the regiment.

Speaking of Lochiel's character, Sir Walter Scott says, that he was one of the most honourable and well-intentioned persons in whom the patriarchal power was ever lodged. "Far from encouraging the rapine which had been, for a long time, objected to the men of Lochaber, he made the most anxious exertions to put a stop to it by severe punishment; and while he protected his own people and his allies, he would not permit them to inflict any injury upon others. He encouraged among them such kinds of industry as they could be made to apply themselves to, and in general united the high spirit of a Highland chief with the sense of a well-educated English gentleman of fortune. Although possessed of an estate, of which the income hardly amounted to seven hundred a-year, this celebrated chief brought fourteen hundred men into the Rebellion, and he was honourably distinguished by his endeavours on all occasions to mitigate the severities of war, and deter the insurgents from acts of vindictive violence."* The same writer says, referring to the chief's generous decision to join the Prince at the outset, against his own better judgment:—"Thus was Lochiel's sagacity overpowered by his sense of what he esteemed honour and loyalty, which induced him to front the prospect of ruin with a disinterested devotion, not unworthy the best days of chivalry. His decision was the signal for the commencement of the Rebellion; for it was generally understood that there was not a chief in the Highlands who would have risen had Lochiel maintained his pacific purpose"; and he adds that, as an example to the rest of his followers, he went the length of ordering one of his men to be shot. After passing the Forth, on the march from Perth to Edinburgh, abuses were committed by the army,—taking sheep in the neighbourhood, and shooting them against orders. It has been stated that he actually

* *Tales of a Grandfather.*

shot this man by his own hand, but the statement is not credible. It is, no doubt, founded on Dougal Graham's *Metrical History of the Rebellion.* The Glasgow Bellman, who appears to have been present, says :—

> Here for a space they took a rest,
> And had refreshment of the best
> The country round could then afford,
> Though many found but empty board,
> As sheep and cattle were drove away,
> Yet hungry men sought for their prey ;
> Took milk and butter, kirn and cheese,
> Of all kinds of eatables they seize ;
> An he who could not get a share,
> Sprang to the hills like dogs for hare ;
> There shot the sheep and made them fall,
> Whirled off the skin, and that was all ;
> Struck up fire and boiled the flesh,
> With salt and pepper did not fash ;
> They did enrage the Cameron Chief,
> To see his men so play the thief ;
> And finding one into the act,
> He fired and shot him through the back ;
> Then to the rest himself addressed :
> "This is your lot, I do protest—
> Whoe'er amongst you wrongs a man ;
> Pay what you get, I tell you plain ;
> For yet we know not friend or foe,
> Nor how all things may chance to go."

Referring to the part Dr. Archibald Cameron took in improving the habits of the people of Lochaber, before Culloden, the author of the Historical Account of his Life says, that he exercised " his talents among a people whose manners and fierceness resembled them very much to the wild beasts of a forest; yet by his gentle and humane carriage among them, many were taught to follow a more honest course of life than is generally ascribed to the Highlanders, especially the Camerons, who have been reckoned the most infamous of all the clans for their thefts and plunderings. The Doctor therefore took as much pains in cultivating the minds of those poor ignorant wretches as he did of their bodies, in prescribing them proper remedies in all their illnesses. So that the whole clan, by means of his and his brother's instructions and regulations, were greatly reformed in their morals ; honesty and industry increased everywhere by the encouragement given by their patrons, who took all imaginable pains to instruct them in the principles of justice and religion, and to civilize their manners by teaching them to behave like rational and sociable creatures." The same writer records the change which came over the people, under these influences, before the battle of Culloden :—"At the breaking out of the Rebellion," he says, "the clan was judged to consist of about 800 fighting men, fit to bear arms, bold, stout fellows, and trained up in the exercise of arms ; but what was most to their praise, they were not so addicted to pilfering and robbing their neighbours, which most of the other clans in the Highlands were notorious for, particularly the Macdonalds ; for young Lochiel being a man of honour and probity himself, took abundance of pains, nor was his brother the Doctor less assiduous in reforming the people of his clan and to infuse into them true notions of justice and honesty ; and as Lochiel was the chief magistrate amongst them, he punished their excesses with a becoming severity, and at the same time endeavoured to inculcate into them better principles, and juster notions of right and wrong than they had hitherto learned. So that though he was both beloved and feared by great numbers of them, yet there were many who hated both him and his brother, because they would not suffer them to spoil and plunder their neighbours, which was allowed by most of the other chiefs of the clans ; but Lochiel little regarded their clamour on that account. He knew his authority was sufficient to keep them in subjection, and he gave himself no trouble about anything they should report against his administration."

Lochiel seems to have kept up a regular correspondence, both with the Chevalier and the Prince during his residence in France. The following, extracted from the *Stuart Papers*, will be found interesting, and will help to illustrate many incidents in Lochiel's latter days not generally known. They will especially show how urgently he advocated another expedition to the Highlands, to regain the British

Crown for the Stuarts, and how his services had been appreciated by the Chevalier and Prince Charles; how a patent of peerage was made out in his favour, though his father was still alive; and various other facts in connection with himself, his family and friends, worthy of record in this connection.

Donald Cameron wrote, from Paris, on the 16th of January, 1747, to the Chevalier de St. George :—

> I most humbly beg leave to renew my duty and respect to your Majesty in the beginning of the year, which I pray God may prove more prosperous to your Royal Family and cause than the present face of things give reason to expect. By what I took the liberty to write on the twenty-sixth of last month, and what your Majesty must have from other hands, it will appear that the present misfortunes though very great are not irretrievable; but at such a distance I fear your Majesty cannot be so fully informed as would be necessary to form a judgment of the real state of affairs, and the true disposition of your Majesty's friends, both here and in Britain, for which reason I am grieved it is not in my power to enable Lord Sempill to wait on your Majesty at this critical juncture, because I am persuaded his informations would determine your Majesty to accept of the succours that can be obtained, rather than expose your faithful Highlanders to utter destruction, and your whole kingdom of Scotland to the slavery with which it is threatened. I even flatter myself that upon such lights as we are now able to transmit in this manner, your Majesty may be graciously pleased to send instructions and directions, since it is visible that the ruin of your Majesty's friends in Scotland would very much discourage, and perhaps totally dispirit, your friends in England, by which means the Restoration would become impracticable, at least so difficult that it could only be effected with an army superior to all the forces of the Government; whereas the landing ten regiments in Scotland before the Highlands are depopulated, will not only unite all the Highlanders, but all other Scotchmen of spirit, in your Majesty's cause, and give so much employment to the troops of the Government, that your Majesty's loyal subjects in England may with small assistance be in a condition to shake off the yoke, and complete their own deliverance and ours by a happy restoration. If it were in my power to represent these circumstances in as clear a light as they appear to me, I am sure that the result of your Royal wisdom would be conformable to my wishes, which will always have the honour and happiness of your Majesty and your Royal Family for their chief object. In whatever situation I may be, of this I have given proofs that I now apprehend may prove fatal to my country; but my comfort is to have acted upon a principle that I am sure is right in preferring the honour of the Royal Family and the public good, which I consider as inseparable to all private conditions whatsoever. According to this principle, from which I shall never deviate, when the Prince, soon after our arrival here, did me the honour to tell me of Lord Ogilvy's application for a regiment, I represented to his Royal Highness that such applications might make the Court of France look on our affairs to be more desperate than they really are, and hinder them from granting the body of troops which they would otherwise be willing to transport into Scotland, because it is not natural that men of any interest or consideration should propose to engage their people in a foreign service, while they can employ them to recover their losses in their own country, for which reason I begged that his Royal Highness's only application might be to obtain the necessary assistance. The Prince seemed to think in the same manner, and I was

persuaded there would be no more mention of regiments for us in this country until there should be no hopes of relieving our own. But his Royal ,s told me, about ten days ago, that there was a grant obtained of a r   r Lord Ogilvy, under your Majesty's approbation. before   Prince   ,,er, as being then the only method thought of to get bread for a gr... ..,, poor gentlemen. His Royal Highness at the same time assured me that all endeavours should be immediately used to obtain another for me, and was pleased on the occasion to use many gracious and kind expressions, of which I shall ever retain a most grateful remembrance, as likewise of the singular marks of favour and probation his Royal Highness, the Duke of York, continues to honour me with. But the more I am sensible of their goodness, the more inconsolable I should be to find designing people suggesting projects that will never be executed, and by these inducing the Prince to lose the glorious opportunity of relieving his distressed friends. I told his Royal Highness that Ogilvy or others might incline to make a figure in France; but my ambition was to serve the Crown and serve my country, or perish with it. His Royal Highness said he was doing all he could, but persisted in his resolution to procure me a regiment. If it is obtained I shall accept of it out of respect to the Prince; but I hope your Majesty will approve of the resolution I have taken to share in the fate of the people I have undone, and, if they must be sacrificed, to fall along with them. It is the only way I can free myself from the reproach of their blood and show the disinterested zeal with which I have lived and shall die.

On the 20th of January, 1747, the Chevalier de St. George wrote to young Lochiel from Rome :—

I received some days ago your letter of the 26th December, and take very well of you your having writ so fully and freely to me. Your great zeal for us and singular attachment to the Prince, joined to your universal good character, will always make what comes from you both acceptable and of weight with me, as it renders me yet more sensible of your losses and sufferings on our account. The honour and reputation the Prince has gained can, no doubt, be a satisfaction to me, but I don't feel the less the hardships and sufferings of my Scots subjects, and the ruin to which the whole kingdom is now exposed. I thank God I had neither hand in, nor knowledge of, the unfortunate undertaking, and whoever encouraged it have much to answer for; but there is no remedy for what is past, and the best way to repair it is to turn our thoughts towards the undertaking some solid expedition, which may have a reasonable prospect of success, and whatever tends to that I shall certainly approve, promote, and encourage as much as depends on me. But as the Prince is now in France, and myself at so great a distance, it is he that must naturally, and indeed necessarily, examine such matters, act, and decide on them. It is not possible I can at present direct in them myself, and should I do it, it might be subject to great inconveniences; though I shall certainly give the Prince the best advice I can betwixt him and me, for advice is the only authority I am inclined to employ with my children; and I now write to the Prince about his giving a hearing to Lord Sempill, and Balhaldy, though I do not think it proper to mention to him your having now writ to me, which I am persuaded you will approve, and not be surprised nor take it amiss if I don't ever enter into more particulars. It is a pleasure to me to think that the Prince has in you so honest and worthy a man about him, and who will, I am persuaded, always act towards him not only with zeal but with a candour and freedom suitable to your character, and the kindness he has for you, while mine for you is as sincere as it will be constant.

The Chevalier de St. George wrote to him again from Rome on the 2nt of February, 1747 :—

I received last Saturday a letter of the 30th January, and take very well of you the freedom with which you write me. By what you say, I am persuaded the Prince has not discovered to you all his motives for his going to Avignon, and I easily feel that that is a step which cannot be relished by those who are not in his secrets : he has delayed writing to me fully on this subject till his arrival at Avignon, on account of his being afraid that his letters might be opened at the post-office at Paris. When I hear from him I shall be better able to judge of the matter ; but whatever lights I may receive from him, you cannot but be sensible, that as long as the Prince is so much nearer the Court of France than I am here, it can never be advisable for me to cut with that Court but in concurrence with the Prince ; and my doing otherwise, would manifestly be subject to the greatest inconveniences, in any case or supposition that can be made, since no project can ever be undertaken and executed without the Prince's approbation, and heading the expedition. I have already writ to the Prince to hear and examine the project in question, and I shall write to him again to the same purpose by this very post, but that is all I can in prudence do, and I should think I was disserting my subjects if I made any other step in that particular. In all this you must be sensible that I can have no other view but the real and the greater good of the cause, in which nobody being so much concerned as the Prince, none can suspect that he should neglect anything that may be for its advantage. This is all I can say on the contents of your letter. I hope this will find Lord Sempill and Balhaldy well again. I shall always be glad to hear from you, for my constant good opinion and kindness will ever attend you.

Lochiel wrote from Paris on the 23rd of February, 1747, to Prince Charles Edward :—

As soon as your Royal Highness was pleased to let me know your intention of moving from hence, my respectful and tender attachment to your person, as well as your cause, obliged me to represent some of the bad consequences that I apprehend might ensue upon your leaving the only country whence you could have a prospect of obtaining any assistance towards retrieving your affairs and relieving your distressed friends. But since reasons that I cannot pretend to understand determined your Royal Highness to proceed, I am very glad to hear that your journey has proved agreeable, and that you are safely arrived at Avignon.

Though your going hither was, and still is, matter of the greatest affliction to all your true friends, and me in particular; yet, upon considering that step in every shape, I persuade myself that your Royal Highness may give it such a turn, and make such use of it, as will not only make your apology to the king of France, but in the end effectually confute the disadvantageous opinion that the world has conceived of it, and force the public to admit your Royal Highness' abilities in the cabinet, as well as your courage and heroism in the field. To render what I would suggest in this view as clear and distinct as possible, I must beg your Royal Highness will be pleased to observe, that, since you left this place, the talk and expectation of peace is become more general and popular. It is said the Marshall de Belleisle, who is quickly expected here, will be sent as Plenipotentiary to the conference of Breda, and from thence into England ; so that, though the king's equipages are getting ready for the field, few people make any doubt but a peace will be soon concluded ; and I remark such are the universal desires of it in this country, that there is reason to fear the Elector of Hanover and his allies will obtain any terms they please to ask in relation to your Royal Highness, which the Court of France will think they can grant with a good grace, since your Royal Highness has, of your own accord, left their dominions. If this should be the case, the many dismal consequences of it are too plain ; and if your Royal Highness be pleased to reflect on them, I am sure there is nothing practicable, nothing so dangerous or desperate, that you would not do to prevent them. But, sir, I am far from proposing anything of that kind to your Royal Highness. I am persuaded it is still in your power to prevent a peace by means that are both wise and honourable. A cursory view of the present state of your affairs will demonstrate that, at least, there is a great probability of your succeeding, if you will be graciously pleased to enter into the measures that are necessary for that end.

Your Royal Highness is not ignorant that, both before and during the time of your last attempt, your English friends were ready and willing to declare for you, if you could either have furnished them arms, or brought a body of troops capable to protect them. There is good reason to believe their disposition is still the same, and it is only for your Royal Highness to get proofs of it. As for the disposition of Scotland, if we could return to the Highlands with artillery, arms, and ammunition, and only four or five battalions of foot, we would not only relieve our distressed friends and save the remains of the country, but deliver the whole kingdom of Scotland from the slavery to which it is, or soon will be, reduced, and put in condition to act uniformly under your Royal Highness, who is so justly become the object of the affections and desires of all ranks of the people, even of many that have hitherto appeared most active against your cause. Indeed I hear from all hands, and have great reason to believe, that all Scotsmen, not excepting those who are most distinguished in the Government's service, are so incensed at the inhumanity with which the Elector has proceeded, and the neglect they have met with since the unhappy action of Culloden, that they only want an opportunity to shew their resentment.

For heaven's sake, sir, be pleased to consider these circumstances with the attention that their importance deserves, and that your honour, your essential interest, the preservation of the Royal cause, and the bleeding state of your suffering friends, require of you. Let me beg of your Royal Highness, in the most humble and earnest manner, to reflect that your reputation must suffer in the opinion of all mankind, if there should be room to suppose that you had slighted or neglected any possible means of retrieving your affairs. Since you cannot obtain such an embarkation of troops as would be necessary to land in England and overturn the Government with one blow, it is surely advisable to try if you can compass what may be sufficient for Scotland. If your Royal Highness were master of that kingdom you could assert your dignity with a high hand, and treat with foreign courts upon equal footing, whereas till you acquire some degree of power, which you can only do by possessing some part of the three kingdoms, the reason of state and necessary policy will always be adduced by every Court in Europe, for the omission of such respects and regards as are due to your Royal birth and just rights.

I hope, and cannot but persuade myself, upon the knowledge both of the goodwill of your heart and the greatness of your spirit, that your Royal Highness will seriously enter into these important considerations, which I am sure will immediately determine you to apply for such succours as the king of France, in the present state of his marine, thinks himself in a condition to support. Your Royal Highness knows that he had condescended in March last, to embark six or seven battalions, with all other necessaries, for your assistance—providing the secret could have been kept within the limits he thought proper, and that, upon Mr. Sullivan's return from Scotland, he actually ordered preparations for the embarking of ten battalions. I hope his Majesty's goodwill is still the same—at least it is fit to make trial of it in the most discreet and prudent manner that can be thought of, and, above all, to do it by hands that will not be disagreeable to him, or to any of the ministers that are necessary for the execution. By this caution, sir, I do not pretend to point out Lord Sempill or my cousin Macgregor [Balhaldy], because your Royal Highness has unhappily conceived a prejudice at those gentlemen. Though I know the king and his ministers have a particular confidence in them, yet I doubt not but your business may be done without directly employing them, if your Royal Highness will be graciously pleased to enter into the following measure: which is to write a proper letter, with your own hand, to the king of France, in which you tell his Majesty that you retired to Avignon in order to avoid observation and suspicion of the present government, because you are sensible that, in the present state of his Majesty's marine, it is impossible to transport even a small body of troops into Britain, unless the embarkation be made with the utmost secrecy. But as you have still the same confidence in his Majesty's friendship and generosity, you have therefore sent the bearer with orders to lay before his Majesty what you judge necessary for retrieving your affairs in Scotland. In my opinion, sir, Mr. Sullivan would be the properest bearer of this letter, because the Court of France has already trusted him, and because the king himself has ordered him to confine the secret within the boundaries he was then pleased to prescribe. If your Royal Highness obtains an embarkation of a small body of French troops for Scotland, the Court of France, being once more engaged with your Royal Highness, will not refuse to reinforce you by wafting your brave Irish regiments, as soon as you are master of the coast of Scotland, and I am persuaded that they will also be willing to transport three or four thousand into Wales, or any place where your English friends shall desire; and I know your English friends will be glad of that small body, as soon as they see your Royal Highness master of the field in Scotland.

The Chevalier de St. George, writing to Prince Charles, from Albano, on the 7th of November, 1747, says:—

I have received my dearest Carluccio's of the 16th October, and am very glad Lochiel has at last got a regiment. I remark, and take well of you, that you do not directly ask of me to declare Lochiel's title, for after what I already wrote to you on such matters, you could not but be sensible that these were things I could not do at this time, were I not to declare all the latent patents (which are in great number), and which it would be highly improper to do. I should please but one, and disgust a great many other deserving people, and in Lochiel's case I should particularly disoblige the other clans, who have all warrants as well as he. Neither is Lord Lismore's case a precedent for others, since his title had not been declared without he had come to be about me in the way he is. Lochiel's interest and reputation in his own country, and his being at the head of a regiment in France, will make him more considered there than any empty title I could give him; and as he knows the justice both you and I do to his merit and services, I am sure he is too reasonable to take amiss my not doing now what would be of no use to him, and would be very improper and inconvenient for us.

Donald Cameron was "a man of good parts, great probity, of an amiable disposition, universally esteemed, and was at great pains to soften and polish the manners of his clan".*

* *Douglas's Baronage.*

He married Anne, daughter of Sir James Campbell, fifth Baronet of Auchinbreck, with issue—

1. John, his heir and successor, born in 1732.

2. James, a man "of great hopes and spirit," a captain in the Royal Regiment of Scots in the service of France, commanded by Lord Lewis Drummond. He died, unmarried, in 1759.

3. Charles, who succeeded his brother John, as chief of the clan.

4. Isabel, who married Colonel Mores of the French service.

5. Janet, who died a nun in the Carmelite Convent, Paris.

6. Henriet, who married Captain Portin of the French service, without surviving issue.

7. Donalda, who died unmarried.

The "Gentle Lochiel" died on the 26th of October, 1748, at Borgue, of inflammation in the head, having been chief for less than a year, when he was succeeded by his eldest son,

XX. JOHN CAMERON,

Described as "a man of extraordinary parts and merits," who "inherited all the virtues of his worthy ancestors, and was esteemed by all who knew him." When his father died he was only sixteen years old. He held the rank of captain in his father's regiment, and afterwards in the Royal Scots. His position in France will appear from the following correspondence, which will also throw additional light on the events surrounding the death of his father, and conclusively establish the esteem in which Lochiel and his family were held by the ex-king and his son.

On the 4th of November, 1748, Drummond of Balhaldy, under the signature of "Malloch," wrote from Paris to the Chevalier de St. George :—

> It is so long since the situation of affairs I had any concern in permitted my troubling your Majesty directly with accounts from this place, that it becomes cruel

in me now to be obliged to begin to inform you of the loss your Majesty has of the most faithful and zealously devoted subject ever served any prince, in the person of Donald Cameron of Lochiel. He died the 26th of last month of an inflammation within his head at Borgue, where he had been for some time with his regiment, and where I had the melancholy satisfaction to see all means used for his preservation, but to no valuable effect. There is no great moment to be made of the death of people who continue in their duty to your Majesty, having no temptation to swerve from it, or of others who have an affectation of zeal and duty to procure themselves subsistence, nor even those whose distresses, when personal, or flowing from oppressive tyranny, determine to be freed of the load by all reasonable means. Lochiel was not in any of their cases. He had all the temptations laid in his way that government could. The late Duke of Argyll, Duncan Forbes, the President, and the Justice Clerk, never gave over laying baits for him, though they knew his mind was as immovable as a mountain on that article; and since he came here he has not been left at ease. The Duke of Cumberland caused information that, if he applied in the simplest manner to him, he would never quit his father's knees, until he had obtained his pardon and favour: this he disdained, or rather had a horror at. I need say no more; his own services and the voice of your Majesty's enemies, speak loudly the loss. The Prince has very graciously interested himself in procuring the regiment Lochiel had for his eldest son, which his Royal Highness has charged Mr. Lally to solicit for along with other officers. It is very unhappy that this Lally has been for some time heartily hated by the minister. I am afraid his appearance will hurt the youth as well as the other affair he is charged with, but there is no help for it. The Prince was positive, and would not allow Sullivan to be employed in it, notwithstanding he had all along agented with the Court all the public affairs Lochiel had since his arrival here. All I can do is to go to Fountainbleau privately, and give what assistance I can for the support of that numerous afflicted family. Had I had the lieutenant-colonelcy of that regiment, as your Majesty graciously inclined I should, and my deceased cousin [Lochiel] wished, above everything on this side of the water, this nomination could have met with no difficulty, because the king and the minister of war would have confided in me for conducting the regiment until Lochiel was of age to do it himself; but my being named to that or any other thing while his Royal Highness continues here and keeps Mr. Kelly to advise him, is inconsistent with the duty and respect both Lochiel and I owed him, and either of us would have suffered anything rather than oppose his will in what regarded ourselves. . . . I am afraid that I shall not be able to continue the connexion and correspondence Lochiel and I had with the Highlands; what was easy for us to have done while he lived and had a regiment, without putting your Majesty to any expense.

To this letter the Chevalier replied from Rome, on the 3rd of December, 1748, as follows :—

I received last week yours of the 4th November. I had already heard of Lochiel's death : it is a loss to the cause, and I am truly concerned for it ; if my recommendation to the Court of France comes in time and has its effect, young Lochiel will have his father's regiment, and on this and all other occasions I shall be always glad to shew him the great sense I retain of the merits of that family . . . I desire Lochiel's lady, his brother, and his son, may find here my condolence on their late loss, which I sincerely share with them.

On the 16th of December, 1748, Dr. Archibald Cameron wrote to the Chevalier de St. George from Paris :—

I, upon having the honour, for the first time of troubling your Majesty with a letter, or rather an apology for not writing sooner, to acquaint your Majesty that my brother Lochiel died on the 26th of October last of ten days' sickness, at a time the most fatal and unlucky for his family and his clan it could have happened, having just completed his regiment at great expense and considerable exertions, and upon the way of reaping the benefits of it towards the maintaining his wife and six children, and providing for some of his friends and dependents, who lost comfortable living to join him in the late desperate and unsuccessful struggle we had in behalf of his Royal Highness in Scotland, and for a little time in England; but now, by his death, they are reduced to the miserable situation they were in before the king of France was pleased, through the application of his Royal Highness, to grant the regiment. Next day after my brother's death, I brought my nephew, of sixteen years of age, in order to lay him flat at his Majesty's feet; then, by his Highness' approbation, to present him to the king of France. Accordingly his Highness made application, and on the 7th of November gave in a memorial asking the regiment for my nephew, and if thought too young, that I, being at present captain of Grenadiers, commandant (in absence of the lieutenant-colonel), and his uncle, would manage the regiment till he was of age, as I am resolved to attend and serve my brother's children and my own, especially as that of Spain does not answer. I would have forwarded a letter I wrote more regular and more fully on the 12th of November, designed for your Majesty; but rather than add in the least to your Majesty's uneasiness by subjects of this kind, and thinking that the Court of France would determine the fate of the regiment long ere now, I kept it from being sent, knowing his Royal Highness would be so good as acquaint your Majesty before the present situation of affairs would induce his Highness to leave Paris. All our corps, and the remains of Lochiel's family, are unanimously inclined to have my nephew, and regiment if obtained, under my directions at present, as is my nephew himself. I beg your Majesty will give assistance towards it.

On the 23rd of the same month, Dr. Cameron wrote him again, urging similar reasons to those stated in his letter of the 16th, as above.

On the 23rd of "February" (? December), 1748, John Cameron himself wrote to the Chevalier de St. George, in the following terms :—

Mr. Macgregor of Balhaldy was so good as to show me a paragraph of a letter from your Majesty this day. It gives me the greatest pleasure to find your Majesty has such a sense of the sufferings of the family I now represent and the death of my father, and could anything add to my loyalty and attachment to your Majesty's royal cause, your seasonable interposition to the Court of France in my favour requires it. In principles of loyalty to your august family I was educated from my tenderest years, and in the same (through God's assistance), I steadfastly purpose to live. And as my nonage doth make me incapable of rendering your Majesty's service all the assistance that could be expected from me and my family, I have appointed Archibald, my uncle, curator and sole manager in all my affairs. I beg leave to inform your Majesty the motives that induced me to this step, which are : he is my full uncle, so that I believe his sincerity to be unexceptionable. He also, from the Prince's going to Scotland, was equally concerned with my father, and then got so much the heart of the clan I represent, that the cruelties committed on them by their barbarous enemies, would not deter them from cheerfully engaging in the royal cause at any time, if, during my minority, they should be commanded by him : to this step I have the unanimous consent of all my friends from Scotland, by express, upon hearing of my father's death, and the officers of the regiment.

The Chevalier replied to these letters from Rome, on the 14th of January, 1749, addressed to Dr. Cameron :—

I received, some days ago, your letters of the 16th December, and, since, that of the 23rd, with one from your nephew, Lochiel, of the same date. It is true I took a very particular share in the great loss you have lately made, being well acquainted with your brothers, and your family's merit with me, and truly sensible of the many marks they have given us of it, as I now am of the sentiments expressed in your letters. By what I lately heard I am afraid Lochiel's regiment will be reformed, but in that case I understand that the officers will be still taken care of, and your nephew and his mother have pensions. I should be very sorry for this reform, neither do I see what I can well do to prevent it, after the very strong recommendation I had already made that the said regiment might be given to your nephew ; but you may be sure that nothing that can depend upon me will ever be neglected which may tend to the advantage of your family, and of so many brave and honest gentlemen. This would be a very improper time to mention you to the Court of Spain, but some months hence I shall be able to recommend you to that Court, and in such a manner as I hope may succeed, if they are any wise disposed to favour you. The Duke [of York] takes very kindly of you the compliments you make him, and I have often heard him speak of you with much esteem and in the manner you deserve. I don't write in particular to your nephew, since I could but repeat what I have here said, and to which I have nothing to add, but to assure you both of my constant regard and kindness.

On the 27th of April, 1753, John Cameron of Lochiel wrote to the Chevalier de St. George, from Paris :—

As your Majesty's enemies have taken possession of my estate in Scotland, and since I have nothing to depend upon in that country till it please God to restore the Royal family, I have now no resource but to push my fortune in the French service. I have been a captain since the year 1747, and am told, that, upon proper application, I might obtain a colonel's brevet, especially as the recommendation his Royal Highness, the Prince of Wales, gave my father, has made our family and their sufferings known to them. If your Majesty would be graciously pleased to write in my favour, I am hopeful it will have the desired effect.

In 1759, John returned to Scotland, where his affable and obliging manner made him universally regarded and beloved. He died of a lingering illness at Edinburgh, in October, 1762, unmarried. His next brother, James, having died before him, in 1759, John was succeeded as representative of the family, by his next surviving brother,

XXI. Charles Cameron,

Third son of the "Gentle Lochiel". He had a commission in the Old 71st, or Fraser Highlanders, when it was first embodied, on which occasion he raised a company, numbering 120, of his clansmen. He obtained leases of parts of the forfeited family estates on easy terms from the Crown. When his regiment was ordered on foreign service, in 1776, he was lying dangerously ill in London, but hearing that his clansmen objected to embark in Glasgow, where they were quartered, without him, he hastened north; but on his arrival in that city, he was pleased to find that the persuasive eloquence of Colonel Simon Fraser of Lovat, commander of the regiment, had the desired effect upon his men, in getting them to return to their duty, especially as Captain Charles Cameron of Fassiefern had been appointed to command them; but the exertion put forth on the journey from London to Glasgow was too much for his then delicate state of health, and he died a few weeks after, universally respected and lamented. He was received in Glasgow, on his arrival, with great demonstration and enthusiasm, where it was generally believed that it was his father who prevented the city from being burnt and plundered in 1746, by the followers of Prince Charles, on their return to the Highlands.

In 1767, he married Miss Marshall, with issue—

1. Charles, born in 1768, and died young.
2. Donald, his father's successor, born in 1769.
3. John, born in 1771.
4. Archibald, born in 1774.
5. Charles, born in 1776.
6. Anne, born in 1773, and married Vaughan Foster, a major in the army, with issue—a son, Charles Foster, married, with issue.

Charles died in 1776, when he was succeeded by his eldest surviving son,

XXII. Donald Cameron,

A minor, seven years old, to whom the estates, previously

vested in the Crown by Act of Parliament, were restored, subject to a fine of £3432, under the Act of General Indemnity, passed in 1784. This Lochiel built the mansion house of Achnacarry, early in the present century, after a design by Mr. Gillespie, a distinguished architect. In *Reminiscences of My Life in Highlands*, by the late Joseph Mitchell, C.E., Inverness, we find a description of a visit to Achnacarry in 1837, in which he says:—"We went through the rooms. The house had been built some thirty-five years previously, and was all but finished when Lochiel's father became disgusted with the place, left it, and never returned. We found that the plaster ornaments of the ceiling lay all that time on the floor ready to be fixed, and the doors of the rooms, of beautiful Highland pine, grown brown with age, leaned against the wall ready to be screwed on. They had remained in this position for thirty-five years. The present year [1837] Lochiel arranged to have the house completed, which has been done, and it is now a handsome residence worthy of the chief. With his French training and education (he was then 54 or 55 years old), and his want of acquaintance with the old clan, and the customs of the country, it can easily be imagined how distasteful a Highland life must have been to him."

He married on the 23rd of April, 1795, Anne, eldest daughter of the famous General, Sir Ralph Abercrombie, Baronet, of Tullibody. She died on the 17th of September, 1844. By her Lochiel had issue—

1. Donald, his heir, born on the 25th of September, 1796.
2. Rev. Alexander Cameron, born in 1806, and educated at Edinburgh and Oxford Universities. He graduated B.A., in 1834, and, in the same year, was ordained clerk in holy orders. He married, on the 1st of September, 1835, Charlotte, daughter of the Hon. and Very Reverend Edward Rice, D.D., Dean of Gloucester. She was raised to the rank of a peer's daughter on the succession of her brother, the Rev. Francis William Rice, in 1869, to the title of Baron Dynevor. Mr. Cameron died in

1873, and his widow, the Hon. Charlotte Cameron, in 1882, leaving issue—(1) Ralph Abercrombie, who was born in 1839, and married, in 1869, Charlotte Anne H. Yea, daughter of the Rev. Henry Thompson, and grand-daughter of the late Sir William Walter Yea, Bart. of Pyrland Hall, Somerset, with issue: Archibald Rice, born in 1870; John Ewen, born in 1874; Ralph Abercrombie, born in 1877; Eleonora Yea; and Christina Charlotte. (2) Edward Alexander, C.E., who, born in 1843, married in 1873, Emma, daughter of the late Rev. Edward Bankes, of Soughton Hall, Flintshire, Canon of Gloucester and Bristol, and of the Hon. Maria Bankes, sister of the late Baron Dynevor, without issue. (3) Anne Emily; (4) Catharine Charlotte.

3. Mary Anne, who, on the 2nd of September, 1846, married Lord John Hay, Rear-Admiral, R.N., C.B., third son of James, seventh Marquis of Tweeddale, without issue. She died on the 30th of November, 1850; and he on the 27th of August, 1851.

4. Matilda.

Lochiel died in 1832, when he was succeeded by his eldest son,

XXIII. DONALD CAMERON,

A captain in the Grenadier Guards. He was present at Waterloo; and he retired from the army in 1832. Of him Mr. Mitchell says, that "unfortunately he was equally ignorant of the habits of Lochaber and its people," with his father, and that he "was obliged from ill-health to reside in England, and the administration of his estates was entrusted to his relative, Sir Duncan Cameron, under whom Mr. Andrew Belford, a writer in Inverness, acted as factor, Sir Duncan placing implicit confidence in his management. With a view to increasing the rental, Mr. Belford followed the then prevalent custom of removing the people and converting the hill-sides of Loch Arkaig into sheep-farms." This Belford afterwards purchased the estate of Glenfintaig. "From time immemorial eight or nine families had lived on this estate. They were a remarkably fine race, distinguished for good dispositions, great size, and athletic frames. 'The Dochenassie men,' as they were called, were the beau-ideal of magnificent Highlanders. They had their cottages and arable crofts on the low ground near Loch Lochy, and their sheep-farm was in common divided into nine parts, of which Mr. Belford, when he purchased the estate, acquired one part. He granted these men leases of nine years, by which, according to the first Reform Act, he acquired nine votes in the county, and expected, no doubt, that the tenants would vote for him. Unfortunately at the first election the votes were found to be of no value, as Mr. Belford, from his economical habits, omitted to have the leases stamped. By having a share of the sheep-farm Mr. Belford discovered that it was a very profitable concern, yielding about £100 per annum to each tenant, or £900 in all, which he thought he might as well secure to himself. Accordingly at the termination of their leases, all these men got notice to remove, and were cleared off." He retained the farm in his own hands, and in the first winter of his occupancy, in 1852, he lost not less than 600 of his sheep in a severe snow-storm.

On the 31st of July, 1832, Lochiel married Lady Vere Catharine Louisa Hobart, daughter of the Hon. George Vere Hobart, sister of Augustus Edward, sixth and present Earl of Buckinghamshire, and grand-daughter of Alexander MacLean, fourteenth of Coll, by his wife Catharine, eldest daughter of Cameron of Glendesseray. By this lady Lochiel had issue—

1. Donald, his heir, now of Lochiel, born on the 5th of April, 1835.

2. George Hampden, born October, 1840; died on the 23rd of June, 1874, unmarried.

3. Anne Louisa, who died, unmarried, on the 24th of June, 1864.

4. Julia Vere, who married, on the 14th of June, 1870, Colonel Hugh Mackenzie, Commandant, Royal Military

Asylum, Chelsea, with issue, a son, Kenneth Donald, and a daughter, Mary Vere Charlotte.

5. Sibella Matilda, born in 1838; and married the Rev. Henry George John Veitch, eldest son of the Rev. William Douglas Veitch, of Eliock, Dumfriesshire, with issue, a son, George Douglas, and two daughters, Vere Matilda Lisette, and Sybil Eleanor.

6. Albinia Mary, born 1840, and died in 1861.

Lochiel died on the 4th of January, 1859, when he was succeeded by his eldest son,

XXIV. DONALD CAMERON,

Now of Lochiel, and M.P. for the County of Inverness since 1868. In 1883-4, he was a member of the Royal Commission appointed to inquire into the Grievances of the Highland Crofters. He was educated at Harrow, and was in the Diplomatic Service, first as Attache to Lord Elgin's Mission to China, in 1857, and afterwards to the Embassy at Berlin. From 1874 to 1880, he was Groom-in-Waiting to the Queen. He is D.L. and J.P. for the County of Inverness, and D.L. for the County of Argyll. On the 9th of December, 1875, he married Lady Margaret Elizabeth, second daughter of Walter, fifth Duke of Buccleuch and seventh of Queensferry, K.G., with issue—

1. Donald Walter, his heir, born in 1876.
2. Ewen Charles, born in 1878.
3. Allan George, born in 1880.

The following document, courteously supplied to us by the Lyon Depute, Edinburgh, will be found interesting in more respects than one :—

"Donald Cameron of Lochiel Esquire, son and heir of Charles Cameron Esquire, who was lawful son and heir of Donald Cameron of Lochiel Esquire, the undoubted Representative and Chief of the antient family of Lochiel and Chief of the Clan Cameron, *Bears* Gules two Bars or, *Crest*, a Sheaf of Five arrows proper, tied with a Band Gules, *Motto* Unite. On a compartment below the Shield on which are these words *Pro Rege et Patria* are placed for Supporters Two Savages wreathed about the heads and middles with Oak Branches proper each holding in his exterior hand a Lochaber axe of the Last: Which Armorial Ensigns above blazoned We do hereby ratify confirm and assign to the said Donald Cameron Esquire, and the Heirs male of his body as their proper Arms and Bearing in all time coming.

"And whereas in the Month of February 1792 Allan Cameron of Erracht, in consequence of a misrepresentation of Facts made to the late Keeper of the Lyon Records, now deceased, found means to obtain a Patent from this Office declaring that the Male representation of the above Family had devolved upon him and assigning to him the Arms of said Family in the Character of the Representative thereof, which Patent though signed and Unduly Impetrated from the said Keeper of The Records was not recorded in the Lyon Register, nor any Fees of Office paid for the same, the Misrepresentation above-mentioned having been previously discovered and the Registration and Receipt of Fees of Course immediately prohibited.

"Notwithstanding whereof, and of a formal Intimation and requisition made to the said Allan Cameron on the subject, he, the said Allan Cameron does, as is alledged, still hold and make use of said Patent so improperly obtained as a Legal and Effectual Deed.

"Therefore we do not only hereby declare the said Patent to have been, from the Beginning, Ineffectual, Void, and Null as having never been Recorded, but also, and Separately that the said Patent having been obtained upon Misinformation and Misrepresentation as above-mentioned and Retained by the said Allan Cameron contrary to good Faith and without Authority from Us, is not and shall not be entitled to any Credit or Authority whatever in judgment or out of the same in all Time Coming, and we appoint this Declaration to be inserted in the Public Records of the Lyon Office along with the Present grant. In Testimony of All which these presents are Subscribed by Robert Boswell Esquire, and the Great Seal of the Lyon Office Appended.

(Signed)   "RO. BOSWELL,
"Lyon-Dep."

(1795.)

DR. ARCHIBALD CAMERON.

DR. ARCHIBALD CAMERON was the fourth son of John Cameron, eighteenth of Lochiel, the grandson of Sir Ewen Dubh, and brother of the "Gentle Lochiel" of 1745. He was born in 1707, and was originally educated for the Bar, but "observing that in order to be properly qualified for an advocate he must be master of all the quirks and sophistical reasonings that are usually made use of to puzzle a cause and hoodwink the understanding with factitious arguments," he applied himself to the study of a science "more agreeable to his natural genius and bent of mind"—the medical profession, which was finally chosen by him. He studied anatomy under Dr. Alexander Munro, then a distinguished professor, like his father before him, in the University of Edinburgh; while he studied physic under Dr. Sinclair, one of the most eminent professors of his day. He afterwards travelled abroad, and studied for some time in Paris. Having thus fully qualified himself for the practice of his profession, he returned to Lochaber, where he married and settled among his own people. According to one authority, his services were much required morally, as well as physically. The author of *The Life of Dr. Archibald Cameron*, published in London in 1753, says that he "who might have made a considerable figure even in a Court, or a populous and well-cultivated city, contents himself with exercising his talents among a people whose manners and fierceness resembled them very much to the wild beasts of a forest; yet by his gentle and humane carriage among them, many were taught to follow a more honest course of life than is generally ascribed to the Highlanders, especially the

Camerons, who have been reckoned the most infamous of all the clans for their thefts and plunderings. The Doctor therefore took as much pains in cultivating the minds of these poor ignorant wretches as he did of their bodies in prescribing them proper remedies in all their illnesses. So that the whole clan, by means of his, and his brother's instructions, were greatly reformed in their morals. Honesty and industry increased everywhere by the encouragement given by their patrons, who took all imaginable pains to instruct them in the principles of justice and religion, and to civilize their manners, by teaching them to behave like rational and sociable creatures." The author of the booklet from which we quote is not known; but it is beyond question that he was as wofully ignorant of the character of the Highland people as he undoubtedly was of the history of that family to whom Dr. Cameron belonged. Considering how severely the author writes against the Highlanders generally and the Camerons in particular, it is agreeable to find him writing so favourably of Dr. Cameron, who, he informs us, "was a man of no ambition but of a quiet and easy temper," whom the reader must not expect to find "engaged in any notable exploits, his only or chief business in the army" of Prince Charles "being to attend his brother Lochiel, and to assist him with his skill if any disaster should happen to befal him in battle". The same writer also informs us that "the doctor could not for a good while be prevailed upon to join" Prince Charles, and that he strongly urged upon his brother Donald to keep out of the rebellion. "He remonstrated in the strongest terms upon the insurmountable obstacles that he foresaw would attend the undertaking, and the terrible consequences of a miscarriage. Lochiel, however, would take no denial, telling him, that he did not want the assistance of his sword or his valour, but only desired he would attend him as his companion, that he might always have the advantage of his advice and skill, in case the fortune of war should render either of them necessary. The doctor, how ill-soever he thought of the cause, yet his affection for his brother, and the many signal obligations he lay under to him, at length prevailed over all other considerations, and he submitted to share his brother's fate whatever it should be. But though the doctor was, with great reluctance, and, in a manner, forced to join his brother's measures, yet he absolutely refused to accept any commission in the army; neither did he act there, as ever I could learn, in any other capacity than as a physician.* He was perfectly unacquainted with the military art, and therefore wholly unqualified to give his advice, or even his vote in council, upon any operations that were proposed by the chiefs or general officers. Yet as he was always among them, it is supposed, at least in the eye of the law, that he countenanced, encouraged, and, as much as it was in his power, assisted the rebels, in all their outrages against the government. Dr. Cameron was of so humane a disposition that, if credit be given to general report, when any wounded prisoners were brought to him, he was as assiduous in his care of them, as if they had fought in the cause he espoused; and it is affirmed that he never refused his assistance to anyone that asked it, whether friend or foe." This appears to be a very fair estimate of Dr. Cameron's character.

At Falkirk, Lochiel in the heat of the action was wounded by a musket-ball in the heel, "which being observed by his brother the doctor, who always kept near his person, he begged him to retire to have it dressed, which he accordingly did; but as the doctor was lending him his assistance he himself received a slight wound". Lochiel's wound was, however, slight, for we have seen that he was able to lead his men into Falkirk after the battle.

We have also seen that Lochiel was severely wounded at Culloden, in both ankles, when he was carried off the field by his two henchmen, assisted by the doctor, who dressed his wounds with every possible care, and followed him in his wanderings for some months after, doing everything

---

* The writer is clearly wrong here, as will be seen hereafter.

that filial affection and medical skill could suggest to effect a speedy cure of his wounds.

Dr. Cameron finally escaped with Prince Charles, Lochiel and others, on the 18th of September, to France, where he received an appointment as physician and captain in Albany's regiment—to which his brother had been appointed Colonel—in which position he remained until Lochiel's death in 1748, when Dr. Cameron was transferred to a similar position in Lord Ogilvy's regiment, in the same service. We have already given some of Dr. Cameron's letters, referring to the death of his brother Lochiel, and to the position in which his family and friends were left, in consequence of that event. In a letter to the Chevalier de St. George, dated, Paris, 23rd of December, 1748, he says, referring to a previous one of the 16th of the same month, and already given in full:—

Upon my laying my nephew at his Royal Highness's feet, his Highness was so good as to recommend to the Minister of War, Comte D'Argenson, the giving the regiment to my nephew, in lieu of his family's sufferings, upon which I, by the advice of general officers of the army, and at the unanimous desire of all the captains of the Albany Regiment, I gave in a memoir to the minister, asking the regiment for my nephew; but if thought too young to command it, I would take charge of it in his name during his minority, as his uncle, captain of Grenadiers, and commandant of the Regiment of Albany, now upon the peace being concluded, I would undertake to recruit the regiment of our numerous, though much reduced clan, and other Scotch we have interest with. Though the Comte has not given their answer as yet, in relation to the regiment, yet as they all are well known to the merit and readiness to serve of my brother and family when your Majesty's cause is in hands, and his suffering upon the misgiving of the late attempt in Scotland; also they are sensible of my share in it, and of my having a wife and throng family of children to maintain. I plainly understand they have compassion for us, which will give my nephew the better chance for the regiment—which I attribute to your Majesty's being so good as to recommend my nephew to them, of which I was advised this day by a letter from my wife, from Graveline's being told so by Major Ogilvie of our regiment, as also by our cousin, Balhaldy, who acquainted me of your Majesty's sympathy in our loss through the death of my brother, which gives us, the remaining part of Lochiel's family, great pleasure to think that any assistance or little services our family was ready to offer towards the royal cause should have such a grateful impression on your Majesty; but as there is no return in my power, for your Majesty's constant care of us, but what in my duty I, as well as others, at all times will promise, which is my readiness to serve your Majesty, the sincerity of which your Majesty cannot have proofs of except the royal standard was displayed in British fields,—but if that was the case, I hope I will have the loyalty and courage to draw my sword,—whereas, on this side of Dover, I can be of no use, rather a trouble to your Majesty. As that of the Cabinet is above my capacity and ambition, I never attempt dabbling in state affairs; my whole study, while abroad, is to keep as free as possible from being a burden on your Majesty, but sorry to be obliged to trouble your Majesty in recommending the maintenance of me, my wife, and family to this court, to whom I am much obliged for my support, having got no pay, nor no appearance of it as yet, from the court of Spain ; and the reason I was not named lieutenant-colonel of my brother's regiment, as his Highness and my brother intended long before the regiment was obtained, was, that at the time the regiment was granted, it was thought my pay in Spain would punctually answer, though I even all that time had not absolute faith in its being paid duly, which my family would require. However, how soon Clunie was named upon the supposition of my being provided for in Spain, both in obedience to his Royal Highness, and the regard I had for Clunie, as a worthy, honest, and brave man, who suffered by the common misfortunes, I not only succumbed but approved, and does still, of Clunie's enjoying it,—especially as it is reported that he will be over this winter; but if either he do not come over, or if the court, despairing of him, will propose to name another lieutenant-colonel, it's allowed by everybody as well as all our corps that I have the best title to expect it, especially as my nephew puts his whole confidence in me, in relation to the management of his affairs during his minority.

On the 16th of January, 1750, Alexander Macdonald, younger of Glengarry, writing from Boulogne-sur-Mer to Mr. Edgar, referring to his recent visit to Scotland, says : " It is with regret I find myself obliged to acquaint you, in order that you inform his Majesty, of the conduct of Dr. Archibald Cameron, brother to the late Lochiel, whose behaviour, when lately in the Highlands, has greatly hurt his Majesty's interest by acquainting all he conversed with that now they must shift for themselves, for his Majesty and Royal Highness had given up all thoughts of ever being restored. I have prevented the bad consequences that might ensue from such notions ; but one thing I could not prevent, was his taking 6000 Louis-d'ors of the money left in the country by his Royal Highness, which he did without any opposition, as he was privy to where the money was laid, only Cluny Macpherson obliged him to give him a receipt for it. . . . I am credibly informed that he designs to lay this money in the hands of a merchant at Dunkirk, and enter partners with him." In another letter, addressed to Prince Charles, young Glengarry refers to this subject and says, " as to the account I sent of the embezzling of the money by Clunie and Dr. Cameron, with some others of his family, most of that money is still in the country ". He, however, appears to have been himself charged with a similar offence, for he complains that people " have spread a report that I touched considerably of it when last in Scotland". And this is apparently true, for he hopes his Royal Highness will "approve of the trifle I or any of my friends received". In the same connection, Ludovick Cameron of Torcastle wrote to Prince Charles, from Paris, on the 21st of November, 1753, thus :—

> I would not have troubled your Highness with these lines if I did not think my honour was engaged to clear myself of an imputation which has prevailed too much among my countrymen, and I am afraid may have made some impression on the generous mind of your Royal Highness. My nephew, Dr. Cameron, had the misfortune to take away a round sum of your Highness's money, and I was told lately that it was thought I should have shared with him in that base and mean undertaking. I declare, on my honour and conscience, that I knew nothing of the taking of that money until he told it himself at Rome, where I happened to be at the time, and that I never touched one farthing of it, nor ever will, having been mostly ignorant of the Doctor's proceedings, he never consulting me about anything he undertook since we first came in this side of the water.

Dr. Cameron's wife, writing to Mr. Edgar, from Paris, on the 25th of January, 1754, makes a charge against young Glengarry, showing that a bad feeling existed between the parties; which must be held to account to a considerable degree for their reflections upon each other. She says that "Henry Pelham, brother to the Secretary of State, declared to Sir Duncan Campbell of Lochnell that in 1748-49 young Glengarry came to him offering his most faithful and zealous service to the government in any shape they thought proper, as he came from feeling the folly of any further concern with the ungrateful family of Stuart, to whom he and his family had been too long attached, to the absolute ruin of themselves and country". She intimated this information under pressure from her friends, who thought it ungrateful on her part to conceal it any longer from those who had so befriended herself and her family.

In a letter to Mr. Edgar, dated Douay, the 11th of June, 1751, Dr. Cameron, after intimating the death of Sir William Gordon of Park, lieutenant-colonel of Lord Ogilvy's regiment, proceeds :—

> I cannot in justice to myself, but acquaint you, that, at the forming of it first, in January, 1747, a little before I went with the Prince to Spain, my Lord Ogilvie having his Royal Highness's approbation, gave me a commission as oldest captain

in his regiment, which I enjoyed till, in October thereafter, I was made captain of Grenadiers in my brother's regiment, and ever since I got a company a second time in this regiment, it is allowed by the most experienced officers of the army, that it is my due to be oldest captain now, and as there is a lieutenant-colonel awanting, I cannot help being so vain as to think myself more entitled to it than any other in the regiment, and I find all the gentlemen in the regiment think it a great hardship upon them if any shall be named who has not already a commission in the regiment, as it may prove a precedent for a step of preferment being lost (both now and upon any vacancy hereafter), to every individual from the lieutenant upwards, so if you think it proper, I wish you would apply to the king for a recommendation to my Lord Clare and my Lord Ogilvie (who were always my good friends) towards naming me lieutenant-colonel. The principal advantage I propose by this is to be a means to procure me a retreat if at any time I see occasion for it according as things turn out, especially if the ball received at Falkirk, and is still in my body, give me as much trouble and pain as it did in winter and spring last, which helped the continuance of my sickness at that time,—so I should propose, in case it may render me incapable of serving, to live in the way it may give me least trouble. However, I leave all to your prudence.

When the Chevalier de St. George was informed of the execution of Dr. Cameron, he wrote, on the 9th of July, 1753, to Lord George Murray—"I am stranger in particular to the motives which carried poor Archibald Cameron into Scotland ; but whatever it may have been, his hard fate gives me the more concern, that I own I could not bring myself to believe that the English government would have carried their rigour so far". On the following day, Mr. Edgar wrote Prince Charles a letter from Rome, in which he says :—

I had the honour to write you on the 19th December last by the king's command, which I hope has gone safe to your hands. As there happens now a subject of great charity to write you about, and having still no other way than by you to mention it to the Prince, I beg you will let his Royal Highness know as soon as you can, that the king is persuaded he would be very much concerned for poor Archibald Cameron's untimely and cruel death, and for the forlorn condition his wife and seven children are left in, especially since the appointments of a Spanish colonel, in consequence of a commission his Royal Highness obtained when he was at Madrid, for Archy, now fails. It was a long while before his Majesty could, by frequent and strong recommendation, bring the court of Spain to begin the payment of these appointments. Archy's family needs now the continuance of it more than ever. The king, therefore, designs to recommend it in the strongest terms to the court of Spain, to renew the commission of colonel to Dr. Cameron's eldest son, and that the appointments of it should be paid at Paris, or to give an equivalent pension to his mother to be paid at the same place. But as his Majesty foresees that this is a grace that will be very hard to be obtained, he thinks, that, as the first favour was granted to the Prince, his Royal Highness would write to him a few lines in French, such as he may send to the court of Spain in recommending also the affair in his Royal Highness's name, that if anything could do, might prevail on that court to grant the charity so much wanted for poor Archy's family, when you inform the Prince of the contents of the letter, I humbly beg. If the Prince should think fit to write, as is proposed, it will be charity to do it as soon as he can, and the king, in expectation of his letter, will wait ten or twelve weeks before he recommends the affair in question in Spain.

It is stated that a collection was made in 1749, "among those who were friends to the Pretender's cause, for the support of his unhappy adherents abroad. Dr. Cameron came over to England to receive a part of the money contributed. And a collection was set on foot, in 1753, for the same purpose, and the doctor made advances to his friends in England for a part of it, representing by his letters, that his pay in the army was not sufficient to support him and his numerous family. But after many solicitations, not receiving any satisfactory answer, he came over himself; and this, according to some authorities, was the business that brought him to Scotland, when he was discovered, apprehended, and taken to London." We have the following account of the manner of his apprehension :—" On Monday, March 26th, Dr. Cameron, brother to Lochiel, who was engaged in the last rebellion, and attainted, was brought prisoner to the Castle of Edinburgh ; he was taken by a party of Lord George Beauclerk's regiment, who was detached from the fort of Inversnaid in search of him ; this detachment was commanded by one Captain Graven. They had information of the house where he was to stay some days, but in their march to it, were obliged to pass through two small villages ; at the end of the first they saw a little girl, who, as soon as she perceived soldiers, ran as fast as she could ; a sergeant and two or three men pursued her, but she reached the other village before they could overtake her ; and there she sent off a boy, who seemed to be placed there to give intelligence of the approach of the soldiers. The soldiers then pursued the boy, but finding they were not able to come up with him, the sergeant called out to his men to present their pieces, as if they intended to shoot him ; the boy on this, turning round, begged his life ; they secured him, and then went to the house where the doctor was, which they beset on all sides. The disposition the captain made was admirable; he, with some of his men, marched up to the front of the house, but was soon discovered from the window, where he was immediately secured by the sergeant above-mentioned, who was placed there, as the captain very judiciously suspected the doctor might attempt an escape from that part of the house." After a short confinement in Edinburgh Castle, Dr. Cameron was sent up to London, and condemned on the attainder passed against him, and the others engaged in the Rebellion, shortly after Culloden.

The author of the doctor's Life, though quite unreliable when dealing with proceedings in Scotland and in the Highlands, appears to have been well-informed as to the details of Cameron's imprisonment and execution in London. His account of these we shall give at length. He says that, on "Thursday, May 17th, Dr. Cameron was carried from the Tower, attended by several of the warders and a party of the Guards, to the Court of King's Bench, and then arraigned upon the Act of Attainder passed against him and others, for being in the late rebellion, and not surrendering in due time. The four Judges were on the Bench, and the prisoner not being desirous to give the Court any trouble, readily acknowledged himself to be the identical person; whereupon, after due deliberation, the Lord Chief Justice Lee pronounced the following moving sentence: 'You, Archibald Cameron of Lochiel, in that part of Great Britain called Scotland, must be removed from thence to his Majesty's prison of the Tower of London, from whence you came, and on Thursday the 7th of June next, your body to be drawn on a sledge to the place of execution, there to be hanged, not till you are dead; your bowels to be taken out, your body quartered, and your head cut off, and affixed at the king's disposal, and the Lord have mercy on your soul'. On receiving the sentence, he made a genteel bow, and only desired he might have leave to send for his wife, who with seven children, entirely dependent on him for support, are now at Lisle in Flanders, which was granted. He said, that in 1746, he came from France to surrender himself, agreeable to the Proclamation, but was prevented by an accident happening to his family. He behaved with great resolution before the Court, and answered to every question with a becoming decency. During the interval between the sentence and his execution, his wife used all possible means to obtain a pardon, by delivering a petition to his Majesty, another to her Royal Highness the Princess of Wales, and to several of the nobility; but without effect, for on Thursday, June 7th, he was conveyed in a hurdle from the Tower to Tyburn, and there executed agreeable to his sentence. His behaviour was all along firm and intrepid, yet decent and solid, and becoming a man who expected, yet feared not, the stroke of death. On Wednesday, orders were sent to the Tower that the gates should be shut at six o'clock in the evening, and no persons whatever admitted after that hour, to prevent any attempt that might be made to favour his escape. As soon as his wife arrived from Flanders, she immediately repaired to her husband, in the Tower, who received her with all that tenderness and affection which the greatness and solemnity of the occasion could inspire. The grief and anguish of her soul is much more easily imagined than described. She came to take her last farewell of him, who, by all the ties of mutual affection, was dearer to her than all the world. And as an aggravation of her affliction, she not only saw herself about to be deprived of an affectionate husband, but to be left destitute of a support for herself, and her numerous family. Their children, the dear pledges of their love, must now be exposed to all the necessities and casualties of life, without the patronage of a kind and indulgent father to have recourse to for advice and assistance. The consideration of this train of evils now hastening upon her, made such a strong impression on her mind, as to force a flood of tears from her mournful eyes. The doctor comforted her as well as he could, and desired her to use all the means in her power to save his life; which was to present a petition in his favour, to his

Majesty, who, perhaps, might be prevailed upon to save him. On the morning of his execution, she took her last leave of him; indeed it was a very mournful one, and melted those who saw it into tears. The excess of her grief has so affected her senses, that she is now distracted; so great was her love for her husband, and so intense her sorrow for his sad catastrophy. As soon as she was gone, the doctor put himself in readiness to receive the Sheriff and those who were sent to conduct him to his execution. Accordingly, about ten o'clock he was brought out of the Tower, by a party of the Horse Guards, who delivered him to the Sheriffs of London and Middlesex, as soon as he was come without the Tower-Gate. He was then put into the hurdle, to which he was fastened by the executioner. In this manner, he was drawn through the city, attended by Sir Richard Glynn, one of the Sheriffs, and under the care of the Sheriff's officers and constable, to the place of execution. Sir Charles Asgill left the prisoner at the Tower, and Sir Richard Glynn followed the sledge from the Tower, in his chariot, to Tyburn. The doctor was dressed in a light-coloured coat, red waistcoat and breeches, and new bag-wig. In his passage though the streets, he was observed to look about, as if in admiration of the vast multitude of spectators that crowded the streets, windows, and balconies to see him pass, and bowed to several persons; about twelve o'clock he arrived at the place of execution. Having arrived there, and helped into the cart, he desired to speak with the Sheriff; who being come to him, the doctor entreated the favour of him, that he would give orders to his officers to let his body hang till he was quite dead, before the executioner began his further operation. The Sheriff promised to oblige him in his request; and accordingly the body was permitted to hang full three quarters of an hour, and was not cut down before it was very certain that no life was remaining in him. He had likewise some discourse with the executioner about the disposal of his body after the execution was performed, which he desired might be decently put in a coffin, and conveyed to Mr. Stephenson's the undertaker, and that his clothes might be given to his friends, in lieu of which, that he might not lose his usual perquisite, he bid him take what money was in his pockets. While he was in the cart, a gentleman in a lay-habit, came to him, and prayed with him for about a quarter of an hour, and then left him to his private devotions. From this incident, the spectators imagined that the doctor was a Roman Catholic, and that the gentleman who prayed with him was a priest. But whatever his religion was, he died with great steadiness, constancy, and resolution, without any visible alteration in his countenance or behaviour, but perfectly resigned to the will of Heaven, and cheerfully acquiescing with the sentence which the laws of his country had passed upon him. He made no public profession of his faith, nor declared what religion he was of; nor did he address the people in a speech ; nor did he give any letters or papers to the Sheriff, or any other gentleman present at the execution, so that if anything of this kind should hereafter be published, we may look upon it as spurious. His body being taken down from the gallows, the executioner cut off the head, and took out the bowels, but did not quarter the body. His body and head were put into a coffin, with this inscription upon it: 'Dr. Archibald Cameron, suffered the 7th of June, 1753, aged 46'." A hearse conveyed it to Mr. Stephenson's, undertaker, opposite Exeter Change. *

It has been repeated by several writers that his visit was in connection with the money left in the Highlands by Prince Charles, mention of which has been already made ; while others maintain that he came over in connection with another projected rising in favour of the Prince. For the latter there does not seem to be any foundation whatever. Respecting the former, T. L. Kingston Oliphant, in *The Jacobite Lairds of Gask*, states distinctly that it was the French money "that lured" him back to Scotland; and, in an account which the same writer gives of what became of the money, immediately after the battle of Culloden, he

* *Life of Dr. Archibald Cameron*, London, 1753.

says that £5500 was "keept by Captain Archibald Cameron". From this, as well as from several other known facts, it is quite clear that he held a commission in the Highland army, notwithstanding what has been said by others to the contrary. That he conducted himself at the last in a manner worthy of his race, is admitted by all. His fate was universally lamented; the friends and best-wishers of the government considered his execution, so long after the attainder, a most unnecessary and wanton act of barbarous cruelty, and the king himself when asked to sign his death-warrant, partook of the same feeling; for he expressed his unwillingness to sign it, and exclaimed, "Surely there has been too much blood spilt on this account already". His Majesty's advisers must have been a cruel, blood-thirsty set.

Sir Walter Scott says that his execution, so long after all hostilities were over, on his old attainder, "threw much reproach upon the government, and even upon the personal character of George II., as sullen, relentless, and unforgiving;" for the doctor was a man of mild and gentle disposition, and had uniformly exercised his skill as a medical man in behalf of the wounded of both armies.* The government of France settled a pension of 1200 livres per annum upon his widow, and 400 upon two of his sons, then in the French service, in addition to their regimental pay.

Though it is quite true that, at the place of execution, he did not hand any documents or papers to those about him, he did so to his wife, before he left the prison; and a copy of what he "intended to have delivered to the Sheriff of Middlesex at the place of execution, but which he left in the hands of his wife for that end," has been found among the Gask papers, and is printed in the appendix to the *Jacobite Lairds*, as follows:—

On the first slip of paper:—

TOWER, *5th June, 1753.*

Being denied the use of pen, ink, and paper, except in the presence of one or more officers (who always took away the paper from me, when I began to write my

* *Tales of a Grandfather.*

complaints), and not even allowed the use of a knife, with which I might cut a poor blunted pencil, that had escaped the diligence of my searchers, I have notwithstanding, as I could find opportunity, attempted to set down on some slips of paper, in as legible characters as I was able, what I would have my country satisfied of, with regard to myself and the cause in which I am now going to lay down my life.

As to my religion, I thank God I die a member, though unworthy, of that church in whose communion I have always lived, the Episcopal Church of Scotland, as by law established before the most unnatural rebellion began in 1688, which for the sins of these nations hath continued to this day: and I firmly trust to find, at the most awful and impartial tribunal of the Almighty King of kings, through the merits of my Blessed Lord and Saviour Jesus Christ, that mercy (though undeserved) to my immortal part which is here denied to me by my earthly by an usurper and his factions, though it be well known I have been the instrument in preventing the ruin and destruction of many of my poor deluded countrymen who were in their service, as I shall make appear before I have done, if opportunities of writing fail me not.

On the second slip of paper :—

In order to convince the world of the uprightness of my intentions while in the Prince of Wales's army, as well as of the cruelty, injustice, and ingratitude of my murderers, I think it my duty in this place to take notice how much better usage I might have expected of my country, if humanity and good-nature were now looked upon with the same eyes as in the times of our brave and generous ancestors; but I'm sorry to observe that our present men in power are so far sunk below the noble spirit of the ancient Britons, as hardly at this day to be distinguished from the very basest of mankind. Nor could the present possessor of the throne of our injured sovereign, if he looked on himself as the father and natural prince of this country, suffer the life of one to be taken away who has saved the lives and effects of above 300 persons in Scotland, who were firmly attached to him and his party; but it seems it is now made a crime to save the lives of Scotsmen. As neither the time nor the poor materials I have for writing, will allow me to descend to a particular enumeration of all the services I have done to the friends of the Usurper, I shall therefore only mention a few of the most known and such as can be well attested. In July, 1745, soon after the setting up of the Royal Standard, before our small army had reached Corayarick, it was moved by some of the chiefs to apply to the Prince for a strong detachment of clans to distress Campbell of Invera's house and tenants in that neighbourhood, which my brother Lochiel and I so successfully opposed, by representing to our generous leader (who was always an enemy to oppression), that such proceeding could be no way useful to his undertaking, that the motion was entirely laid aside, to the no small mortification of the proposer. My brother and I likewise prevented another such design against Breadalbane, to the great satisfaction of our dear Prince. And on our return from Glasgow

ARCHIBALD CAMERON.

On a third slip of paper :— *

My brother and I did services to the town of Glasgow, of which the principal gentry in the neighbourhood were then, and are to this day sensible, if they durst

---

* Note by Gask. "Mr. Cameron's custom was, when interrupted, to subscribe his name, in order (as he told his wife) to authenticate what he had written, lest he should not have another opportunity of adding anything further."

own the truth; but that might be construed disaffection to a government founded on and supported by lies and falsehood. On our march to Stirling, I myself (though I am like to meet with a Hanoverian reward for it) hindered the whole town of Kirkintulloch from being destroyed and all its inhabitants put to the sword by my brother's men, who were justly incensed against it for the inhuman murder of two of Lady Lochiel's servants but two months before.

Here was a sufficient pretence for vengeance, had I been inclined to cruelty, but I thank God nothing was ever farther from my nature, though I may have been otherwise represented. Mr. Campbell of Shawfield likewise owes me some favors done to himself and family, which at least deserve some return in my behalf; and Lady Campbell of Lochnell, now in London, can, if she pleases, vouch for the truth of some of the above facts.

ARCHIBALD CAMERON.

June 6th, 1753.

On a fourth slip of paper :—

I thank kind Providence I had the happiness to be early educated in the principles of Christian loyalty, which as I grew in years inspired me with an utter abhorence of rebellion and usurpation, though ever so successful; and when I arrived at man's estate I had the joint testimony of religion and reason to confirm me in the truth of my first principles. As soon therefore as the royal youth had set up the king his father's standard, I immediately as in duty bound repaired to it, and I had the honour from that time to be always constantly about his person till November, 1748, excepting the short time his Royal Highness was in the Western Isles after the affair of Culloden. I became more and more captivated with his amiable and princely virtues, which are indeed in every instance so eminently great as I want words to describe. I can further affirm (and my present situation and that of my dear prince can leave no room to suspect me of flattery), that as I have been his companion in the lowest degrees of adversity ever prince was reduced to, so have I beheld him too, as it were, on the highest pinnacle of glory, amidst the continual applauses, and, I had almost said, adorations of the most brilliant court in Europe, yet he was always the same, ever affable and courteous, giving constant proofs of his great humanity and of his love for his friends and his country. What great good to these nations might not be expected from such a prince, were he in possession of the throne of his ancestors! And as to his courage, none that have heard of his glorious attempt in 1745, I should think, can call it in question. I cannot pass by in silence that most horrid calumny raised by the rebels under the command of the inhuman son of the Elector of Hanover, which served as an excuse for unparalleled butchery, committed by his orders, in cold blood, after the unhappy affair of Culloden, viz. : that we had orders to give no quarter; which if true must have come to my knowledge, who had the honour to serve my ever dear master in the quality of one of his aide-de-camps. And I hereby declare I never heard of such orders. The above is truth.

ARCHIBALD CAMERON.

I likewise declare on the word of a dying man, that the last time I had the honour to see his Royal Highness, Charles Prince of Wales, he told me from his own mouth, and bid me assure his friends from him, that he was a member of the Church of England.

ARCHIBALD CAMERON.

On a fifth slip of paper :—

To cover the cruelty of murdering me at this distance of time from the passing of the unjust Attainder, I am accused of being deeply engaged in a new plot against this government (which if I was, neither the fear of the worst death their malice could invent, nor the blustering and noisy threatenings of the tumultuous council, nor mnch less their flattering promises could extort any discovery of it from me), yet not so much as one evidence was ever produced to make good the charge. But it is my business to submit, since God in His all wise providence thinks fit to suffer it to be so. And I the more cheerfully resign my life as it is taken away for doing my duty to God, my king, and my country; nor is there anything in this world I could so much wish to have it prolonged for, as to have another opportunity to employ the remainder of it in the same glorious cause.

ARCHIBALD CAMERON.

I thank God I was not in the least daunted at hearing the bloody sentence which my unrighteous judge pronounced with a seeming insensibility till he came to the words, "*But not till you are dead*," before which he made a pause, and uttering them with a particular emphasis, stared me in the face, to observe, I suppose, if I was as much frightened at them as he perhaps would have been in my place. As to the guilt he said I had to answer for, as having been instrumental in the loss of so many lives, let him and his constituents see to that; at their hands, not at mine, will all the blood that had been shed on that account be required. God of His infinite mercy grant they may prevent the punishment that hangs over their guilty heads, by a sincere repentance and speedy return to their duty.

I pray God to hasten the restoration of the Royal Family, without which these miserably divided nations can never enjoy peace and happiness, and that it may please Him to preserve the King, the Prince of Wales, and the Duke of York, from the power and malice of their enemies, to prosper and reward all my friends and benefactors, and to forgive all my enemies, murderers, and false accusers, from the Elector of Hanover and his bloody son, down to Samuel Cameron the basest of their spies, as I freely do from the bottom of my heart.

ARCHIBALD CAMERON.

I am now ready to be offered; I have fought a good fight, all glory be to God.

The following is added, at the foot, by his widow:—"The above is a faithful transcript of what my husband left with me as his dying sentiments". A monument was erected to Dr. Cameron, by her Majesty's permission, in 1846, in the Chapel Royal, Savoy, by his representative, the late Charles Hay Cameron, for several years Legal Member of the Supreme Council of India.

Boswell, in the *Life of Dr. Johnson*, relates the following incident:—Johnson used to be a pretty frequent visitor at the house of Richardson, the author of *Clarissa*. Hogarth one day, soon after the execution of Dr. Cameron, came to see Richardson, and, being a warm partizan of George II., he observed to Richardson, that certainly there must have been some very unfavourable circumstances lately discovered in Dr. Cameron's case, which had induced the king to approve of his execution for rebellion, so long after it was committed, as this had the appearance of putting the man to death in cold blood, and "was very unlike his Majesty's usual clemency". While Hogarth was talking he perceived a person standing at a window in the room, shaking his head, and rolling himself about in a strange and ridiculous manner. He concluded that this person was some idiot whom his relations had placed under the care of Richardson. To his great surprise, however, this figure stalked forward to where he and Mr. Richardson were sitting, and all at once took up the argument and burst out into invective against George II., as one who, upon all occasions, was unrelenting and barbarous, mentioning several instances, particularly that, when an officer of high rank had been acquitted by court-martial, George had with his own hand struck his name off the list. In short, the peculiar figure displayed such a power of eloquence, that Hogarth looked at him with astonishment, and actually imagined that this idiot had been at the moment inspired. Dr. Johnson, for it was he, and Hogarth were not introduced to each other on this occasion. To this story, Boswell adds the following footnote: —" Impartial posterity may perhaps be as little inclined as Dr. Johnson was to justify the uncommon rigour exercised in the case of Dr. Archibald Cameron. He was an amiable and truly honest man, and his offence was owing to a generous, though mistaken principle of duty. Being obliged, after 1746, to give up his profession as a physician and to go into foreign parts, he was honoured with the rank of Colonel both in the French and Spanish service."

Dr. Archibald Cameron married Jean, daughter of Archibald Cameron of Dungallon, with issue—

1. John, a colonel in the French service.

2. Donald, a partner in the banking house of Harley Cameron & Son, George Street, Mansion House, London. He resided for several years at Valentine, Essex, of which county he was Sheriff in 1791. He married Mary Guy, the daughter of a noted Jacobite, with issue—(1) Charles, who carried on the male representation of the family, and

of whom presently, with other members of his family ; (2) a daughter, who died unmarried.

3. Margaret, who married Captain Donald Cameron of Strone, with issue—a son, Captain Donald Cameron, an officer in the 21st Scots Fusilier Guards, who fought throughout the whole of the Peninsular campaign. He married Anne, daughter of Duncan Campbell, factor for Maclean of Ardgour, widow of Allan Cameron, Inverscadale, well known among his countrymen as " Alein Mac Sheumais," with issue—(1) Donald, late a lieutenant in the Bombay Fusiliers, since retired, and emigrated to Australia, where he resides, unmarried ; (2) Colin John Macdonald Campbell, late captain in the 24th Bombay Native Infantry, who died, in 1884, at Nairn, unmarried ; (3) Charles, a squatter, Netley, Wentworth, Australia, unmarried ; and (4) Margaret Anne, who married the Rev. Mr. Beaumont, Greenwich, without surviving issue. Dr. Cameron had four other children, of whom we have been unable to secure any trace.

He was succeeded as representative of the family by his eldest son,

II. JOHN CAMERON, a colonel in the army, who married Elizabeth, daughter of the honourable George Hamilton (sixth son of James sixth, and brother of James seventh Earl of Abercorn), M.P. for Wells, and Deputy-Cofferer for the Prince of Wales, by his wife, Bridget, daughter and heir of Colonel William Coward, Wells, county of Somerset. In Douglas's *Peerage*, where the marriage is recorded Colonel Cameron is described as " a general in the French service ". He predeceased his wife, who, as her second husband, married the Comte de Fari.

By his wife Colonel Cameron had issue—

1. John.
2. Another son, who died unmarried.
3. Peggy, who died unmarried.

On his death Colonel Cameron was succeeded as representative of the family, by his eldest son,

III. JOHN CAMERON, a captain in the army, who died

unmarried, when the male representation devolved upon his cousin-german,

IV. CHARLES CAMERON, eldest son of Donald, second son of Dr. Archibald Cameron, Civil Commissioner of Malta, and, afterwards, on the 22nd of December, 1803, appointed Captain-General and Governor-in-Chief of the Bahama Islands. He married in 1789, Lady Margaret Hay (who died in 1832), daughter of James, fourteenth Earl of Erroll, with issue—

1. Charles Hay.
2. Donald, who died young.
3. Isabella Hay, who married General Darling, Lieutenant-Governor of Tobago, with issue—several sons, all of whom died without surviving issue, except Sir Charles Darling, K.C.B., Governor of Victoria, who married three times, leaving issue—Charles, a lieutenant in the Royal Engineers, and several other sons; also a daughter, who married Colonel Tyler, R.A.
4. Mary Hay, who, on the 7th of May, 1814, married Admiral the Hon. Philip Wodehouse (born on the 16th of July, 1773, and died on the 21st of January, 1838), with issue—(1) Edwin, born in 1817, C.B., and A.D.C. to the Queen; a colonel in the Royal Artillery, and a Knight of the Legion of Honour, who, on the 16th of October, 1845, married Catharine, only daughter of the late Captain John Street. Colonel Edwin Wodehouse died on the 6th of October, 1870, leaving issue—(*a*) Edwin Frederick, born on the 20th of February, 1851, now a captain in the Royal Artillery, married, with issue; (*b*) Catherine Mary Phillipa, who, on the 27th of June, 1877, married James Andrew Thomas Bruce, commander, Royal Navy, youngest son of Sir Henry Bruce, Baronet of Dowanhill, County of Londonderry; and (*c*) Alice Katharine, who, on the 9th of December, 1875, married James M. Carr Lloyd, only son of Colonel Carr Lloyd of Lancing Manor, Sussex. (2) Constantine Griffith, who, born on the 21st of March, 1847, married, on the 7th of April, 1858, Fanny Isabella, eldest daughter of the Rev. Edward H. Sawbridge, rector

of Thelnethan, Suffolk. (3) Phillip Cameron, chaplain at Hampton Court Palace, born on the 22nd of January, 1837, and married, on the 12th of April, 1866, Mary, second daughter of the Rev. Edward H. Sawbridge, of East Haddon Hall, county of Northampton. Admiral Philip Wodehouse and Mary Hay Cameron had also four daughters —Margaret, Agnes, Jane, and Eleanor Mary, all of whom died unmarried. (4) Margaret Hay, who died unmarried.

Charles Cameron was succeeded as representative of the family by his only surviving son,

V. CHARLES HAY CAMERON, Legal Member of the Supreme Council of India. In 1838, he married Julia Margaret Pattle, with issue—

1. Eugene Hay.

2. Ewen Hay, of St. Regulus, Ceylon, who married Annie, daughter of Edward Chinnery, M.D., Lymington, Hants, with issue—(1) Ewen Hay ; (2) Julia Hay.

3. Hardinge Hay, of Her Majesty's Civil Service, Ceylon. He married Katharine Anne, daughter of the Rev. Dr. Norman Macleod. She died without issue.

4. Charles Hay, still unmarried.

5. Henry Herschell Hay, still unmarried.

6. Julia Hay, who married Charles Lloyd Norman, Bromley Common, Kent, with issue—six children.

Charles Hay Cameron was succeeded as representative of the family by his eldest son,

VI. EUGENE HAY CAMERON, major, Royal Artillery, who married Caroline Catherine, daughter of John Denis Browne, sometime M.P. for County Mayo, with issue—

1. Archibald Denis Hay.

2. Donald Hay.

3. Caroline Beatrice.

4. Caroline Margaret Hay.

THE CAMERONS OF FASSIEFERN.

I. JOHN CAMERON of Fassiefern, second son of John Cameron, eighteenth of Lochiel, by his wife, Isabella, sister of Sir Duncan Campbell of Lochnell, was the first of this family. He entered the mercantile profession and resided for a considerable period of his life in the West Indies, where he became a successful merchant. He was a Burgess of the City of Glasgow, his Burgess ticket being still in existence, and dated in July, 1735. Though he did not actually join in the Rising of 1745, he is said to have materially aided his brother Donald at that time with money to provide him with the sinews of war. He was suspected by the Government, who charged him with having abstracted documents connected with claims upon the forfeited estates of Lochiel, which were alleged to have been forged. Of this charge he was found guilty, "on very slender evidence, and after very arbitrary proceedings," was banished from Scotland, by an Act of Sederunt of the Court of Session, for ten years, during which period he resided at Alnwick in England.* He married Jean, daughter of John Campbell of Achallader, with issue—

1. Ewen Cameron, created a Baronet on the 8th of March, 1817, for the distinguished military services of his son John, colonel of the 92nd Gordon Highlanders.
2. Donald.
3. Archibald, who died without issue.
4. Charles, killed at Savannah in 1779, during the

* The Rev. Dr. Clerk of Kilmallie says, "that he was imprisoned for a period of seven years and exiled for another".—*Memoir of Colonel John Cameron of Fassiefern.*

American War, in the Old 71st regiment. General Stewart of Garth describes his death on the landing of the regiment, in December, 1779, in the river Savannah, a little below the town of the same name, in the following terms:—" Captain Cameron immediately pushed forward to attack the advanced post of the enemy stationed beyond the landing place. As the light infantry advanced, the enemy fired a volley by which Captain Cameron, an 'officer of high spirit and great promise,' and three men were killed."*

5. Catharine, who married MacIan, chief of the Macdonalds of Glencoe, with issue—(1) Alexander, who married his cousin Mary, daughter of Sir Ewen Cameron of Fassiefern, with issue—six sons and two daughters.—John, Ewen, Colin, Alexander, Ronald (who married a Miss Thomson, by whom he had a son and daughter), Alister, Louisa, and Jane. Jane married —— Macdougall, with issue—two children. (2) Anne, who married W. Stewart, without issue. (3) Jane, who married Mr. Kennedy. (4) Catharine.

6. Isabella, who married Alexander Campbell of Ardshiel.

7. Margaret, who married Dr. Foster, with issue—several children.

8. Mary.

9. Lucy, who married the Rev. Dr. Ross, minister of Kilmonivaig, with issue—five sons and two daughters.

10. Johanna, who married Ewen Campbell of Corrie, with issue—some of whose descendants settled in America.

John Cameron was succeeded in Fassiefern by his eldest son,

II. SIR EWEN CAMERON, created a Baronet, as already stated, in 1817. He resided at Inverscadale House, since the property of Maclean of Ardgour. He married Lucy, daughter of Duncan Campbell of Barcaldine and Glenure, with issue—

1. John, a colonel in the army, born at Inverscadale on the 16th of August, 1771; killed at Quatre Bras, and of whom presently.

* *Sketches of the Highlanders*, Vol. II., p. 121-2.

THE CAMERONS OF FASSIEFERN. 283

2. Duncan, afterwards Sir Duncan Cameron, Baronet.

3. Peter, commander of the East Indiaman "Balcarras," H.E.I.C.S., who died unmarried.

4. Mary, who married her cousin, Alexander Macdonald of Glencoe, with issue—John, and others.

5. Jean, who, in 1787, married Roderick MacNeil of Barra, with issue—(1) Roderick, a general in the army and colonel of the 78th Highlanders, who married, in 1818, Isabella, daughter of Lieutenant-Colonel Charles Brownlow of Lurgan, County of Armagh, and sister of the first Baron Lurgan, with issue—a daughter, Caroline, who married an officer in the 78th Highlanders. (2) Cameron; (3) Ewen; (4) Anne, who married John Campbell of Achallader, with issue—John and Jane; (5) Louisa; (6) Jane, who, on the 15th of July, 1828, married the Right Hon. Charles Brownlow, created Lord Lurgan in 1839, with issue—Charles Edward, the present Baron, and Clara-Anne-Jane, who married William Macdonald of St. Martin's Abbey, Perthshire, with issue—one son, Montague William Colquhoun Farquharson, late of the Grenadier Guards, born in 1852.

6. Catherine, who, in 1798, married Colonel Duncan Macpherson of Cluny, with issue—(1) Ewen Macpherson, C.B., the present chief, who married Sarah Justina, daughter of Henry Davidson of Tulloch, with issue—*(a)* Duncan, C.B., late colonel of the 42nd Royal Highlanders (Black Watch), who married Emily, daughter of Major-General Philips Harris, without issue; *(b)* Ewen Henry Davidson, late colonel commanding the 93rd Sutherland Highlanders, unmarried; *(c)* George Gordon, late captain, Coldstream Guards, who married Bertha Maria, second daughter of the late Matthew Marsh of Ramridge, sometime M.P. for Salisbury, Wilts, with issue—one daughter, Georgina; *(d)* Albert Cameron, who married Frances, eldest daughter of the late Rev. Henry Addington Howton, Grange, Bedfordshire; *(e)* Caroline, who married George Dartmouth Fitzroy, late captain, Royal Navy, with issue—two sons and three daughters—Ewen, Symon, Emily, Georgina, and Mar-

garet ; (*f*) Catherine, unmarried ; *(g)* Lucy, who married Edward Fitzroy, major, Royal Artillery, a brother of her eldest sister's husband, with issue—a daughter, Eva.

Colonel John Cameron having died before his father, Sir Ewen (who died in 1828) was succeeded in the Baronetcy by his second son,

III. SIR DUNCAN CAMERON, W.S., who married Mary Cameron, with issue—an only daughter,

IV. CHRISTINA CAMERON, who, in 1844, married the late Alexander Campbell of Monzie and Inverawe, sometime M.P. for the County of Argyll, with issue—

1. Christina, who, in 1865, married Henry Spencer Lucy of Charlecote Park, Warwick, with surviving issue — four daughters, Ada Christina, Constance Linda, Sybil Mary, and Joyce Alianore.

2. Louisa, who married, first, Captain Alexander Macdonell Bonar, R.A., second son of Andrew Bonar of Kimmerghame, Berwick, and Marsali, second daughter of the famous Glengarry who died in 1828, without issue. She married, secondly, on the 10th of August, 1875, John Peter William Campbell of Barcaldine, retired major-general, Bengal Staff Corps, and third son of Sir Duncan Campbell of Barcaldine and Glenure, with surviving issue—Ian Alastair, and Christina.

3. Jane, unmarried.

Mr. Campbell of Monzie died in 1869. Mrs. Campbell succeeded her father in 1863, as heiress of entail.

COLONEL JOHN CAMERON OF FASSIEFERN.

The family removed from Inverscadale to Fassiefern while John was yet quite young. He was nursed by Mrs. Macmillan, whose husband was provided with a holding at the head of Loch Arkaig. Of his foster-brother, Ewen Macmillan, and his devotion, we shall learn much to his credit as we proceed. During Lochiel's exile in France, Ewen Cameron of Fassiefern became his legal representative in Lochaber. John was thus brought up on the most intimate relations with the clan. He went first to the

Grammar School of Fort-William, at that time considered a very good educational institution, after which he had the services of a private tutor. He subsequently completed his education at King's College, Aberdeen. Dr. Clerk informs us that though during the whole of his educational course he was attentive to his studies, and made respectable progress in every branch to which his mind was directed, "he was by no means distinguished for scholarship, nor did his youth afford any prognostication of future eminence. He spent his vacations in those sports and exercises which then formed, as they still do, much of the pastime of every Highland gentleman, fishing, shooting, and especially stalking the deer." These sports formed a very different school to what they do now, requiring "vigour of will and of muscle, resolution and activity," whereas now the noble monarch of the forest, after having been fed on turnips and hay like cattle, is, in most cases, driven to the muzzles of the rifles of drawing-room and easy-chair sportsmen, like sheep to the slaughter. In following the native sports of his country, John Cameron became inured to every description of hardship, thus accustoming a naturally strong constitution to the hard life that was in store for him, in after years, in the service of his country.

He loved to converse in his native tongue, and his mind was well stored with its lore and songs. He had a partiality for Highland bagpipe music, and "it was his delight, after he got the command of a Highland regiment, to march at its head, surrounded by the entire band of pipers, to some of whom he often showed personal regard". All this naturally endeared him to his men, when he came to command them as an officer.

He was apprenticed to the Law, with James Fraser of Gorthlick, W.S., Edinburgh, but the profession did not prove congenial to his tastes, and, having expressed a strong desire to enter the army, his father, in 1793, purchased a commission for him in the 26th or Cameronian Regiment, he being then twenty years of age. At this time Mr. Campbell of Ardchattan raised an Independent Highland Company, and instead of joining the Cameronians, John Cameron entered this Company, afterwards incorporated with the 93rd Sutherland Highlanders, as lieutenant. When the Marquis of Huntly resolved upon raising a regiment in 1794, he offered Ewen Cameron of Fassiefern a commission for his son, John, in this regiment, at first designated the 100th, but afterwards the 92nd Gordon Highlanders. Fassiefern at first declined the offer, pleading his inability to raise the number of men which would entitle his son to the rank proposed, whereupon the noble Marquis intimated that he would be glad to have young Cameron a captain in his regiment, though he should not bring a single recruit along with him. The father was not the man to accept such an honour without doing his part if possible, and so, by the aid of his chief Lochiel, and his brother-in-law, MacNeill of Barra, who sent him twelve stalwart men, John Cameron was able, in a short time, to join the Gordon Highlanders with a company of one hundred brave Highlanders. With these he arrived in due course in Aberdeen, where it was proposed to draft them into separate divisions of grenadiers and light infantry. This they refused, and it was with great difficulty that Cameron prevailed upon them to submit to the rules of the service; for they at first declared that they would not on any conditions be separated from each other, nor would they serve under any other commander than John Cameron, whom they had followed hither as their leader.

The regiment was ordered, shortly after, to Gibraltar, where a dispute arose between Captain Cameron and Lieutenant (afterwards Sir John) Maclean, of the same regiment, which ended in a duel, in which neither of the combatants were much the worse. In 1798, the regiment went to Ireland, where Captain Cameron met a young lady, with whom he fell in love, and whom he engaged to marry. His father, on learning of the proposed alliance, peremptorily objected to it, subject to his sternest displeasure, whereupon the young captain wrote to the lady's father, explaining his position, releasing the lady from her engagement, at the same time declaring that he considered himself bound to her while he lived, and regretting the life-loss to which, in the circumstances, he was doomed by his father's displeasure. He had informed his father that the sacrifice made in giving obedience to his will was at the expense of his own future happiness; but it was of no avail, the old gentleman was inflexible. The young lady soon after married another, with whom she lived happily; but Cameron continued disconsolate, kept single, and declared to his father, on repeated occasions, the saddened state of his mind; at one time writing to him, when he applied for active service, that he was "utterly indifferent whether it should be in Otaheite or Botany Bay". In 1799 he served with his regiment in Sir Ralph Abercromby's expedition to Holland, and under Sir John Moore. On the 2nd of October in the same year, Captain Cameron was severely wounded in the knee at the battle of Egmont-op-Zee. It was he who sent two men of his regiment to carry Sir John Moore off the field, when he was very severely wounded on that occasion. Referring to this incident Sir John Moore writes to Lieutenant-Colonel Napier from Richmond, on the 17th of November, 1804, for a drawing of arms. He says: "I have chosen [for supporters] a light infantry soldier for one, being colonel of a light infantry regiment, and a Highland soldier for the other, in gratitude and commemoration of two soldiers of the 92nd, who, in action, on the 2nd October, raised me from the ground when I was lying on my face wounded and stunned (they must have thought me dead), and helped me out of the field. As my senses were returning, I heard one of them say, 'Here is the General, let us take him away,' upon which they stopped, and raised me by the arm. I never could discover who they were, and therefore concluded they must have been killed. I hope the 92nd will not have any objection—as I commanded them, and as they rendered me such service—to my taking one of the corps as a supporter." Sir John offered a reward of £20 to the men who carried him off the field, but no one ever claimed it, clearly showing that his assumption as to their having fallen was correct.

Cameron's foster-brother, Ewen Macmillan, who accompanied him throughout, was wounded by a Frenchman, whom he noticed, while on outpost duty, at some distance. Stalking him, as he was in the habit of doing with the deer on Loch Arkaig side, Macmillan got within shot of him, and deliberately aiming at him from behind a low wall, the Frenchman noticed him, and quicker than the Highlander, who considered himself in fair security, he fired sooner than Macmillan, and shot away his ear. The Highlander instantly returned the fire ; the Frenchman fell, but to make sure work of him, Macmillan rushed forward to where he lay, and transfixed him to the ground with his bayonet. Returning to the ranks, and finding his master, he informed him, in Gaelic, of what had occurred, saying : "The devil's son, do you see what he did to me?" "You well deserved it, Ewen, for going beyond your post," replied Captain Cameron ; whereupon his foster-brother declared, "He'll not do it again, faith"; which was true enough, and seemed almost to have quite satisfied Macmillan for the loss of his ear.

On the conclusion of this service the regiment came home, and Captain Cameron returned to Lochaber, on leave of absence, accompanied by his devoted foster-brother. Having again joined his regiment, which embarked for the coast of France, on the 27th of May, 1800, he served under Generals Maitland and Lord Dalhousie in succession, in the Mediterranean. This expedition did not prove a success, and Cameron writes, " I shall ever regret, and feel perfectly ashamed that I belonged to this army ". They were soon after, however, ordered to Egypt, under Sir Ralph Abercromby, arriving at Aboukir on Sunday the 1st of March, 1801, embarking on the 8th, when they victoriously fought the battle of the Sand-hills.

After the battle of Mandora, where Cameron's company

held an advanced position, and on which occasion the gallantry of the 92nd called forth special commendations from the Commander-in-Chief, Captain Cameron was promoted to a majority. He was wounded at the battle of Alexandria, where he signally distinguished himself, receiving a gold medal from the Sultan for his gallant services. After the Egyptian Campaign, Major Cameron returned home with his regiment, when they were ordered to Scotland, and quartered for a time in Glasgow. In 1805 we find them in Feversham and Canterbury, in the County of Kent, forming part of a brigade commanded by Major-General John Hope, who, on the 24th of June in that year, wrote to the Duke of York, "strongly recommending Major Cameron as highly-deserving of his Royal Highness's favourable notice". He was on duty in St. Paul's Cathedral at Lord Nelson's funeral. On the 11th of January, 1806, he writes, on this subject, from London, that he "had the honour to lead the procession with a small detachment of cavalry, and four light companies of the line. When we arrived at St. Paul's, I formed my party within the railings. The rest of the troops, with the exception of the Grenadiers, passed on to Moorfields. Though the honour was great, the trouble was by no means slight, as we were under arms from six in the morning till half-past seven at night, during most of the time of which I was on horseback."

Soon after this he accompanied the regiment to Ireland. In 1807 he applied for permission to join the First Battalion, one hundred picked men from his own, the Second Battalion, having been transferred to the first, but the Commander-in-Chief positively refused to grant his request. On the 23rd of May, 1808, he was promoted to a brevet lieutenant-colonelcy, and, in the following June, was appointed lieutenant-colonel. At this time he wrote home—"I would rather than a thousand pounds that I was with our regiment in Spain," the First Battalion of which was crowning itself with glory under Sir John Moore. At Corunna, the 92nd lost its commander, Lieutenant-Colonel

Napier of Blackstone, and Cameron succeeded to the command of the First Battalion of his regiment as senior lieutenant-colonel, at the early age of thirty-seven.

The Walcheren expedition, under Lord Chatham, was entered upon in July, 1809, and Colonel Cameron, with his regiment, composed of a thousand men, formed part of it; but this fine body was afterwards reduced by fever and ague to an effective force of about three hundred men. This severe loss was, however, soon made up by recruits from the Second Battalion. The regiment, with the other remnants of this fine army, was recalled from Walcheren, and the 92nd quartered at Woodbridge, in the County of Suffolk. From this place Colonel Cameron writes, on the 14th of December, 1809, a letter from which Dr. Clerk makes the following interesting quotation:—" The poor little Bo-man's (cattle herd's) son is alive, and doing well. He is our quarter-master sergeant, and Kennedy's son from Moy, Peter Mor's friend, is our sergeant-major. I do all I can, of course, to keep our own people uppermost if they at all deserve it. The Bo-man's son has begged of me to forward you (enclosed) one-half of a ten-pound note to assist his father's family. The other half he will forward to his brother by next post. He is a very *siccer* lad. Not one of the poor fellows who came with me has ever behaved ill—none of them has even a questionable character. Poor Mackenzie from Balachulish, or rather from Ounich, was taken prisoner on the retreat through Spain, and has not since been heard of." This letter shows the personal interest Colonel Cameron took in and the knowledge he had of all his men. He never lost an opportunity of promoting his Lochaber friends, many of them having obtained commissions by his influence and interest in their behalf.

In the beginning of 1810, his father wrote to Colonel Cameron, urging him to retire on half-pay, and at the same time offering to make every provision to maintain him in a good position for the remainder of his life. This did not at all suit the views of the gallant soldier. He gave several reasons for remaining in the army, among others, his unfitness for any other profession than the one he was in, being now "in the very situation to which for sixteen years he had been aspiring. It is probable," he continued, "in the present aspect of affairs, that every man who wishes well to his country will soon have to fight her battles on her own soil; and what situation more becoming, or of greater trust or honour, could I occupy than that which I hold? In short, it would disappoint me beyond measure were I obliged to quit my present post in the present times. But I have laid it down as a *rule through life, to sacrifice my dearest feelings to the pleasing of the best of fathers.* Therefore, if you *absolutely insist* on it, I will endeavour to quit on half-pay." The father did not absolutely insist, and Colonel Cameron was destined to die a glorious death in defence of his country. In July, 1810, he received leave of absence for three months, when he paid a visit to his family and friends in Lochaber, but he was not allowed to enjoy their society long when he was called away to perform more arduous duties than ever.

In the end of 1810, the 92nd, with its gallant Colonel at its head, joined Wellington at the Lines of Torres Vedras, and throughout the whole of the Peninsular Campaign Cameron and his regiment not only signally distinguished themselves, but their deeds added materially to the glory of the British army. At the battle of Fuentes D'Onor, fought on the 5th of May, 1811, the 92nd occupied a trying position, exposed to a heavy cannonade, and they lost considerably. On the 28th of October the regiment took part in the battle of Arroyo del Molino, on which occasion Colonel Cameron was wounded, at the head of his men. The wound was not severe, but the escape of the gallant hero was almost miraculous. Dr. Clerk informs us that, "while holding his sword, a musket ball struck him in the middle-finger of the right hand, passed through the hilt of the sword, and hit him on the breast". The resistance offered by the hilt, however, was so good as to deprive the ball of its force, so that he suffered no injury except the loss of his finger, and a contusion of the breast. On this occasion the Prince D'Aremberg was taken prisoner, in a half-naked state, by a sergeant of the 92nd. We next find the regiment distinguishing itself at Almaraz, on the 19th of May, 1812; from the 10th to the 16th of November following, at Alba de Tormes, and at Vittoria on the 20th of June, 1813, where the services rendered were most conspicuous.

Colonel Cameron some time before obtained command of the First Brigade of Rowland Hill's Division. The heights of Puebla were occupied by a strong French force, and Colonel Cameron was ordered with his Brigade to seize the heights and "to hold them while he had a man left". The gallant fellows were soon up the face of the hill, and a hand-to-hand struggle of a fierce and deadly character ensued. The French fought desperately, receiving reinforcements as their ranks were thinned by the Highlanders. Hundreds of the Brigade fell in the deadly contest, though the loss of the 92nd was only four rank and file killed and sixteen wounded; but the survivors, headed by Cameron, redoubled their daring, crowned the heights, and retained them, though exposed for a considerable time to a most destructive fire. In acknowledgment of Colonel Cameron's distinguished services and those of his Brigade on this occasion, a medal was conferred upon him.

In the absence of Lieutenant-General Sir William Stewart, the command, at the sanguinary engagement between the British and the French in the Pass of Maya, devolved upon Colonel Cameron. Dr. Clerk graphically describes the incidents of this deadly contest as follows :—On the 23rd July, 15,000 French troops, in the highest order, attacked the British, not amounting to a fifth of that number, and considerably scattered. For a time the enemy advanced rapidly, driving the outposts and skirmishers easily before them, but Cameron, making the most skilful dispositions which his small force allowed of, speedily checked their course. "That fierce and formidable old regiment," the 50th, not merely checked the French column, but drove it back a considerable distance. The 92nd he divided into two wings, which did all that men could do. The overpowering numbers of the French, however, proved irresistible, and the British were obliged to draw back, until they reached the rock of Maya, where the valley contracted, and where, consequently, a stand was more easily made. Here the scene was appalling, and such as must sadden anyone to relate or to contemplate. For *ten hours* that brave band maintained the conflict against five times their number. "That officer (Cameron) still holding the Pass with the left wings of the 71st and 92nd, then brought their right wings and the Portuguese guns into action, and thus maintained the fight; but so dreadful was the slaughter, especially of the 92nd, that it is said the advancing enemy was actually stopped by the heaped mass of dead and dying; and then the left wing of that noble regiment coming down from the higher ground, smote wounded friends and exulting foes alike, as mingled together they stood or crawled before its wasting fire. Never did soldiers fight better—seldom so well. The stern valour of the 92nd would have graced Thermopylae."*

At length just as the ammunition was about being expended, and as some of the soldiers had recourse to stones, which they hurled at the enemy, they received succour from General Barnes, who advanced with a considerable body of men. The shattered remnant of the 92nd was forbidden to charge; but whether from the determination to avenge their slaughtered comrades, or from being suddenly seized by that *battle delirium* frequently spoken of in their native tongue as "mire catha," causing, as it is thought, insane joy, even exultation, in the fiercest fight, and resistlessly urging on to the deadliest danger, these warriors dashed forward at the very head of the charge, and hurled their enemies back over the ground that had been lost. This charge was led by Captain Seton, and animated by the war-tune of the "Haughs of Cromdale," one of Cameron's favourite pipe tunes. It was indeed "stern

* Napier, Vol. V., pp. 219-221.

valour," but the loss to the regiment was frightful ; 324 privates, out of about 750, fell there ; 19 officers were killed or wounded. Colonel Cameron received three wounds. His horse was killed, and his cloak, strapped on the front of his saddle, was pierced in several places. His faithful follower, Ewen Macmillan, who fortunately escaped unhurt, led him forth from the battle, and guided him to some shelter, where his wounds were dressed. Major Mitchell, who succeeded to his command, was likewise struck down. Ewen Kennedy, who had left Lochaber as a private, but had, through Cameron's influence, been promoted to a commission, was killed, as were many other officers of the highest character and promise.* Captain Seton survived to lead the remnant of his splendid regiment from the sanguinary field ; and for the distinguished gallantry displayed on the occasion, Colonel Cameron was authorised to bear "Maya" upon his shield.

In the passage of the Pyrenees, the 92nd took a prominent part, and during the four days' fighting no less than 53 rank and file were killed, while 36 officers and 363 rank and file were wounded. Colonel Cameron, who had meanwhile got better from his wounds, was the first, at the head of the 92nd, to cross the Nivelle. The regiment did excellent service at the crossing of the Nive, where the Colonel's favourite piper was knocked down. Finding that he was killed, Cameron exclaimed that he would rather have lost any other twenty men than this piper, who had so often inspired and led his brave corps to victory. This was on the 9th of December, 1813, and the fighting continued incessant and fierce in the extreme until the 13th, when the battle of St. Pierre, the most desperate since the war began, was fought and won by the British. We shall again quote Dr. Clerk. He says :—" The 92nd charged early in the day against two regiments of French, who gave way completely before the onset ; but Soult brought such a storm of artillery to bear on them, that they, in their turn, were obliged to retreat. Their old comrades,

* *Memoir of Colonel John Cameron, Fassiefern, K.T.S.*

the 71st, gave way also; but the fierce and formidable 50th and the Portuguese fought desperately to give time to the 92nd to rally and re-form. Then its gallant Colonel Cameron once more led it down the road, with colours flying and music playing, resolved to give the shock to whatever stood in the way. At this sight, the British skirmishers on the flanks suddenly changing from retreat to attack, rushed forward, and drove those of the enemy back on each side. A small force was the 92nd compared with the heavy mass in its front, but that mass faced about and retired across the valley. . . . How gloriously did that regiment come forth again to charge, with their colours flying and their national music playing as if going to a review! This was to understand war. The man who in that moment, and immediately after a repulse, thought of such military pomp, was by nature a soldier."* For his services on that day, Cameron received an honorary badge marked with the word "Nive," and Royal authority was granted to the regiment to bear the same word on its colours and appointments.

Dr. Clerk also records the following incident which occurred on this occasion at St. Pierre. "The faithful Macmillan signalised not only his devotion to his master's person, but his care for his master's property, in a manner worthy of being commemorated, and with a contempt of danger worthy of all honour. Colonel Cameron, during the first advance, had his horse killed under him, and the sudden fall entangled him so as completely to disable him for a moment. A Frenchman rushed on him, and was on the very point of transfixing him with his bayonet, when the ever-present Macmillan transfixed the Frenchman. He instantly liberated his master, led him forward till he reached his own men, then suddenly turning round, he made his way back to the dead horse, cut the girths, and raising the saddle on his shoulders, rejoined the 92nd, displaying his trophy, and exclaiming, 'We must leave them the carcase, but they shan't get the saddle where Fassiefern

* Napier, Vol. V., pp. 408-416.

sat!' All this was done in the midst of hot and heavy firing, during the progress of one of the fiercest and deadliest fights that occurred during the whole war."

In the course of the day the regiment made four distinct charges with the bayonet, on each occasion driving the enemy to his original position in front of his entrenchments. Sergeant Robertson, who kept a journal, in his description of one of these charges, says—" The order was given to charge with the left wing of the 92nd, while the right should act as riflemen in the fields to the left of the road. The left wing went down the road in a dashing manner, led by Colonel Cameron, who had his horse shot under him, and was obliged to walk on foot. As soon as we came up to the French, many of them called out for quarter, and were made prisoners. After the enemy had maintained their ground for a short time, they saw that it was impossible for them to stand against us. The road was soon covered with the dead and dying. The French now broke off to their own right, and got into the fields and between the hedges, where they kept up the contest until night. Although the action ended thus in our favour, we did not gain any new ground. After the battle was over, we were formed on a piece of rising ground about a mile to our own rear, when Lord Wellington came in person to thank the 92nd for their gallant conduct and manly bearing during the action, and ordered a double allowance of rum, and that we should go into quarters on the following day." The regiment in this action lost 3 officers and 28 rank and file killed, and 10 officers and 143 rank and file wounded.

The 92nd and its Colonel earned further laurels for their conduct at Hellete, Garris, and Arriverate. In honour of the latter, Colonel Cameron received a royal warrant to bear for his crest a Highlander of the 92nd up to the middle in water, grasping in his right hand a broadsword, and in his left a banner inscribed " 92nd " within a wreath of laurel, and as a motto over it the word " Arriverate". The idea of having the Highlander shown up to his middle in water will be understood from the following account of the fording of the river from Dr. Clerk's Memoir :—"Their Colonel was asked to make a demonstration at some distance up the river, with the view of inducing the enemy to withdraw part of their number from the bridge which they held in great force. He asked permission to turn the feint into a real attack if he should see cause. Discretionary power was given him. Discovering a fordable place he plunged into the stream, led his undaunted followers across, under a storm of shot from the French artillery, rushed upon the enemy in the village, which they strongly held, and rapidly routed them ; more than this, continuing the impetuous charge, he drove them from the bridge-head, and thus enabled the whole division to cross." In this daring movement he only lost 10 rank and file wounded. At Orthes, on the 27th of February, and Aire on the 2nd of March, Colonel Cameron and his irresistible Highlanders were again to the front, adding in both cases to their previous laurels. For Orthes, Cameron obtained another badge, and for Aire a Royal Patent was issued in his favour authorising him to bear on his arms "above the cognisance of Lochiel, a representation of the town of Aire, in allusion to his glorious services on the 2nd of March last." In this patent it is also set forth that he had "the honour to receive an address from the inhabitants, expressive of their gratitude for the maintenance of discipline, by which he had saved them from plunder and destruction," a fact which reflects no small credit on the men and their commander. The loss of the regiment at Aire was only 2 rank and file killed, and 3 officers and 35 rank and file wounded.

After the battle of Toulouse, in which the 92nd was not actively engaged, and the abdication of Napoleon, Colonel Cameron and his regiment returned home, disembarking at Monktown, in Ireland, on the 28th of July, 1814, after which they proceeded to Fermony Barracks, where the thanks of Parliament, accorded some time previously, was conveyed to the regiment, for "the meritorious and eminent services it had rendered to the king and country during the course of the war". Acknowledging a vote of thanks, for his conduct at the battle of Vittoria, by Parliament, on the preceding 24th of June, General Sir William Stewart gallantly said—" I should be ungrateful for the services rendered me by Colonel Cameron and by General Byng on that, as on all occasions, if I were not to advert to them in my present place; for to their exertions and support am I indebted for the success of those measures of which I am reaping the rich reward from my country at your too generous hands this day ". On receiving similar thanks for his services in the Pyrenees, Sir William was equally complimentary in his references to the 92nd and its gallant Colonel.

On the return home of the Peninsular Army, peerages, baronetcies, knighthoods, and other rewards, were distributed among those who occupied the highest posts, and who were considered the most distinguished. When the list of these honours was published, Colonel Cameron was not among them, much to the surprise of his friends and naturally his own great disappointment, for he considered himself at least entitled to the rank of knighthood, when his services and those of his regiment were compared with others for which honours of this kind had been conferred. He at once wrote a letter to the Horse Guards, calling attention to his claims, and received a reply from the Duke of York, to the effect that it was a fixed principle that no officer holding the rank of colonel or lieutenant-colonel received such honours as he claimed, who had not been previously "recommended for five badges of distinction in commemoration of important victories" obtained in the field. Colonel Cameron, on receipt of this reply, wrote direct to the Duke of Wellington, then at the Congress of Vienna, stating that the regiment considered the conduct of the authorities towards their commander a "reproach to themselves". The Duke replied that—" Not having received orders to recommend medals for Arrozo, Molinos, Aire, or Arriverate, it was impossible to recommend you for a medal for your services on these occasions; nor for Fuentes D'Onor or the Pyrenees; according to the rules I was bound to make out lists ". As to the knighthoods, he continues—" I have had nothing to do with the selection of the officers recently appointed Knights Commanders of the Bath. I did not know their names until I saw them in the *Gazette.*" He then complains of the "harshness" of the Colonel's letter, which he attributes solely to the irritation which he naturally felt, and concludes :—" However, the expression of this irritation, however unjust towards me, and unpleasant to my feelings, it has not made me forget the services which you and your brave corps rendered upon every occasion on which you were called upon ; and although I am afraid it is too late, I have recommended you in the strongest terms to the Secretary of State". Notwithstanding this recommendation, as the Duke anticipated, nothing came of it.

Colonel Cameron had also written to several of his most distinguished brother officers on the subject. Lieutenant-General Sir William Stewart, already quoted, referring to his name being omitted from the list of K.C.B.'s, says in a letter dated 23rd of January, 1815—" I have myself felt every degree of regret, and, I will add, of indignation, at seeing your name omitted in that list. I may say truly that it was the first name I looked for there." He then describes an interview he had on the subject with General Torrens, Secretary to the Commander-in-Chief, when he says, that he was "warm with him and expressed his feelings freely," and "assured him that I could not with patience see your name omitted—you, whose services, zeal and steady adherence to duty, at the head of one of the finest regiments of H.M.'s service, had invariably acquired the admiration of our Peninsular and allied armies ". The writer of these eulogiums was Cameron's superior officer at Vittoria, and he knew, from personal knowledge, his distinguished prowess on that occasion.

On the 31st of the same month, Lord Hill writes :—" I assure you I never can forget the eminent services rendered to me by yourself and your excellent regiment, during our late campaign "; and he expresses " the pleasure and satisfaction" which it would have given him to have seen Colonel Cameron's name in the list of the Military Knights of the Bath.

General Hope, then Lord Niddry, on the 21st of January, 1815, writes—" I can assure you that I felt almost as much concern as you will yourself on seeing that you were not included in the late arrangements for extending the honour of the Bath, and I have written to the Commander-in-Chief's Secretary, as strongly as it is in my power to do, in support of your claim. On what principle the arrangement has been made, or what is the rule followed, I know not; but it appears to have given more general dissatisfaction than anything within my remembrance. I have requested General Torrens that if any opening yet remains, or if any chance is to be expected, he will bring your case before the Commander-in-Chief." On the 5th of February, Lord Niddry sent him an extract from the reply of General Torrens to his lordship's communication, in these terms— "Suffice it to say that Colonel Cameron has been excluded, not from want of a thorough conviction of his peculiar merits and distinguished gallantry, but because he did not come within the line—namely, that he had been recommended for five medals". The Highland Society writes to him on the 24th of February, 1814, saying how gratifying it is to them that "you should have so signalised yourself in the immediate command of a brigade of these regiments, as to merit the handsome encomiums bestowed upon you by the Lieutenant-General". These encomiums are contained in a letter from Sir Rowland Hill, K.B., to the Right Hon. Sir John Sinclair, of which the Society enclosed a copy to Colonel Cameron. In it Sir Rowland says—" The conduct of the officers and men [of the 71st and 92nd] has been so uniformly good, as to make it almost unnecessary for me to select particular individuals for praise. Lieutenant-Colonel Cameron of the 92nd does, however, demand that distinction; during the greater part of the battle of Vittoria, he commanded my first brigade, 50th, 71st and 92nd regiments, and also at Maya, and several other operations in the Pyrenees. I am also much indebted to him for leading the gallant 92nd in several successful charges against very superior numbers of the enemy's troops in the battle of the 13th of last month, near Bayonne." An officer who could command such testimonies to his distinguished services as these might have felt satisfied, though military red-tape had robbed him of what was due to him, and what his country would gladly have seen conferred upon him.

A royal patent, dated the 25th of May, 1815, conferring armorial bearings, sets forth in an authentic form the services rendered by the Colonel, as follows :—

"Whereas taking into our royal consideration the able and highly-distinguished services of our trusty and well-beloved John Cameron, Esq., Colonel in our army, and Lieutenant-Colonel of our 92nd Highland Regiment of Foot, upon various occasions in Holland in the year 1799, in Egypt in the year 1801, and the recent glorious and ever-memorable campaigns in Portugal, Spain, and France, under our Field-Marshal, Arthur Duke of Wellington ; and more especially the signal intrepidity and heroic bravery displayed by him in the action of Aroyo Moulino on the 28th October, 1811, in defence of the Pass of Maya on the 25th July, 1813, and more particularly in the brilliant action of the 13th December, 1813, near Bayonne, in crossing the Gava de Moulino at Arriverate, on the 17th day of February, 1814, and compelling a very superior force of the enemy to abandon the town of Aire on the 2nd March, 1814 ; and being desirous of conferring upon the said Colonel John Cameron such a mark of our royal favour as may, in an especial manner, evince the sense we entertain of his distinguished merits, we have thought fit to grant unto him our royal licence and permission for his wearing certain honourable armorial distinctions allusive thereto, whereby his faithful and zealous exertions in our service may be transmitted to posterity ; know ye, that we, of our princely grace and especial favour, having given and granted, and by these presents do give and grant, unto the said Colonel John Cameron, our royal licence and authority that he, and his descendants, may as a lasting memorial of our royal approbation of his highly-distinguished services, bear the crest of honourable augmentation following; that is to say, on a wreath, a demi-Highlander of the 92nd Regiment armed and accoutred, and up to the middle in water, grasping in his dexter hand a broadsword, and in his sinister a banner inscribed 92nd, within a wreath of laurel, and in an escrol above, 'Arriverate,' in allusion to the signal intrepidity displayed by him at the passage of the river Gava de Moulino, on the aforesaid 17th day of February, 1814," etc., etc.

In the same month he was created a Knight of the Royal Portuguese Military Order of the Tower and Sword " in testimony of the high sense which the Prince [Regent of Portugal] entertains of the great courage and intrepidity" displayed by him in the Peninsula.

Colonel Cameron spent a few happy months during this period among his friends in Lochaber, and with his father at Arthurstone, in Perthshire, a property which he had recently purchased, and whither he had gone to reside; while the Colonel, hoping to spend his latter years in the home of his youth which he loved so well, took a new lease of Fassiefern. He was destined, however, not to derive much enjoyment from it. On the 7th of March 1815, news reached the Vienna Congress that Napoleon had escaped, and that he was on his way to Paris, his old veterans joining him in legions as he marched in triumph to the French Capital. What followed is already known; how he again ascended the throne of France, supported by an army of 200,000 men; and how the allied powers determined that he should not continue to hold it. Colonel Cameron, among the rest, was called upon to join his regiment at Cork, which he did, and at its head joined the allied army, under the Duke of Wellington, at Brussels, early in June, 1815. He dined with the great Commander on the evening of the 13th, and he was also present at the famous ball given by the Duchess of Richmond, during which he and the other officers present were ordered to retire privately from the ball-room and proceed at once to Quatre-Bras, from which he was not destined to return. By two o'clock in the afternoon he was with his brave 92nd in front of the enemy. It is unnecessary to recapitulate at length the proceedings of that sanguinary day. It is known to every school-boy; but we must give Dr. Clerk's account of the part taken in the day's engagement by Colonel Cameron and the 92nd, and how gloriously he ended his career.

The regiment was terribly cut up, having lost about 300 rank and file in deadly contest with the enemy. The reverend author relating how Cameron fought, and "in the shock of steel, died like the offspring of Lochiel," and here "closed his life of fame by a death of glory," informs us that his narrative is taken from an eye-witness of the scene, who says—" The regiment lined a ditch in front of the Namur Road. The Duke of Wellington happened to be stationed among them. Colonel Cameron, seeing the French advance, asked permission to charge them. The Duke replied, 'Have patience, and you will have plenty of work by and by'. As they took possession of the farm-house, Cameron again asked leave to charge, which was again refused. At length, as they began to push on to the Charleroi Road, the Duke exclaimed, 'Now, Cameron, is your time—take care of that road'. He instantly gave the spur to his horse; the regiment cleared the ditch at a bound, charged, and rapidly drove back the French; but while doing so their leader was mortally wounded. A shot, fired from the upper storey of the farm-house, passed through his body, and his horse, pierced by several bullets, fell dead under him. His men raised a wild shout, rushed madly on the fated house, and, according to all accounts, inflicted dread vengeance on its doomed occupants. Ewen Macmillan, who was ever near his master and his friend, speedily gave such aid as he could. Carrying him, with the aid of another private, beyond reach of the firing, he procured a cart, whereon he laid him, carefully and tenderly propping his head on a breast than which none was more faithful. The life-blood, however, was ebbing fast, and on reaching the village of Waterloo, where so many other brave hearts were soon after to bleed, Macmillan carried Fassiefern into a deserted house, by the road-side, and stretched him on the floor. He anxiously inquired how the day had gone, and how his beloved Highlanders had acquitted themselves. Hearing that, as usual, they had been victorious, he said, 'I die happy, and I trust my dear country will believe that I served her faithfully'. His dying hour was soothed by that music which he always loved, and which, while harsh and unmeaning to a stranger, is so intimately blended with a Highlander's deepest feelings, and most sacred memories, as to awaken his whole heart, to rouse up his whole being, and thus is highly-esteemed in the hour of sorrow or of danger, in every great crisis of life. Better still, his dying hour was soothed, and, we trust, blessed by earnest prayer. And worthy of remark it is that these dying supplications were uttered in that mountain tongue, the first which he had heard in youth, and now, as we have known in kindred instances, at the close of life, naturally offering itself as the vehicle of the deepest aspirations of the soul in the most solemn of all situations." Thus died gloriously, at the early age of forty-four years, a Highlander, who, had he lived, would, we doubt not, have attained to the highest honours of his profession.

He was temporarily buried in a green valley on the Ghent Road, on the 17th of June. Macmillan, who attended with a few wounded soldiers and his old friend Mr. Gordon, afterwards General Gordon of Lochdhu, carefully marked the spot. In April, 1816, the Colonel's youngest brother, Peter, accompanied by Macmillan, proceeded to the place, opened the grave, placed the remains in a leaden coffin, and brought them to Leith, from which they were carried to Lochaber in one of his Majesty's ships, granted for the purpose, on the application of the Colonel's eldest brother, Duncan, then a W.S. in Edinburgh. The remains were kept for a few days at Fassiefern House, after which they were interred, within a ruinous aisle of the old church of Kilmallie, in the same place where lies a meet companion, the late Sir Ewen Dubh of Killiecrankie renown, and other chiefs of the Cameron Clan. It is scarcely necessary to say that the remains of the distinguished soldier were followed to their last resting-place by his own relations, the leading men and the whole manhood of Lochaber, including Lochiel, Macneill of Barra, Macdonald of Glencoe, Campbell of Barcaldine, and "by three thousand Highlanders, who with feelings responsive to the wailing notes of the lament poured forth from many bagpipes, sincerely mourned for the early death of one whose brave deeds were worthy of his high ancestry, and shed additional lustre on their country".

Moralising on the splendid sight, Dr. Clerk says, that such a scene shall never again be witnessed in Lochaber, even supposing there was another Colonel Cameron. "Neither the chiefs nor the men to grace any funeral thus are now [1848] to be found in Lochaber. The men have passed away to other countries and climes, and the wild wail of the Highland Lament is more frequently to be heard amid the woods of Canada, and over the plains of Australia, than amid the glens and mountains which, of old, so oft re-echoed its thrilling notes, and which undoubtedly formed the fitting abode of the pibroch."

Colonel Cameron had the reputation of being a very strict, indeed severe, disciplinarian, though most attentive to the welfare of his men in every respect. His love of the music, language and traditions of his home and early youth continued with him to the last.

It is no common testimony to his merits, that the great Duke of Wellington, after the terrible conflict was over, and when the country and he were mourning over the loss of numbers of its greatest heroes and thousands of its bravest sons, should have specially mentioned the brave Fassiefern. Writing to the Lords of the Treasury from Orville, under date, 25th of June, 1815, only a week after

Waterloo, he says—" Your Lordships will see in the enclosed lists the names of some most valuable officers lost to his Majesty's service. Among them I cannot avoid to mention Colonel Cameron of the 92nd Regiment, and Colonel Sir H. Ellis of the 23rd Regiment, to whose conduct I have frequently called your Lordships' attention, and who at last fell, distinguishing themselves at the head of the brave troops which they commanded. Notwithstanding the glory of the occasion, it is impossible not to lament such men, both on account of the public and as friends." This is a monument more enduring than marble itself, and no one will dispute that it was well earned.

On the 6th of July following, Lord Niddry writes a letter of condolence to Colonel Cameron's father, in which he speaks of " the glorious circumstances in which his son had fallen," and " the feelings of mingled admiration and regret experienced by his fellow-soldiers at his loss. But," he continues, " if any such reflections can alleviate the grief of relatives, Colonel Cameron's family have an abundant store; for no man ever fell under circumstances more glorious, or more memorable; nor is it possible that any man can be more lamented than he is, not only by the gallant corps which he so often led to victory and honour, but by the whole army and the country at large." This is only a specimen of many other communications of a similarly complimentary and gratifying nature from men holding high positions in the army and in the State.

In acknowledgment of his distinguished services to his country a Baronetage was conferred on his father on the 8th of March, 1817.

A monument—a large obelisk—which cost £1400, has been appropriately raised to his memory at Kilmallie, his native parish, bearing the following inscription, composed by Sir Walter Scott :—

"Sacred to the memory of Colonel John Cameron, eldest son of Ewen Cameron of Fassiefern, Bart., whose mortal remains, transported from the field of glory where he died, rest here with those of his forefathers. During twenty years of active military service, with a spirit which knew no fear, and shunned no danger, he accompanied or led, in marches, sieges, and battles, the 92nd Regiment of

Scottish Highlanders, always to honour, and almost always to victory, and at length in the forty-second [? forty-fourth] year of his age, upon the memorable 16th of June, 1815, was slain in command of that corps, while actively contributing to achieve the decisive victory of Waterloo [Quatre Bras], which gave peace to Europe. Thus closing his military career with the long and eventful struggle, in which his services had been so often distinguished, he *died*, lamented by that unrivalled general, to whose long train of success he had so often contributed; by his country, from which he had repeatedly received marks of the highest consideration; and by his sovereign, who graced his surviving family with those marks of favour which could not follow, to this place, him whom they were designed to commemorate. Reader, call not his fate untimely, who, thus honoured and lamented, closed a life of fame by a death of glory!"

The following lines are from the same author's "Dance of Death":—

  Apart from Albyn's war array
  'Twas there grey Allan sleepless lay—
  Grey Allan, who for many a day
   Had followed stout and stern,
  Where through battle, rout, and reel,
  Through storm of shot, and hedge of steel,
  Lay the grandson of Lochiel,
   The valiant Fassiefern.

  Through steel and shot he leads no more,
  Low-laid 'mid friends' and foemen's gore;
  But long his native lake's wild shore,
  And Suinard rough and wild Ardgour,
   And Morven long shall tell;
  And proud Ben-Nevis hear with awe,
  How at the bloody Quatre Brâs
  Brave Cameron heard the wild hurrah
   Of conquest as he fell.

This sketch of the distinguished hero cannot more appropriately be concluded than in Professor Blackie's spirited lines, worthy of the subject and of the author:—

  At Quatre Bras, when the fight was hot,
  Stout Cameron stood and eyed the shot,
  Eager to leap as a mettlesome hound
  Into the fight with a plunge and a bound;
  But Wellington, lord of the cool command,
  Held the reins with a steady hand,
  Saying, "Cameron, wait; you'll soon have enough;
  The Frenchman shall taste your fervid stuff
   When the Cameron men are wanted!"

  Now hotter and hotter the battle grew,
  With tramp and rattle and wild haloo:
  And the Frenchmen poured like a fiery flood
  Right to the ditch where Cameron stood.

Then Wellington flashed on his Captain brave
A lightning glance, and the order gave,
Saying, "Cameron, now have at them, boy;
Take care of the road to Charleroi,
    Where the Cameron men are wanted!"

Brave Cameron shot like a shaft from a bow
In the midst of the plunging foe,
And with him the lads whom he loved, like a torrent
Sweeping the rocks in its foamy current;
And he fell the first in the fervid start,
Pierced with a shot in a mortal part;
But his men pushed on, where the work was rough,
Giving the Frenchmen a taste of their stuff,
    Where the Cameron men were wanted!

Brave Cameron then from the mortal fray
His foster-brother bore away—
His foster-brother with service true—
Back to the village of Waterloo.
And they laid him on the soft green sod,
And he breathed his spirit there to God;
But not till he heard the loud hurrah
Of victory bellowed from Quatre Bras,
    Where the Cameron men were wanted!

By the road to Ghent they buried him then,
This noble chief of the Cameron men;
And not an eye was tearless seen
That day beside the alley green:
Wellington wept, the iron man;
And from every eye in the Cameron clan
The big round drop in bitterness fell,
As with the pipe he loved so well,
    The funeral wail they chanted!

And now he sleeps (for they bore him home,
When the war was done, across the foam)
Beneath the shadow of Nevis Ben;
With his sires, the pride of the Cameron men,
Three thousand Highland men stood round,
As they laid him to rest in his native ground—
The Cameron brave, whose eye never quailed,
Whose heart never sank, and whose hand never failed,
    Where the Cameron men were wanted!

THE CAMERONS OF WORCESTER.

THE progenitor of the Camerons who settled at Worcester was,

I. JOHN CAMERON, minister of Dunoon and Kilmun. According to Scott's *Fasti Eccl. Scoticanae*, "John Cameron is said to have been here" in 1566, and "prior to the Reformation to have adopted the Protestant faith". He was a member of the General Assembly in 1610; and "was a person of great probity and learning". He is said to have been a brother of Allan Mac Ian Duibh, sixteenth of Lochiel. He had at least three sons: John, born about 1579, the famous Principal of the University of Glasgow, the most famous Protestant divine of his day; Archibald, minister of Inchcalzeoch (or Buchanan), in 1617; and

II. THOMAS CAMERON, who settled in Glasgow. He married Margaret, daughter of Robert Boyd of Portancross, by Margaret, daughter of Sir Robert Montgomery of Skelmorlie by Dorothea, daughter of Robert, third Lord Semple, by his second wife, Elizabeth Carlysle, daughter of Lord Torthorwold. By Margaret Boyd, Thomas Cameron had issue,

III. THOMAS CAMERON, who married Jean, daughter of Walter Macaulay of Ardincaple, by his wife, Jean, daughter of Hugh Montgomery of Hazelhead, by Arrabella, daughter of John Wallace of Dundonald and Ackans, by Jean, daughter of Sir John Stewart of Minto, ancestor of Lord Blantyre. By Jean Macaulay, Thomas Cameron had a son,

IV. JOHN CAMERON, minister of Callendar, and of Kincardine in 1682, who married, first, on 3rd of October,

1682, Janet Barclay, and, secondly, in January, 1701, Elizabeth, daughter of John Luckly or Lucklow (a wealthy citizen and a Bailie of Coupar), by Elizabeth, daughter of Alexander Scott, minister of Melrose, son of Sir William Scott of Balweary (county of Fife), by Jean Elizabeth Graham, daughter of John, third Earl of Montrose (Lord High Chancellor, and Viceroy of Scotland under James VI., after his Majesty became King of England), by Jean Lillias, daughter of David Lord Drummond, ancestor of the Earls of Perth. He refused to take the oath of allegiance to King William, and lost his preferment. The offence charged against him was, "not reading the proclamation of the Estates, not praying for their Majesties William and Mary, employing one who prayed for King James, not observing the thanksgiving, not reading the proclamation for the collection, bringing down the rebels to rob his parishioners, and saying, if God would not give him amends of them he would make the devil do it ".*

He died at Edinburgh, on the 6th of June, 1719, at the age of sixty-five.

By Elizabeth Luckly or Lucklow he had a son,

V. DR. THOMAS CAMERON, born in 1704. He left Scotland, and commenced practice as a physician in Worcester about 1727. He was educated in the High School of Edinburgh, and afterwards went to Oxford, he having been elected an Exhibitioner to Baliol College on a foundation by John Warner, Bishop of Rochester, who, in 1666, "founded four exhibitions for scholars of the Scottish nation, who, when they had taken the degree of M.A., were to return to their native country in Holy Orders, that there may never be wanting in Scotland some who shall support the ecclesiastical establishment of England"; and "in 1679, John Snell, Esq., of Ayrshire, left the manor of Ufton, in Warwickshire, to the College, to support from five to twelve more exhibitioners, having the same object in view as Bishop Warner, the support of Episcopacy in Scotland". When Episcopacy was abolished in Scotland

* Scott's *Fasti Eccl. Scoticanae*, Vol. II., p. 727.

on the accession of King William, the trustees threw the scholarships open, and allowed the exhibitioners to adopt any profession they chose. Mr. Cameron was the first who took advantage of this change, and, instead of going into Holy Orders, he adopted the medical profession. He is said to have been a great master of the Latin language, writing and speaking it with great fluency. From 1727 he "laboured assiduously in his profession for the term of fifty years, with great reputation to himself and benefit to mankind, during which time he was one of those gentlemen who promoted the first establishment of the [Worcester] Infirmary in 1745, to which institution he was elected physician".

He wrote learnedly on small-pox and on the measles in 1752. Dr. Percival, in the fifth volume of *Medical Observations and Enquiries*, in 1776, bears testimony to his superior method of treating the latter, and informs us that "the practice of using the bark in this disease was first introduced by Dr. Cameron". He further says—"It is many years since I first adopted the method of cure recommended by Dr. Cameron, and experience has afforded me the fullest conviction of its safety and efficacy in all ordinary cases".* Other medical authorities speak very highly of his medical skill and success as a physician. Mrs. Cameron, the wife of his grandson Charles, says of him that, after he settled as a physician in Worcester, "he was brought into notice by attending a poor family in a very dreadful fever, which other medical men would not visit". She also relates the following anecdote:—"On one occasion he was kept waiting by a very young medical man. On his arrival, he apologised to Dr. Cameron, saying he had so much to do. 'When, sir, you have as much to do as I have, you will learn to be punctual to your engagements.'" On another occasion, while walking in the streets of Worcester, he saw a scavenger throwing a shovel full of dirt into his cart, in such a way as purposely

* *Biographical Illustrations of Worcestershire*, by John Chambers, 1820, pp. 364-366.

to splash the white dress of a lady who was at the time passing. Dr. Cameron, " coming up at the moment, seized the man by his waistband, and flung him into his own mud cart," to teach him better behaviour.*

He married, first, Elizabeth Severn, who died without issue. He married, secondly, on the 17th of September, 1747, Barbara Ann, daughter of William Plowden of Plowden, county of Salop (and an officer in the Guards of James II.), by Maria, his wife, daughter of Sir Charles Lyttleton, Baronet, of Hagley, Worcestershire, with issue—

1. Charles.

2. Henry, who married Mary Amphlett of Clent, Worcestershire, with issue, of whom nothing is known.

3. Mary, who married the Rev. John Lyster, D.D., of Rocksavage, Co. Roscommon, Ireland, with issue, one of whom, Marion, the eldest daughter, married Sir James Crofton, Baronet, of Longford House, County of Sligo, with issue.

On the 25th of August, 1730, he matriculated arms in the Lyon Office, Edinburgh.

He died on the 21st of November, 1777, and was buried in St. Peter's Church, Worcester, where there is an inscription to his memory. He was succeeded, as representative of the family, by his eldest son,

VI. CHARLES CAMERON, M.B. of Baliol College, Oxford, where he took his degree of B.M. on the 10th of July, 1774, and settled in Worcester. He was born on the 25th of July, 1748. He had his early training at Eton, matriculated at Oxford on the 8th of November, 1764, and studied at Edinburgh in 1769. In 1773 he was appointed physician to the Worcester Infirmary, " which he attended with unremitting assiduity for more than forty years, when impaired health and strength obliged him to resign his situation, in 1816". He died two years later, when a notice of him appeared in a local paper, from which we take the following: —" On Sunday, December 27th, 1818, died, after a protracted illness, in the 71st year of his age, Charles Cameron,

* *Life of Mrs. Cameron*, second edition, p. 102.

M.B., for more than forty years physician to the Worcester Infirmary. He was the elder son of Dr. Thomas Cameron, a name eminent in the history of medical science, and still highly endeared to all who retain a remembrance of his superior talents and acquirements, or his moral worth. His son Charles was educated at Eton, graduated at Baliol College, Oxford, and completed his course of medical study in London, and at the University of Edinburgh. As a physician, he was distinguished by sound judgment and accurate discrimination, and his own acquirements were enriched by the resources he derived from the profound skill and experience of his father. . . . A certain delicacy of sentiment, and a modesty of mind, which had made him shrink from all appearance of obtruding upon the notice of others, or pushing himself into practice, led him into conduct which was often misunderstood, and exposed him to the censure of pride, or of neglect, to his worldly disadvantage. The distinguishing qualities of his heart were sensibility and affection; and those who knew him most intimately, feel better than they can express, the moral excellence of his character. One striking feature in it must not be passed over; under all the trying circumstances of life, he felt and he expressed a degree of confidence, too rarely manifested even by persons apparently of superior piety, in the kind and providential care of a Heavenly Father, Who never suffered him to be disappointed in that trust." His daughter-in-law, Mrs. Charles Richard Cameron, says of him in her autobiography, that he "was a man of singularly pleasing appearance, handsome and elegant in manner and carriage—having been bred amongst high connections".

He married, on the 20th of April, 1778, Anne (widow of Edward Chambers, surgeon), only daughter of Richard Ingram of White Ladies, Worcester, with issue—

1. Charles Richard, born on the 7th of May, 1779.
2. Francis, Lieutenant R.N., who died in Jamaica, of yellow fever, without issue.
3. Archibald, a solicitor in Worcester, born on the 2nd

of January, 1782. He married on the 31st of March, 1819, Mary, daughter of the Rev. Wm. Hancock Roberts, D.D., rector of Broadwas, Worcestershire, with issue, an only son—(1) Archibald Henry Foley Cameron, M.R.C.S. Eng. and L.R.C.P.E., lately of Lakefield, Co. of Inverness, and now Shiel Road, Liverpool; born on the 28th of June, 1829, and married, first, in 1862, Charlotte Eden, daughter of John Theodore Wilcox of the H.E.I.C.S., with issue—Archibald Evan, born in 1865; and Donald George, born in 1866. He married, secondly, in 1873, Sarah Peterson, with issue—a daughter, Fanny Mary. (2) Mary Emily, Innseagan House, Fort-William, author of a well-written novel—*The House of Achendaroch.*

4. Donald, born on the 24th of August, 1796, who married Frances, daughter of Thomas Ross Broomfield of Marston, Warwickshire, with issue—one son, Donald, M.A. of Oxford, and now vicar of Little Dewchurch, Herefordshire, who married Fanny, daughter of Samuel Lediard, solicitor, Cirencester, with surviving issue—one son, Stuart, and a daughter. Donald had also three daughters, one of whom—Mary Christina—survives.

5. Mary Anne, who died unmarried on the 14th of November, 1852.

6. Jane, who married Captain Thomas Turner Roberts, H.E.I.C.S., sprung from an ancient Cornish family for many years settled in Worcestershire. He bought the estate of Llwyndderw, in Breconshire. He died in 1855, leaving (with two daughters, Jane and Lucy) a son, Thomas Archibald, barrister-at-law, author of a work on the Principles and Practice of Equity. The latter died in 1883, leaving a son, Cameron, now at Oxford, and several daughters.

Mrs. Cameron died on the 9th November, 1815, and Dr. Cameron on the 27th of December, 1818, when he was succeeded, as representative of the family, by his eldest son,

VII. The Rev. CHARLES RICHARD CAMERON, M.A. of Christ Church, Oxford, rector of Swaby, Lincolnshire, who married on the 12th of June, 1806, Lucy Lyttleton, daughter of the Rev. George Butt, chaplain to George III., rector of Stanford and vicar of Kidderminster, Worcestershire. She was remarkable for her piety, and was a voluminous author of popular religious books. Her Life has been published, and has reached a second edition—a most fascinating book of its kind. It exhibits Mrs. Cameron as a woman of extraordinary devotion and earnestness of purpose in good work during the whole of her long life. By her the Rev. Charles Richard Cameron had issue—

1. Charles, M.A. of Oxford.
2. Ewen Henry, B.A., barrister-at-law. He was born on the 17th of March, 1813, and, on the 21st of August, 1845, married Mary Eugenia, daughter of William Taylor Money, Consul-General of Venice, without issue. He died on the 22nd of January, 1846, at Brighton, and was buried there.
3. George Thomas, M.A. of Christ Church, Oxford. He was born on the 28th of May, 1821, and ordained, in 1844, curate of St. Peter's, Saffron Hill, afterwards of St. Ebbes, Oxford, and now vicar of Heckington, Lincolnshire. He married, first, Emily Marian Sophia, daughter of the Rev. J. Short, with issue—a daughter, who died young. He married, secondly, Maria Elizabeth, daughter of F. F. Goe of Louth, without issue.
4. Francis Marten, M.A. of Christ Church, Oxford. He was born on the 14th of September, 1824, ordained on the 19th of September, 1847, and on the 10th of January, 1850, married, first, Miss Goe, daughter of F. F. Goe of Louth, with issue—(1) Francis Ewen, born on the 10th of December, 1854, in Holy Orders; (2) Mary Amelia, who died young in 1863; (3) Emma Jane; (4) Maria Louisa; (5) Lucy Elizabeth. His first wife died on the 19th of January, 1859, and on the 9th of October, 1860, he married, secondly, Hannah, daughter of Edward Dale, with issue— (6) George Henry, born on the 28th of August, 1861, a member of Christ College, Cambridge; (7) Archibald Edward Marten, who died in infancy; (8) Archibald Thomas Butt, born on the 17th of January, 1873; (9) Percy Lyttleton, born on the 29th of May, 1875; (10)

Charles Moor Marten, born on the 3rd of July, 1877; (11) Alice Sophia; (12) Annie Beatrice; (13) Clara Margaret; (14) May Evelyn; and (15) Kathleen Edith. He was presented, first, to the church of Brockham, in the County of Surrey, and is now rector of Bonnington, Hythe, County of Kent.

5. Lucy, who, on the 20th of September, 1838, married the Rev. Stephen Richard Waller, M.A. of Oxford, with surviving issue, the Rev. Charles Henry Waller. She died on the 13th of May, 1842.

6. Mary Anne, who, on the 10th of August, 1837, married the Rev. J. H. C. Moor, B.D. of Oxford, and vicar of Clifton-on-Dunsmore, near Rugby, with issue—(1) Charles Thomas, born in 1843; (2) Henry Peter, born in 1844; (3) George Isaac, born in 1846; (4) Lucy Martha; (5) Susan Emma; and (6) Sophia Salome. She died on the 14th of May, 1847.

7. Martha Elizabeth, who died, unmarried, on the 24th of September, 1847.

8. Emma Jane, who, in January, 1849, married the Rev. Frederic G. Lugard, chaplain, H.E.I.C.S., and a clergyman in Vepery, Madras, where she died of cholera a few years after, leaving issue—two daughters, Lucy Jane and Emma Charlotte. She died on the 26th of December, 1851.

9. Barbara Sophia, who, on the 5th of November, 1850, married the Rev. Theodore Percival Wilson, M.A., Principal of St. Peter's Collegiate School, Adelaide, Australia, afterwards vicar of Pavenham, Bedfordshire, with issue—
(1) Charles Thomas, born on the 14th of October, 1851;
(2) Percival Ewen, born on the 10th of June, 1853;
(3) Donald Marten, born on the 1st of August, 1854;
(4) Theodore Cameron, born on the 30th of April, 1856;
(5) Edmond Algernon, born on the 21st of August, 1863;
(6) Sophia Lucy Martha; and (7) Sophia Mary—all of whom survive except the last-named.

10. Charlotte, who died, unmarried, on the 10th of June, 1846.

THE CAMERONS OF WORCESTER. 317

11. Frances Amelia, who married James Herbert O'Donoghue, without issue.

A son, Archibald, died in infancy, in 1814.

The Rev. Charles Richard Cameron was succeeded, as representative of the family, by his eldest son,

VIII. CHARLES CAMERON, M.A. of Oxford, minister of St. James's Church, Dudley. He was born in 1807, and married, in 1851, Marcia, daughter of the Hon. Merrick Burrell, and sister of the fourth and present Lord Gwydyr, with issue—

1. Charles, his heir.
2. Marcia Frances Lyttleton.
3. Georgina Emma.   } Twins.
4. Clara Charlotte, who, }

in 1883, married the Rev. John William Margetts, rector of St. Edmonds, Leeds.

5. Lucy Amelia.

He died at Heckington in 1861, and was succeeded, as representative of the family, by his only son,

IX. CHARLES HAMILTON HONE CAMERON, medical practitioner, Harlesden, Willesden, London, born in 1852. He is a M.R.C.S. Eng., and L.R.C.P. Lond. In 1878, he married Mary Louisa Savile, daughter of the late Robert Walter Mexborough Shepherd, with issue—a daughter,

Stella Willoughby Savile, born in 1880.

THE CAMERONS OF ERRACHT.

WE have found it impossible to give a continuous genealogical account of the Camerons of Erracht. No material exists from which it could be prepared. Though several members of the family have at various times taken a prominent part both in the wars and civil affairs of the clan, no record of these remains beyond what has already appeared in connection with the family of Lochiel.

The first Cameron of Erracht was Ewen, eldest son of Ewen, thirteenth of Lochiel, by his second wife, Marjory Mackintosh. The family were always known as "Sliochd Eoghainn 'ic Eoghainn, or the descendants of Ewen, son of Ewen". The residence of the family was within a short distance of the castle of the chief, situated on an elevated plateau at the entrance to Glenlui, and seen from the Caledonian Canal between Gairlochy and Banavie. One of the most distinguished members of the whole clan was an Erracht Cameron, the famous General Sir Allan Cameron, and were he alone among the race as a gallant soldier he would have made the name of Cameron illustrious. We shall notice his glorious career at considerable length. His father,

DONALD CAMERON of Erracht, was born shortly before 1715; for we are told that, when Allan's grandfather joined the Earl of Mar in that year, Donald was an infant in his mother's arms. The grandfather was killed at Sheriffmuir, but the father joined Lochiel and Prince Charles as second in command of the Camerons at Glenfinnan, in 1745; for Fassiefern, who was a step nearer in blood, did not join his chief on this memorable occasion, and Donald of Erracht took his place as second in command. His son, Allan, was at the time an infant in his mother's arms, as he himself had been when his father joined the Earl of Mar, thirty years before. Like many others, who took a part in the Rising of 1745, Donald of Erracht was a wanderer from his family and friends for about three years after Culloden, during which time his family, like others in the Highlands, were subjected to cruelties and indignities which have fixed indelible disgrace upon the soldiers of the king and their commanders, and the eternal reprobation of humanity.

Donald married Marsali or Marjory, daughter of Mac-Lean of Drimnin, Morvern, with issue—

1. Allan, afterwards famous as General Sir Allan Cameron of the 79th Cameron Highlanders, and of whom presently.

2. Donald.

3. Ewen, known as "Eoghainn Mòr," whose name will often appear in the narrative of Sir Allan's career. He died unmarried.

Donald had also three daughters, one of whom married Mr. Cameron of Scamadale (who died in Inverness in 1833), with issue, among others, Major Alexander Cameron, who, while holding the rank of lieutenant, commanded the 79th at Waterloo, for the last three hours of the action, and led the regiment off the field, all his superior officers having been killed or wounded. When his conduct on that occasion was reported to Wellington, he recommended him for promotion, and in consequence he was gazetted captain on the 30th of June, and in September following, brevet-major. Brevet-Lieutenant-Colonel Duncan Cameron, of the 79th, writing from Brussels, where he lay wounded, on the 26th of June, 1815, to General Allan Cameron, intimated his nephew's bravery to the old veteran, and after describing their great loss and the manner in which Alexander Cameron behaved, he says—
"Both himself and your other nephew (Archibald) escaped

being seriously wounded, as they have continued with the regiment and are off with it to *Nivelles*. This will be gratifying to you, and also that I can add, they conducted themselves with the utmost gallantry and coolness throughout the terrible attacks made on us, notwithstanding that it was the first time either had faced the enemy."

We shall now return to

GENERAL SIR ALLAN CAMERON, K.C.B.,

Colonel of the 79th Cameron Highlanders, who made the family patronymic of Erracht so distinguished. The absence of any adequate notice of his services, except what appeared in two pages of the *Gentleman's Magazine*, at his death, in 1828, may be attributed largely to his own reticence in supplying information. Sir John Philliphart and Colonel David Stewart of Garth, who applied to him when collecting materials for their respective "Military Annals," expressed regret that his reply for particulars of his career was of the most meagre character. Although, in common with many other distinguished men, averse to giving publicity to the various incidents of his life, he was not so among his personal friends; and he was never happier than when surrounded by them. His house in Gloucester Place was a general rendezvous, during many years, for his companions in arms, where his "Highland cousins," as he fondly termed them, were always received with a genial welcome.

Notwithstanding the very general absence of his name from unofficial publications, it may be affirmed, without hesitation, that, in his day, few men were better known, and there was no one whose fame stood higher as a soldier than that of *Ailean an Earrachd*. In the army he was held universally popular, where, in consequence of his familiar habit of addressing the Irish and Highland soldiers with his Gaelic salute of "*Cia mar tha thu?*"—How are you? he was known as "Old *Cia Mar Tha*". He is so styled even in Lever's *Charles O'Malley*, where he is presented (Vol. I., Chap. X.) as one of the friends of General Sir George

Dashwood. Miss Sinclair, in *Scotland and the Scotch*, refers to him as "a frequent visitor at her father's house in London, and a celebrity of the past generation, who was said to have been one of the principals in the last duel fought with broadswords; and also known to his friends for the more than hearty grasp he shook their hands with".

He was remarkable for his great size and powerful structure. In a verse from one of the many Gaelic songs written in his honour, alluding to his majestic form and figure when in the Highland costume, the bard says :—

> Nuair theid thu'n uidheam Gaidheil
> Bu mhiann le Ban-Righ sealladh dhiot,
> Le t-osan is math fiaradh,
> Do chalp air fiamh na galluinne.
> Sporan a bhruic-fhiadhaich,
> Gun chruaidh-shnaim riamh ga theannachadh,
> Gur tric thu tarruing iall as
> 'S ga riachadh a measg aineartaich.

He was a firm friend of the soldier, and considered every man in his regiment committed to his personal charge. In health he advised them; in sickness he saw that all their wants were supplied; and when any of them became disabled, he was incessant in his efforts until he managed to secure a pension for them. Numerous stories are told of the many encounters between him and Sir Harry Torrens, Military Secretary to the Commander-in-Chief, and his persistent applications for pensions and promotions. The poor fellows, for whom he was never tired of interceding, were naturally grateful for his fatherly feelings and actions towards them.

During the turbulent times of the 'Forty-five Allan Cameron passed his infancy. He was four years of age before he saw his father, and although it was hoped that the final settlement of the difficulties which then existed would favour his career in life, exempt from the evils and strifes of civil war, that was not to be, as the sequel will show.

He was the oldest, as we have seen, of three sons and three daughters, some of whom subsequently found meet employment in his regiment. Their education was conducted, as customary in those days, by resident tutors from Aberdeen and St. Andrews. With one of those Allan, on reaching a suitable age, went to the latter University for one or two sessions, to complete his education. As the eldest son, it was intended that, on arriving at a proper age, he should relieve his father of the care and management of the lands and stock, and become the responsible representative of the family at home; while it was arranged that of the other sons, Donald was to enter the naval service of the Dutch East India Company, and the youngest, Ewen, was to get a commission in one of the Fencible Corps of the county of Argyll. But this arrangement was not to be, especially as regarded the eldest and youngest. A circumstance of melancholy interest occurred before the former succeeded to the management of the farm, or the other arrived at an age to be an effective officer of a regiment, which had the effect of exactly reversing their prospects. The occurrence referred to was of a tragic nature, and caused the utmost sensation among the families of the district, for relationship was so general there that whatever brought affliction to the hearth of one family would leave its portion also at the threshold of the others.

Allan employed much of his earlier years in the sports of a Highland country life—fox-hunting, deer-stalking, and fishing for salmon on the Lochy, at all of which he was more than ordinarily successful. The nearest house to his father's was that of another Cameron chieftain of a considerable tribe (*Mac Ile' Onaich* or Sliochd Ile' Onaich), who had recently died of wounds received at Culloden. His widow and children occupied Strone House. The lady is reputed to have been very handsome, and would apparently answer *Donnachadh* Bàn's description of *Isabel og an oir fhuilt bhuidhe;* and she was styled *par excellence, a Bhanntrach Ruadh.* Allan, like a friendly kinsman, was most generous in sharing the successes of his gun and rod with the widowed lady, for which, no doubt, she was grateful to the youthful sportsman. The course of this commendable friendliness was unexpectedly interrupted by some words which occurred between Allan and a gentleman, also a Cameron, closely related to the widow's late husband, and known as *Fear Mhorsheirlich*. He had been out in the 'Forty-five when quite a youth, and escaped to Holland, from which he had only returned a few months previous to the date of the incident which terminated his life. Contemporaries spoke of him as a most accomplished gentleman, of gallant bearing. The exact nature of the dispute has not been preserved in a sufficiently authentic form to justify more detailed reference than that rumour assigned it to have been an accusation against Allan of being on too intimate terms with the young and handsome widow of Strone. The insinuation was resented by Allan in plain and forcible terms. Morsheirlich was Allan's senior by more than twenty years, but, notwithstanding, his high spirit could not brook the rough retort of his young clansman; and, much to Allan's confusion, he received a peremptory demand from his opponent to apologise for his language, or to arrange a meeting for personal satisfaction. Having declined the one, he felt bound to grant the other and more desperate alternative.

Allan's chief anxiety was, how to keep his position from coming to the knowledge of his parents and family, and he quietly repaired to a relative to request his attendance the following morning as his friend or second on the occasion. This gentleman used his utmost powers of dissuasion without success. Determination had, in the short interval of a few hours, become too settled for alteration. Allan, as the challenged, according to duelling etiquette, was entitled to the choice of weapons and place of meeting. Although by this time the pistol had in a measure superseded the rapier in England on such occasions, the broadsword remained the favourite weapon in the north. Highlanders had always a preference for the arm styled by Ossian—*An Lann tanna*—and by the modern bards—*Tagha nan arm*. Allan decided on the steel blade, and named an obscure spot on the banks of the Lochy for the meeting, on the following day, at the grey hour of morning.

His next difficulty was how to get possession of a good sword without exciting suspicion or inquiries. These numbered, at that period, more than one in the armoury of every Highland gentleman's household, and those in his father's house were preserved with a care due to articles which had been often used with good effect in what was considered sacred occasions in the past. Among the favourites was one which had been out in the campaigns of 1689 under Dundee, in 1715 under Mar, and in that of 1745-6. Of Spanish manufacture, and remarkable for the length and symmetry of its blade, it received the sobriquet of *an Rangaire Riabhach*. Failing to find the keys of the armoury, Allan determined to take into his confidence an elderly lady who had been a member of the family since the days of his childhood. The aged Amazon not only promised her aid, but highly approved and even encouraged the spirit of her youthful relative. Having access to the keys of the armoury, the *Rangaire* was soon in Allan's possession, and with it he repaired to the appointed place, to vindicate his honour and to afford satisfaction to his antagonist.

The time of year when this event took place was in the early days of autumn. Daylight and the combatants were on the scene together. Vague particulars of the preliminaries between them have been variously given. The elder Cameron was reputed a skilful swordsman, and it was said that this was not the first occasion on which he had met his foes in the field for a similar purpose. If the knowledge of this had any effect on the nerves of his young opponent, there was no outward sign of it. The home-taught countryman, however, must have felt that he was to stand face to face with no ordinary foe. Allan, like the generality of the young men of his day, had sufficient practice in the use of the weapon to make him acquainted with the cuts and guards. No sooner were the combatants engaged than the superiority of the elder Cameron was apparent, and it was soon placed beyond doubt, for he not only kept himself for some time uninjured, but inflicted a severe cut on Allan's left arm—a cut which may be said to have brought the conflict to its sudden and fatal conclusion. The pain and the humiliation roused Allan's wrath to desperation. It became at once manifest to the two friends present that the life of one, if not of the two principals, was to be sacrificed; but they were quite powerless to restrain the rage of the wounded youth. Their anticipations were not long in being confirmed. The elder Cameron fell from a blow delivered on the head by the powerful arm of his antagonist, the force of which may be imagined when we state that it was what is known as No. 7 cut, and that Morsheirlich's sword, in the act of defending himself, was forced right into his forehead. He only lived long enough to reach Strone House, distant about a mile.

The state of feeling which such a painful result produced on the three survivors of the scene may be imagined. Time, however, was not to be trifled with, for, although there were no "men in blue" to take in charge the breakers of the peace, yet the vanquished combatant had friends who would not hesitate even to take life for life. That possibility at once occurred to Allan's friends. They therefore hurried him away from the field and across the river Lochy. After a short consultation they decided that he should immediately leave the Cameron country for a time. In this he concurred, and girding on his claymore he resolved upon making direct for his uncle's house in Morvern—Maclean of Drimnin, about sixty miles distant, where he arrived without a halt. The decision arrived at proved a wise one, as the sequel proved. The fallen man being a cadet of a numerous tribe, it was natural, and in accordance with the habit of the times, to seek to avenge his death. They sought for Allan far and wide with diligence and zeal; but, fortunately for the fugitive, and thanks to the vigilance of his relatives, his pursuers failed in their attempt to capture him.

The consternation of the uncle at Drimnin, on learning

the cause of his nephew's sudden visit, may be imagined; but what was done could not be undone. When the laird was satisfied with Allan's version, that *Morsheirlich* fell in fair fight, brought about by himself, his displeasure relented. Affection and sympathy mingled in the old man's bosom, and he decided to befriend his unfortunate relative at all hazards. He conjectured that the search of the avengers would be directed towards his district, where Allan's relatives were numerous, and where they would naturally expect him to betake himself in this emergency. That he might elude his pursuers with greater certainty, Drimnin had him escorted across the Sound of Mull by some trusty kinsmen, and placed him under the charge of Maclean of Pennycross, with whom he was to remain until he should receive further instructions as to his future destination. The grief and revenge of *Morsheirlich's* friends had not yet subsided, and would not, for years to come, so that Allan would be unwise to return home, or place himself in their path.

The Collector of His Majesty's Customs at Greenock was a near relation of Drimnin, by marriage, and a correspondence was entered upon, with the view of ascertaining his opinion as to what was best to be done with Allan. Negotiations occupied more time at that period than we can imagine in the present day, and in the end nothing satisfactory was proposed to Allan, so that, for two years, he continued wandering up and down the island of Mull, and through the glens of Morvern, under the guidance of his uncle. At last a request came from the Collector to send the fugitive on to him, that he might find employment in his own office. The uncle decreed, rather against Allan's grain, that this offer of a clerkship should meanwhile be accepted. He remained in this occupation for several months, until he received an invitation from another friend residing in Leith. This gentleman wrote, intimating that there was now an opportunity of giving him service in an enterprise likely to be more congenial to "a man of metal" such as he conceived Allan to be. The war of American Independence had commenced, and the employment which the Leith friend proposed was that Allan should join a privateer which was fitting out in an English port, armed with letters of marque, to capture and destroy American shipping. Allan answered by repairing to Leith in person, with all speed. The nature of the service offered, however, did not accord with his ideas of honourable warfare; in fact, he considered it more akin to piracy, and not such as a gentleman should take part in. He had no affection, he said, for clerkship, but he had still less for the life of a pirate.

While he was thus oscillating he learned that a relative of his mother's, Colonel Allan Maclean of Torloisk, who had emigrated to one of the North American Colonies, some years previously, had received a commission to embody a regiment of those of his countrymen "who had become residents on free-grants of land at the same time with himself". To this gentleman Allan decided on going. Soldiering was more congenial to his nature than marine freebooting, and he calculated on Colonel Maclean's assistance in that direction.

Arrived in America, Allan was received kindly by his relative, and, being a soldier himself, he viewed the past event in Allan's life as of a nature not without a certain amount of recommendation to a wanderer in search of fame. Allan was not long in the country when Colonel Maclean added him to his list of volunteers, in a body which was soon afterwards enrolled as the "Royal Highland Emigrant Corps".

During the progress of the war the Americans were guilty of many acts of cruelty to whosoever fell into their hands, some of which fell to the share of Allan Cameron. The Royal Highland Regiment, to which he was attached, was stationed in Quebec when Canada was threatened with invasion by General Arnold at the head of 3000 men. Maclean, who had been detached up the river St. Lawrence, returned by forced marches and entered Quebec without being noticed by Arnold. The fortifications of the city had been greatly neglected, and were scarcely of any use for the purposes of defence. The strength of the British within its walls was under 1200, yet they repulsed the repeated attacks of the American generals. It was here that Allan Cameron came for the first time into hostile contact with the enemy, and both his regiment and himself acquitted themselves with great gallantry.

On the approach of spring, General Arnold, despairing of success, withdrew his forces, raised the siege, and evacuated the whole of Canada. Released from this defence the battalion entered on enterprises in different parts of the province, and to enable it to do so more effectually, Colonel Maclean transformed a limited number of it into a cavalry corps, for outpost duty and scouts. Of this body Cameron got the command. Daring, and sometimes over-zealous, he often led himself and his company into situations of desperate danger. On one occasion they were surrounded by a strong force of the enemy, from which they escaped with the utmost difficulty, and only by the personal prowess of each individual and the fleetness of their steeds. The Americans communicated with the British commander to the effect that "this fellow and his men had been guilty of the *un*military proceeding of tampering with the native Indians in their loyalty to American interests," stating a determination of vengeance in consequence. It is not known whether Allan was apprised of this charge against him or not; at any rate he continued his incursions for some time. The threat was not unintentional, as the succeeding events proved, and an unfortunate opportunity enabled the enemy to give it effect. Allan and nearly half his company were seized. The latter were made prisoners of war, and he was committed to the jail of Philadelphia as a common felon, where he was kept for two years and treated with the most vindictive harshness. This proceeding was denounced by the British General as "contrary to all military usage," but his representations proved unavailing.

The ardent nature of the imprisoned Highlander chafed

under restraint, and finding no hope of release he was constant in vigilance to procure means of escape. This he at last effected through his jailer neglecting to fasten the window of his place of confinement, which was on the third storey. Allan's ingenuity was put to the severest test. He, however, managed to tie part of the bed-clothes to the bars of the window, and descended with its aid. The blanket was either too short, or it gave way; Allan came to the ground from a considerable height, and, being a heavy man, he, in the fall, severely injured both his ankles. In this crippled state he was scarcely able to get away to any distance, but he managed to elude the search of his enemies.

Although the Americans, as a nation, were in arms against Great Britain, still among them were many families and individuals who were slow to forget their ties of kinship with the people of the "old country," and Philadelphia especially contained many who possessed that feeling. Allan, on his first arrival in that country, became acquainted with and obtained the friendship of more than one of these families. To the house of one of them, in his emergency, he decided on going. This was a Mr. Phineas Bond, afterwards Consul-General in that city, who received him without hesitation, and treated him with the utmost consideration. Allan, however, before he would accept shelter and hospitality, explained to Mr. Bond his condition and how he became a prisoner, adding that he merely desired rest for a day or two to enable him to escape towards the British cantonments. Mr. Bond made him welcome and promised him every assistance. Both were fully impressed with the danger and delicacy of their position, and Allan, like an honourable soldier, was more anxious about that of his host than about his own. He, therefore, embraced the first opportunity of relieving his chivalrous friend of so undesirable a guest.

Without entering into details as to the nature of his escape, it may be stated that after frequent chances of being recaptured, Cameron arrived at a station where some

British troops were quartered. Among these were some officers and men with whom he had served in the early part of the campaign, but he had become so altered in condition that they scarcely believed him to be the Allan Cameron they knew. His relative, Colonel Maclean, sent his aide-de-camp to convey him to headquarters, on arrival at which he was most attentive to do everything that could be done for him. After medical inspection, however, Allan was pronounced unfit for active service for at least a year. This was most disappointing to him, as he feared his career in the army was in consequence to come to an untimely end. Colonel Maclean recommended him to repair at once to Europe and procure the most skilful advice he could get for the treatment of his wounds and broken limbs. Allan concurred, and returned to England on sick leave, where he arrived in 1780.

He had not been many months at home when news arrived of the conclusion of the war; and, with that consummation, Colonel Maclean's corps was reduced; the officers were placed on the "provincial list"—a grade not known in the army at the present day—Government, in addition to their pay, giving them and the other men grants of lands in the following proportions—5000 acres to a field officer; 3000 to a captain; 500 to a subaltern; 200 to a sergeant; and 100 to each soldier. These conditions were applicable only to those who remained in, or returned within a given time to the colony. In the case of absentees only one-half of this number of acres was granted, but they were allowed to sell their lots. As Allan had been promoted to the rank of captain, he had 1500 acres, which he turned into cash. This money and his pay were the only means he possessed. He was, however, only one of many similarly situated on the termination of the American War.

The transport ship brought home other invalids besides Cameron, one of whom, Colonel Mostyn, and himself came to be on terms of the warmest friendship. This gentleman, descended from one of the best families in Wales, and having many relatives resident in London, was of considerable service to Allan in introducing him to the society of these relations and other friends. "American officers," as those returned from the war were termed, were welcomed wherever they went. Among them Allan was not the least distinguished, perhaps the more so on account of his unfortunate adventure with his Lochaber adversary in the duel already described; and his subsequent chequered career in America.

At the house of one of Colonel Mostyn's relatives, Allan met a young lady who was destined a few months after to become his wife. She was the only child of Nathaniel Philips of Sleebeich Hall, Pembrokeshire. The heiress of a wealthy squire was beyond Allan's expectations; besides, he understood there were more than one aspirant for her hand, who were themselves possessors of many broad acres; and it could scarcely occur to the mind of the "provincial officer" to enter the lists against such influential competitors.

Notwithstanding, Cameron became the favoured suitor of Miss Philips, but both thought the barrier of her father's consent to be insurmountable. Nor was there any circumstance likely to arise in favour of Allan's worldly position to make him acceptable to the squire as his son-in-law. He therefore made his visits to the house of their mutual friend at greater intervals. Philips was at the time, and had been for a few years, a widower; and it was reported that he was contemplating a second marriage. Moreover, his intended spouse was scarcely yet out of her teens, while he was past middle age, and even his daughter was her senior. The father's intentions created disappointment, if not dissatisfaction, in his daughter's mind, which, it is alleged, was one of the causes that induced her not to view even elopement with serious objection, and Allan Cameron and Miss Philips betook themselves to Gretna Green without the knowledge or consent of her father. Notwithstanding that a vigorous pursuit ensued, it was not successful in interrupting the marriage of the runaway pair.

Instead of returning to London with his bride, Allan went to the capital of his native country, where he and his wife remained for several months. It now, however, became necessary that he should get into some office, the emoluments of which would add to his slender income. After some delay he was fortunate in securing an appointment, through a friend with whom he had served in America, on the militia staff of one of the English counties. Allan retained it until the fortune of events reduced the displeasure of his father-in-law to that state when mutual friends thought they could do something to induce the injured squire to forgive and forget. These friends did not fail to take advantage of this state of feeling, and embraced the opportunity to obtain for Allan an interview with Mr. Philips, his wife's father, which resulted in full forgiveness to the son and daughter. This was important to Allan, as the allowance to his wife, which followed, enabled him to live in affluence, in comparison with his past position.

Mr. Philips did not marry at the time rumour had formerly assigned, but he did so some time later, after he had become a sexagenarian. By the second marriage he had another child, who is still living, in the person of the venerable Dowager Countess of Lichfield, herself the mother of a numerous family of sons and daughters, including the present peer of that name, as also the wife of the present Earl of Wemyss.

Two years before Allan's return from America, the Highland Society of London was instituted for "promoting objects of advantage to the Highlands generally; and good fellowship, with social union, among such of its natives as inhabited the more southern part of the island," and several other specific objects, such as the restoration of the Highland dress; the preservation of the music of the Highlands; cultivation of the Celtic language, etc., etc. An institution for the support of such objects had particular attractions for Allan Cameron; and now that he was not otherwise specially employed, he was able to give some attention to their promotion. The members of the society were composed of almost all the men of rank and position belonging to, or connected with, Scotland. From the list, Allan appears to have been elected at a meeting held on the 21st of January, 1782, and, with the names of other gentlemen on the same occasion, John Home, author of *Douglas*, is included.

The Act of Parliament which enacted the suppression of the Highland dress was in force in Scotland during Allan's childhood, and up to the time of his departure, after the encounter with *Morsheirlich*, so that he had never worn the dress of his ancestors until he joined his regiment in America. Its use was still (1782) prohibited at home. On his return Allan and many of his friends became the most active members for promoting the objects of the society. Having found that one of these was the restoration of the Highland dress, they formed a committee, of which Cameron was a member, to co-operate with members of the Legislature to have that obnoxious Act removed from the Statute Book. Within a few months after this date, the legal restriction placed on the dress of the Highland people for the previous thirty-five years, was obliterated for ever.

The next action of national importance which engaged the attention of the society was the publication of the Poems of Ossian in the original. In the prosecution of this project Cameron was most zealous, but before it was completed he was called away to duties of a sterner nature. About the same time the controversy respecting the authenticity of the Poems was running its rancour unabated. During the few days of Allan's sojourn as a fugitive in Mr. Bond's house, they had conversed on the merits of Ossian's poems, and the latter informed Allan that he had such evidence in favour of their ancient existence as convinced him of their being the genuine remains of poetry of a very remote period, adding that he owed his intimacy with them to the acquaintance of the Rev. Colin MacFarquhar, a native of one of the Hebrides, at this time minister in Newhaven of Pennsylvania.

It occurred to Allan that it would be desirable to get the testimony of this gentleman, and he decided upon addressing himself to his friend in Philadelphia on the subject. In due time Mr. Bond replied with a communication from Mr. MacFarquhar, dated, "Newhaven, Penn., January, 1806," stating that :—" It is perfectly within my recollection when I was living in the Highlands of Scotland, that Mr. James Macpherson was there collecting as many as he could find of the poems of Ossian. Among those applied to was a co-presbyter of mine, who knew that a man of distinguished celebrity had resided in my congregation, and he requested the favour of me to have an interview with him and take down in writing some of these poems from his lips for Mr. Macpherson, which I did, but cannot recollect at this distance of time the names of the poems, though I well remember they were both lengthy and irksome to write, on account of the many mute letters contained in almost every word. Indeed, it would be difficult to find one among ten thousand of the Highlanders of the present day who could or would submit to the task of committing one of them to writing or memory, though in former ages they made the repetition of the poems a considerable part of their enjoyment at festive and convivial entertainments. Well do I remember the time when I myself lent a willing ear to the stories of Fingal, Oscar, Ossian, and other heroes of the Highland bard. I cannot, therefore, forbear calling that man an ignorant sceptic, and totally unacquainted with the customs of the history of the Highlanders, and the usages prevailing amongst them, who can once doubt in his mind their being the composition of Ossian. And as to being the production of Macpherson or any of his companions, I have no more doubt than I have of the compositions of Horace or Virgil to be the works of these celebrated authors."

The secretary laid Mr. Bond's letter and the statement of the Reverend Mr. MacFarquhar before the Highland Society, which they considered so important as to adopt them in Sir John Sinclair's *Additional Proofs of the Authenticity of the Poems of Ossian.**

Allan, although now, 1792, surrounded by a young family, and in circumstances independent of the emoluments of his profession, was not disposed to live a life of idleness. Nor had he relinquished the intention to enter again on active service. This was most difficult of accomplishment, on account, principally, of the reduction of the army on the termination of the American War; and that no additions were made to it for the past five or six years.

Britain was at the time at peace; but the state of affairs in India was causing so much concern that the home government decided on increasing the military force in all the Presidencies; and to enable that to be effected, an augmentation of the army of five battalions was ordered, commencing with the 74th regiment. Two of these were to be raised in Scotland and three in England. Into one of the new corps Allan hoped to be transferred from the provincial list. In this, however, he was disappointed, owing to other applicants being his seniors in the service; notwithstanding that the Marquis Cornwallis, whose friendship he had previously gained in America, recommended him to the Commander-in-Chief.

After remaining a few years longer at home, an event impended, which was to shake Europe to its foundation—the French Revolution.

The force which was sent to Flanders in 1793 was a serious drain on the strength of the army, which had to be made good without delay. The government ordered commissions to be issued forthwith for the enrolment of twenty-two regiments for general service, from the 79th to the 100th, sixteen of which were subsequently made per-

---

* In connection with this subject, another reference was made to Mr. Bond. The Highland Society in acknowledging the receipt of his communications, alluded to the services he had rendered to their fellow-countryman (Erracht) when in distress. The Marquis of Huntly, who was President, moved that the Society's Gold Medal be conferred on Mr. Bond; also that he be elected an *Honorary* member of the Society. The propositions were unanimously approved, and thus his friendship to the benighted prisoner was not forgotten by the members of this noble and patriotic Society.

manent, and added to the establishment. Other bodies were also raised for home service, known as Fencibles. Now was the time for Allan to bestir himself. Applicants, with influence and claims on the War Office, were greatly in excess of the number required. The previous recommendation by Lord Cornwallis in his favour was found of advantage in support of his present application, for the Letter of Service granted in his favour was among the first of the batch gazetted on the 17th of August, 1793. Although Major-Commandant Cameron (for he will now be named by his successive ranks in the army) had reason to be satisfied with the success of his application for the Letters, yet the terms and conditions embodied were not only illiberal, but exacting; a circumstance he had an opportunity some time afterwards of pointing out to one of his Majesty's sons, the Duke of York. The document is not sufficiently interesting for quotation at length, and the following extract must suffice :—" All the officers—the ensigns and staff-officers excepted — are to be appointed from the half-pay list, according to their present rank, taking care, however, that the former only are recommended who have not taken any difference in their being placed on half-pay. The men are to be engaged without limitation as to the period of their service, and without any allowance of levy money, *but they are not to be drafted into any other regiments.*" On receipt of this communication from the War Office, Major Cameron received intimation from his father-in-law—Mr. Philips —that money to the extent of his requirements for the expenses of attaining his ambition, would be placed at his disposal. This relieved him from one of his principal difficulties. The next consideration was, how far it might be prudent to make the recruiting ground his own native district of Lochaber, remembering how he had left it as a fugitive from the vengeance of a considerable portion of its inhabitants. The terms of his Letters of Service restricted him in the disposal of the commissions which might have been offered them as means of pacification, but the few left at his disposal he at once decided to confer on the sons of families in influential positions and otherwise eligible for appointments. With this view he despatched several copies of the *London Gazette* containing the "authority to raise a Highland regiment" to his brother Ewen, known in later years as *Eoghann Mor an Earrachd*, with a letter, both of which he enjoined him to make as widely known as possible. The letter is, if somewhat plausible, frank enough, and characteristic of his conduct throughout his varied career. He states that, "having been favoured with the honour of embodying a Highland regiment for his Majesty's service, where could I go to obey that order but to my own native Lochaber; and with that desire I have decided on appealing to their forgiveness of byegone events, and their loyalty to the sovereign in his present exigencies. The few commissions at my disposal shall be offered first to the relatives of the gentleman whose life, unfortunately, was sacrificed by my hand."

The printing press, even of the capital of the Highlands, was not so far advanced in those days as to enable him to have circulars printed of this proclamation. The brother had to transcribe copies as best he could, which he did to such effect that, before Allan arrived in Lochaber, Ewen had already enlisted a company to start with, all of whom he retained on his farm at Erracht until the arrival of Allan. Thus the credit of gathering the nucleus of the now long famous 79th is due to *Eoghann Mor*, for which service his brother, Major Allan, procured for him a commission as captain and recruiting officer for the regiment in Lochaber.

The first duty which Cameron had now, 1794, imposed upon him by his Letter of Service, was to recommend the officers from the half-pay list to be associated with him in raising the regiment. In the disposition of these he was, to a certain extent, under the guidance of his own inclination, to have as many as he could of his old American brother-officers with him. After the selection was made, the names were submitted to the War Office and approved.

Reference to the list of officers selected will show that Cameron was not unmindful of his brother-officers of the Royal Emigrant Regiment, his choice consisting of five officers of the Clan Maclean, while two only belonged to his own. When the half-pay list was exhausted, by distribution among the numerous corps being embodied, and Allan was released from the War Office regulations, the commissions in the regiment were always given to his Lochaber relatives, as the army list of subsequent years will fully testify.

Although Major Cameron had, by this time, been absent from the district for a number of years, yet he was not an entire stranger; for he was from time to time heard of. He was informed by his brother that the rage and irritation occasioned by the result of the famous duel had greatly subsided, if not, indeed, entirely disappeared, and that his arrival in the country was not at all likely to revive them. On receipt of this intelligence Allan, with careful calculation, arranged that he should arrive in his native Lochaber on one of the first days of November, which would give him an opportunity of meeting the greater part of the country people of all classes, at the winter market, at Fort-William. The idea also occurred to him that, as he was to be engaged in his Majesty's service, the government might give him, for his own and his officers' accommodation, quarters in the garrison. His application to the Board of Ordnance, to this effect, proved successful, and the building known as Government House was placed at his disposal. His family, at this time, consisted of three sons, respectively named Philips, Donald, and Nathaniel; the first and last after their mother's father, and the other after his own father. The eldest two accompanied him to the Highlands, and remained there long enough to acquire some acquaintance with the Gaelic language, an acquisition which they often declared afterwards to have served them well in their relationship with the soldiers of the 93rd.

The day at last arrived when Allan, after an absence of

twenty-five years, was to look again on his native hills, an event which gladdened and warmed his Highland heart. It is said that he timed his first appearance to take place on the last day of the market, and he observed it punctually. This enabled the people, if so inclined, to meet him without interfering with their business affairs. His brother, Ewen, was most useful to him in making proper preparations for his reception. Quite a multitude went out to meet him and his companions, about a mile, and accorded him a most enthusiastic reception. It has, indeed, been said, that the ovation and the escort of that day resembled more that usually awarded to an illustrious conqueror than that to a mere field-officer of the British army. Allan gave instructions to make that and subsequent days a carnival of hospitality — feasting and rejoicing without limit. After a reasonable time, however, the festivities must terminate, and business had to commence.

A writer of experience adverts to the anxious state of the public mind at this period.* "In 1793, and the succeeding years," he says, "the whole strength and resources of the United Kingdom were called into action. In the northern corner a full proportion was secured. A people struggling against the disadvantages of a boisterous climate and barren soil, could not be expected to contribute money. But the personal services of young and active men were ready when required for the defence of the liberty and independence of their country." Producing so many defenders of the State, as these glens have done, they ought to have been saved from a system which has changed the character where it has not altogether extirpated their hardy inhabitants.

The business of raising the regiment was now, 1793-94, to commence in real earnest, and as it was Cameron's desire that the complement should be made up of as many as he could induce to join him from his own and the adjacent districts, his officers and himself visited every part round about, with so much success that, between Lochaber,

* *Colonel Stewart's Sketches*, Vol. II., pp. 245-6.

Appin, Mull, and Morvern, 750 men were collected, at Fort-William, within less than two months; at any rate the official accounts record that number to have been inspected and approved by General Leslie on the 3rd of January, 1794.* Colonel Stewart states that, "in the instance of the embodiment of the 79th no bounty was allowed by government, and the men were therefore recruited at the sole expense of Allan Cameron and his officers; nevertheless the measure of the success will be understood by the early date of their inspection at Stirling, where they received the denomination of the 79th Cameron Highlanders". The Major was now desirous to repair as quickly as possible to the place appointed for inspection, that he might get his corps numbered, and with that determination, ordered every man to be in readiness for the journey southwards.

Great was the excitement in the little village, adjoining the garrison of Fort-William, on that winter's morning, when Cameron and his followers collected on its parade-ground, to have the roll called by "Old Archie Maclean," their first adjutant, preparatory to bidding farewell to Lochaber—a last farewell by the greater part of them. The nearest and dearest must part, and such was the case with the Lochaber men and their friends, now that "they promised to help King George". With Allan at their head, this devoted band filed off in well-regulated order, marching with steady step through the village, the pipers leading, playing the well-known march—"*Gabhaidh sinn an rathad mor*" (We will keep the high road), while large numbers of the country people convoyed them a considerable distance, reluctant to give the final farewell. A string of horses preceded them, to different stages, with creels well provided with creature comforts desirable for their long journey, along different paths, and over bleak mountains, to Stirling.

At that season of the year, the weather was very severe,

* *Historical Record of the 79th Regiment*, by Captain Robert Jamieson; Edinburgh, 1863.

and the absence of any habitations on the way did not admit of any halt; therefore it was decided to continue the onward course without interruption, except short intervals necessary for refreshments. This decision enabled them to reach the rendezvous at noon of the third day, when after a day or two's rest, drilling was resumed, without intermission, in consequence of which, the corps were in a fair state of order by the time the inspecting officer arrived. The Cameron Highlanders underwent the ordeal of military and medical inspection to the General's entire satisfaction, who duly reported the result to the War Office; and, being the first to be so reported, the corps received the first and subsequent number of 79th (the 78th, Mackenzie's Ross-shire regiment, having been completed in the month of March of the previous year). Meanwhile the exigencies of the service becoming pressing, the "Office" was induced to dispatch urgent orders to Cameron to augment the regiment with the necessary 250 men, so as to raise it to a total strength of 1000 rank and file. In obedience to this summons, he, with others of his officers, lost no time in returning to the districts of the Highlands from whence they came. If further proof were needed of his popularity, the fact that he collected the 250 recruits required, and reported them at Stirling in the short space of five and twenty days, will be sufficiently convincing. When the 1000 men were completed, on the 30th January, 1794, Allan was advanced to the lieutenant-colonelcy of the regiment!*

This marvellous rapidity of success may be contrasted with the fact, that when Cameron of Fassiefern was offered a company in the corps being raised by the Marquis of Huntly in the following month of February, he was obliged to have recourse to the assistance of his brother-in-law, Macneil of Barra, to complete the complement of 100 men. He was only able to secure nineteen men in his own district of Lochaber, notwithstanding that he was aided by the personal influence of his cousin, Lochiel, from whom

* *Captain Jamieson's Historical Record;* Blackwood, Edinburgh, 1863.

Allan Cameron did not seek, nor receive, the slightest favour.

The colours for the 79th had been prepared, and immediately on registration they were presented, in 1794, after which the regiment received the route for Ireland. There they remained until the following June, where their uniform reached them, which, being the Highland dress, was similar to that of the other Highland corps, except in the facings, which were green. Although the Cameron tartan is one of the handsomest patterns, the ground and prevailing colour being red, it was thought unsuitable for wear with a scarlet jacket; but that could not have been a sufficient reason for its non-adoption as the tartan of the Cameron Highlanders, the tartan worn, the Stewart, by the 72nd being of still brighter colour than the Cameron. Allan chose to have a tartan of his own, or rather of his mother's design. That pattern is so well known as to need no description. The first supply was provided by Messrs. Holms of Paisley (now of Greenhead, Glasgow), and designated the "Cameron Erracht," as distinguished from that of the Cameron proper. It is the pattern chosen by the Highland company of the Liverpool Rifle Corps, and by the 2nd Lochaber Company, of which Lochiel was captain.*

The Cameron regiment had scarcely completed its equipment, when it was ordered to embark for Flanders to reinforce the British and Austrian armies under the command of the Duke of York, against the French. They were joined in this expedition by their countrymen of the 42nd and the 78th. Their arrival proved of the utmost consequence, inasmuch as that by their support, in reserve, they helped, by a victory over Pichequr, to retrieve a disaster experienced by the Duke shortly before. This

---

* "It was returned to the Lord-Lieutenant by this company under the designation of "Cameron Lochiel". The captain's attention was drawn to the misnomer, who disclaimed any knowledge of the error. It has transpired since, to have been the act of an officer of the corps, now deceased, who must have committed this piece of piracy, either from ignorance or subserviency."—*The late John Cameron MacPhee.*

engagement lasted from an early hour till the afternoon, and its decision was weighing in the balance, when the Duke charged with the British troops into the centre of the French army, bayonet in hand, and thus brought hostilities to an end for the day. This success, however, was of small advantage, as the Allies were subsequently compelled to retreat before the overwhelming forces of the French, and, retiring towards Westphalia, endured the most dreadful hardship and suffering, both from its inhospitable inhabitants and the rigour of its climate—the winter and spring of 1794-95—the elements of which proved more fatal to the British army than the fire of the enemy. The Camerons lost 200 men. The British army withdrew from the Continent after this fruitless campaign, embarking in April at Bremen. The 79th was ordered for quarters to the Isle of Wight, where it remained till the month of July, when it received the route for India ; and Colonel Cameron was again ordered to recruit the regiment to the extent of its losses in Flanders.

The destination of India was suddenly countermanded and exchanged for the Island of Martinique. With this change the following incident is said to have had something to do. While Colonel Cameron was making the most laudable endeavours to complete his regiment to the required strength, he received private information that it was intended to draft one of the newly-raised corps to others at the time serving in India, to make up for deficient numbers, and that the measure was resorted to solely on the plea of economy. Rumour, moreover, gave it that the Camerons were those to be sacrificed. This report reached the Colonel, and though through an unofficial channel, yet he considered the source of his information too important to be treated with indifference, and it caused him much uneasiness. While in this state of uncertainty he learned that the Duke of York, Commander-in-Chief, was expected on a tour of inspection ; he determined to await his arrival at Portsmouth, and seek an interview with reference to the truth or falsehood of the rumour regarding the drafting of the 79th. Of the nature and result of this audience we have two accounts which we shall give as briefly as possible. The first is from the Record of the 79th.*— "Colonel Cameron respectfully, yet firmly, remonstrated on the extreme hardship and injustice of the proposed measure, which, besides being a breach of faith towards himself personally, would also be in open violation of a specific clause in his Majesty's 'Letter of Service' for raising the regiment. These representations had their effect, and, if an order so vexatious ever existed, it was rescinded, as nothing was afterwards heard of drafting." To this account the following footnote is added :—" At this interview Colonel Cameron plainly told the Duke 'that to draft the 79th was more than his Royal father dare do'. The Duke then said, 'The King will certainly send the regiment to the West Indies'. The Colonel, losing temper, replied, 'You may tell the King from me that he may send us to h—l if he likes, and I will go at the head of them, but he *daurna draft us*,' a line of argument which proved perfectly irresistible." The following is the version of the incident given by Mr. Thompson, the chaplain.†—" The regiment had not returned many weeks from the Continent when it was rumoured that it was to be drafted among others in India. Colonel Cameron, however, was not the man to be disposed of in a manner so summary, and he lost no time in waiting on the Commander-in-Chief, who admitted that it was contemplated to distribute one of the young regiments to reinforce those in India, but that its officers would not suffer in rank or pay meanwhile. The Colonel then unfolded a copy of his 'Letter of Service,' and begged the Duke would listen to the last clause of its terms, viz., '*No levy money will be allowed by the Crown, but in consideration of which it will not be drafted into other regiments*'. His Royal Highness remarked, that 'if the 79th would be thus exempted, you must not be disappointed if your Highlanders are sent to a climate more trying than

---

* *Jamieson's Historical Record of the 79th Cameron Highlanders.*
† *Military Annals*, compiled by Sir John Philliphart (Colburn, London, 1819).

India—Martinique will probably be the destination'. To this Colonel Cameron answered, 'I have performed my duty to collect corps for general and permanent service, therefore that you may order us to the hottest spot in the king's dominions, and it will be cheerfully obeyed, and myself at the head of them; but I trust his Majesty will not be advised to compromise his commission'. After some complimentary allusion to the appearance of the regiment, the Duke shook hands with the Colonel, saying, 'Your protest will be taken into consideration'." It is not of much consequence which version is the correct one. There is a rudeness and defiant tone throughout the first that Colonel Cameron would not be likely to commit himself to. He was by nature too courteous, and he would be politic enough to avoid language that might be construed into an act of insubordination. Whether it was from the necessities of the service, or as a matter of punishment for his remonstrance against the drafting, has not transpired, but, within a few days after the interview, the regiment was directed to sail for the Island of Martinique.

In this place they remained for two years, where disease carried off more officers and men than did the swords of the enemy in any of their subsequent battles. The regiment was reduced to less than 300 men, and Sir Ralph Abercromby, commanding the station, ordered Colonel Cameron, with his remaining officers and sergeants, home, while he directed the convalescent soldiers to be attached to other corps in the adjacent island. However welcome the order was to quit such sickly quarters, the Colonel demurred to the unreasonable proposition of the General, in detaining the men on stations where they had lost so many of their comrades by fever. Sir Ralph's command, however harsh and cruel, was supreme, and the result was, that few returned alive.

In addition to grief for the loss of so many of his gallant soldiers, the Colonel had also the misfortune to lose his wife while stationed in Martinique. Between fevers and the orders of Abercromby, drafting was accomplished most effectively, and Colonel Cameron had but a scanty number of his regiment to return home with. On their arrival at Gravesend, Chatham was assigned as their station, but they did not rest long there when they received orders to proceed to the North of Scotland, to recruit 800 men. As no place was specified in the warrant, Colonel Cameron selected the town of Inverness as his headquarters, from whence he, his officers, and sergeants, travelled over the northern counties as far as Sutherland, where they were most successful (the 93rd had not then been raised), and westward through the districts of the Great Glen. These exertions were rewarded by his being able to leave Inverness for Stirling at the head of 780 men ready for inspection. Thus, in less than nine months after his return from Martinique, he recruited a fresh body, equal to a new regiment, and procured them, notwithstanding that the 91st and 92nd had nearly denuded the country, a few years before, of all the men eligible for soldiers!

Colonel Cameron and his new regiment were now, 1798, ordered to occupy the military stations of the Channel Islands, where they lay for twelve months, until they received instructions to hold themselves in readiness to join another expedition, for the recovery of Holland from the French. The Duke of York again commanded-in-chief, while his generals of division were Sir Ralph Abercromby and Sir James Pultney, his brigadiers being Coote, Dundas, and Moore. The 79th formed part of Moore's brigade, with their countrymen, the First Royals and the 92nd. Several actions took place with varying success, and considerable loss on both sides. The principal engagements were, one near a village named Egmont-op-Zee, on the 2nd of October, and the other, in the vicinity of Alkmaar. The loss of the 79th in this, their first encounter with the enemy, was two officers and several men killed, with nearly half the officers and men wounded. Among the latter was the Colonel, and so severe was his wound considered that his recovery was despaired of. The brigade received the thanks of his Royal Highness, the Commander-in-Chief,

who, in passing it the day after the battle, approached the 79th, addressed Major Maclean, inquired for the Colonel, and expressed a hope that his wound was not so severe as reported; then taking off his hat, and turning to the regiment, he said, " Major Maclean, nothing could do your Highlanders more credit than their conduct yesterday ".*
By this time the season was so near winter that the Duke, sensible that operations during it would not be attended with advantage, entered into a capitulation, and thus ended the second expedition to the Continent, which was almost as ineffectual as the previous one of 1793-4.

It has been observed that although this was not the first campaign in which the Cameron Highlanders served, yet it was their maiden one, so far as coming into personal conflict with the enemy.

In connection with this engagement an incident occurred which, not being without interest, may be introduced into the narrative. It need not be denied now, that, for centuries, and down to a considerable period in the reign of George III., there existed in the breasts of the Highlanders, and especially those of the Jacobite clans, a feeling of kinship towards their ancient allies, the French, as against their mutual foes, the English. That amity, however, would last only so long as the French did not provoke the wrath of the king, to whom the 79th had now sworn fealty. Allan Cameron and his officers had already proved *their* loyalty in defending the rights of the British crown in the American War, but that test had not yet been applied to his Highlanders, and there was no suspicion that the slightest defection existed; nor was there any when the moment for action arrived. The incident referred to is given on the authority of a gentleman, himself one of the heroes of Albuera, from an interesting work on congenial subjects,† who says—" Without quoting the other verses of this song,‡ I cannot help remarking that the feeling against

---

* *Captain Jamieson's Historical Records of the 79th Regiment.*

† *Traditions of the Highlands, its Poetry, Music, &c.*, page 130, by Captain D. Campbell, late 57th Regiment; Collie, Edinburgh, 1862.

‡ An old Gaelic song of inimical sentiments towards the opponents of the Stuart dynasty.

the English nation expressed in the song, came down, at least, among the adherents of the Stuart family, to my own time, the commencement of the war resulting from the French Revolution. This was shown by the 79th Highland Regiment at a critical moment, on its first meeting the French under its illustrious founder and chief, Allan of Erracht. This splendid officer heard a murmur passing through its ranks as the enemy was in front—'The French are our old friends, and of our own race'. Colonel Cameron said not a word, but ordered a slight movement forward, which brought his Lochaber men within range of the fire—upon which he exclaimed in his own thundering voice, 'Now, my men, there they are, and if you don't kill them, by ——, they will kill you'. The Camerons, on hearing this threat, and finding the bullets whistling freely in their midst, soon gave a speedy account of their ancient allies. From that day (Egmont-op-Zee) there has not been in the army a regiment more distinguished for loyalty and bravery."

The prowess of the British on this occasion, 1800, is commemorated by the Gaelic bard, Alexander Mackinnon, an enthusiastic soldier, who shared in the campaign, as a non-commissioned officer in the 92nd Regiment. In his epic, *Blar-na-Holaind*, he celebrates the deeds of the two Highland regiments (79th and 92nd) and their leaders, the Marquis of Huntly and Colonel Cameron, thus—

> 'S dh'fhag iad sinne mar a b' annsa,
> Fo'n cheannardach, Morair Hunndaidh,
> An t-og smiorail, fearail, naimhdeil,
> N'an leannadh ain-neart ga'r ionnsuidh.
> * * * * * *
> Bha'n leoghann colgarra gun ghealtachd,
> 'S a mhile fear sgairteil lamh ruinn,
> An Camshronach garg o'n Earrachd
> Mar ursainn chatha 's na blaraibh.

The army left Holland and arrived in England, where they remained undisturbed until the following August, when a demonstration against Ferrol was determined upon. The force sent included Colonel Cameron and his regiment,

SIR ALLAN CAMERON OF ERRACHT.   349

but the attendant laurels were too slight to deserve notice. Another and more important expedition followed, of which the then almost unknown land of the Pharoahs was the destination.

A French army under Bonaparte arrived in Egypt, preparatory to a movement on India. To drive this force out of Egypt was determined on by the British ministry. The comparative failures hitherto experienced in Holland had not impaired the confidence of the country in its soldiers, or in the skill of its leaders. Sir Ralph Abercromby proceeded with a force of 12,000 men, arrving at Aboukir in March, 1801. Bonaparte meanwhile departed to look after his personal interests in France, leaving the command in Egypt with General Menou. The British fleet had scarcely appeared in the bay before Menou was prepared for resistance. The demonstration, however, did not daunt the former from attempting to leave their ships. To land in the face of an opposing army was a task of great danger. A murderous fire galled them as they approached the beach. The men nevertheless landed, forming in order as best they could, bravely charged, and drove back the enemy, with great gallantry. The French retired and entrenched themselves in the vicinity of Alexandria. Abercromby followed them. Generals Hutchinson and Moore ably assisted. The French commenced the attack on the night of the 20th. The 42nd Highlanders, who displayed their accustomed valour, were the first encountered. The commander was in their midst encouraging them, and it was on that occasion that he, with such effect, reminded them of "their ancestors". As day dawned a numerous body of cavalry bore down again on the shattered ranks of the Black Watch. Simultaneously the brigade, of which Colonel Cameron and the 79th Regiment formed part, met dense swarms of the enemy's riflemen, with whom a contest lasted, more or less, throughout the whole 21st. Their ammunition was expended, and charges with the bayonet became their only recourse. The enemy, despairing of success, collected his scattered columns, and withdrew to his original position. The British, laying siege to Alexandria, closely invested it, and in a few days it surrendered. Thus ended a short but arduous campaign, the result being, the total and rapid expulsion of the French from Egypt. The four Highland regiments, 42nd, 79th, 90th, and 92nd, gained imperishable honour in this campaign, as did also their comrades, the Welsh Fusiliers, the 50th and 28th (the Slashers). The last-named regiment was attacked before and behind; the rear faced about and fought valiantly in this double position, and for this act of splendid discipline they are honoured by being permitted to wear their number on the back as well as on the front of their regimental caps.

Few of Colonel Cameron's regiment were killed in the Egyptian campaign, but he was badly wounded himself, and the greater portion of his men were wounded more or less severely.

On their return from Egypt, the 79th were settled for a year in the Island of Minorca, from which they embarked for Britain, where they remained till 1804. By this time, in view of further active service, Colonel Cameron was favoured with a Letter of Service to raise a second battalion, which he completed within twelve months of the date of his missive. While the Colonel was recruiting for the completion of this battalion, a considerable amount of feeling and controversy had arisen about superseding the kilt, in the Highland regiments, by the tartan trews, and from the following correspondence between the Horse Guards and Cameron, it will be seen that an intention to that effect existed. The Adjutant-General wrote:—

> I am directed to request that you will state for the information of the Adjutant-General your *private* opinion as to the expediency of abolishing the kilt in Highland regiments and substituting the tartan trews, which have been represented to the Commander-in-Chief from respectable authority as an article now become acceptable to your countrymen—easier to be provided, and calculated to preserve the health and promote the comfort of the men on service.
>
> Colonel Allan Cameron.   (Signed)   HENRY THORPE.

Colonel Cameron replied as follows:—

GLASGOW, *27th October, 1804.*

Sir,—On my return hither, some days ago, from Stirling, I received your letter of the 13th inst., respecting the propriety of an alteration in the mode of clothing Highland regiments, in reply to which I beg to state freely and fully my sentiments upon that subject, without a particle of prejudice in either way, but merely founded upon facts as applicable to these corps—at least as far as I am capable from thirty years' experience, twenty of which I have been upon actual service in all climates with the description of men in question, which, independent of being myself a Highlander, and well knowing all the conveniences and inconveniences of our native garb in the field and otherwise; and, perhaps, also aware of the probable source and clashing motives from which the suggestions, now under consideration, originally arose. I have to observe progressively that in course of the late war several gentlemen proposed to raise Highland regiments, some for general service, but chiefly for home defence; but most of these corps were called from all quarters and thereby adulterated with every description of men that rendered them anything but real Highlanders, or even Scotchmen (which is not strictly synonymous), and the colonels themselves generally unacquainted with the language and habits of Highlanders, while prejudiced in favour of and accustomed to wear breeches, consequently averse to that free congenial circulation of pure wholesome air (as an exhilarating native bracer), which has hitherto so peculiarly befitted the Highlander for activity, and all the other necessary qualities of a soldier, whether for hardship, on scant fare, *readiness in accoutring*, or making *forced marches, etc.*, besides the exclusive advantage, when halted, of drenching his kilt in the next brook as well as washing his limbs, and drying both, as it were, by constant fanning, without injury to either; but, on the contrary, feeling clean and comfortable, while the buffoon tartan pantaloon, with all its fringed frippery (as some mongrel Highlanders would have it), sticking wet and dirty to their skin, is not easily pulled off, and less so to get on again in *cases of alarm* or any other hurry, and all this time absorbing both wet and dirt, followed up by rheumatism and fevers, which ultimately make great havoc in hot and cold climates, while it consists with my knowledge that the Highlander in his native garb always appeared more cleanly, and maintained better health in both climates than those who wore even the thick cloth pantaloon. Independent of these circumstances, I feel no hesitation in saying that the proposed alteration must have proceeded from a whimsical idea more than the real comfort of the Highland soldier, and a wish to lay aside the national martial garb, the very sight of which has upon many occasions struck the enemy with terror and confusion, and now metamorphose the Highlander from his real characteristic appearance and comfort, in an odious incompatible dress, to which it will, in my opinion, be difficult to reconcile him, as a poignant grievance to, and a galling reflection upon Highland corps, as levelling that material distinction by which they have been hitherto noticed and *respected;* and from my own experience I feel well-founded in saying, that if anything was wanted to aid the rack-renting landlords in destroying that source which has hitherto proved so fruitful for keeping up Highland corps, it will be that of abolishing their native garb, which his Royal Highness, the Commander-in-Chief, and the Adjutant-General, may rest assured will prove a complete death-warrant to the recruiting service in that respect. But I sincerely hope that his Royal Highness will never acquiesce in so painful and degrading an idea (come from whatever quarter it may) as to strip us of our native garb (admitted hitherto our regimental uniform) and stuff us into a harlequin tartan pantaloon which, composed of the usual quality that continues as at present worn, useful and becoming for twelve months, will not endure six weeks' fair wear as a pantaloon, and when patched makes a horrible appearance; besides that the necessary quantity to serve decently throughout the year, would become extremely expensive, but above all, would take away completely the appearance and *conceit* of a Highland soldier, in which case I would rather see him *stuffed in breeches* and abolish the distinction at once.—I have the honour to be, etc.,

    (Signed)   ALLAN CAMERON, Colonel 79th Cameron Highlanders.

To Henry Thorpe, Esq., Horse Guards, London.

The reader will, we fear, be driven to the conclusion that the gallant Colonel had not strictly adhered to his promise of strict impartiality at the outset; at any rate it is manifest that the Adjutant-General applied to the wrong quarter for sympathy or favour for his views of abolishing the kilt as part of the uniform of the Highland regiments.

Colonel Cameron and the 79th formed part of the force sent at this time to the Baltic. Arrived at Elsinore, negotiations were opened for the delivery of the Danish fleet, under solemn engagements that it should be restored on the conclusion of a peace with France. The proposal being indignantly rejected by the Crown Prince, preparations were made to enforce it. The fleet proceeded up to Copenhagen, the troops were landed, batteries were constructed, and a bombardment was immediately commenced both by sea and land, which lasted three or four days, after which the Danish commander surrendered. Colonel Cameron, at the head of the flank companies of the army, with two brigades of artillery, was directed to take possession of Copenhagen.*

Both Houses of Parliament passed votes of thanks to the generals, admiral, army, and navy engaged in this expedition; and in addition, Colonel Cameron received a special letter from Lord Cathcart, concluding:—"In communicating to you this most signal mark of the approbation of Parliament, allow me to add my own warmest congratulations upon a distinction which the force under your command had so great a share in obtaining for his Majesty's service, together with the assurance of the truth and regard with which I have the honour to be, etc."

Scarcely had the army returned from Denmark when another demonstration was directed towards Sweden. Sir John Moore had the command-in-chief, and Colonel

---

* *Life of the Duke of Wellington;* Kelly, London, 1814.

Cameron was promoted to the command of a brigade. It was a bloodless campaign, and they returned pretty much as they went.

Soon after the battle of Vimiera, Sir John Moore was appointed to the command of 20,000 men destined to co-operate with the Spaniards in driving the French from the north of Spain. Of this force the 79th and other Highland regiments formed part. At this period the services of Colonel Cameron were closed as a regimental officer, the appointment of Commandant of Lisbon, with the rank of Brigadier, having been conferred on him. His personal command of the 79th therefore ceased, after fifteen years' unremitting and unwearied zeal, sharing its every privation; and his almost paternal care for his native Highlanders had never permitted him to be absent from their head. He finally resigned the command of the regiment into the hands of his eldest son, Lieutenant-Colonel Philips Cameron.*

At Corunna, the 79th, under Lieutenant-Colonel Philips Cameron, and the 92nd, under Lieutenant-Colonel Napier, were in the brigade of General Fraser, "a fine specimen of an open generous Highland chieftain, a good soldier, with plain common sense, whom everybody loved".† The British—or rather the remnant left from the retreat and the fight—embarked for England the same evening, and left Spain, for a season, a prey to the French.

General Cameron, who had been relieved as Commandant of Lisbon by General Sir John Craddock, was advancing towards Spain with a reinforcement to Moore's army, when he was placed in a most critical position by the unexpected retreat on Corunna. Nevertheless he succeeded in conducting his force back to Lisbon, undergoing great difficulties from the nature of the country, and the inclemency of the weather. It was considerably augmented by stragglers from Moore's army, collected as they went along. For this act General Cameron received the acknowledgments and personal thanks of the Commander-

---

* *Historical Record.*
† *Stocqueler's History of the British Army.* London, 1854.

in-Chief. The preservation of so large a number of men under the circumstances was fortunate, for in about a week Sir John Craddock, with them and those at Lisbon, was able to give considerable assistance to Wellington on his return to Portugal.*

Soon after, the British Government decided on making another effort to clear the Peninsula of its invaders. The chief command was conferred on Sir Arthur Wellesley, who arrived at Lisbon in April. A force under the direction of Sir John Craddock had previously moved from the capital towards Oporto, in which General Cameron commanded a brigade, consisting of the 79th, 83rd, and 95th regiments. Sir Arthur overtook this body at Coimbra, and immediately set about dislodging Soult from Oporto. His army amounted to 20,000, six thousand of whom were allotted to act as a separate corps under Marshal Beresford; Generals Hill and Cotton, with brigades, were directed towards it by way of Aveira, and Generals Sherbrooke and Cameron by Ovar; while Wellesley himself and the remainder took another route. All arrived at the rendezvous as designed, but found that as the bridge for crossing the Douro had been destroyed, and every boat removed, it became no easy matter to effect a passage. This difficulty was shortly removed by Colonel Waters finding, at some distance higher up, a small boat, and standing near it, the prior of a convent and three peasants. He prevailed upon these to row him across. The deed was a daring one, for the patrols of the enemy passed to and fro constantly. Colonel Waters returned with the peasants, and four barges, into which General Paget and three companies of Buffs threw themselves. The French were surprised, became confused, and, before they scarcely realized the state of matters, the British force had crossed; and soon after they were pursuing Soult out of Oporto. The slaughter was great, for a panic had evidently overtaken them. The enemy was not far advanced when headquarters were established in the house which Soult had so recently

* *Annual Register for 1828.*

occupied, and Sir Arthur and his staff partook of the dinner which had been prepared for the French Marshal.*

The British now entered Spain to form a junction with the Spanish forces, but the condition of the latter was so miserable that no dependence could be placed on their co-operation. Both were in position before Talavera, when two French *corps d'armée* (Victor's and Sebastian's) attacked them with the utmost fury. The Spaniards, from the nature of the ground, were nearly out of harm's way, so that the weight of the combat fell entirely on the British. The battle occupied two days (27th and 28th of July), and is reckoned to have been the best contested during the war. The French lost 7000 killed and wounded, and the British upwards of 5000. The victory gained for Sir Arthur the title of Viscount Wellington of Talavera. Writing to his friend, Mr. Huskisson of the Treasury, he says, "We have gained a great and glorious victory, which has proved to the French that they are not the first military nation in the world"†; also adding that nearly every one of the generals were seriously wounded; and in the same despatch he says, "I have particularly to lament the loss of General Mackenzie, who had distinguished himself on the 27th".‡

Brigadier Cameron is included among the general officers mentioned, as "meriting the Commander-in-Chief's unqualified praise for their gallantry during the contest". He had three horses killed under him—two on the first, and one on the second day, and he himself was twice wounded—severely on the 28th.

The defeat of the Austrians at Wagram having released Napoleon's army from that country, he resolved now to put the finishing stroke upon "British effrontery and Peninsular independence". His army across the Pyrenees was augmented to an enormous extent, and under the most renowned of his Marshals, among whom were Soult, Ney,

---

* *The Marquis of Londonderry's Narrative*, Vol. I. (Colburn, London).
† *Greenwood's Select Despatches*, Nos. 296 and 315.
‡ General Mackenzie had commanded the 78th, and will be recognised in the North as of "Suddie" (Ross-shire). A monument is in St. Paul's to his memory.

and Massena. The latter boasted that he would drive the British out of Portugal within three months. His first move was on Almeida, which he took, and Wellington fell back on the strong but irregular ranges of Busaco, near Coimbra. The British army numbered not much more than half the French; but this, with Wellington, was not of so much consequence as a good position fortified by nature. With this conviction he assembled the flower of his army and disposed of it along the hill-tops, there to await "the spoilt child of victory," as Massena was termed. These ranges, for a length of eight miles, were studded with Wellington's troops. Among his generals of divisions were Hill, Picton, and Lightborne, his brigadiers being Leith, Park, Mackinnon, Crawfurd, and Cameron. The plains below were thick with the enemy. Two months exactly to a day had elapsed since the last combat at Talavera, when now, on the early morning of September the 27th, the French commenced their ascent towards the heights with their accustomed *elan;* and, notwithstanding that the guns of the horse artillery made serious gaps in their ranks, their impetuous progress was not checked till they came in contact with Cameron's brigade (79th, 7th, and 61st), and Crawfurd's (43rd, 52nd, and 95th). The efforts of the enemy to force the British positions were unsuccessful, and these brigades suffered little during the rest of the day.*

This was the signal for the various divisions to engage. Unflinching valour was maintained on both sides, until, as evening closed, the contest ended with the disappearance of the French, and Busaco was added to the list of British triumphs.

Cameron escaped any mishap in this action, but as he was leading off his brigade his horse stumbled, and both came heavily to the ground, when he received a severe contusion of the chest, from which he suffered considerable

* In this affair the 79th lost Captain Alexander Cameron, who commanded a picquet and could not be prevailed on to withdraw. He was last seen fighting hand to hand with several French soldiers, to whom he refused to deliver up his sword. His body was found to be pierced with seven bayonet wounds.—*Historical Record.*

inconvenience for a long time afterwards. After this victory Wellington made his way towards Lisbon. It was on this occasion that he planned that wonderful system of intrenchment, known as the "Lines of Torres Vedras," where he lay during the winter of 1809-10.

After remaining here for a time with the army, General Cameron, finding his health to be in a dilapidated state, was most reluctantly compelled to apply for leave to resign his command, that he might return to England. The resignation was accepted in a letter from the Commander-in-Chief, in which he expressed sincere regret for the cause of the retirement; also his having heard from Captain Burgh *(aide-de-camp)* of the accident that befel General Cameron at Busaco, which would have had his sympathy at the time but from the pressing circumstances of affairs.*

This closed the military career of the veteran, after a period of thirty-six years—twenty-two of which were spent in active service in the field. "He first served in the American War of Independence, and next accompanied his own regiment to Flanders, the West Indies, Holland, Egypt, Portugal, and Spain, at a period of life when men of less strength of mind or of ordinary constitution and habit would be incapable of encountering such changes of climate and exhausting duties."† His heart was still with his Highlanders, and he left his son at their head, whom he had the misfortune to lose three months after they parted, to which event a reference may presently be made, as well as to the services of the 79th.

When, in 1811, Massena followed Wellington to the Lines of Torres Vedras, and found himself checkmated by his astute opponent, he retired sulkily towards Santarem, and having received large reinforcements, directed his movements with the view of relieving Almeida, which Wellington had meantime invested. The latter sent a portion of his army in pursuit, during which several actions took place. The light companies of the 79th were part of

---

* Letter in possession of General Cameron's family.
† *Stewart's Sketches*, p. 281, Vol. II.

the pursuers, and in its progress they overtook the 39th French regiment at Fozd Aronzee, and after a spirited encounter, Lieut. and Adjutant Kenneth Cameron * took its colonel prisoner and conveyed him to headquarters.

Massena hurried on to Almeida, but on the way thither the village of Fuentes D'Onor lay in his path. This position was occupied by the 24th, 71st, and 79th Highlanders, the whole being under the command of the colonel (Philips Cameron) of the latter.

Against this small band Massena brought an imposing force—including his "Giant Guards".† To obtain possession of the village was the determined object of the French Marshal—for it was the key to Almeida. The retention of the place, therefore, became matter of the deepest interest to Wellington. A frightfully sanguinary battle was the result. It commenced on the afternoon of May 3rd, and, with but little cessation, continued till the evening of the 5th. Chroniclers tell how valiantly the French attacked the village, and how nobly they were resisted by the Highlanders and by the 24th Regiment.

The contest raged furiously, and a serious of hand-to-hand encounters continued till darkness ended it for that evening, only to recommence within a few hours afterwards. French superiority of numbers enabled Massena to press the British out of the lower part of the village, after which he attacked the upper portion, but without success. It was a personal combat again; the ammunition was spent; the bayonet was doing its deadly work, and some whose bayonets became disengaged had to use the butt-end of their muskets. Bonaparte's Giant Guards were among the assailants, notwithstanding which the Highlanders and their gallant comrades, or rather remnants, drove them

---

* Lieutenant Cameron was of the family of Camerons of Clunes in Lochaber. He died a colonel after retiring to Canada. There is a fine monument erected to his memory in the Churchyard of Thorah, on Lake Simcoe, Ontario, with the following inscription—"In memory of Colonel Kenneth Cameron, formerly in Her Majesty's 79th or Cameron Highlanders, who died June 20th, 1872, aged 84 years". He is said to have joined the regiment as ensign in 1802.

† The enemy never had such a superiority of numbers opposed to British troops as in this action.—Note in *Wellington's Despatches* (Gurwood), No. 615, p. 545.

back and maintained their position. It was then that one of the French grenadiers was observed to step aside into a doorway and to take deliberate aim at Colonel Philips Cameron, who fell from his horse mortally wounded. A cry of grief, intermingled with shouts for revenge, rapidly communicated to those in front, arose from the rearmost Highlanders, who witnessed the fall of their commanding officer. This act caused great commotion, during which two companies of the 79th, that became separated from the main body, were surrounded and made prisoners.*

As Colonel Cameron was being conveyed to the rear by his sorrowing clansmen, General Mackinnon, at the head of the 74th Highlanders and 88th Connaught Rangers, was passing at the double, and his men, on hearing who was in the blanket—that it was *Ciamar tha's son*,† raised a yell, and redoubling their pace, dashed into the village, and, with this impetus, made a charge which cleared the enemy entirely out of it, with great slaughter. Captain Stocqueler ‡ writing of this engagement says :—" The 71st and 79th formed a very wall of their dead and wounded in defending their position. Here their chivalrous colonel fell—Philips Cameron, the *beau ideal* of a soldier, and the pride of his corps; and to this day a monument near a church at Villa Formosa records his virtues and his heroism."

Colonel Philips Cameron was held in the highest esteem as an officer of superior professional talent. So highly was he valued by Wellington that he and his staff, and all the general officers within reach, attended the funeral, which was conducted with military honours; and this at a most critical period of the campaign, and when they were urgently required elsewhere. § Notwithstanding the

* The largest proportion of the two regiments (71st and 79th) were Gaelic speaking men (indeed spoke English but imperfectly), and when the exclamation of *Thuit an Camshronach* (Cameron has fallen) was heard, the excitement became intense. This was followed by additional cries of Gaelic revenge.—*Historical Records*.

† The soldiers of the 88th being natives of Connaught, spoke Gaelic more like the Highlanders than any of the provinces.

‡ *Stocqueler's History of the British Army*, 1854.
§ *Historical Records by Captain Jamieson*.

pressure of other important matters that must have occupied Wellington at the time, he was so considerate towards the feelings of General Cameron, father of the deceased, that he wrote him two letters—the first intimating his having been wounded, and the other announcing his death. The latter is as follows :—

VILLA FORMOSA, *15th May, 1811.*

MY DEAR GENERAL,

When I wrote you last week (7th inst.), I felt that I conveyed to you information which would give you great pain, but I hoped that I had made you acquainted with the fullest extent of the misfortune which had befallen you. Unfortunately, however, those upon whose judgment I relied were deceived. Your son's wound was worse than it was supposed to be—it was mortal; and he died the day before yesterday at two in the morning.

I am convinced that you will credit the assurance that I condole with you most sincerely upon this misfortune, of the extent of which no man is more capable than myself of forming an estimate from the knowledge which I had, and the just estimate which I had formed in my own opinion of the merits of your son. You will, I am convinced, always regret and lament his loss; but I hope you will derive some consolation from the reflection that he fell in the performance of his duty, at the head of your brave regiment, loved and respected by all that knew him, in an action in which if possible the British troops surpassed anything they had ever done before, and of which the result was most honourable to his Majesty's arms.

At all events, if Providence had decreed to deprive you of your son, I cannot conceive a string of circumstances more honourable and glorious than those under which he lost his life in the cause of his country.

Believe me, however, that, although I am fully alive to all the honourable circumstances attending his death, I most sincerely condole with you upon your loss, and that I am yours most truly,

(Signed) WELLINGTON.

To Major-General Allan Cameron, etc., etc., London. *

Comment on this letter would be superfluous. No one will doubt the sincerity of the expressions of sympathy it contains, when they remember the character of the man who wrote it. And, while it is most honourable to the writer, we cannot withhold our admiration for one of whom Wellington could write in such terms of unqualified praise,† also our regret that his brilliant career, and the distinction

---

* Letter in possession of General Cameron's family. It is also in Gurwood's *Select Despatches*, No. 539, p. 478.

† Colonel Gurwood in his compilation of Wellington's select despatches records only five letters of condolence, viz., on the deaths of the Hon. G. Lake, 29th Regiment; Philips Cameron, 79th; Hon. S. Cocks, 79th; Hon. H. Cadogan, 71st; and Hon. A. Gordon (Staff); all of which bear unmistakable proofs of his sympathies, but the one quoted surpassed the rest in its tone of sorrow.

he must evidently have attained, was cut off at the early age of thirty.

In addition to the grief expressed for Colonel Cameron's loss by Wellington, the Man of War, he was lamented also by the Man of Letters—the Colonel's illustrious countryman, Sir Walter Scott—both in poetry and prose. In the Vision of Don Roderick, Colonel Cameron's death is thus bewailed :—

> What avails thee * that for Cameron slain?
> Wild from his plaided ranks the yell was given,
> Vengeance and grief gave mountain rage the rein,
> And, at the bloody spear point headlong driven,
> Thy despot's † giant guards, fled the rack of heaven. ‡

General Cameron was but slowly recovering from the effects of the injuries received at Talavera, and the accident at Busaco, when the news of the death of his son reached him. This laid him completely prostrate; his cup of sorrow was overflowing. Two of his sons had now fallen during the war, and he had previously been deprived of his wife, who had fallen a sacrifice to the climate of Martinique. His third son, Nathaniel, commanded the 2nd battalion of the 79th, and his household now consisted only of two daughters. Great consideration was extended to him by the authorities. Wellington's letter came with official communications from the seat of war to Lord Bathurst, Minister for War, which his lordship forwarded, accompanied by a note expressive of his own personal sympathy for the melancholy nature of its contents. He had also numerous letters of condolence from other distinguished persons. But the burden of sorrow uppermost with him was that he had survived Talavera, and so did not escape his present domestic calamity.

* Massena. † Napoleon.
‡ Colonel Cameron was wounded mortally during the desperate contest in the village of Fuentes D'Onor. He fell at the head of his native Highlanders, who raised a shriek of grief and rage; they charged with irresistible fury the French grenadiers, being a part of Napoleon's selected guard. The Frenchman who stepped out of his rank to take aim at the Colonel was bayoneted and pierced with wounds, and almost torn to pieces by the furious Highlanders.—*Note to Don Roderick.*

The following letter from General Cameron to his son was found in the pocket of the latter when he fell at Fuentes D'Onor :—

LONDON, *20th February, 1811.*

I arrived at home some few days ago after rather a rough passage to Falmouth. Captain Stanhope favoured me with his best cabin, for which I was thankful.

I am glad to say that I found your sister quite well ; and now my own health has so much improved, I begin to regret having resigned my command in the army. Let me, however, charge you to appreciate your own position at the head of a fine regiment : be careful of the lives of the gallant fellows, at the same time that you will also hold sacred their honour, for I am sure they would not hesitate to sacrifice the one in helping you to maintain the other. I will not trouble you with more at present, but write when you can.

Wellington, in his despatch, alluding to the gallantry of General Pack and his brigade in driving the French out of their redoubts at Toulouse, adds—" But we did not gain this advantage without severe loss, particularly in the Sixth Division. The 36th, 42nd, 79th, and 61st regiments lost considerable numbers, and were highly distinguished throughout the day."*

The 42nd had four officers and eighty men killed, and twenty officers and three hundred and ten wounded. Their colonel (Macara) was honoured with K.C.B., he having commanded the regiment in three general engagements. The 79th had five officers and thirty men killed, and fourteen officers and two hundred men wounded.

Colonel Douglas and Brevet-Colonel Duncan Cameron of the 79th received marks of distinction for the conduct of the regiment at this decisive action. In the course of the forenoon of 12th (Tuesday), intelligence was received of the abdication of Napoleon ; and had not the express been delayed on the journey by the French police, the sacrifice of many valuable lives would have been prevented. A disbelief in its truth occasioned much unnecessary bloodshed at Bayonne, the garrison of which made a desperate sortie on the 14th. This was the last action of the Peninsular War, and in the course of a couple of months afterwards the British army embarked for home—some of the

---

* *Wellington's Despatches*, No. 894.

regiments having previously been ordered to augment our forces in America.

General Cameron received the following letter from Lieut.-Colonel Duncan Cameron, giving him information about the battle :—

TOULOUSE (FRANCE), *13th April, 1814.*

My dear General,—I take the very first opportunity I could command since our coming to this place on the 10th to write you. We fought a heavy battle with Soult that day (Sunday) which we fervently trust will finish this interminable contest. I am sorely grieved at the loss of so many dear relatives and comrades in this action—in which I know you will join—your two nephews (John and Ewan), my cousin (Duncan), and Captain Purves were killed, and Lieutenant Macbarnet is not likely to outlive his wounds. Adjutant Kenneth Cameron * is also severely wounded, indeed I think Colonel Douglas and myself are the only two among the officers that escaped. We buried Captain Purves, John, Ewan, and Duncan in the one grave in the Citadel of Toulouse, and I have ordered a memorial slab to mark their resting-place. News is about that Napoleon has abdicated, but not confirmed. I will, however, write again and acquaint you of anything. I hope your own health is improved. My best regards. I am, yours ever sincerely,

DUNCAN CAMERON, Brevet Lieut.-Colonel.

To Major-General Cameron, Gloucester Place, London.

Among the general officers on whom the Prince Regent (George IV.) conferred the honour of knighthood after the war, and to whom the Houses of Parliament accorded their thanks, General Cameron was included, "in acknowledgment of long and meritorious services".

It is unnecessary to recapitulate Napoleon's imprisonment in Elba, his escape in spite of the vigilance of his guardians, his arrival at Cannes on the 1st of March, his entry into Paris on the 20th, at the head of an army, and the consternation among the representatives of the Allied Powers assembled at Vienna to regulate the dismembered state of Europe, when the astounding intelligence reached them that their imperial captive had escaped, and was already in possession of the Tuilleries. Nor is it necessary to refer in detail to the arrangements made by the Powers to meet their enemy again in the field, and the events which led to the battle of Quatre Bras, on the 16th of June. The history of the ball to which the Duchess of

* This gentleman is referred to by the Rev. Dr. Masson, as Colonel Cameron of Thorah, in his address before the Gaelic Society of Inverness (Transactions, p. 37).

Richmond (sister of the Duke of Gordon) invited Wellington, his generals, and other officers on the evening of the 15th, is already well known to the reader. At midnight, in the midst of revelry and mirth, from which, however, the generals and other officers had quietly and secretly retired, the bugles were sounded throughout the city of Brussels, summoning the troops to assemble for further orders. Sir Thomas Picton's division was the first to march. It was composed of Kempt's Brigade (28th, 32nd, and 79th), and Pack's (42nd, 44th, and 92nd). The colonels of the Highland regiments were Neil Douglas, Sir Robert Macara, and John Cameron (Fassiefern). At two o'clock A.M. the generals were informed that the troops were assembled and ready under arms. Perhaps no portion of British history has engaged so many writers as Wellington's campaign in Flanders. Southey, Scott, and Byron have devoted several stanzas to Waterloo. One stanza celebrates the gathering of the troops on that eventful morning :—

> And wild and high the "Cameron's gathering" rose !
> The war-note of Lochiel, which Albyn's hills
> Have heard, and heard, too, have their Saxon foes
> How, in the noon of night, that pibroch thrills,
> Savage and shrill ! But with the breath which fills
> Their mountain pipe, so fill the mountaineers
> With the fierce native daring, which instils
> The stirring memory of a thousand years,
> And Evan's, Donald's, fame rings in each clansman's ears.

At four o'clock on the morning of Friday, the 16th June, Kempt's Brigade was the first to start—its two senior regiments, 28th and 32nd, leading, and after them the 79th. To these succeeded Pack's Brigade and the Hanoverians, taking the road to Waterloo by the Forest of Soignes, where they rested at mid-day and refreshed. The Duke appeared among them at this early hour, and ordered them to proceed direct to Quatre Bras (twenty-one miles from Brussels).

> Soigne waves above them her green leaves,
> Dewy with nature's teardrop as they pass,
> Grieving—if aught inanimate e'er grieves—
> Over the unreturning brave.

Picton and his division, with the Hanoverians and a corps of Brunswickers, arrived there at two o'clock, every man of whom became immediately engaged with more than double their number, and continued so until six o'clock, when Sir Colin Halkett's Brigade most opportunely came to their aid ; still it was an unequal contest. The British had no cavalry present, except a few Brunswick and Belgians, which were soon scattered like chaff before the veteran French Cuirassiers. We read how a regiment of Lancers galloped into the midst of the 42nd, and how the latter stood back to back, every man fighting on his own ground, till they repulsed them, but with the loss of their intrepid colonel (Macara), who fell pierced and mortally wounded with lances. And when the Duke ordered the 92nd to "charge these fellows," how they sprung over the ditch and cleared them out of their position. It was in this charge their colonel fell also mortally wounded. Leaving Pack's Brigade, the Duke rode off to Kempt's position, where he directed the 79th "to cover the guns and drive these fellows from their places". The regiment accordingly "cleared the bank in front at a bound and charged with the bayonets, drove the French with precipitation to a hedge, where the latter attempted to reform, but were driven from that with great alacrity, and a third time scattered them in total confusion upon their main column". Their comrades of the 32nd and 28th were, at the same time, performing heroic feats of gallantry, the latter sustaining the reputation won in Egypt. The enemy failed in every attack, and at nightfall withdrew to a considerable distance. The action of Quatre Bras would have been sufficient of itself to be sounded by the trumpet of fame, but it was overshadowed by the subsequent and greater victory of Waterloo.

Wellington, in a paragraph of his despatch, pays his tribute of praise to Picton's men for their valour at Quatre Bras :—" The troops of the Fifth Division, and those of the Brunswick corps, were long and severely engaged, and conducted themselves with the utmost gallantry. I must particularly mention the 28th, 42nd, 79th, and 92nd regiments, and the battalion of the Hanoverians." Napoleon was in person at Ligny, from which he compelled Blucher and the Prussians to retire on Wavre. This retrograde movement necessitated a similar one on the part of Wellington, in order to keep up the communication of the allied armies. On Saturday (17th) the Duke made a leisurely retreat, undisturbed except by a few cavalry skirmishes, to the plains of Waterloo, which he had previously selected for a battlefield.

On the same day Napoleon formed a junction with Ney, when their united forces amounted to 78,000. Wellington's effective strength on the morning of the 18th was 68,000. The two portions of the field which appear to have claimed the greatest desire on the part of Wellington to preserve were the house and gardens of Hougoumont, an advanced post situated on the right, and the other, the village of Planchenoit on the left. The importance of holding the latter position will be understood when it is stated that it commanded Wellington's line of communication with Blucher. The first of these posts was occupied by the Brigade of Guards, among the commanding officers of which were Colonels James Macdonell of Glengarry, D. Mackinnon, and Lord Saltoun. The defence of the second was entrusted to Picton's division, but more immediately to Kempt's brigade, a wing of the Rifles under Major Alexander Cameron, the 28th under Colonel Belcher, the 79th under Colonel Douglas, and the Royal Scots under Colonel Campbell. Although, during the Peninsular War, Wellington met and fought almost all Napoleon's Marshals, the two principals had not hitherto met. Napoleon is said to have been confident, and to have expressed his gratification that he was "to have an opportunity of measuring himself against Wellington". About ten o'clock the respective armies were ready for action, and near enough to see each other. The scene must have been imposing—Napoleon the Great at the head of the chosen troops of

France, against those of Britain * and her allies, under the renowned British commander! The Emperor was observed with his staff passing along the lines, the troops hailing him with enthusiasm and loud shouts of *Vive l'Empereur;* the infantry raising their caps upon their bayonets, and the cavalry their *casques* upon their swords and lances! "The force of the two armies," said the Emperor, "cannot be estimated by a mere comparison of numbers; because though one Britisher might be counted for one Frenchman, two of their allies were not equal to one Frenchman." The first attack was made by Prince Jerome with a strong force upon Hougoumont, which continued more or less persistently throughout that day, † but the gallant Guards defended it successfully till the last, even when the whole place was in flames!

The enemy's next move was to wreak its vengeance on the British left position (Picton's). Ney, with four massive columns, made towards it, and meeting with some Netherland troops, which he dispersed easily, was descending upon a portion of Kempt's brigade, the 28th and 79th. The artillery on both sides were blazing away at each other, regardless almost of friends or foes. There was a hedge between the combatants, and Picton, seeing the impetuosity of Ney's columns, ordered these regiments to meet them, which was obeyed with a volley that stemmed their further progress, and then, with a cheer, they rushed through the hedge, receiving a murderous encounter in return. This caused but a momentary delay, as the leading regiment, the 79th, quickly rallied, and, levelling their bayonets, charged Ney's columns back to their position. It was during this repulse of the enemy that Picton fell, struck in the right temple, and he died almost immediately. His life had been spent in the service of his country; and no officer on the field that day was held in greater admira-

* The majority of the British regiments were composed of young men drafted from their reserve battalions. The peninsular regiments had not returned from America.

† This day of terrible strife was Sunday, and it was on the same sacred day, fourteen months before, that the battle of Toulouse was fought.

tion than this immortal son of Wales. His last words were: "Thornton (his *aide-de-camp*), rally the Highlanders" —the Camerons.* During the battle of Waterloo, Pack's brigade was not so hotly assailed as that of Kempt's. The 92nd was, however, an exception, but that occasion alone would be sufficient to immortalise their bravery. It was when some one of the foreign corps gave way,† before a column of several thousand French, who, in consequence, came directly in front of the 92nd, whose strength did not then exceed three hundred. Sir Denis Pack rode up, exclaiming, "Ninety-second, you must charge that body". The regiment formed four deep, and in that compact order advanced until within twenty paces, when it fired a volley, and instantly darted into the heart of the French column, in which it became almost invisible. The Scots Greys seeing the desperate situation of their countrymen, galloped to the rescue, shouting, *Scotland for ever!* The impetuosity of the Greys broke up the column, and in pursuing it Sergeant-Major Ewart captured two of their standards. After this brilliant affair, Sir Denis, complimenting Colonel D. Macdonald, added, "Highlanders, you have saved the position, retire and rest yourselves". Neither the 92nd nor 42nd, from the nature of the ground they occupied, were molested to any extent at Waterloo; but not so with Kempt's brigade, for Ney did not relax his utmost efforts to annihilate the devoted band that composed it, in hopes of interposing the co-operation of the Prussians expected from that quarter. The desperate trials to which they were exposed will be understood when it is stated that the 79th lost all its superior officers, and the command, for the last three hours of the day, was conducted by Lieutenant Alexander Cameron, and that of the 28th and Rifles to captains. While Ney directed his energies towards this part of the field, Napoleon and his generals ordered their resources on the whole line of the Allies, but more directly on their centre. This de-

* Captain Seborne's detailed account of Waterloo.
† Some writers say they were Belgians, others that they were Germans.

monstration brought the contending forces into general conflict—more especially the cavalry. It would be superfluous here to record the brilliant charges of Ponsonby, Vivian, Anglesey, and Somerset, with their respective brigades.

It was now seven o'clock in the evening, and the Prussians made their appearance, after which they attacked the French right (Planchenoit). Napoleon's chances were growing desperate, and as a last effort he ordered the advance of his magnificent Old Guard against the British position at La Haye Saint, Napoleon himself and his lieutenant, Ney, at their head. They went up a gently sloping ridge, at the top of which the British Guards were lying down, to avoid the fire of the artillery, but, as the columns approached, Wellington gave the word, "*Up Guards*," which was instantly obeyed, and, at a distance of about fifty yards, delivered a terrible volley into the French ranks. This was followed by a charge which hurled the Old Guard down the hill in one mingled mass with their conquerors. The result of that repulse threw the whole French line into confusion. Napoleon galloped to the rear, and Wellington, availing himself of the French dismay, ordered a general advance. The French were now in complete rout; Blucher followed and overtook Wellington at La Belle Alliance, when it was agreed to leave the pursuit to the Prussians, who were comparatively fresh.

Many prisoners were made, and Napoleon himself narrowly escaped. It was computed that, during the two days' engagement, the French lost 30,000 men, while it was also estimated that nearly half the Allies were either killed or wounded. Among the killed, besides Picton, were Sir William Ponsonby and the Duke of Brunswick.

The battles of the 16th and 18th may be described as a succession of assaults of unabated fury, which put even the steadiness of the British to a severe test. Every attack diminished their numbers, and still their survivors yielded not an inch of ground. No other troops would have endured for so long such a terrible struggle with an enemy of undaunted courage, and hitherto much accustomed to victory. It is a well-authenticated fact, that Napoleon repeatedly expressed admiration of the incomparable firmness of his opponents.

The wounded were in most instances conveyed to Brussels and Antwerp, while the remnant of the survivors bivouacked that night (Sunday) on the ground which had been the French position. Thus closed that eventful day, in a conflict, the first of which had commenced upwards of twenty years before, and which resulted in peace between the British and the French for over half a century. Notwithstanding the fatigues of the three previous days, the allied army marched off the field at an early hour the following morning to Nivelles, where they remained till joined by Wellington on the 21st, who had been to Brussels to see the wounded were cared for. After a short interruption they entered Paris on the 7th of July. Napoleon had, meanwhile, on the 22nd of June, abdicated in favour of his son, under proclamation, with the title of " Napoleon the Second"; but this submission was of no avail—the terms of the conquerors being the unconditional removal of the Bonaparte family and the restoration of the Bourbons.

For many years the field of Waterloo continued to be visited by men most eminent in the arts and sciences, civil and military, and of every nationality. Among the earliest visitors to it were Sir Walter Scott and Lord Byron, and both have commemorated their pilgrimages in verses that will co-exist with the memory of the battle itself.*

After the wounded reached Brussels, and were recovering somewhat, General Cameron received the following communication from Brevet-Colonel Duncan Cameron of the 79th Regiment:—

---

* Sir Walter and Byron met each other for the second and last time on this occasion. The former was on his way back, and the other was leaving the following day (15th September, 1815) for Waterloo and Paris. And this was Byron's *last* in England, as he never returned.

SIR ALLAN CAMERON OF ERRACHT.

BRUSSELS, *June 26th, 1815.*

My Dear General,—You will have heard of our great battles and our losses at them. I am here under the doctors, suffering rather severely from two wounds, and it is only with difficulty I can write these few lines. Our division was desperately engaged on both days, in fact I believe we suffered more than any of them. The colonels of the 42nd and 92nd were killed, besides heavy losses among their officers. I understand that our own regiment exceeded even them; in fact all our superior officers are either killed or wounded, and Colonel Douglas among the latter. You will understand *that* when I mention a lieutenant (your nephew Alexander) commanded it for the last two or three hours. Both himself and your other nephew (Archibald) escaped being seriously wounded, as they have continued with the regiment and are off with it to Nivelles. This will be gratifying to you, and also that I can add, they conducted themselves with the utmost gallantry and coolness throughout the terrible attacks made on us, notwithstanding that it was the first time either had faced the enemy. This town is quite an hospital, and what between prisoners and invalids, it is crowded. Medical gentlemen, both from London and Edinburgh, have generously come to our aid, and I have been fortunate enough to have had the attention of Mr. George Bell of the latter, who gives me hope of recovery, after which it is my intention to follow the regiment.—Meanwhile, believe me, yours very sincerely, DUNCAN CAMERON.

To Major-General Cameron, 28 Gloucester Place, London.

On receipt of this letter General Cameron, accompanied by one of his daughters, started for Brussels to see his suffering countrymen, where he remained a fortnight, and shortly after his return to London received letters from his two nephews from Paris, one of which is as follows:—

HEAD QUARTERS, CLINCHY, NEAR PARIS. *July 15th, 1815.*

My Dear Uncle,—I have to ask your indulgence for not writing sooner, but I was so closely on duty ever since we left Brussels on the 15th ult. that I really had not a moment to think of anything but to attend to it. I had a note from Colonel Duncan to say that you had been to see them there, and that he told you about Archie and myself. We both escaped getting badly hurt, which was a miracle, and we are thankful for it. In consequence of all my superior officers being either killed or wounded, the honour of taking the 79th out of the field devolved on me. We got frightfully attacked in getting through a hedge, the only time we got somewhat disordered. Our brave colonel was seriously wounded on the 16th; but during the day he was always reminding us of Toulouse, and General Kempt rode up saying, "Well done, Douglas," and then added, "79th, keep together and be firm"; and *we did*. Archie and myself are very anxious to have a look at Paris, but cannot get leave. Our strength is reduced very much—we do not number 220 effectives out of 740 the night we left Brussels. We lost on the 16th (Quatre Bras) 304 men, and on the 18th (Waterloo) 175. (I don't know *how many we killed*). I am sure your visit to Brussels was welcome to the poor fellows, and that it did more good to them than the doctors. I beg now to conclude with my dutiful affection to our cousins and yourself, and believe me to be your faithful nephew,

ALEXANDER CAMERON.

General Cameron, London.

He purchased the lands of Erracht from Lochiel, in 1790, but the disposition was afterwards annulled by the Courts, at the instance of Lochiel's trustees. It is, however, deemed best to give the particulars at length in the form of an Appendix.

Allan Cameron of Lundavra, in his depositions in this action of Declarator by Lochiel against Allan Cameron of Erracht, declares, "that the defender (Erracht) was always esteemed to be particularly attentive to every gentleman from the Highlands of Scotland, and was at pains to have them frequently at his house; that it consists with his knowledge, that the defender has been of great assistance to his poor countrymen, and particularly to such of them as had occasion to come to London, to get up the Chelsea Pension List, and the deponent has frequently seen numbers of them feeding in the defender's house, and once or twice has seen a dozen of them there at a time. Depones, that, previous to the present business, the deponent has always heard the defender express the highest regard for Fassiefern and his family, and that it consists with his knowledge, that the defender, out of regard to Fassiefern and his family, exerted himself, and procured a comfortable provision for a brother of Fassiefern's in the West Indies; and he also knows that the defender strongly recommended several young gentlemen, his countrymen, and who were accordingly provided for in the West Indies." There is no doubt that General Cameron was a great benefactor to his countrymen at that time.

The following is from a notice, on the occasion of Sir Allan's death, by Colonel Sir William Napier, in the *Gentleman's Magazine* for April, 1828:—

Died at Fulham, on the 9th ult., at an advanced age, General Sir Allan Cameron, Colonel 79th Regiment. By birth a Highlander; in heart and soul a true one; in form and frame the bold and manly mountaineer. His adventurous career in early life, and subsequent distinguished gallantry in the field, gained him considerable celebrity, together with the unbounded admiration of his countrymen, The son of a private gentleman, but ardent and determined in accomplishing whatever he undertook, he brought to the ranks of the British army more men, and in less time than any other, who, like himself, were commissioned to raise regiments in 1793-4. During the American war he had the misfortune of being taken prisoner, but from which he escaped after two years' confinement, by an act of desperate daring. Fate, however, brought him, in the course of his life, the rare distinction of being successively commandant of the capitals of two countries (Denmark and Portugal, 1807-8). Although of late years he was not able to go among his friends, yet they were always, and to the last, found at his house, and around his hospitable table. The number of this man's acts of friendship to his countrymen cannot be estimated, therefore the blank his death has created will be understood better than described.

General Sir Allan Cameron married Anne, eldest daughter of Nathaniel Philips of Sleebeich Hall, Pembrokeshire, with issue—

1. Philips, who afterwards succeeded his father as Lieutenant-Colonel of the 79th Cameron Highlanders, and was killed at Fuentes D'Onor. He died unmarried.

2. Nathaniel, Lieutenant-Colonel, 2nd battalion of his father's regiment, appointed on the 24th of June, 1813.

3. Ewen, killed in the Peninsula, unmarried.

4. Marcella,
5. Anne, } all of whom died unmarried.
6. Diana,

Sir Allan Cameron, who died at Fulham, Middlesex, on the 9th of March, 1828, was succeeded, as representative of the family, by his only surviving son,

NATHANIEL CAMERON, Lieut.-Colonel 2nd Battalion 79th Cameron Highlanders, of Dan-y-Graig, Glamorganshire. He married Lœtitia Pryce, only daughter of the Rev. John Cuny, cousin of the late Duke de Coigney, who possessed property in her own right in Glamorganshire—the Gellyhyr and Countycarne estates, now called the Cameron estates—with issue—

1. Nathaniel Pryce.
2. William Booth Joseph, St. Agnes, Cornwall, who married Elizabeth, daughter of W. Morris, without issue.
3. Lœtitia Pryce, residing in Brighton.
4. Mary Anne, who married J. W. Bruce, Duffryn, St. Nicholas, Glamorganshire, with issue—(1) Allan Cameron Bruce Pryce, who married, first, Louisa, only daughter of Sir John Slade, Baronet, with issue—three sons and three daughters, and, secondly, Miss Maunsell, with issue—three sons and three daughters. Mrs. Bruce died in 1880. (2) John Bruce, Commander, Royal Navy, who married Annie Maria, daughter of the Rev. George Boyes, the Parsonage, Aberchirder, Banffshire, with issue, four children—Thomas, Allan Cameron, George Wyndham, and Edith Marion. He was drowned at sea. (3) A daughter, Edith, who married R. Dick, of Tullymet.
5. Charlotte Mayzod Marcella, who married E. M. Elderton, of the Temple, London, and the Grove, Surrey, without surviving issue. She resides at Petersburg, Innellan. In addition to her husband's name she assumed that of de Coigney, one of the family names.
6. Georgiana,
7. Caroline Augusta,
8. Frances Ann Grey,
9. Alan Louisa Catherine,
} 4 Albert Road, Brighton.
10. Rosetta Phillippa, who married Charles T. Eustace, Robertstown, Co. Kildare, Ireland, and Grosvenor Street, London, without issue.

Lieutenant-Colonel Nathaniel Cameron was succeeded, as representative of the family, by his eldest son,

NATHANIEL PRYCE CAMERON, of Murton, Glamorganshire, and 5 Broadwater Road, Worthing, who married Charlotte Mary, only daughter of the late Loftus Tottenham, Glenade, Co. Leitrim, with issue—two children, who died young.

THE CAMERONS OF INVERAILORT.

THE Camerons of Inverailort claim to have originally sprung from the family of Erracht. The first that we know anything of is

DONALD CAMERON, who resided at Murligan, in Lochaber. He married Helen, daughter of Alexander Macdonald of Achatriachtan, Glencoe, with issue, eight sons, the six eldest of whom died young or unmarried. The seventh, the Hon. Hugh Cameron, went to Canada, where he became a member of the Legislative Council. The eighth and youngest was

SIR ALEXANDER CAMERON, K.C.B. and K.C.H., born in 1778, a distinguished Major-General in the British Army, which he first entered in 1797. We take the following account of his career from a publication issued by authority in 1816, when he held the rank of Major in the Rifle Brigade, and Brevet Lieutenant-Colonel in the Army :—In 1797, this officer was appointed to an ensigncy in the Breadalbane Fencibles, and continued to serve with them for two years. In 1799, he accompanied the expedition to Holland under the command of the Duke of York, as a volunteer (an officer of Fencibles), and soon after received an ensigncy in the 92nd Regiment, and served the whole of that campaign. In March, 1800, he volunteered to serve in the Rifle Corps, then forming under the superintendence of Colonel Manningham, and in the following August succeeded to a lieutenancy. In the course of that year he accompanied the expedition to Ferrol, and was engaged with a detachment of Rifle Corps under the Hon. Colonel William Stuart. Immediately after, he volunteered to accompany the 92nd Regiment to Egypt, and was severely wounded in the arm and side, on the 13th March, 1801, at the battle of Alexandria, after which he returned to England and rejoined the Rifle Corps. In 1805, he was promoted to a company. In the latter end of this year he went with the expedition to Germany under Lieutenant-General Lord Cathcart. The following year he once more returned to England. In 1807, he again was under the command of Lord Cathcart at Copenhagen, and was present during the whole of the operations before that place, and engaged in the action of Kioge under Major-General Sir Arthur Wellesley. In 1808, he landed in Portugal, and was present at the battle of Vimiera; marched into Spain with Lieutenant-General Sir John Moore; was constantly with the rear-guard of the army during the retreat; and engaged in the affair of Calcaballos, where he had two companies placed under his orders; and on the 16th of January, 1809, was at the battle of Corunna. In May, 1809, he again embarked for the Peninsula, under Brigadier-General Crawford, and joining the army under Lord Wellington, early in the morning after the battle of Talavera, formed the rear-guard of the army in falling back on the Guadiana.

Between the months of January and June, 1810, he was constantly on outpost duties with the Light Division, and engaged in various skirmishes on the rivers Coa and Agueda. On the 24th June, when the enemy attacked the division, he was posted with two companies of riflemen to occupy the bridge upon the Coa, which he held during the day, although the passage was repeatedly and severely attacked by the enemy. He formed the rear-guard when the army fell back on the Sierra de Busaço. On the day previous to the battle of Busaço he was engaged with the enemy's advanced guard, and commanded two companies during that battle; he composed the rear-guard when the army retired to the lines of Torres Vedras, and was present till the enemy broke up and retired to his position in Santarem; was on outpost duty in front of that place till the 6th of March, 1811, when the enemy retreated; he was then placed in advance and was frequently engaged with the enemy's rear-guard. The Rifle Corps were on this occasion formed into wings, and attached to separate brigades of the Light Division. The left wing came under his orders after the fall of Major Stuart, and was twice led into action by him, when the command devolved on a senior officer. On the 3rd of April, he commanded three companies in the action on the Coa, under Colonel Beckwith, and after the operations of that day was recommended for the brevet rank of major. During the blockade of Almeida, he was placed in front of the army, with a separate command of 200 picked sharp-shooters, and half a troop of horse artillery, for the purpose of narrowly watching the enemy, and of cutting off any supplies; again joined the Division, and was engaged at the battle of Fuentes D'Onor. In May, 1811, Captain Cameron received the brevet of major; and shortly after, the left wing of the regiment was placed under his command for outpost duty in front of Ciudad Rodrigo. He was present during the whole of the siege, and commanded the covering party at the storming of the fortress, on the night of the 18th January, 1812. He continued with the army, and proceeded to the siege of Badajoz; was present at the whole of the operations, and, with Colonel Williams of the 60th, was thanked in general orders for having repelled a sortie made by the enemy. On the night of the assault, he commanded the covering party, composed of the left wing of the Rifle Corps with 200 Cacadores, and after the fall of Major O'Hara, during that night, succeeded to the command of the battalion. On this occasion he was recommended for the brevet rank of lieutenant-colonel, and the regimental majority. On 27th April, 1812, he was appointed brevet lieutenant-colonel, and on the 14th of May following was promoted to a majority in his regiment. He still continued in command of the battalion, on the advance of the army to the Douro, and during its subsequent movements till its arrival on the heights of

Salamanca; commanded the 1st Battalion Rifle Corps, and 300 Cacadores in the battle of Salamanca; formed the advance guard after the action; followed the enemy to the Douro; and entered Madrid with the Marquis of Wellington. He retired from that capital with a corps under the command of Sir Rowland Hill, of which he formed the rear-guard; joined the army under the Marquis of Wellington, still in the rear-guard, in command of the regiment; and was occasionally sharply engaged with the enemy. He continued in command till the battalion took the field in May, 1813, when a senior officer joined. He was present and severely wounded at the battle of Vittoria in June of that year, and obliged to return to England. In the latter end of that year, he volunteered to proceed to Holland with the army under Lieutenant-General Sir Thomas Graham, when a provisional battalion of the Rifle Corps was formed by orders of the Commander-in-Chief and placed under his command.

In that campaign he commanded the outposts of the army, and was engaged at the affair of Merxem, upon which occasion he was thanked in general orders, and mentioned in the public despatch. He continued with the army during the operations before Antwerp, and only returned to England on peace being concluded. In January, 1815, Lieutenant-Colonel Cameron was appointed a Companion of the Military Order of the Bath; and in the spring of that year he embarked for Flanders, and was engaged with Lieutenant-General Sir Thomas Picton's Division at the battle of Quatre-Bras on the 16th June. He was present on the 17th, and commanded the light companies of the Brigade that day. On the 18th June—the battle of Waterloo—after Colonel Sir A. Barnard was wounded, he commanded the 1st Battalion of the Rifle Corps, and continued to command till near the close of the action, when he was compelled to quit the field in consequence of receiving a severe wound in the throat, from the effects of which he still [1816] greatly suffers, the ball having lodged in his body, where it is likely to be sometime longer confined. In October, 1815, he received from the Emperor the appointment of Knight of the Military Order of St. Anne of Russia.

In addition to the crosses of the two above-mentioned Military Orders, Lieutenant-Colonel Cameron has received a medal for the campaign in Egypt, and others for Ciudad Rodrigo, Badajoz, and Salamanca.* He was also awarded the Peninsular medal with five clasps—Vittoria, Fuentes D'Onor, Busaco, Corunna, and Vimiera—and the Waterloo medal.

Consequent on the wound he received at Waterloo, he was never again fit for active service.

On the 22nd July, 1830, he was promoted to the rank of full colonel, and on the 28th of June, 1838, to that of major-general. On the 19th of July, 1838, he was nominated a Knight Commander of the Most Honorable Military Order of the Bath, and on the 24th of April, 1846, he was appointed to the colonelcy of the 74th Highlanders.

Major-General Sir Alex. Cameron, K.C.B. and K.C.H., was a most intimate personal friend of the great Duke of Wellington, under whom he so long served in the field.

In 1818, he married Christian, only daughter of Colonel Macdonell, of Barrisdale, with issue, five children—

1. Duncan, his heir.
2. Colin William, born in 1823, and died young in 1840.
3. Arthur Wellington Cameron, Colonel, 92nd Gordon Highlanders, born in 1827. He served with his regiment in India during the Mutiny; is unmarried, and now resides at Inverailort.
4. Helen, who died young, in 1839.
5. Jane, who also died young.

He died at Inverailort, on the 26th of July, 1850—the bullet with which he was wounded, in the neck, at Waterloo, being still in his body—when he was succeeded, as representative of the family, by his eldest son—

DUNCAN CAMERON of Inverailort, born on the 28th of May, 1819. On the 23rd of October, 1835, he entered the

* *Royal Military Calendar*, Vol III. pp 286-287, 1816.

42nd Highlanders (Black Watch), as Lieutenant, and was Adjutant from the 30th of October, 1838, until he retired from the regiment, on the 8th of May, 1840.

He married, first, in 1849, Louisa Campbell, daughter of Mackay of Brighouse, with issue—

1. Louisa Campbell Christian Campbell, who died in infancy.

He married, secondly, in 1857, Alexa Marion Macleod, second daughter of Thomas Gillespie, Ardachy, with issue (with a son who died in infancy)—

2. Christian Helen Jane.
3. Frances Alexandra.

He died on the 26th of June, 1874, when he was succeeded in the property by his daughter,

CHRISTIAN HELEN JANE CAMERON, now of Inverailort.

THE CAMERONS OF CALLART.

THIS family is the first that branched off from the main stem, and is therefore the oldest cadet family of Lochiel. The Camerons of Callart are descended from John, second son of Allan "Mac Dhomh'uill Duibh," twelfth chief, by his wife, Mariot, daughter of Angus Macdonald, second of Keppoch, and great-grandson of Robert II. of Scotland through his daughter, Lady Margaret, who married John, first Lord of the Isles. [See page 34.] From this family sprung the Camerons of Lundavra, Cuilchenna, and other cadets, many of whom have distinguished themselves in the Army, Navy, Civil Service, at home and abroad, and in the learned professions. They are generally known in the Highlands as "Sliochd Ian 'ic Ailein," or the "Descendants of John, son of Allan" of Lochiel. They followed the banner of their chief under Montrose and Dundee, as well as in the 'Fifteen and 'Forty-five. It is impossible now to trace some of them at all genealogically, and none of them beyond the last Stuart Rising, in 1745-46. There are several branches of the family, but the following are the only two that we have been able to trace to date:—

ALLAN CAMERON OF CALLART, fought at the Battle of Culloden,* was married, and had a son—

JAMES CAMERON, who, on the 23rd of June, 1762, married Mary, daughter of Colonel Alexander Cameron of Glenevis, at the house of Acharn, the residence of her

* Among those in attendance on Prince Charles, Cluny and Lochiel in the Cage after Culloden, was "a young genteel lad of Calard's family, who was principal servant to Lochiel". *Donald Macpherson's Narrative* M.S., quoted in foot-note *Chambers' Rebellion*, p. 368. A "Major Charles Cameron, late captain 76th Regiment of Foot," died, at Callart, in 1784.

cousin, Cameron of Glendesseray, by the Rev. J. Macintyre. By this lady James Cameron had issue—four sons and two daughters.

1. Ewen, a banker in London, born on the 20th of October, 1763, who married, first, on the 23rd of March, 1793, Catharine, daughter of Captain F. H. T. Fortesque of the Royal Navy, London, by whom he had two daughters—Catharine and Mary. Catharine married a Mr. Nairn, and went to Australia, and Mary married Mr. Walkinshaw, a solicitor, and died without issue. Ewen married, secondly, in Glasgow, Mrs. King, a widow, with issue—two sons, Hyndman, an ensign in the army, and James, both of whom died unmarried.

2. Allan, born 27th of February, 1765.

3. Alexander, born 26th of April, 1767. He died in infancy.

4. Charles, born 21st April, 1769. He also died in infancy.

5. Isabel, born on the 14th of November, 1768, and married Alexander Cameron, brother of Major Allan Cameron of Lundavra, with issue—Allan, George, and John.

6. Jean, born 21st July, 1771. She died unmarried.

ALLAN CAMERON, the second son of James, as above, was Captain and Paymaster in the Lochaber Fencibles, raised in 1799, by Donald Cameron of Lochiel, and disbanded, after a few years' service in Ireland, at Linlithgow, in July, 1802, when some of the men were drafted into the 79th Regiment. Captain Cameron was afterwards factor for Lord Macdonald in North Uist, for a period of twenty-seven years, and resided at Lochmaddy. In 1799, he married Mary, daughter of Duncan Campbell, Ardgour House, with issue—

1. James, born at Lifford, in Ireland, on the 8th of February, 1801; died, unmarried, at Lochmaddy in 1822.

2. Duncan Campbell, born at Lochmaddy, on the 4th of July, 1804; died in infancy.

3. Ewen Alexander, born on the 28th of January, 1806; married in 1831, Sybella, daughter of Colonel Murray of Kirkleton, Dumfriesshire, with issue—Matthew James, who married Edith Cotes, with issue—one daughter, Eveline, who resides at Park House, Holmwood Park, Brighton.

4. Allan, who became the representative of the family.

5. John, born on the 7th of October, 1817, and emigrated to New Zealand, where he married Anne Sutherland, with issue—four sons, Allan, John, Hector, James, and a daughter, Mary.

6. Colin John, born on the 19th of March, 1819, and died young.

7. Anne Abercromby, born at Ardgour House on the 10th of September, 1788. She died unmarried.

8. Mary Isabella, who, in 1833, married the Rev. John Lees, chaplain to the Royal Caledonian Asylum, London, and afterwards minister of Stornoway, with issue—(1) the Rev. Dr. James Cameron Lees of St. Giles Cathedral, Edinburgh, who married, on the 7th of February, 1872, Rhoda Clara, second daughter of Major Rainsford Hannay of Kirkdale, Kirkcudbrightshire, with issue—John Cameron, born on the second of December, 1878; Arthur Stanley, born on the 8th of November, 1881; Mary Constance; and Mary Isabella Cameron. Dr. Cameron Lees is the author of the *History of the Abbey of Paisley*, and of several other works. (2) John; (3) Allan Cameron, who went to New Zealand, and married Fanny, daughter of Stent of St. John's Hill, Wanganui; and (4) Donald.

9. Louisa, born on the 7th of September, 1807.

10. Jane, who, in 1842, married Donald MacLean, M.D., son of the Rev. Neil MacLean, minister of Tiree, without issue.

Allan was succeeded, as representative of the family, by his eldest surviving son,

ALEXANDER WENTWORTH CAMERON, born on the 9th of October, 1810, and married, on the 8th of July, 1852, Isabel Margaret, daughter of the Rev. Neil MacLean, minister of Tiree, with issue—

1. Allan, born on the 3rd of July, 1857, and emigrated to New Zealand in 1879.

2. Neil MacLèan, born on the 23rd of November, 1858, and emigrated to the United States of America in 1883.

3. Mary Jane, who on the 9th of October, 1873, married W..A. MacLeod, late tenant of Scorrybreck, with issue— one son and five daughters, Donald, Mary Anna, Isabel Alexa, Helen, Louisa, and Mabel. Mr. MacLeod went, with his family, to New Zealand in 1883.

4. Isabel Macdonald.

5. Mary Flora.

6. Harriet Louisa, who accompanied her brother Allan to New Zealand in 1879.

7. Lillias Margaret.

8. Mary Isabella Lees, who died in infancy.

He was succeeded, as representative of the family, by his eldest son,

ALLAN CAMERON, who, in 1879, emigrated to New Zealand, as above.

THE CAMERONS OF LUNDAVRA.

THE Camerons of Lundavra are cadets of the family of Callart, descended, as we have seen, from John, second son of Allan "MacDhomh'uill Duibh," twelfth of Lochiel, by his wife, Mariot, daughter of Angus Macdonald, second of Keppoch, and grandson of Lady Margaret, daughter of King Robert II. of Scotland.

LIEUTENANT ALLAN CAMERON of Lundavra, of Lochiel's regiment, was one of the four Highland officers of the army of Prince Charles, killed at the battle of Preston, on the 21st of September, 1745. It is impossible, in the absence of any family papers, all of which were destroyed by the English soldiers, under Cromwell, after the 'Forty-five, to trace this family, step by step, back to the Camerons of Lochiel. The Camerons of Callart, Lundavra, and Cuilchenna, however, are universally admitted to have sprung from the family of Lochiel, and consequently a complete genealogy is of little consequence. They are invariably spoken of in Gaelic, even at the present day, in Lochaber, as "Sliochd Ian 'ic Ailein," or the "Descendants of John, son of Allan" of Lochiel.

ALLAN CAMERON, killed at the battle of Preston, was married, with issue—

ALLAN CAMERON OF LUNDAVRA, accidentally killed at Colleag. Bridge, on his way home from Fort-William, on horseback, and buried in the famed Island of St. Mungo, in Lochleven, opposite the entrance to Glencoe. He was most popular in the district, and on his death, about 1790, Allan MacDougall, widely known as *Ailean Dall*, family bard to the famous Glengarry of George the Fourth's time, composed a Gaelic Elegy, in which he refers to the subject of his eulogy in the most laudatory terms. In the following lines, he alludes to his descent from Allan Cameron, twelfth of Lochiel :—

> "'Nam an cruadal a tharruinn,
> Bha do dhualchas ri fallaineachd sll,
> Bho Chloinn Chamshroin an daraich,
> 'S tu ' Shliochd Ian mhic Ailein' nam pios."

He married Jessie Stewart, niece of Stewart of Glenbuckie, Perthshire, with issue—

1. Allan.

2. Alexander, an extensive sheep farmer in Ross-shire, who married Isabel, eldest daughter of Allan Cameron of Callart, with issue, among others—George, successively Sheriff-Substitute at Fort-William, Tain, and Dingwall.

3. John, a shipowner, trading with the West Indies.

He was succeeded, as representative of the family, by his eldest son,

ALLAN CAMERON OF LUNDAVRA, born in 1760 or 1761. He joined the army at a very early age and went to India, from whence he returned to Britain in 1781 or 1782, just about the time when he came of age. In the minutes of an action of Reduction and Declarator by Lochiel's Trustees against General Allan Cameron of Erracht, in 1792, Lundavra is designed as " Lieutenant Allan Cameron, late of Colonel Tarleton's dragoons, unmarried, aged thirty years and upwards ". On his return from India, he visited his father at Lundavra, and remained for some time in Lochaber. He then returned to London, where he remained for a few years, met Lochiel, then a minor, and became very intimate with him. In 1785 he went back to India, returning home again in about a year and a half; and, after a short stay in London, he visited Lochaber. Soon after this, Lochiel, who had then come of age, visited his property for the first time, in the autumn of 1790, and Allan accompanied him, with several others of the leading gentlemen of Lochaber, on a tour among his friends and principal tenants. On this occasion, the Earl of Errol, and Donald

Cameron, son of Dr. Archibald Cameron of the 'Forty-five, a banker in London, and one of his trustees, accompanied Lochiel to Lochaber, and on his visits to his friends.

Major Cameron of Lundavra appears to have been in very good circumstances; for he states in his depositions, that he "allowed some hundreds of pounds, and sometimes above a thousand, to remain in the defender's [Allan of Erracht's] hands, without a voucher; that his confidence in him was unbounded, and that he never had cause to repent it". He also lent young Lochiel, at the time in straitened circumstances, £163 12s., in various sums, between September, 1786, and March, 1787, all of which was duly repaid on the 3rd of March, 1792. Allan afterwards entered the 83rd Regiment, where he succeeded to the rank of major, but having had a difference with his commanding officer, he left the army and procured an important post in the Civil Service.

In his *Memoir of Colonel John Cameron of Fassifern*, the Rev. Dr. Clerk informs us that the Colonel, who was, in May, 1808, stationed at Drogheda, "writes in warm terms of the hospitable kindness of *Allan Lundavra*, a Lochaber gentleman who held an important civil office in Drogheda". He often visited Lochaber. After leaving Ireland, where he married, he resided in Edinburgh. He married, first, Lady Jane Dundas, who, with her only child, died, at its birth, about a year after; and secondly, at Drogheda, about 1802, Bridget, only daughter of Beauchamp, and seventh in descent from Sir Anthony Colclough—who had a grant from the Crown of the Abbey and lands of Tintern, in the County of Wexford, in 1576—widow of Colonel George Urquhart of Meldrum and Byth, Aberdeenshire, with issue—

1. Allan John Russell Bedford.
2. Adelaide, born at Drogheda about 1808, and married Dr. Maharge of the 70th Regiment, without issue.

Allan, who died about 1829, was succeeded, as representative of the family, by his only son,

ALLAN JOHN RUSSELL BEDFORD, County Inspector,

Royal Irish Constabulary. In connection with this office, the distinguished seventh Earl of Carlisle, Chief Secretary, from April, 1835, to September, 1841, and afterwards, for eight years, Lord-Lieutenant of Ireland, wrote, on the 18th of October, 1851, a letter in which he says, that he "was acquainted with Mr. Cameron when he filled a prominent place in the Constabulary Service in Ireland, and he has had many opportunities of seeing how well he was qualified to discharge its duties, and in what a singular degree he enjoyed the esteem of his neighbours and acquaintances as a man of honour and a gentleman". He was born at Drogheda about 1805, and on the 18th of April, 1839, married Helen, second daughter of Lieutenant-Colonel Charles Cox, of the 87th Regiment, with issue—

1. George Frederick Howard Carlisle, born in 1840; died in infancy.

2. Allan Ewen Charles.

3. Henry St. George De Halberg, Manager of the Provincial Bank of Ireland, Cootehill, County Cavan. He was born in 1842, and married, on the 3rd of September, 1874, Mary Atkinson, youngest daughter of William Crawford Poole, J.P., M.D., of Glendysart, Ardmore, County Waterford, with issue—Douglas Crawford Poole, born in 1880; William Bedford St. George, born in 1881; and a daughter, Dora. His wife died in 1881.

4. William Justin Beauchamp, of Uanda, Queensland. He was born in 1845, and married, on the 14th of June, 1881, Elizabeth Patricia, third daughter of Donald Charles Cameron of Barcaldine, Queensland, with issue, a son and daughter—Donald, born in 1882; and Margaret.

5. Richard Standish Le Bagge, Batavia, Java. He was born in 1850, and married in 1874, with issue—one son and a daughter. He died at Batavia, on the 24th of June, 1883.

6. George Francis Blundell, born in 1853, and drowned at sea, on the 24th of April, 1875, unmarried.

7. Russell Bedford Colclough, Sourabaya, Java, born in 1856; still unmarried.

8. John Alexander Staples, of Napa, Canada, born in 1858. He married, in 1877, Mary, daughter of Andrew MacCloughery, of Dromod, County Leitrim, with issue—Florence and Helen.

9. Georgina Barbara Harriet, who, in 1869, married John Stewart, Kemang-Banca, Java, eldest son of the Rev. John Stewart Gumley, head of the ancient family of Gumley of Gumley, Yorkshire, England, and Bailieboro' and Belturbet, County Cavan, Ireland, and Prebendary and Rector of Tarmonbarry, County Roscommon, with issue—two daughters, Helen and Kathleen Mary. She died in 1875.

10. Helen Anna, who, in 1871, married David MacNair, Batavia, with issue — two sons and three daughters, Donald, Allan, Helen, Eveleen, and Beatrice.

11. Adelaide Anita Arabella, who, in 1883, married Donald, younger son of Donald Charles Cameron, of Barcaldine, Queensland, with issue.

Allan John Russell Bedford Cameron died at his residence, Aughamore House, County Leitrim, on the 1st of November, 1863, when he was succeeded, as representative of the family, by his eldest son,

ALLAN EWEN CHARLES CAMERON, present County Inspector, Royal Irish Constabulary, for Mayo. He was born in 1841, and married, first, on the 16th of January, 1867, Gretta, eldest daughter of the Rev. John Stewart Gumley, Prebendary and Rector of Tarmonbarry, County Roscommon, already mentioned, with issue, three sons and six daughters—

1. Allan John Russell Bedford, born in 1869.
2. Ewen, born in 1877.
3. Allan, born in 1878.
4. Arabella Le Bagge.
5. Anna Maria.
6. Gretta Helen Mary.
7. Sophia, who died in infancy.
8. Clare.
9. Georgina Barbara Harriet.

His first wife died on the 13th of November, 1878, and

on the 16th of December, 1882, he married, secondly, Rosa Elizabeth,* eldest daughter of the Rev. Edward Loftus Fitz-Gerald, a scion of the ducal house of Leinster, Rector of Temple-Michael, County Waterford, with issue—

10. Donald, born in 1883.
11. Evan, born in 1884.

* Mrs. Cameron, by her paternal grandmother, Maria Loftus, descends rom the celebrated Adam Loftus, Lord Archbishop of Dublin and Lord Chancellor of Ireland, in Queen Elizabeth's reign; and by her mother, Lily Maxwell, through the noble house of Farnham, from Henry VII., King of England.

THE CAMERONS OF GLENEVIS.

THIS family is found in Lochaber, possessing lands of their own, as far back as we have any record. It would have been seen that they held these lands from the family of Gordon, who, until very recently, kept their ancient hold in Lochaber. It was also seen how the Camerons of Glenevis and Lochiel were generally at feud with each other; and this feeling of antagonism came down even to modern times. Indeed it has been maintained that the Glenevis family were originally not Camerons at all but Macdonalds, who settled there, under the Macdonalds of the Isles, before the Camerons had any hold in the district. Whether there is any foundation for this theory or not, the family are described as Camerons ever since anything is known of them in the history of the country, and they constantly intermarried with the other leading families of that name in the district.

Beyond what appears in the general history of the clan, under the Camerons of Lochiel, little is known of the family of Glenevis before the Stuart Risings of 1715 and 1745. The head of the family, like that of the Camerons of Fassiefern, kept out of the 'Forty-five from prudential motives, though members of the family and most of the followers of Glenevis joined the standard of the chief on that occasion. This action of Glenevis has been attributed to the influence of the Gordon family, who then supported the Whigs and opposed the Stuarts. Glenevis did not, however, escape from the cruel persecutions indulged in by the representatives of the Government after Culloden, and

ALEXANDER CAMERON of Glenevis was imprisoned for about a year for the share his family had taken and his own active sympathy in the affairs of Prince Charles in 1745-46. His brother Allan was killed at Culloden, and most of his relations fought throughout the whole campaign, while he no doubt privately extended to them all the aid and information that his position admitted of; in consequence of which Alexander was taken prisoner. In the *Gentleman's Magazine* for 1747, we are told that on " Tuesday, 7th July, were discharged from Edinburgh Castle, Alexander Macdonald of Kingsburgh, and Alexander Cameron of Glenevis". During his imprisonment, his wife and family suffered severely at the hands of Cumberland's troops, and like those of the other leaders, Glenevis House was burnt, while Mrs. Cameron, her family and friends, had to find shelter in mountain caves; and even here they were not able to escape the brutality of the human hounds of the Royal Butcher, who desolated the land and perpetrated unspeakable brutalities and crimes wherever they went. There are endless accounts of such carried down by tradition among the people.

The Rev. Alexander Stewart, F.S.A. Scot., relates the following in *Nether Lochaber*, at pages 188-189 :—" Calling on the Misses Macdonald of Achtriachtan the other day at Fort-William, we were shown some very fine old silver plate, having a history of its own, to the recital of which we listened with no small interest. After the battle of Culloden, a party of 'redcoat' soldiers entered Lochaber, and employed themselves in pillaging and plundering in all directions. Hearing that visitors so unwelcome were in the neighbourhood, Mrs. Cameron of Glenevis, a lady of great spirit and decision of character, had all her silver plate, china, and other valuables buried deep in the ground outside the garden wall, after which she removed, with her children and personal attendants, to a spacious cave called *Uaimh Shomhairle*, (Samuel's Cave), far up the glen, in the south-western shoulder of Ben-Nevis. Meanwhile the soldiers visited Glenevis House, but, disappointed at not finding the valuables they looked for in such a residence, they burned and plundered the glen without mercy, the terrified inhabitants taking to the mountains, only too glad to escape with their lives, while their homesteads were in flames, and their cattle either driven away or slaughtered on the spot. Lady Glenevis was at last discovered in her cave by a party of soldiers, who had somehow heard of her place of retreat, and had to undergo much rude treatment at their hands, because, in defiance of all their threats, she refused to tell where the valuables of which they were in search had been hidden away. As they were about to leave the cave, one of the soldiers, observing that she had something bulky in her breast, of which she seemed very careful, and over which her plaid, fastened with a silver brooch, was carefully drawn, made a snatch at the trinket, and when the lady resisted, drew his sword and made a thrust, which cut open the plaid at its point of fastening, wounding her infant son at the moment in the neck; for the hidden treasure in her bosom, though the soldier doubtless thought it might turn out to be something of more marketable value, was a child only a few months old. The soldiers at last departed, carrying with them the brooch and plaid as the only trophies of their victory over the defenceless lady of the cave. The wounded child recovered, though he bore the mark of the sword-thrust to his dying-day. He lived to be laird of Glenevis, was father of the late much-respected Mrs. Macdonald of Achtriachtan, and grandfather of the ladies above mentioned. We remember hearing our friend, the late Dr. Macintyre of Kilmonivaig, repeating some very fine Gaelic lines to a waterfall, something in the style of Southey's address to *Lodore*, which he said was by Mrs. Cameron of Glenevis above mentioned, and composed by her while in hiding in the cave. When quieter times came round, the buried valuables were of course exhumed, and were found to be none the worse of their temporary interment."

On another occasion her presence of mind, exhibited in a striking manner, was the means of saving her life at the hands of one of her own devoted retainers. Walking up the glen one day, during this troublous period, she observed one of her clansmen, at a considerable distance, on the other side of the river, slowly but carefully taking deliberate aim at her with his musket. The man mistook her scarlet cloak for one of Cumberland's "redcoats" from Fort-William. Perceiving that the man was acting under a misapprehension, she at once sat down on a large stone, spreading out her cloak as widely as she could, that the Highlander might see that he was aiming at a woman and not at a redcoated soldier. This had the desired result; the man discovered his error, and, throwing down his musket, he ran where the lady was, to assure her of safety and to express his regret for having alarmed her. The lady was herself a Cameron of the Lochiel family, a daughter of Archibald Cameron of Dungallon, by his wife, Isabel, daughter of Sir Ewen Dubh of Lochiel.

Alexander's mother was a daughter of Fraser of Foyers, by his wife, Janet, daughter of John Macpherson of Nuide, third son of Ewen Macpherson of Cluny. According to Burke, the last-named lady married not less than five husbands, by all of whom she had issue—namely, first, Fraser of Foyers; second, Angus Macpherson of Dalraddie; third, Grant; fourth, Angus Macpherson of Invereshie; and fifth, MacQueen.

Alexander Cameron of Glenevis married Mary, daughter of Archibald Cameron of Dungallon, by his wife, Isabel, daughter of the famous Sir Ewen Cameron of Lochiel, with issue—

1. Ewen, his heir.

2. John of Achnasaul, a Lieutenant-Colonel in the army, who fought in the American War of Independence, and was afterwards Governor of Fort-William. He married Louisa, daughter of Campbell of Glenmore, with issue—(1) Ewen, a Captain, 79th Cameron Highlanders, who afterwards settled in, and died at Glenfaba, Isle of Man. He married Miss Brydson, a Manx lady, with issue—several daughters. (2) Colin, of Her Majesty's

Customs, Liverpool. He married, without male issue.
(3) Alexander, a Colonel in the 42nd Royal Highlanders
(Black Watch) from the 9th of October, 1855, to the
9th of August, 1858. He commanded the regiment
at the Relief of Lucknow, and was wounded at Bareilly.
He died in India on the 9th of August, 1858, from
fever, it is said, brought on by his wound, which was
inflicted by a poisoned dagger. He married Emily,
daughter of General Ashworth, with issue, two sons—
Ewen Hay, a Captain in the Royal Engineers; Maurice
Alexander, a Lieutenant in the same Corps; and one
daughter, who married Mr. Jackson, son of an Irish
Dean. (4) Jessie, who married Captain Moses Campbell,
son of John Campbell of Inverliver, with issue. (5) Margaret, who married Thomas Macdonald, Fort-William,
with issue, sixteen children, the only survivor of whom is
John Cameron Macdonald, manager of the *Times* newspaper, still unmarried. He had also a daughter, Augusina,
who married Captain George Fraser, son of W. J. Fraser
of Ladhope, Roxburghshire, with issue—William James.
(6) Isabella, who married John Cameron MacGregor,
solicitor and bank agent, Fort-William, with issue, among
others, John Cameron Macgregor, still unmarried, in India.

3. Anne, who, on the 14th of July, 1772, married John
Cameron, tacksmen of Kinlockbeg, Argyllshire, grandson
of Angus Cameron of Kinloch-Leven, with issue—(1)
Angus, a Captain in the 21st Regiment, or Royal Scots
Fusiliers, born on the 2nd of June, 1777, and died unmarried on the 28th of June, 1809, from the effects of a
wound received two days before at the capture of the
Island of Procida, in the Bay of Naples. In recognition
of his services his father received a pension of £40 per
annum from the government, which was after his death, on
the solicitation of General Sir Allan Cameron of Erracht,
continued to his mother. The father also received an
annuity of £15 from the Patriotic Fund. (2) Jean, who, on
the 17th of November, 1800, married Robert Campbell
tacksman of Finnart, in Rannoch, a cadet of the Camp

bells of Glenfalloch, with issue—four sons and one daughter. (3) Anne, who died unmarried. (4) Helen, who married Angus Rankine, tacksman of Dalness, Glenetive, with issue—one son and three daughters. (5) Christian, who married Ronald Macdonald, a Lieutenant in the army, descended from the family of Keppoch, with issue. Five other daughters died young.

4. Mary, who, on the 23rd of June, 1762, married James Cameron, Fort-William, with issue—(1) Allan, a Captain in the Lochaber Fencibles, factor for Lord Macdonald, and latterly residing at Calgarry Castle, Mull. [See "Camerons of Callart".]

Alexander Cameron of Glenevis was succeeded by his eldest son,

EWEN CAMERON of Glenevis, a Lieutenant in the Old 78th, or original Fraser Highlanders, which he joined in 1757, and from which he retired, in consequence of a wound which unfitted him for active service. He married, on the 22nd of September, 1778, Helen, eldest daughter of Patrick Grant of Glenmoriston (by his wife, Henrietta, second daughter of Patrick Grant of Rothiemurchus), with issue—

1. Patrick, his heir.

2. John, a Planter in Berbice, British Guiana, who succeeded his brother in the property.

3. Donald, an Ensign in the 21st Regiment (Scots Fusiliers), who, after he had retired from the army, was for many years resident at Fort-William. He died unmarried.

4. Isabella, who married Sir Colin Mackenzie, eighth of Kilcoy, Baronet, with issue—(1) Charles, ninth of Kilcoy; (2) Evan, the late Baronet; (3) Colin, who died unmarried in 1868; (4) Jane, who married the late Major James Wardlaw, of the H.E.I.C.S., Belmaduthy, with issue—(*a*) John Colin, born on the 19th of July, 1856, Lieutenant and Adjutant, Border Regiment; (*b*) George Lake, born on the 19th of April, 1864; (*c*) James Robert Preston, born on the 22nd of September, 1867; (*d*) Geraldine Anne Isabella Mary

Jane, who, in 1876, married George F. Gillanders, now of Highfield, Ross-shire, with issue—Frances Geraldine ; (*e*) Horatia Georgiana Ramsay, who, on the 19th of July, 1877, married William Gordon Cumming Asher, Belmaduthy Mains, with surviving issue—William Augustus, and Isabella Mackenzie ; (*f*) Jane Frances Harriet.

5. Harrietta, who, on the 5th of October, 1813, married James Murray Grant, of Glenmoriston and Moy, with issue—(1) John Grant, a Captain in the 42nd Highlanders, who predeceased him on the 17th of August 1867, at Moy House, Forres. He married first, in 1850, Emily, daughter of James Morrison of Basildon Park, Berks, without issue ; and secondly, Anne, daughter of Robert Chadwick, of High Bank, Prestwick, in the County of Lancaster, with issue— Ian Murray James Grant, now of Glenmoriston ; born in 1860 ; succeeded his grandfather in 1868 ; and is a Lieutenant in the First Battalion Queen's Own Cameron Highlanders ; Ewen Grant, born in 1861 ; Heathcoate Salisbury Grant, born in 1864, in the Royal Navy ; Frank Morrison Seafield Grant, born in 1865 ; and Emily Grant. (2) Evan Grant, who distinguished himself in India and the East as Colonel in the Bombay Army. He married the eldest daughter of Colonel Pears of the Royal Madras Artillery, with issue—one son and four daughters, and died in London shortly after his return from the East. (3) Patrick Grant, of the H.E.I. Civil Service, who married Elizabeth, second daughter of Donald Charles Cameron of Barcaldine, with issue—two sons and four daughters. (4) Hugh Grant, a Lieutenant-Colonel in the Bengal Army, married, with issue—a son and a daughter. (5) James Murray Grant, a Major-General in the Madras Army, who married Helen, third daughter of Donald Charles Cameron of Barcaldine, with issue—four sons and three daughters. (6) Jane Grant, who married William Unwin, of the Colonial Office, Barrister-at-Law, London, and had, with other issue, an only daughter, Henrietta Mary, who, on the 6th of April, 1863, married Sir John Heathcoate Amory, Baronet of Knightshayes Court, County

Heathcoate Amory, Baronet of Knightshayes Court, County of Devon, M.P. for Tiverton (born on the 4th of May, 1829), with issue—John Murray, who died in infancy ; Ian Murray Heathcoate, born on the 16th of April, 1865 ; Harry William Ludowick, born on the 7th of June, 1870 ; Geoffery, born on the 12th of November, 1873 ; Muriel Mary Heathcoate, Anne Christel Lucy Heathcoate, and Dorothy Helen.   (7) Elizabeth Grant, who married James Alexander Pierson of the Guynd, Forfarshire, without issue. (8) Helen Grant, unmarried.   (9) Harriet Grant, who married Frank Morrison, of Holepark, Kent, without issue; and (10) Isabella Grant, who died unmarried.

6. Helen, who married Adam MacDonald, Achtriachtan, Glencoe, with surviving issue—John Cameron, Isabella Jane, and Jane Fraser.

Ewen Cameron of Glenevis, died on the 12th of December, 1797, when he was succeeded by his eldest son,

PATRICK CAMERON OF GLENEVIS, who died unmarried ; when he was succeeded by his next brother,

JOHN CAMERON OF GLENEVIS, who, in 1851, sold the estates to Sir Duncan Cameron of Fassiefern, Baronet. He was a planter in Berbice, British Guiana, where he married, with issue—several sons, among whom John, Charles, and Donald ; also two daughters. After he sold the estate he went to reside in the Island of Jersey.

THE CAMERONS OF SPEYSIDE.

THIS branch of the clan is descended from a cadet of the Camerons of Glenevis, who left Lochaber in charge of his infant chief, and settled in Banffshire. The circumstances are detailed, in such an interesting manner, in a letter from Ewen Cameron of Glenevis, in 1785, addressed to Captain Alexander Cameron of Milton of Balvenie, Banffshire, then head of the family, that we shall give it in full. It is as follows :—

"GLENEVIS, *6th September, 1785.*

"Dear Sir,—My cousin, Mr. Cameron, Kinrara, wrote me some time ago he had the pleasure of yours and your brother's company at his house last July for some days, and that you was so kind as to express a wish of paying a visit to your Duchas at the foot of the Big Hill and seeing your friends in this country. My brother (the bearer of this) goes to see his cousin at Kinrara, and to escort you and your brother to this country ; I flatter myself it may be convenient for you to accompany him here, and that I will have under my roof the descendants of the man who, under God, was the preserver and protector of the second founder of this family. As Mr. Cameron informs me you left Scotland at an early age, possibly you may not know by what means your predecessor came to leave my native land, and settle in the north. I have often heard my father (who certainly knew more of the history of the Highland families around him, and of his own in particular) speak with warmth and gratitude of your predecessor, and give a detail of the cause which induced him to forsake this country and settle on Spey banks.

I wish I was able to do justice to this history he gave me of this transaction, which, indeed, I must own I can do but imperfectly. I proceed now to inform you, the family of Gordon claimed the property of the lands of Mamore, which finding they could not peaceably keep, possession being disputed by a powerful family in this country. This and other causes induced them to give a charter of the said lands of Mamore to my predecessor, which, consequently, entailed upon him the enmity of that powerful family, and nearly lost him his paternal inheritance of Glenevis. In this quarrel my predecessor and yours frequently bled, and at last were extirpated all but one child, a son of Glenevis, with whom his then nearest of kin (your predecessor) fled to Gordon Castle, and put himself under the protection of his superior, where he remained to the age of manhood, when he was, by a fortunate change of times and circumstances, enabled to resume the property of Glenevis, which was also seized upon, and, by relinquishing his grant of Mamore, to establish peace between said family and Huntly. The lands given up, though at a later period, were divided equally between them, as they continue to be at this day. Those were the causes that induced your predecessor to forsake Lochaber and settle on Speyside, but he and his friends here for a long time kept a friendly and close intercourse with each other; and so did his descendants, of which there is now no evidence, but tradition; nor is this at all to be wondered at, when it is considered the knowledge of letters in those days, and, indeed, long after, fell to the lot of few, for, so late as my great-grandfather, Sir Ewen Cameron of Lochiel, he could only sign his name. But my grandfather, who was Baillie of Regality for the Lordship of Lochaber, in his frequent journeys to Gordon Castle, as my father has told me, cultivated a proper intercourse with your friends, and so did my father at a later period, the less frequent since the Rebellion, 1745. Forgive me then to say it would be a shame to me and you to suffer the connection betwixt us to die away. The same blood still flows in our veins, and I should be sorry either of us should degenerate so far from the virtue of our fathers as to allow the friendship that subsisted so long to be lost or forgot by us.

"Indeed it is my earnest wish to improve the good old connection by a personal acquaintance, and I trust you will not disappoint me. An epistolary correspondence is at best a cold substitute; nor will I be satisfied with it from you and your brothers. I shall, therefore, flatter myself with the expectation of seeing you here when my brother returns. Meantime, I entreat you, make my kind respects acceptable to Mrs. Cameron, your mother, and to your brothers also; and believe me, very sincerely, dear sir,

"Your affectionate friend and cousin,

"EWEN CAMERON,

"Glenevis."

CAPTAIN ALEXANDER CAMERON of Balvenie, with two of his brothers, in early life served in the Dutch service, in what was then called the "Scotch-Dutch Brigade," until the war between Great Britain and Holland broke out, near the end of the last century, when they at once declined to fight against their own country, threw up their commissions, and returned to Scotland. After a long correspondence with the War Office, and with much difficulty, they obtained commissions of a similar rank in the British army to what they held in the service of the Dutch, and were placed on half-pay. Captain Cameron, after serving with the 95th, then a kilted regiment, settled in Banffshire, and married Miss Gordon, daughter of Patrick Gordon of Aberlour, with issue (among several others who emigrated, and died abroad, without issue)—

PATRICK CAMERON, who was, in 1828, appointed Sheriff-substitute of Elginshire, an office which he filled for about thirty-five years. He died in 1865.

He married, first, Anne, daughter of George Fenton, Sheriff-substitute of Elginshire, with issue—

1. George Fenton Cameron, M.D., for some time acting as assistant-surgeon in the 3rd Buffs, during the Irish Rebellion of 1848, and in the Carabineers. He retired from the army and settled in London, where he now resides. Born in 1824, he married Ann, daughter of the late Alexander Johnston, New Mill, Elgin, and widow of the late Robert Grigor, Jamaica, with issue—Ewen Gordon, Alexander Patrick George, and Alice.

Patrick Cameron married, secondly, Mary, daughter of the Rev. William Leslie of Belnageith, and of St. Andrews, Llangbride, with issue—

2. Alexander Cameron, Highfield, Elgin, and of Mainhouse, Roxburghshire. He was Provost of Elgin for six years. He married Elizabeth Louisa, daughter of the late Ralph Compton Nesbit, Banff, and of Mainhouse, Roxburghshire, with issue—Ralph Compton George, and Mary.

Captain Alexander Cameron of Balvenie had also a daughter, Clementina, who married Robert Grigor, writer, Elgin, with issue—Dr. Grigor, Nairn.

THE CAMERONS OF DAWNIE.

THIS is a branch of the Camerons of Glenevis. According to the traditions of Lochaber, "Eoghainn MacAilein, mhic Dhomh'uill Duibh, mhic Alastair a Ghlinne"—"Ewen, son of Allan, son of Donald the Black, son of Alexander of Glenevis," occupied Dawnie in 1745. Ewen is said to have led a body of Glenevis Camerons in the Highland army, and to have received special recognition for gallantry from Prince Charles. The tradition in the family is that he was knighted by his Royal Highness on his return from some skirmish in which he displayed great valour. The story goes that the Prince addressed Ewen, saying, " Give me your sword, Captain Cameron," who replied, " There is little but the hilt left, as it was broken in your Highness' service ". " Never mind," replied the Prince, " my cane will do." With this he touched Captain Cameron lightly as he knelt, saying, " Rise up, Sir Ewen," and he then presented him with the cane, adding, " that it may never be used less worthily ". According to the same story, the Prince afterwards sent Ewen a sword of his own to take the place of the broken one, and " both staff and sword were in the family until the sword was stolen and afterwards sold to the Marquis of Breadalbane, about 1835 or 1836 ". The staff was retained, and was for some time in possession of the late Captain John Cameron, Lianassie, Kintail, the representative of the family; and it is now in the possession of his descendants in Australia. The Prince was present at the baptism of Dawnie's eldest son, on which occasion the name Charles was introduced into the family, the infant having been named Donald Charles, by special command, after his Royal Highness. The Camerons of Dawnie held lands in Lochaber, from the Duke of Gordon, for a pepper-corn rent, but they were claimed by the Duke's creditors, and, in consequence of some flaw in the title, were lost to the family.

EWEN CAMERON OF DAWNIE, who fought with Prince Charles at Culloden, married, with issue—

DONALD CHARLES CAMERON. He married a daughter of Cameron of Letterfinlay, with issue—

1. John, his heir.
2. Ewen, a sheep-farmer in Glenelg, and subsequently in Tallisker, Isle of Skye. He married Johanna, daughter of the Rev. Colin MacIvor, minister of Glenelg, with issue—(1) the late Captain Donald Colin, who succeeded his father at Tallisker, and who married Jane, daughter of James Thomas Macdonald of Balranald, with issue—Ewen, James Thomas, Donald, Mary, and Jeanie. He died at Tallisker, Isle of Skye, in December, 1883.
3. Donald Charles, first of the Camerons of Barcaldine, Argyllshire, of whom presently.
4. Allan, who accompanied his second brother, Donald, to the West Indies, where he died of yellow fever, unmarried.

Donald Charles had also five daughters.

He was succeeded, as representative of the family, by his eldest son,

JOHN CAMERON, an officer in the 79th Highlanders. After Waterloo he retired, and took a lease of the farm of Lundavra in Lochaber, and subsequently of Lianassie, in Kintail. Captain Cameron married a daughter of Kennedy, Lianachan, Lochaber, with issue—

1. Donald Charles.
2. Ewen, M.D., who died without issue.
3. John, M.D., died, unmarried, in Berbice.
4. Angus, who went to Australia.
5. Alexander, M.D., in Demerara.

He died in Kintail, about 1852, when he was succeeded, as representative of the family, by his eldest son,

THE CAMERONS OF DAWNIE.

DONALD CHARLES CAMERON, of Barcaldine, Queensland, who first went to the West Indies, and from thence, in 1852, to Australia, where he was engaged in squatting, on an extensive scale, during the remainder of his life. He married Miss Moore, with issue—

1. John Cameron, of Kensington Downs, New Zealand, married, with issue—three sons.

2. Donald, of Caledonia, Queensland, who married Adelaide Anita Arabella, youngest daughter of Allan John Russell Bedford Cameron of Aughamore House, Co. Leitrim, Ireland, with issue—one child.

3. William.

4. A daughter, who married Mr. Crombie, of Greenhills, Queensland.

5. A daughter, who married Mr. William Crombie, Sydney, N.S.W., brother of her sister's husband.

6. Elizabeth Patricia, who married William Justin Beauchamp, of Uanda, Queensland, fourth son of Allan John Russell Bedford Cameron of Aughamore House, Co. Leitrim, Ireland, with issue—Donald and Margaret.

7. Adèle, still unmarried.

Donald Charles Cameron was succeeded, as representative of the family, by his eldest son,

JOHN CAMERON, now of Kensington Downs, Queensland, married, with issue—several children.

Mrs. Donald Charles Cameron now resides at Barcaldine, Queensland, the residence of her late husband.

THE CAMERONS OF BARCALDINE.

THE first of this family, who, in 1842, purchased the estate of Barcaldine from the trustees of Sir Duncan Campbell of Barcaldine and Glenure, was,

DONALD CHARLES CAMERON, third son of Donald Charles Cameron of Dawnie, Lochaber. When quite a young man he joined the Letterfinlay Company of the 4th Battalion of the Inverness-shire Volunteer Infantry, and afterwards, in 1806, he obtained a commission in the army and proceeded to the West Indies; but on reaching Berbice he threw it up, on the advice of his relative, John Cameron of Glenevis, went into a government office, and afterwards bought an estate there. In 1822, he returned to Scotland and purchased, in that year, the estate of Foxhall, Linlithgowshire, where he resided until, in 1842, he bought the estate of Barcaldine in the county of Argyll. Years before this he was anxious to purchase the Lochaber properties, purchased by Lord Abinger and George Walker, " but from some mistake as to instructions, when he was in the West Indies, his agent let them slip by, much to his disappointment". When afterwards one of his sons visited Mr. Walker, who possessed the lands of his ancestors, in Lochaber, " the people could not make enough of him, when they knew who he was. They seemed to think he had a right to the shooting and other sports greater than his entertainer, so far did their memories take them to those who reigned there in the old times," when his predecessors possessed the lands of Dawnie.

He married Elizabeth Rupert Fraser, third daughter of Colin Matheson of Bennetsfield, with issue—

1. Donald, who died in infancy.
2. Alexander, who died in infancy.
3. Colin, who died in infancy.
4. John, who succeeded his father, as second Cameron of Barcaldine and Foxhall.
5. Allan Gordon, who, in 1857, succeeded his brother, as third Cameron of Barcaldine and Foxhall.
6. Donald Charles, late Captain in the Inverness-shire Militia, and tacksman of the farm of Glenbrittle, Isle of Skye. He married Anne, daughter of Charles Shaw, W.S., late Sheriff-substitute at Lochmaddy, with issue—Donald Charles, Charles Shaw, Annie Elizabeth, and Elizabeth Henrietta.
7. Patrick Evan, who died unmarried in 1854.
8. Grace Maria, who married James Archibald Campbell of Inverawe, with issue—four sons and five daughters.
9. Elizabeth, who married Patrick, third son of James Murray Grant of Glenmoriston, with issue—two sons and four daughters.
10. Helen, who married Major-General James Murray, fifth son of James Murray Grant of Glenmoriston, with issue—four sons and three daughters.

Donald Charles Cameron died in 1848, when he was succeeded in the property by his fourth and eldest surviving son,

JOHN CAMERON, second of Barcaldine and Foxhall. He died of yellow fever, in the West Indies, in 1857, unmarried, when he was succeeded in the estates by his next brother,

ALLAN GORDON CAMERON, third of Barcaldine and Foxhall, born in 1827. He was educated at Harrow and Oxford, was B.A. of Trinity College, and was ordained a clergyman of the Church of England in 1852. In January, 1854, he married Mary Colebrooke, only daughter of George William Traill of Viera and Rousay, Orkney, with issue—

1. Ewen Somerled, his heir.

2. Allan Gordon, born in June, 1856, M.A. of Trinity College, Oxford, and a barrister of the Inner Temple, London.

3. Mary Colebrooke, who died unmarried in the twenty-first year of her age in 1878.

The Rev. Allan Gordon Cameron died in November, 1871, leaving the estates to his widow in life-rent. He was succeeded, as representative of the family, by his eldest son,

EWEN SOMERLED CAMERON, late an officer in the Royal Lanark Militia. In January, 1881, he married Julia, only daughter of J. B. Wheelock, Boston, United States of America.

SIR RODERICK W. CAMERON'S FAMILY.

THE progenitor of this branch was Donald Cameron, a cadet of Glenevis, who, according to the traditions of Glenmoriston, secured the lands of Morsheirlich from Lochiel. This intrusion from Glenevis was resented by Lochiel's own immediate clansmen so much that, when another Lochiel succeeded, he sent for Cameron, and asked, in a friendly way, to see his titles, which, on being handed to him, he instantly threw into the fire, and coolly asked their late possessor by what rights he could now claim to remain among the Lochiel Camerons on that side of the Lochy. In those days might was right. Instead, however, of returning to Glenevis, Cameron removed to Glenmoriston—with which a close Lochaber alliance had been established in 1698, by the marriage of Janet, daughter of Sir Ewen Dubh of Lochiel, to John Grant of Glenmoriston [see p. 210],—where his descendants long after lived in prosperity. The first of whom we have authentic record is—

ALEXANDER CAMERON, who, born at Glenmoriston, Inverness-shire, in 1729, emigrated to the colony of New York, before 1776, and in that year, like many more who had settled in the States, crossed the St. Lawrence into Canada, and settled in the township of St. Charlottenburg, in the county of Glengarry. He married, about 1760, Margaret Macdonell, Glenmoriston, with issue—

1. Duncan Cameron.

2. A daughter, who married Hugh Macdonell, a cadet of the family of Glengarry.

Alexander Cameron died at his residence in Glengarry,

Canada, in 1825, at the age of ninety-six,* his wife having died in 1817, aged 87 years, when he was succeeded by his only son,

DUNCAN CAMERON, born at Glenmoriston, Inverness-shire, in 1764. He was one of the founders of the North-West Fur Trading Company, in connection with which he spent several years in the great North-West. From 1813 to 1815, he commanded at Fort Gibraltar, afterwards Fort Garry, on the Red River, where now stands the city of Winnipeg, Manitoba. During his command there, in 1815, a feud broke out between the Hudson Bay and North-West Companies, and Mr. Temple, who claimed to have been appointed Governor by Lord Selkirk, was killed in a skirmish. Cameron was arrested, by strategy, with several others, and tried for the death of Mr. Temple, but as the Selkirk party attacked, and it being shown that Mr. Cameron had no share in the fight, the jury did not find a true bill against him, and he subsequently obtained a verdict for damages against Lord Selkirk, which he, however, never collected.

In 1818, he visited Britain, when he was presented at Court, and was elected a member of the Highland Society of London, after which he visited the Highlands, remaining some time in Lochaber, Glenquoich, and Achnacarry, on which occasion he made the acquaintance of the lady who, two years later, became his wife. When he retired from active life in the North-West, he settled down in the township of Lochiel, in the county of Glengarry, Canada, calling his residence, after the home of his ancestors in the Highlands of Scotland, Glenevis House. He represented the

---

* The following inscriptions are on his tombstone, and that of his son, Duncan Cameron :—" In memory of Alexander Cameron, a native of Glenmoriston, Inverness-shire, Scotland, who died in Williamstown, January, 1825, aged 96 years, and of Margaret Macdonell, his wife, also a native of Glenmoriston, who died 1817, aged 87 years. Mr. Cameron was one of the early settlers of the then colony of New York, but true to the principles of his education, preferred seeking a new home in Canada, rather than to identify himself with the revolutionary movement against his flag."

" In memory of Duncan Cameron, a native of Glenmoriston, Inverness-shire, Scotland, who died in Williamstown, on the 15th of May, 1848, aged 84 years."

county of Glengarry, in the Parliament of Upper Canada, from 1820 to 1824.

Margaret, daughter of Captain William Macleod of Hammer—and grand-daughter of John, and sister of Neil Macleod of Gesto, cadets of Macleod of Macleod, Isle of Skye—whose acquaintance Mr. Cameron made while on a visit to the Highlands in 1818, accompanied her brother, Dr. Roderick Macleod, to Canada in 1820, and there Duncan Cameron, then advanced in years, married her.

He died at Williamstown, Glengarry, Canada, on the 15th of May, 1848, at the age of eighty-four, leaving issue—

1. Duncan, born in January, 1822, and died in 1826.
2. Roderick William.

Duncan Cameron was succeeded, as representative of the family, by his second son,

SIR RODERICK WILLIAM CAMERON, born on the 25th of July, 1825. In early youth Sir Roderick was known in Canada as an expert trapper and hunter. In 1852 he resolved upon going to Australia, and went to New York to make the necessary arrangements for the passage, when he made the acquaintance of the famous American shipowner, Lewis Tappan, with the result that, instead of going to Australia, he established a line of ships between New York and Australia. In his business Mr. Cameron succeeded in making a fortune, at the same time gaining the respect of the Americans as well as that of his own countrymen in Canada. In 1883 he was, on the recommendation of the Marquis of Lorne, Governor-General of Canada, knighted by the Queen, on her sixty-fourth birthday.

In 1856, he became a member of the Highland Society of London. In 1863, he travelled through the Highlands, visiting Lochiel at Achnacarry, and his mother's friends in the Isle of Skye.

He married, in 1860, Anne Fleming, daughter of Nathan Leavenworth, directly descended from an old Puritan divine, a gentleman of culture and independent means, who went over to America on the early settlement of the

New England colonies, by his wife, Alice Johnstone, the daughter of a Scottish gentleman, who settled in the Colony of New York about a century ago. By this marriage Sir Roderick had issue—

1. Duncan Ewen Charles, born on the 11th of December, 1866. He was educated, for the last four years, at Harrow, and is entered for the 2nd Life Guards.

2. Roderick MacLeod, born on the 7th of January, 1868, studying at St. Paul's School, Concord, New Hampshire, United States of America.

3. Alice Leavenworth, who died in August, 1880, in the tenth year of her age.

4. Margaret Selina Erne, presented at the British Court in May, 1883.

5. Catherine Nathalie.
6. Anne Fleming, and
7. Isabella Dorothea.

Mrs. Cameron died on the 2nd of July, 1879, in her fortieth year. Sir Roderick Cameron is, and his father, Duncan Cameron, was, a United Empire Loyalist.

THE CAMERONS OF CUILCHENNA, AND OTHERS.

THERE are several other Cameron families, that can only be referred to briefly.

THE CAMERONS OF CUILCHENNA, a branch of the family of Callart, produced some very distinguished men. The late Sir John Cameron, K.C.B., belonged to this family. He entered the 43rd Regiment of Foot on the 25th of April, 1787, as Ensign. He became Captain on the 11th of July, 1794; Major on the 9th of October, 1800; Lieutenant-Colonel in the 7th West India Regiment on the 28th of May, 1807; on the 4th of June, 1814, he received the brevet rank of Colonel. He served in the West Indies under Sir Charles Grey; was at the Siege of Fort Bourbon, at the capture of Martinique, St. Lucia, and Guadalope, and at Fleur D'Epée. While serving under Brigadier-General C. Graham in Guadalope, he commanded his regiment in the action of the 30th September, 1794, and in several others up to the 4th of October, when he was taken prisoner, and was afterwards detained in captivity for two years. He served in Portugal in 1808, and was at Vimiera, after which he went to Spain and fought at the battle of Corunna. He next served in the Walcheren Expedition, and, subsequently, in the Peninsula. He was present at Talavera, Busaco, Salamanca, Vittoria, Nive, and the Siege of St. Sebastian, for which services he received a cross and two clasps, and was created a K.C.B.

His veteran son, Sir Duncan Alexander Cameron, K.C.B., is now Colonel of the 42nd Royal Highlanders (Black Watch). He joined the regiment as Ensign on the 8th of April, 1825, and never served in any other. He became

Major on the 23rd of August, 1839; Lieutenant-Colonel, 5th of September, 1843; Brigadier in Turkey (local rank) on the 24th of October, 1854; Major-General (local) on the 5th October, 1855; Major-General (local) in England on the 24th of July, 1856; Major-General on the 25th of March, 1859; appointed to the Colonelcy of the 42nd on the 9th of September, 1863; and became a Lieutenant-General in the Army on the 1st of May, 1868.

Sir Duncan served through the Crimean Campaign, commanded the 42nd at the battle of the Alma, and the Highland Brigade at Balaklava, was at Kertch, and at the siege, the assault on the outworks, and the fall of Sebastopol. He was appointed President of the Council of Education in 1857; was Commander-in-Chief in Scotland in 1860; Commander of the Forces in New Zealand, with the local rank of Lieutenant-General, in 1861; and of the Australian Colonies and New Zealand in 1863. In 1865, he was appointed Governor of the Royal Military College at Sandhurst.

THE CAMERONS OF KINLOCHIEL are often referred to in the body of the work. The family produced several notable men, among whom may be named the brilliant and world-renowned War Correspondent of the *Standard* —J. A. Cameron.

THE CAMERONS OF CLUNES AND CAMISKY are of the Sliochd Ian 'ic Eoghainn, or Erracht, and both have produced some very good men. The present representatives of these families, however, do not appear to have enough interest in the history of their ancestors to have induced them to aid us in any way in placing their history and genealogical connection with the main stem on record in this work; and we naturally concluded that what seemed of so little interest to themselves, could not be expected to prove more interesting to the general public, and we, therefore, did not concern ourselves any further about them.

THE CAMERONS OF STRONE have been repeatedly mentioned. For the later members of the family, see p. 278.

There are many prominent men now living belonging to this renowned and historic clan, such as, Commander Verney Cameron, R.N., the famous African explorer; Dr. Charles A. Cameron, the eminent analyist of Dublin, and F.R.C.S.I.; Dr. Charles Cameron, M.P. for Glasgow; and many others, who have added in our own time to the historic fame of the Cameron clan, but our present plan does not admit of their history being given at length in this work.

APPENDICES.

APPENDIX I.

LOCHIEL'S TRUSTEES AGAINST ERRACHT.

Action of Reduction and Declarator, at the instance of the Trustees of Donald Cameron of Lochiel, against Allan Cameron of Erracht.

ON the 2nd of November, 1790, Donald Cameron of Lochiel sold the lands of Erracht and others to Allan Cameron, afterwards so well known as General Sir Allan Cameron of Erracht, from whom he had borrowed considerable sums of money during the latter years of his minority and soon after he came of age. On the 12th of May, 1791, Lochiel, who repented his bargain, conveyed his whole estates in trust, to the Right Hon. Henry Dundas, one of his Majesty's Principal Secretaries of State; Robert Barclay-Allardice of Urie; Donald Cameron, banker, George Street, London; and Ewen Cameron of Fassiefern, with special power and authority, "to challenge all or any deeds granted by me, alienating or charging the said lands and estate, or any part thereof, upon any grounds of law, or in equity which I might myself maintain". This was intended to cover the action to be raised against Cameron of Erracht, immediately after the trust-deed should be completed, and which was raised accordingly. After several appearances in Court, an interlocutor was issued, on the 22nd of February, 1792, ordaining the pursuers to "give in a printed condescendence of the facts they averred and would undertake to prove in support of their reasons of reduction, without using one word of argument; and when given in, allowed the defender to see the same, and ordained him to give in answers thereto without delay". The following condescendence and answers given in, in terms of this interlocutor, will fully explain the facts of the case. After quoting the disposition by Donald Cameron of Lochiel in favour of Allan Cameron of Erracht, the pursuers, in obedience to this interlocutor, proceed to state :—

"The grounds on which the pursuers insist that this disposition shall be reduced and set aside, are, that 'The said disposition was elicited and impetrated from the said Donald Cameron of Lochiel by the defender, by fraud and circumvention, without proper consideration or value, and to the great hurt and enormous lesion of the said Donald Cameron and of the pursuers; and besides, at the time the transaction was entered into, and the consideration or price alleged to have been paid, the said Donald Cameron was a minor, under the direction of curators whose consent was not given thereto, and the consideration pretended to be given therefor was not profitably applied for his use; notwithstanding at the time, the said Allan Cameron was in the perfect knowledge of the said Donald Cameron's being under minority, and under the direction of curators to whom, if a fair and onerous transaction had been only intended, it was natural and proper for the defender to have applied for their consent; on the contrary, every means was used by the defender to prevent their being informed of the transaction, and it was insisted on by him, that the same should be kept concealed from them by the said Donald Cameron'.

"For these reasons the summons concludes, that the said disposition and instrument of sasine following thereon should be reduced, and declared 'to have been from the beginning, to be now, and in all time coming, void and null, and of no avail, force, strength, or effect, with all that has followed, or is competent to follow thereon, and to bear no faith in judgment, or outwith the same, and the said pursuers ought and should be reponed thereagainst *in integrum* '.

"In this action, which in every view must be admitted to be very serious and important in its nature and consequences, the defender returned defences, which are verbatim as follows: 'This action is one of the most groundless, vexatious, and irrelevant of any brought into this or any other Court of Law; instigated entirely, and carried on from a spirit of resentment and private pique by two of these trustees, viz., Donald Cameron the *sine qua non*, and Ewen Cameron, who have brought this suit more with a view of founding an attack upon the defender's private character, and injuring his reputation, than any solid expectation of prevailing in setting aside a fair and onerous transaction, entered into *bona fide*, concluded, and homologated by the said Donald Cameron of Lochiel, when of perfect age, and who, conscious of the propriety of the defender's conduct, has not ventured to bring the suit in his own name, though influenced by the machinations of the said Donald and Ewen Cameron to divest himself of his whole estate in their favour; a measure which probably may be attended with more serious consequences to himself in the long run than to the defender. They have stept forward to the attack, but the defender rests humbly confident that he will be assoilzed, even after the strictest investigation.'

"This action having come before his Lordship [on the 22nd February, 1792], he was pleased, upon hearing parties to pronounce the following interlocutor: 'The Lord Ordinary having heard parties' procurators, before answer, ordains the pursuers to give in a pointed condescendence of the facts they aver, and will undertake to prove, in support of their reasons of reduction, without using one word of argument; and when given in, allows the defender to see the same, and ordains him to give in answers thereto without delay'.

"In obedience to this appointment, the following condescendence is humbly offered upon the part of the pursuers:—

".In the first place, they do condescend and say, that the estate of Lochiel, comprehending the lands contained in the disposition now under reduction, was forfeited in the person of Donald Cameron, Esq., in consequence of his accession to the Rebellion, 1745; the estate remained annexed to the Crown till 1784, when an act of Parliament was passed to enable his Majesty to restore the forfeited estates in Scotland to the heirs of the former proprietors. The clause of this act relative to the estate of Lochiel is in these words: 'That it shall and may be lawful to his Majesty, his heirs and successors, to give, grant, and dispone to Donald Cameron, son and heir of Charles Cameron, late Captain in the 71st Regiment of Foot, deceased, who was only lawful son of Donald Cameron, late of Lochiel, and his heirs and assigns, ALL and EVERY the Lands and Estate which became forfeited to his said late Majesty by the attainder of the said Donald Cameron, late of Lochiel, now deceased, subject always to, and chargeable with the sum of £3433 9s. $1\frac{8}{12}$d. sterling of principal money to be paid into the said Court of Exchequer as after directed'.

"In consequence of this act his Majesty was graciously pleased to restore the estate of Lochiel to Donald Cameron, Esq., the present proprietor.

"2$^{do.}$ When the estate was thus restored to Donald Cameron, Esq., he was only in the 15th year of his age; from the time of his father's death, in the year 1776, he had been educated in England under the inspection chiefly of the pursuer Mr. Cameron, banker in London, who was first cousin to his father, and who entertained for his young kinsman and chief all the regard and affection of a father. He and Mr. Cameron of Fassiefern, who was also first cousin to his father, had, alongst with his mother, been appointed guardian to Lochiel by the will of his father.

"3$^{tio.}$ At the time the estate of Lochiel was thus restored, the defender, Allan Cameron, possessed a farm upon the estate, called Erracht, in virtue of a lease from the commissioners of annexed estates, of date 10th of July, 1781, for forty-one years from Whitsunday, 1781. He likewise possessed the lands of Leck and Stradin, not included in the lease, and from which he was of course removable at pleasure. By the lease, the rent payable for the lands of Erracht was £37 17s. 6d., besides relieving the proprietor of public burdens, which may be from £6 to £7 more. The rent payable for Leck and Stradin, held without lease, was £9 14s. 3d.

"The defender was born upon the farm of Erracht, about the year 1750, as it is believed, his father being then tenant on the lands. The defender continued upon the farm assisting his father in the management of it down to the year 1773, when the defender went abroad. His father continued to possess the farm till his death, some years afterwards. From that time a brother of the defender's has possessed the farm for the defender's behoof.

"4to. After the estate of Lochiel was restored to Mr. Cameron, the young gentleman, after continuing some time at Westminster School, went abroad in the course of his education, and he returned to London in summer or autumn, 1789, being then still under age. From the books of the pursuer, Mr. Cameron the banker, it appears that Lochiel, as well when abroad as when in England, was liberally supplied with money.

"5to. Notwithstanding this, it appears that Lochiel, in consequence of some youthful dissipation, which he was unwilling to divulge to his curators, had got into some pecuniary embarrassment, from which he wished to be relieved. With that view he, in October, 1789, applied to Mr. Teasdale (a person who advertises in the public papers in London, to advance money to persons wanting the same) to procure him the sum of £500 sterling, stating to him, that he, Mr. Cameron, was the possessor of the Lochiel estate in Scotland, of the yearly value of £1200 a year and upwards. Mr. Teasdale agreed to procure Mr. Cameron the sum he wanted, but wished Mr. Cameron to refer him to some gentleman who knew him and his estate, to satisfy him that what was told him was true. Lochiel, who knew that the defender was intimately acquainted with the estate, referred Mr. Teasdale to him; Mr. Teasdale accordingly applied to the defender, who, taking advantage of that circumstance, gave such an account of Lochiel's circumstances and situation as induced Mr. Teasdale to think that it would not be safe to lend him any money. In consequence of this, Mr. Teasdale declined to advance the money, although it was ready, and the transaction had proceeded so far that Lochiel's life was insured as a security.

"6to. In November following, Lochiel, in consequence of the former disappointment, applied to the defender to lend him £400. The defender answered, that it was not in his power. In the course of conversation on that business, Lochiel having said, that if he could not raise money otherwise, he would be obliged to sell some of his farms, the defender proposed, that if he would do so, he would willingly purchase the farm of Erracht, which he held in lease, and for which he would give £1000. At this time Lochiel had never been in Scotland, and knew no more of the value of any farm upon his estate than the child unborn. Soon after this conversation, the defender called upon Lochiel, and brought along with him a paper, which he said was a rental of the estate of Lochiel, and pointed out the rent of the farm of Erracht to be there stated at £25 per annum. The defender at the same time observed, that he had a long lease of that farm, with the liberty of cutting down wood. He also mentioned, that there was another farm adjoining, which in the rental appeared to be let at £24 2s. 4d., called Inveruiskvullin, which he would likewise purchase, and give for the same £600, observing that they were the worst farms on the estate. Lochiel, under the immediate pressure of the want of money, which he was ashamed and afraid to disclose to his curators, by whom he had been so liberally supplied, agreed at once to any proposition made by the defender. Next morning, Lochiel went to breakfast with the defender, who, whilst at breakfast, desired Lochiel to write him a letter, saying that his want of money induced him to sell these two farms for £1600. This Lochiel did, in the words dictated by the defender, and then, as desired, sealed the letter and delivered it to the defender, who opened the same, preserving the seal, and then said he had not got the money by him, but would go with him into the city that week, and procure it, and the whole business should then be settled. The letter thus delivered to the defender he is hereby required to produce.

"7mo. In consequence of what passed at this last-mentioned meeting, Lochiel and the defender, upon the 26th of November, 1789, went into the city, to the house of a Mr. Tewer, in Mincing Lane, who acts as agent, attorney, or factor, for Mr. Philips, father-in-law of the defender. Finding Mr. Tewer at home, the defender informed him that Mr. Cameron of Lochiel wished to sell him two farms, and begged he would witness the transaction; and Mr. Tewer answered he had no objection, provided the transaction was fair and just. The defender thereupon pulled out a paper framed by himself, which he read in presence of Lochiel and Mr. Tewer, and then desired Lochiel to copy it over and sign it, which he accordingly did, and then Mr. Tewer signed as witness to it, and thereupon Lochiel received the stipulated sum of £1600 sterling. He desired to be allowed to keep the copy of the agreement which was thus executed, but the defender declined that, and saying it could be of no use, he tore it and threw it into the fire. The defender is hereby required to produce the writing, or minute of sale holograph of Lochiel, and thus signed by him, and witnessed by Mr. Tewer. The precise words of it Lochiel cannot, at this distance of time, recollect; but in general, he remembers it was an agreement to sell the two farms of Erracht and Inveruiskvullin to the defender, for the sum of £1600 sterling.

"8vo. It is material to observe, that when the transaction was thus concluded, and the price of the lands paid upon the 26th of November, 1789, the defender knew that Lochiel was under age, and that he was a minor under curatory. The defender knew that the pursuer, Mr. Cameron, banker in London, was one of the guardians and curators of Lochiel, to whom he, in effect, stood in the relation of a father; but nevertheless, the defender, neither in his defences, nor in his argument at the bar, either said or insinuated that he gave the smallest intimation to Mr. Cameron the banker, although living upon the spot, or to the other guardian, that a transaction of so much importance to his ward was going forward. The defender, indeed, knew enough of the situation, of the character, and of the feelings of Mr. Cameron the banker, to be certain, that if he had had the most distant suspicion that such a measure was in contemplation, it would instantly have been quashed. The defender knew that Mr. Cameron the banker would rather have paid down ten times the value of the lands, than suffer the estate to be dismembered in such a manner, immediately upon its being restored by the benignity and liberality of government, to the heir of a very ancient and respectable family, and before that heir was of age to enter into possession of an estate which he was bound by so many ties to preserve entire and undiminished. For these obvious reasons, the defender not only carefully concealed the whole of this negotiation from Mr. Cameron the banker, and the other guardian, but also exacted a promise from Lochiel that he would not divulge it, either to him or to any human being, for the space of five years. When the transaction was thus concluded, upon the 26th of November, 1789, Lochiel was a week past twenty years of age.

"9$^{no.}$ Thereafter Lochiel, before he came of age, was induced to borrow a further sum of £300 from the defender, for which he gave his note or bill.

"10$^{mo.}$ In autumn, 1790, Lochiel visited Scotland for the first time in his life, and upon that journey was accompanied by his friend and guardian, Mr. Cameron, banker in London, who came down to enjoy the pleasing satisfaction of seeing his young chieftain restored to the estate of his ancestors. They arrived in Lochaber about the 16th of September, 1790, and left it about the 1st of October thereafter, their visit being shortened in consequence of an unfortunate accident which Mr. Cameron, the banker, met with on his way north, which prevented him from moving about when in the country and made him anxious to return to London without delay. During the few days that Lochiel was in the country, his whole time was occupied in receiving and paying visits, and in giving entertainments to his tenants, etc. Neither he nor his curators (for he was then under age) entered upon business of any sort, and the transaction, concluded between him and the defender in November preceding, was concealed, in consequence of the promise of secrecy given by Lochiel, not from his curators only, but from every other person whatever.

"11mo. Lochiel returned to London in the end of October, 1790, and the defender then required him to grant a disposition in his favour, in implement of the obligation granted upon the 26th November, 1789. Upon this occasion the defender said, that he and his brother had made free with some of Lochiel's wood, and used some of his timber in building a house, and that, on that account, he, the defender, would give up Lochiel's note for the sum of £300, and hold the price of the lands to be £1900, instead of £1600, as originally stipulated. Independently of this inducement, it was not in the power of Lochiel to refuse to comply with the defender's requisition, without disclosing his situation to his guardians, which he was as averse from doing as ever. He accordingly went with the defender to Mr. Spottiswoode's, Sackville Street, upon the 2nd of November, 1790, when he was about ten days past majority, and there the disposition now under reduction was produced to Lochiel, and executed by him. Mr. Spottiswoode received his instructions entirely from the defender, who furnished him with the minute and anxious description of the lands contained in the clause of the disposition above inserted. Lochiel was not then in possession of any of the title-deeds or papers of the family, or ever had any occasion to see them, and from his total ignorance of the estate, could have given no information to Mr. Spottiswoode had he been required to do it. On the other hand, the defender, from his having lived constantly upon the estate, from his birth down to the year 1773, was intimately acquainted not only with the situation, but the value of the farms now in question. Besides, in spring, 1790, the defender wrote to his brother, Ewen Cameron (who since his birth has lived upon the farm of Erracht, and since his father's death, managed it for the defender's behoof), to repair to London, which Mr. Ewen Cameron accordingly did, and passed several weeks with the defender there; a circumstance which would alone be sufficient to enable him to furnish Mr. Spottiswoode with the minute and accurate description of the lands contained in the disposition under reduction.

"12mo. By the original bargain concluded in November, 1789, Lochiel only agreed to sell two farms, viz., Erracht, under lease, and Inveruiskvullin, to the defender; but the disposition extended by the orders, and at the sight of the defender, contains no less than five different farms, viz., Erracht, held by the defender under lease; Leck, possessed by him without lease; Stradin, in the same situation; Inveruiskvullin, possessed by John Cameron as tenant without lease; and Achnaneallan, in the same situation; and these, besides the two shealings of Rielone and Garradhirry, of much value as extensive grazings, and which for twenty years have been possessed along with Lochiel's two farms of Moy and Murshelloch, and the value of which two farms will be much diminished should these grazings be separated from them. To this the pursuers must add, that the disposition refers to the possession as in the year seventeen hundred and seventy-one, of which Lochiel could not possibly know anything, although the defender, who had lived upon the lands from his birth down to the year 1773, knew with perfect certainty how every farm upon the estate was possessed in the year 1771.

13$^{tio.}$ The lands contained in the disposition and for which the defender only paid the sum of nineteen hundred pounds, instead of the worst as stated by the defender to Lochiel, are amongst the very best farms upon the estate. They consist in all of above seven thousand Scots acres, and contain great tracts of arable and excellent pasture land, have on them wood to a considerable value, would have then yielded in the market, and were intrinsically worth (even under the burden of the defender's lease of part of these lands), about the sum of £10,000 sterling. The defender had actually, before the date of the disposition to him, received an offer of two hundred and fifty pounds a-year for the farm that he held as tenant, and when it came to be known that he had received the disposition, he soon after received an offer of one hundred pounds a-year for another part of the lands that was not possessed by him as tenant; and the pursuers are informed, that the whole farms and grazings in the disposition to the defender, if let together in one lot, would, on a comparative view with the late sets made by neighbouring proprietors, yield five hundred pounds of yearly rent at least.

"14$^{to.}$ Besides the intrinsic value of the lands, their particular situation renders the transaction peculiarly detrimental to Lochiel. The lands contained in the disposition divide the estate into parts, and completely separate the one from the other for a tract of many miles. If, therefore, the situation of Lochiel's affairs had made it necessary for him to sell any part of his property, every person acquainted with the estate must have been of opinion that the lands contained in the disposition are the very last that should have been sold.

"15$^{to.}$ The defender having obtained this disposition upon the 2nd November, 1790, ten days after Lochiel came of age, kept it in his possession as a latent deed, till the 6th of April, 1791, when it was recorded at Edinburgh, and upon the 23rd of May following, infeftment was taken upon it. For a long time after the disposition was granted, the transaction remained a profound secret, and the first circumstance which led to a discovery of it was the imprudence of the defender's brother, Mr. Ewen Cameron, who, over his bottle, boasted in the country that his brother, the defender, was now Laird of part of the estate of Lochiel, but which insinuation he afterwards endeavoured to retract. This having accidentally reached the ears of the pursuer's guardians, Mr. Cameron, banker in London, took the liberty to question Lochiel upon it, who thereupon disclosed the circumstances of the transaction, as above narrated. It was not till after the matter was thus brought to light, that the defender put the disposition upon record in April, 1791.

"16$^{to.}$ Very soon after the granting the disposition, Lochiel was induced to borrow £500 farther on bond from the defender, who proposed to purchase more farms, which Lochiel declined to agree to. On different occasions afterwards, the defender endeavoured to induce Lochiel to apply to him for money, but without effect; and when Lochiel executed a deed of trust to the pursuers, the defender made a peremptory demand upon him for the £500, which was immediately paid.

"The pursuers have thus, in discharging the trust reposed in them, stated the circumstances of this very important case, without argument or commentary, and they submit that these circumstances, if either admitted by the defender, or established by satisfying evidence, will be fully sufficient to support the grounds of reduction as stated in their summons, and to entitle them to demand from the justice of his Lordship a judgment in terms of the conclusions thereof.

"Before concluding, however, they must submit another view of this case, suggested by the manner in which it was argued, in presence of the defender, by his learned counsel. They stated, that in point of birth the defender yielded to no man whatever, and that he possessed all the fine feelings, and nice sentiments, so suitable and congenial to a gentleman. Such being the situation of the defender, it was argued that he entered into the transaction believing it to be perfectly fair, equal, and honourable. That as he meant to take no advantage of Lochiel, so, in fact, he had not done it, having paid the full value of the lands, and even more than their intrinsic worth.

"Such being the view of the transaction, given by the defender himself, let us suppose that it shall appear that he himself, and Lochiel, were equally deceived as to the value of the lands, and that, instead of £1900 paid by the defender, they were at the time truly worth eight, ten, or twelve thousand pounds sterling; and that independently of the intrinsic value of the lands, parting with them would essentially injure the remaining parts of the estate, and would prove ruinous to the family of Lochiel. If this shall appear to be the case, it may be expected that he will come forward and say, that he entered into the transaction *bona fide*, believing it to be perfectly equal, so, now that it appears to have been very much the reverse, he was above taking the advantage of it, and was ready to give up the bargain, upon getting back his money, with interest from the time it was advanced. If the fact, as to the value of the lands, turns out as the pursuers have reason to believe that it will, this is the conduct which, from the professions of the defender, they must expect that he should adopt, as it would afford the best proof that, from the beginning, he was actuated by no improper motive. In respect whereof, etc., as the said condescendence, signed by Mr. Alexander Abercromby, advocate, procurator for the pursuers, bears."

The case was again called on the 6th of March, 1792, in presence of the Lord Ordinary, when "his Lordship made avizandum to himself with the said condescendence, without prejudice to the defender, to see the same, and to give in answers thereto, between and Thursday then next".

"Accordingly the said Allan Cameron, Esq., defender, gave in to the foregoing condescendence the following answers, bearing, That the estate of Lochiel, which is situated in that part of the Highlands called Lochaber, became forfeited to the Crown, upon the attainder of Donald Cameron, the then possessor, on account of his accession to the Rebellion of 1745, and was afterwards, along with other estates forfeited on the same occasion, annexed to the Crown, and put under management of commissioners named by Parliament.

"This estate, like others in that part of the country, was in general occupied by a number of small tenants and cottars, removeable at pleasure, while at the same time, several of the clan, of more respectability and consideration, connected with the family, had at different periods obtained wadsets, or leases, of particular farms.

"The commissioners, after paying off the debts, and redeeming the wadsets, caused accurate surveys, plans, and mensurations of these forfeited estates, and valuations of the different farms and possessions to be made by the most skilful persons that could be found, and, after thus ascertaining the real value, and dividing the farms properly, leases were granted to the most substantial and industrious of the inhabitants, with the view of promoting improvements, so as to change the face of the country, for the benefits of the inhabitants at large.

"The defender's ancestors had, for many generations, possessed the lands of Erracht, part of the estate of Lochiel, and were distinguished by the designation or title of Camerons of Erracht.

"At the period of the forfeiture, these lands of Erracht were held by the defender's father under a wadset, redeemable upon payment of 4500 merks; and as the profits to be derived from this farm were little enough to support the rest of the family, the defender, after receiving such branches of education as the limited circumstances of an indulgent and an affectionate parent could afford, did, on that account, and for other reasons, unnecessary to be stated, resolve to try his fortune in another clime. He accordingly went to America in the beginning of the year 1773, and upon the breaking out of the war in that country, joined the Royal Army, obtained a commission in one of the

Provincial Corps then levied by government, and on account of his gallant and intrepid behaviour, and uncommon sufferings, was finally promoted to the rank of Major.

"The defender returned to Britain, in the year 1779, for the recovery of his health and wounds, and having married in England, he has, since that time, resided almost constantly in London.

"The defender, after his return to England, received a letter from his father, dated August 14th, 1779, in the following terms :—' As I am growing very old and infirm, consequently not able to undergo the necessary fatigue about business, and the wadset lease of Erracht and Glenmallie being now nearly expired, I wish you would make the proper application to the Commissioners of the annexed estates for a renewal of it, in your own name, for as many years as you can possibly obtain. The rent of it now is about £22 10s. sterling, which in my opinion is as much as the possession will afford at any time. There is a new lease granted of a neighbouring farm, Strone, a far preferable possession to mine. The rent of it formerly was £100 Scots, and by the late augmentation of rents, with the consideration of a long lease, is only £20 sterling, so that it is now a better pennyworth than what mine is for its present rent. But as it now becomes you to think of these matters yourself, I leave you to judge what you ought to do. Inclosed I send you Mr. Butter's discharge in full for the last year's rents and public burdens, and you may get an extract of my wadset lease by applying to Mr. Alexander Hart, writer in Edinburgh, which, together with this letter, will remove every obstacle that might otherwise prevent your transacting matters to your satisfaction ; as I give all up to your own management, I should imagine, your incomparable sufferings in person, and considerable loss of property, during your long and inhuman captivity with the rebels, on account of your attempt and endeavours (however unfortunate) to support the measures of government, that you would find the less difficulty in obtaining any reasonable request from government. I am, etc.'

"The defender accordingly applied to the board of trustees for a lease in his own name, and upon the 26th of February, 1781, the following procedure took place. 'Upon reading a report by Mr. Butter, factor on the annexed estate of Lochiel, upon the petition of Allan Cameron in Erracht, narrated in the minute of 29th January last, the Board resolved to grant to the petitioner upon the usual condition, a forty-one years' lease of said farm and pertinents, exclusive of the pendicles of Lecht and Stradin. The petitioner's mother and younger children to be continued in possession of said pendicles, until the Board shall think proper to inclose the firwood of Garrochyle and grounds contiguous thereto, described in the lease granted to Alexander Cameron in Invermallie, in lieu of which the said pendicles are in event to be added to Invermallie. The rest of Erracht and pertinents, and of said two pendicles, to stand conform to the rental made up by the factor and James Morrison in the year 1774.' (Signed) 'James Morrison, for the secretary'.

"The rental alluded to, in the conclusion of this resolution, was however considered to be too high; a petition was therefore presented to the Board for an abatement, and that petition having been remitted to Henry Butter, the factor on the annexed estate of Lochiel, the following report was made by him upon the 18th of May, 1781 :—'By order from the Honourable Board, Mr. James Morrison and the factor, in September, 1774, settled the additional rents proposed to be paid by the tenants of the annexed estate of Lochiel, and adjusted the several clauses and restrictions to be inserted in the leases intended to be granted, excepting the farms of Glendissary, Fassiefern, Coruanan, and Erracht, which were then under unexpired leases, granted by Donald Cameron, late of Lochiel. The additional rent proposed for these four farms, being inserted in the rental, from the report and estimation only of the land surveyor of that estate, the Honourable Board, in

1780, granted new leases of the farms of Fassiefern and Coruanan, at the additional rents reported by the land surveyor, and stated in the rental. The factor is satisfied that the souming of cattle for the farms of Erracht and Glenmallie, mentioned in the land surveyor's report, is too high, and is humbly of opinion, from the knowledge of that, and the other farms of the Lochiel estate, that if the Honourable Board thinks it proper to grant a deduction of £3 9s. 9d. sterling, from the additional rent of £23 9s. 9d. sterling, it will adequate the rent to the average value of this, and the run of other farms in the neighbourhood. All which is humbly submitted.' (Signed) ' Henry Butter'.

" In consequence of this report, the Board came to the following resolution :—' Upon reading a petition of Allan Cameron in Erracht, in the annexed estate of Lochiel, mentioned in the minutes of 26th February last, praying for an abatement of the additional rent laid on said farm, with a report thereupon by Mr. Butter, the factor ; the Board agreed to grant the abatement mentioned in the factor's report, being £3 9s. 9d.' (Signed) 'James Morrison, for the secretary '.

" The defender accordingly obtained a lease for forty-one years of the lands of Erracht, with its pendicles and pertinents, at the rent of £25 per annum for the first twenty-one years, and of £45 for the remaining twenty years.

" The forfeited estates, having been, through the benignity of government, restored to the heirs of the forfeiting persons, upon the most liberal terms, though under the burden of all the minutes, feus, and leases, that had been granted by the Board of Trustees, the estate of Lochiel came to the possession of Donald Cameron, the grandson of the attainted Donald, and this gentleman being then a minor, the management of this estate, and his other concerns, was assumed by Ewen Cameron of Fassiefern and Donald Cameron,.banker in London, who were his nearest relations, and the next in succession, by the present investitures, after himself and his sister. Whether these gentlemen were legally appointed curators to the young man or not, the defender has no access to know.

"The first act of the administration of these gentlemen was a demand of an additional rent from all the tenants, upon the specious pretext of raising a fund for payment of the debt due to the public, with the burden of which the grant had been made by government, and from the natural and well-known attachment of Highlanders to the place of their nativity and connections, the tenants in general agreed upon this occasion to pay one third of additional rent beyond what they formerly paid to the trustees, and entered into a variety of transactions with Mr. Cameron of Fassiefern, who assumed the absolute management, and, by his residence on the estate, obtained an arbitrary sway among the tenantry, which obliges some of them now, to enter into engagements with others, to seek a retreat in the wilderness of America.

"A similar application was made to the defender at London, for an additional rent of £10 per annum. This, however, the defender, on reflection, did not choose to agree to; first, because he thought the rent payable by his lease sufficiently adequate; and secondly, because he wished not to do anything that might imply the smallest departure from that lease. But, although Fassiefern declared in the presence of the other manager, the banker, that the defender's farm was the dearest on the estate; yet, on their pleading the distress of the young gentleman's family, the defender agreed to make a present of £50, being at the rate of £10 per annum during the period still to run of his minority. With this Fassiefern seemed well pleased, but the banker chose afterwards to refuse this present. On this occasion, too, the defender could not but reflect on a well-known historical fact (which he made no scruple of mentioning), viz.—That his ancestors had been hardly dealt with, and deprived by oppressive measures of the right to the whole estate and chieftainry of the clan. This, however, gave great offence to Fassiefern and the banker, and to that circumstance, and a jealousy of his acquiring an ascendency in that part of the country, in the event of his going to reside there, he can only attribute his being engaged in this present litigation.

"Notwithstanding the dryness which these circumstances gave birth to, the intimacy and friendship that had hitherto subsisted between the young gentleman, his mother and sister, and the defender, who showed them all the civilities and kindness in his power, still remained unbroken. The consequence of which was, the defender's being often obliged to listen to the complaints which the young gentleman made from time to time of his managers, and especially Mr. Cameron, the banker's, refusing to relieve him from the distresses he was reduced to, through want of money, to answer pressing demands.

"On these occasions, the defender pressed him much to lay his situation fairly before his friend the banker, but the only answer he received was, that they had already quarrelled upon that subject, and that he had met with such violent abuse from the banker, that he was resolved to make no further applications to him for money. He accordingly applied to Mr. Teasdale, as mentioned in the condescendence, referring him to the defender for an account of his situation in point of estate. But although the defender gave a fair representation of that matter to Mr. Teasdale, the young gentleman was disappointed in his expectation of getting the money from that quarter, owing, it is believed, to its having been discovered, that in making an insurance upon his life, he had sagaciously stated himself as of full age, although at the time under minority; a fact which came out in a manner he probably did not expect, by the blabbing of some of his companions.

"Thus situated, the young gentleman applied repeatedly to the defender for relief, proposing to sell to him the farm of Erracht and its pendicles, of which he had already a lease not to expire for upwards of thirty years, together with the farm of Inveruiskvullin, upon the defender procuring him £1600 sterling.

"The defender, although he is ready to acknowledge

that a purchase of lands, which had been so long possessed by his ancestors, upon fair and reasonable terms, could not but prove agreeable, knew that a bargain of sale with a minor could not be completely relied on. But as the young gentleman obstinately refused to make any further applications to the banker, the defender was at last, and about the period mentioned in the condescendence, prevailed with to advance the sum of £1600 upon the terms proposed to him.

"With regard to the letter and minute, or other paper said to have been written to the defender on this occasion, the young gentleman must recollect that everything of that kind that had passed between them was destroyed at his own request, when the disposition was executed. But as the defender has no desire to conceal or disguise any part of the transactions that then took place, so he has no difficulty to admit, that in one or two letters written by the young man on that occasion, he did mention his want of money, as an inducement to his selling a part of his estate; and that one of these letters contained an agreement to sell the two farms of Erracht and Inveruiskvullin to the defender for the sum of £1600 sterling, and to grant a proper disposition thereof when he should become major. It is scarcely necessary here to remark, what will obviously occur, viz.—That the defender's wish to accommodate this young gentleman, in the hour of his embarrassment, by advancing so large a sum on a security at least but precarious, favours much more of humanity and friendship than of prudence, and exhibits a conduct by no means consistent with the fraudulent views that are now so improperly and unjustly imputed to him.

"It can indeed hardly be supposed, that a man who had suffered so much torture, in support of a point of honour, in the service of his country in America, when perhaps a small deviation from it might have saved him much pain and persecution from the enemy, while languishing and covered with wounds in a dungeon, upon a scanty allowance of bread and water, for near two years, would, under more easy and independent circumstances, risk a fair and unblemished character for so paltry a consideration as acquiring a purchase of the lands in question, even at a price as inadequate as the pursuers now endeavour to represent what he paid for them.

"In this situation matters remained for some time; and the pursuer's constituent intending to go down to the Highlands along with the banker, of whose company, however, he seemed not over fond, applied again to the defender for a supply of money, who accordingly advanced him £300 upon his letter, acknowledging the receipt of that sum, and promising repayment. This, the gentleman himself cannot fail to acknowledge, was a reasonable supply, not only to bear his expenses on the road, but on account of his mother and sister being then destitute of pecuniary support; and he will also recollect, that £50 of the money was left in the defender's hands for their subsistence, and was drawn for by the mother accordingly.

"Mr. Cameron and the banker accordingly set out for Lochaber, in a post-chaise, etc., purchased with the defender's money, where they remained upon the estate for some weeks, during which time the young gentleman had the best opportunity of receiving complete information with regard to the value of every part of his estate, and particularly of those farms which he had proposed to sell to the defender; and it accordingly appears, that when the bargain between them was completed, some time after he became of age, an additional price of no less than £340 beyond the sum which he had received in the month of November preceding, and which he had then proposed to accept of in full, was given for them.

"The sale was accordingly concluded upon these terms, the disposition having been framed by Mr. John Spottiswoode, and signed in his house, in his own presence, and that of David Robertson, his clerk, who adhibited their subscriptions as instrumentary witnesses, and will, it is supposed, recollect that on that occasion, and after the disposition was delivered, the defender told the disponer that if the transaction was anywise disagreeable to him, it was not yet too late to say so, and put an end to it, or some words to that effect; to which he replied, that it was perfectly agreeable to him, otherwise he would not have done it at all.*

"The defender has reason to believe, that soon after this transaction, Mr. Cameron executed a deed in favour of his mother and sister, by which he gave the former an annuity over his whole estate, excepting, however, the lands now in question, as being previously sold to the defender; and, having occasion soon after to go to France, he borrowed £500 upon his bare note of hand from the defender, to whom he committed the management of his little affairs in London, and with whom, during his absence abroad, he kept up a most friendly correspondence, as can be made to appear from a variety of his letters.

"Mr. Cameron having returned from the Continent in spring, 1791, intended to have gone again to the Highlands, but altered his resolution in that respect, and wrote a letter to Fassiefern, dated in March, 1791, signifying that, as he could not go North that spring, as he first intended, he would be obliged to him to arrange and manage his estate for that year, as might seem most for his advantage, 'barring or excluding the lands of Erracht and Inveruiskvullin, etc., which he had sold to the defender'.

"This transaction with the defender, however, gave

---

* Mr. Teasdale in his depositions declared—"that after the disposition [of the lands in question] was executed, the defender [Erracht] took it up in his hand, and held it across the table where Lochiel was standing, and said, 'Loch', have you done this to your entire satisfaction?' To which Lochiel answered, that if he had not been satisfied, he would not have done it, or used words to that effect." Mr. David Robertson, Mr. Teasdale's clerk, who was also present, "being interrogated upon the part of the defender, whether the deponent recollects that, at the time of executing the foresaid disposition, any conversation or proposition passed from the defender to Lochiel, that if the transaction was not agreeable to him it was not yet too late to be free, or words to that purpose, depones, that words did pass to that purpose between Major Cameron, the defender, and Lochiel, as he thinks, when he was writing his name as witness, and the words used upon that occasion, as nearly as the deponent can recollect, were, that Major Cameron said to Lochiel, I hope you are satisfied with this transaction; if not, it is not yet too late to retract; to which Lochiel made a short answer, purporting that he was satisfied, but that it is impossible for him to be certain of the precise words, though he is certain that such proposition was made, and assented to by Lochiel".

great displeasure to Fassiefern, and his cousin the banker, who were highly offended with their young friend for suffering one, whom they considered so formidable a rival, to obtain a permanent footing in a part of the country where, by residing upon the spot, he might contend for the chieftainship and leading of the clan. Fassiefern accordingly posted to London; and although his young friend had by that time returned again to France, a resolution was immediately formed, to make use of every possible means for preventing the defender from completing his title to the lands which he had purchased; for which purpose, it was known, he intended immdeiately coming down to this country. With this view, Fassiefern returned to the Highlands, without so much as seeing the defender when at London.

"The defender having arrived at Edinburgh about the beginning of April last, the disposition he had obtained was put upon record, and an instrument of seisin written out, and transmitted by post to his brother, who, since the death of his father, had resided on the lands of Erracht along with his mother. But although the defender's brother immediately applied to Ewen Cameron, the only notary public in that part of the country, to execute this business, that notary thought proper to decline to discharge the duties of his office in that respect; and, from what passed afterwards, there is reason to believe that he gave notice to Fassiefern of the defender's intention to complete his title by infeftment; for, so strictly were the motions of the defender's friends watched on this occasion, that as soon as another notary, who was sent for from Inverness, had arrived at Erracht, a body of about forty men, composed of Fassiefern's immediate dependents and menial servants, were gathered together, and, in the most violent and outrageous manner, after breaking open the doors of the house (and throwing the defender's mother and sister-in-law into fits, of which the latter never got entirely the better, and perhaps her death was not a little accelerated by the fright and confusion of that day), dragged the notary away by force; and, after conveying him several miles out of the country, threatened him with death, in case he should ever return to infeft the defender in the lands of Erracht.

"These lawless proceedings seem to have been intended to prevent the defender from getting himself infeft in the lands, until Fassiefern should be able to get another infeftment taken upon the trust disposition, which his constituent was afterwards induced to execute upon the 12th of May, 1791, divesting himself of the whole estate, including the lands sold to the defender, in favour of the now pursuers, for although the defenders, upon being informed of the deforcement of the notary who had been brought from Inverness, sent another from Edinburgh properly attended, he was only able to get his seisin put upon record a few hours before the infeftment which was taken upon the disposition just now mentioned, by the same notary (Ewen Cameron) who had formerly refused the defender's employment.

"This trust disposition, by which Mr. Cameron conveyed the whole estate to the Right Honourable Henry Dundas, one of his Majesty's Principal Secretaries of State; Robert Barclay of Urie, Esq.; Donald Cameron, banker, and Fassiefern, any two of whom were declared a quorum, the banker being always *sine quo non*, appears, *ex facie*, to have been granted chiefly for the purpose of giving to the *sine quo non* trustee a preference for a large debt, said by him to amount to about £10,000; no part of which seems, so far as can be gathered from the deed, to be vouched by any legal documents, and which, at least in part, is, in the deed itself, confessed to consist of money advanced, not to the young man, but to others, which he was nowise legally bound to pay, till it was thus secured. Another reason for taking this trust disposition seems to have been to secure to Fassiefern the factory and local management of the estate (which enables him to monopolize and exercise, as he does at this moment, every advantage of holding and stocking as much of the estate as he may find convenient) during the trust, which is conceived in a very unusual style, having no fixed termination. This disposition, which, at the same time, contained a power to challenge and set aside all deeds granted by the young gentleman himself, was soon brought into exertion, in the view of founding an action of reduction against the defender.

"A clamorous summons of reduction was accordingly executed, charging the defender with having illicited and impetrated the disposition òf the lands of Erracht, etc., by fraud and circumvention, without any proper consideration or value, etc.; and concluding, that the said disposition, and the instrument of seisin following thereupon, should be reduced, and declared to be void and null.

"After the usual steps in such processes, a remit was made to his Lordship to discuss the reasons of reduction; and, after a full hearing of the parties by their Counsel at the bar, the following interlocutor was, of this date (2nd Feb., 1792), pronounced: 'The Lord Ordinary having heard parties procurators, before answer, ordains the pursuers to give in a pointed condescendence of the facts they aver, and will undertake to prove, in support of their reasons of reduction, without using one word of argument; and, when given in, allows the defender to see the same, and ordains him to give in answers thereto, without delay'.

"The pursuers have accordingly given in a condescendence, to which these answers are now humbly offered on the part of the defender; and, after having already given a pretty full detail of the facts relative to the transaction now brought under challenge, he is hopeful that it will be unnecessary to consume much of his Lordship's time in taking notice of the different articles of the condescendence.

"The first article, stating the terms on which his Majesty was graciously pleased to restore the estate of Lochiel to the pursuers' constituent, requires no notice on the part of the defender. It will serve equally well, and will no doubt be admitted, in any action which the pursuers may ever have occasion to bring into Court in their character of trustees.

"The second article seems to be equally foreign to the merits of the present question. The defender shall, therefore, only take the liberty to observe upon it, that if it was meant to assert that the persons therein named were legally named curators, and accepted of the office, they have not explained themselves sufficiently on that head.

"With regard to the third article, it must be sufficient to mention, that the defender has already given an account of the terms of the lease he obtained from the Commissioners of Annexed Estates, and of which there are about thirty years yet to run; and that, although he may have been twenty-one or twenty-two years of age when he left his native spot in October or November, 1772, his attention, from the time he left school, was, as is usual with young men in the same situation, given more to the local amusements of hunting and fishing than to the management of his father's farm.

"Whether the pursuers' constituent was, or was not, liberally supplied with money by his friend the banker, as is stated in the fourth article, it is not the business of the defender to inquire, but most certain it is, that the young gentleman often complained, not only to the defender, but to many others, on that score.

"In answer to the fifth article, the defender knows it to be true, that young Mr. Cameron applied to Mr. Teasdale to procure him, not £500, but £1600 or £1800, and that he referred Mr. Teasdale to the defender for an account of his situation and circumstances; but it is a gross and malicious falsehood to say that the defender gave such an account of his circumstances and situation as induced Mr. Teasdale to think that it would not be safe to lend him any money. This matter has been already stated as it truly happened; and the young gentleman himself cannot fail to recollect, that Mr. Teasdale was perfectly satisfied with the information the defender gave him, and that the only bar to his getting the money from that quarter arose from its being discovered that he was under age, when an insurance was making upon his life, upon the supposition of his having attained the years of majority, as already stated.

"The sixth article of the condescendence is a complete bundle of misrepresentations; and in answer thereto, it is only necessary to refer his Lordship to what has been stated in the narrative part of these answers, and to add, that Mr. Cameron, when he proposed to sell the farms in question to the defender, which he did repeatedly before the defender agreed to purchase them, was in possession of a rental, mentioning even the number of people upon the estate, which had been sent him some time before by Fassiefern; and he had also before him, and in his possession, for some days previous to any settlement about these lands, a concise rental and survey of the whole estate, as taken from the Commissioners' books in 1781, specifying the precise number of acres of arable, pasture, hill, moss, and wood, on each farm, under their respective heads, and the values of each, and had thereby as good access to know the worth of these farms as the defender, who had not been in that country from the time he left it in 1772, and from his father's letter, and the factor's report above inserted, and other circumstances, had no reason to suppose that they were really worth the money which Mr. Cameron then demanded, near two-thirds of the whole being then under a lease, of which upwards of thirty years were still to run.

"In answer to the seventh article of the condescendence, in so far as the same is not already exhausted, it must be sufficient to observe, that, as Mr. Cameron had proposed to sell to the defender the farms in question (and if he had not acquiesced on that occasion, perhaps much more of the estate would have been irretrievably secured by strangers), it would be a matter of no consequence, whether the letter alluded to in this article which the defender has already spoken to, and admitted to be of the purport mentioned in the condescendence, was of his own framing, or written out from a scroll, prepared by the defender, from such materials as he was then accidentally possessed of, the chief of which was an extract of the decree sustaining his father's claim upon the forfeited estate, which he got from Mr. Alexander Hart in the year 1781, and, with regard to what is said of the defender's burning the scroll or draft from which this letter was made out, the gentleman may himself recollect that in writing out the letter he considerably curtailed the original draft, having thought it unnecessary to enter minutely into all the circumstances relative to the transaction, which were there mentioned. It was, therefore, by mutual consent thrown into the fire, and it is difficult even to figure any advantage the defender could derive from refusing to give it to Mr. Cameron, even although the letter itself had been transcribed from it *verbatim*. Had matters rested upon what passed upon this occasion, the defender must have laid his account with submitting to the risk he ran, by entering into any transactions of this kind with a minor, acting for himself, without the consent of curators; but, as the deed now sought to be reduced, and upon which he founds his right to the lands thereby conveyed to him, was executed after the seller had attained the years of majority, and was at full liberty to dispose either of the whole, or of a part of the estate, at pleasure, the transaction here alluded to can be of little consequence to the present question. It is therefore only necessary further to add, in answer to this article of the condescendence, that if, on that occasion, the defender had meant to act unfairly by, or to impose upon the young gentleman, it cannot be supposed that he would have been desirous to call any other party to witness his proceedings, but would rather have settled everything privately, without allowing any other person to be privy to the transaction.

"The eighth article of the condescendence seems to savour more of argument than of allegations, which were the only object of such a paper. The defender, therefore, in answer thereto, shall only state that the young gentleman himself did most violently object to every advice the defender gave him to lay his situation before the banker, who he frequently said had given him (then within a few months of 21 years of age) the opprobrious epithets of a thief, a plunderer, and a rascal, who was coming, day after day, to rob him and his son of their property, whenever he applied for money from him.* It is indeed said, that the defender not only carefully concealed the whole of this negotiation from the banker, and the young man's other friends, but also exacted a promise from him, that he would not divulge it to any human being for the space of five years. This, however, the defender has no scruple to pronounce a downright falsehood. To suppose that the transaction could have been so long concealed, would have been absurd; but it would have been still more so to stipulate such a concealment, as the defender even if he had been acquainted with the law regarding the *quadrennium utile*, must otherwise have known, no length of time could validate a sale made by a minor without the consent of his curators, if he had any, unless it should be homologated or ratified by him after his majority, and that it could be of no consequence whether such homologation or ratification should take place at the distance of four years, or of four days after his becoming of age.

"The ninth article of the condescendence has been already spoken to, and the circumstance to which it relates seems to shew how ready the defender was to assist his young friend in the hour of his distress, upon very slender security.

"Of the tenth article, it seems unnecessary to take any notice, farther than to observe, that during the three weeks

---

* Allan Cameron of Lundavra stated, in his depositions, that Lochiel told him before he left London on his first visit to Lochaber, "that he was in great want of money, and would be under the necessity of parting with a piece of the estate, in order to get money, as he could not procure it otherwise, and behoved to have it before he left town; that he further said, that he had applied to Mr. Donald Cameron for money, a little time before that, and that he had abused him for it, and ordered him to get out of the house, as he was a rascal and a pickpocket; and that he had called his son into the room, and said to him, 'Charles, here is a man come to pick your pocket, for it is your money he wants'. That the deponent dissuaded Lochiel from selling any part of his estate, or burdening it, and advised him to go back to Mr. Cameron, and tell him that he could not leave town without money, and that he must have it; that Lochiel made answer, that he could not think of going back after the usage he had received."

the young gentleman was in Lochaber, he must have had good opportunities to learn the value of the subjects which he had formerly proposed to sell to the defender, more especially as he, in company with Fassiefern and some others of his friends, dined at Erracht, when they amused themselves with walking about and viewing that farm and those adjoining.

"The eleventh article of the condescendence seems to be artfully calculated to evade the force of a circumstance that must of itself be sufficient to put an end to the pursuer's action; namely, that a new bargain was concluded after Mr. Cameron came of age, and was fully master of his own actions, and that, when the disposition now sought to be reduced came to be executed, the defender agreed to pay £1940 instead of £1600, which, while the disponer was in his minority, and before his journey to Lochaber, he appeared willing to accept of. It is there stated, that when he came to execute the disposition in the defender's favour, the defender said that he and his brother had made free with some of his wood, and used some of his timber in building a house, and that, on that account, he the defender would give up his note for the sum of £300 and hold the price of the lands to be £1900, instead of £1600 as originally stipulated. This is, however, too ridiculous a story to gain credit, and is rather inconsistent with the idea which the pursuers are so studious to inculcate, of the defender's having formed a scheme to circumvent the young gentleman, and to elicit from him a disposition of the lands in question at a price far below their real value. The defender does accordingly positively deny that he knew of any claim against his brother, on account of his making free with any wood upon the estate; and the undoubted fact is, that, in addition to the £1600 formerly advanced, it was settled that he should likewise give up the £300 which he had advanced to the young gentleman in the month of August, prior to his setting out for the Highlands. The price actually paid for the lands in question, therefore, stood thus :—

28th Nov., 1789.

To cash advanced him this day, - - - -	£1600	0 0
To interest on ditto, from this date to 11th Nov., 1790, the term of entry, 11 months 14 days, - - - - - - -	76	7 11

21st Aug., 1790.

To cash advanced this day, - - - - -	300	0 0
To interest on ditto, from this date to 11th Nov., 1790, being 28 days, - - - -	3	7 4
	£1979	15 3
From which, deducting the rent and public burdens (£9) of the farm of Erracht to Martinmas, 1790, being - - -	£34	0 0
There still remains, - - - - - - - -	£1945	15 3

—a trifle more than the price mentioned in the disposition.

"What is further stated in this article, with regard to the defender's having furnished Mr. Spottiswoode with the minute and anxious description of the lands said to be contained in the clause of the disposition quoted in the beginning of the condescendence, seems to be of little consequence. The seller trusted to the defender's getting the disposition extended in a proper manner; but it is rather a singular objection to a sale, that the purchaser was enabled to give a just description of his purchase, which certainly was very necessary to prevent any future dispute about the boundaries, of which perhaps advantage might otherwise be taken. It has already been mentioned, that the defender had in his possession an extract of the decree sustaining his father's claim, founded upon his wadset of the lands of Erracht. No mistake could therefore be committed in the description of these lands, which was actually taken from that extract; and, with regard to the other farm of Inveruiskvullin, there could be no impropriety in describing it as it was possessed in the year 1771 by the tenants mentioned in the disposition, and according to the recollection of the defender, who was then near twenty years absent from the country. He had therefore no occasion to desire his brother to repair to London on this account, in spring, 1790; and the fact is, that the brother went there on a very different errand, viz., in order to get some little family disputes adjusted, with which the pursuers have no sort of concern.

"It is said, indeed, in the twelfth article of the condescendence, that the disposition made out by the orders, and at the sight of the defender, contains no less than five different farms. This is, however, a gross misrepresentation of the fact, nothing more being included in that disposition than the two farms of Erracht and Inveruiskvullin, including shealings or summer grazings, forming a part of these farms from time immemorial, as is the case with all other farms in the Highlands, though now attempted to be held forth as so many separate farms.

"The pursuers, in the thirteenth article of the condescendence, are pleased to give a most exaggerated representation of the worth of the lands sold to the defender, which, however, very ill accords with the ideas that appear to have been entertained of their real value, not only by the defender's father, who had the best access to be well acquainted with the farm of Erracht, but also by Mr. Butter the factor, and the other persons in whom the commissioners of the annexed estates did with justice repose confidence. As to the offers alluded to, the defender does not recollect any serious proposition of that kind being made to him. If any such ever was intended, it must have been on the footing of a steelbow contract.

"And, with regard to the farm of Inveruiskvullin, the old rent of it was £16 0s. 6d., with £4 13s. 6d. of addition, amounting in all to £20 14s. 0d., conform to the surveyor's and factor's valuation and report, to which a third more has been added since by Fassiefern; so that it amounted in all to about £27 12s. 0d. And the defender begs leave to add, that the present tenant's father, with the assistance of a pension from Government, died insolvent; and that his successor (his son, the present tenant), notwithstanding many years' possession, with all the advantages ascribed to sheep-farming (while in the hands of a monopolizing few, the curse and scourge of the poor ill-fated Highlanders), cannot boast of either credit, or the means of supporting his family decently or comfortably; and in fact, the rent of this year, as well as for several years past, has been paid by a friend, whose stock is now upon the possession.

"It seems, however, unnecessary to enter much into matters of this kind; for, unless the pursuers can establish some better ground upon which to challenge the transaction, they will find it an arduous task to reduce the sale upon the head of inequality, even although proved to the utmost extent of their allegations. This, at the same time that it is inapplicable to the present purpose, is totally out of their power to do, in spite of the theoretical opinions with regard to the worth of Highland farms, which have been perhaps too loosely entertained since the introduction of sheep into that part of the country; a speculation which teems with oppression, as a serious public grievance, and must ultimately depopulate the country, and leave the proprietors, at last, in the mercy of those who may, perhaps from more distant quarters, wish to take their lands, which will certainly be the case, and they as certainly deserve. The present nominal value of Highland property is therefore not a proper *datum* for fixing a fair and equal price by which the native inhabitants can maintain their families decently. The defender is indeed convinced, notwithstanding of all that is said by the pursuers on this head, that, considering the long period that was still to run of the lease he obtained in 1781, he has paid a very full and adequate price for his purchase.

"In the fourteenth article of the condescendence it is said, that the particular situation of the lands in question renders the transaction peculiarly detrimental to the pursuers' constituent. It is not, however, the defender's business to inquire what part of the estate it would have been most convenient for him to part with. It must be sufficient to observe, that his having already a long lease of the lands of Erracht, and the circumstance of his predecessors having resided on these lands for near 300 years, were motives sufficiently cogent to induce him to prefer them to any other lands of much greater value in that part of the country.

"The fifteenth article of the condescendence seems to be exceedingly immaterial. The defender neither kept the disposition a secret nor boasted of it, but he proceeded to complete his titles upon it, as soon as his business permitted his coming to this country, of which the seller was well informed, and that the purchase was then no secret is sufficiently evident, not only from his writing to Fassiefern, but from the means that were taken to prevent the defender's being infeft.

"In the last article it is said that, soon after granting the disposition, Mr. Cameron was induced to borrow £500 farther on bond from the defender, who proposed to purchase more farms, which he declined to agree to; that, on different occasions afterwards, the defender endeavoured to induce him to apply to him for money, but without effect, and that, when the deed of trust was granted to the pursuers, the defender made a peremptory demand upon him for the £500, which was immediately paid.

"This is, however, another gross misrepresentation. It has been already mentioned, that the defender, on occasion of Mr. Cameron going to France, in November, 1790, lent him £500, not upon bond, but upon his bare note of hand, dated 7th November, 1790, payable six months after date; and so far was the defender from being a harsh creditor, that although the trust-deed, under which the present process is brought, was executed as early as the 12th of May last, about the time of the note falling due, no demand was ever made of that note till the month of September last, when the defender had returned to London; and, after expostulating with the gentleman on the impropriety of his conduct towards him, insisted for, and obtained payment from a Mr. Wall of the Temple, to whom he was desired to apply.

"The defender received several letters from the young gentleman subsequent to this loan, which would satisfy every impartial mind, that the money was advanced from mere friendship, and from no interested motive whatever.

"It is indeed true, that, in consequence of Mr. Cameron, the banker, telling his constituent's mother, on various and particular occasions, that her son was owing him upwards of £10,000, the young gentleman came to the defender, complaining grievously, and expressing an anxious wish to get rid of him altogether, before the family should be totally ruined by his rapacity, and to procure money to pay him off at once. Upon which the defender said, that perhaps he would soon be able to let him have it upon his own bond; but this was all that passed respecting money-matters, beyond the transactions already mentioned.

"The defender, having thus considered every article of the pursuers' condescendence, will, he hopes, be forgiven for further observing, that, taking them either separately or collectively, they afford no relevant ground for setting aside the sale brought under challenge by the present action. The defender is very ready to admit that minority, lesion, fraud, and circumvention, do, each of them, afford relevant grounds of reduction. But it is submitted to his Lordship, that, for the first of these grounds, there is no room in this case, and that no circumstances have hitherto been condescended on from which the other can be inferred.

"Had the transaction rested upon what passed during the minority, it would have been unnecessary for the pursuers, if their young friend was actually under curatory, even to allege lesion, because a minor, who has curators, cannot effectually bind himself without their consent. It will, however, be recollected, that the disposition now sought to be set aside was confessedly granted after he was of full age, and capable not only to judge, but to act for himself. It will not be pretended by these pursuers that the defender could, in consequence of anything that had passed between them during his minority, compel him to part with a single inch of his estate. The case must, therefore, be viewed in the same light as if no communings of any kind had taken place with regard to the sale prior to the seller's becoming of age, in which event it must have been impossible for the pursuers to object to the legality of the transaction in respect of an inequality in the bargain, how easy soever it might have been for them to establish lesion, even to the degree they are now pleased to allege. On the contrary, as they do not pretend to accuse the young gentleman of facility, or such a degree of imbecility as, joined with gross lesion, may raise a constructive fraud, they must have confined their ground of challenge to a charge of direct fraud upon the part of the defender.

"But, although they have made this charge in their summons, it is submitted to his Lordship, that they have not condescended upon facts and circumstances sufficient to support it. They do not pretend that any means were made use of by the defender to impose upon their constituent, by depreciating the value of the subject, or by preventing him from getting sufficient information on that head. But, unless they can prove something of that kind, it would not avail them, although they could show, that the subject was as valuable as they now affect to represent it. From one of these pursuers, viz., Mr. Cameron the banker, a plea of that sort would indeed come rather awkwardly, when it is considered that he concluded a bargain with Mr. Hugh Seton for the estate of Appin at the price of £22,000; and, upon being disappointed in making the purchase at that price, in consequence of a previous inhibition having been used against the seller, came forward shortly thereafter, and offered for the same estate, when exposed to public roup, no less than £34,500. Many other bargains might be pointed out fully as advantageous, upon a comparative view, as that under consideration, both in Argyll and Inverness-shire, within the last ten years, and far better, in many instances, within the last twenty years.

APPENDIX I.

"In short, the only circumstance from which the pursuers attempt to infer fraud, is, that a bargain for the sale of the lands was first made before the seller was twenty-one years of age, and without the participation of curators. But to this, independent of a higher price being afterwards given, when the disposition was granted, it must be a sufficient answer, that the defender was the person who was to run the greatest hazard, upon the supposition that the young gentleman was under curatory, as upon his coming of age he might have refused to stand to that bargain; in which event, the defender would perhaps have found it a difficult matter to recover payment of the sums he had advanced, by these pursuers forcing him to show that the money was profitably employed. It is, however, rather ridiculous to suppose that any man of common understanding would resort to fraudulent means in order to bring about a transaction which was liable to be set aside on other grounds, and on which he could therefore have no reliance.

"The defender cannot conclude without taking notice of an observation made in the end of the condescendence, where, after mentioning what was stated by the defender's counsel at the bar, with regard to his birth, and his being possessed of all the fine feelings and nice sentiments so suitable and congenial to a gentleman, and his having entered into the transaction believing it to be perfectly fair, equal, and honourable; the pursuers are pleased to say, that if it shall appear that the defender and their constituent were equally deceived as to the value of these lands, and that parting with them would essentially injure the remaining part of the estate and prove ruinous to the young gentleman, it may be expected that the defender will come forward and say, that, as he entered into the transaction *bona fide*, believing it to be perfectly equal, so, now that it appears to have been very much the reverse, he was above taking the advantage of it, and was ready to give up the bargain upon getting back his money with interest from the time it was advanced. The defender will beg leave to tell the pursuers, that if they had reflected at all upon their own conduct towards him, they must have been sensible that they had no title to expect any favour at his hand. Had they thought proper to behave to him with common discretion, they might have had a better title to favour; but as, instead of doing so, they immediately declared open war against him, by traducing him, and attacking his character, in the most open and public manner; and as Fassiefern, when at London, showed himself so adverse from holding any sort of communication with him as to return, unopened, a kind invitation to his house, which perhaps might have opened a channel for some terms of accommodation, they can have no title to expect that the defender is to depart from any advantage he may derive from his bargain, although much greater than they affect to represent it. He is, however, at the same time, perfectly convinced, that the circumstance which the pursuers are pleased to think sufficient to induce him to give it up, will never be proved to exist.

"Although, in the course of legal proceedings, the defender is under the necessity of applying the observations which it is necessary for him to state in the way of defence, indiscriminately to all who appear as pursuers, the defender flatters himself that two of the pursuers will believe that he has not the most distant intention, by anything he has said, to throw the least reflection upon them, for appearing in that character in the present action, having by whatever means, being once included in the trust deed, they must, of necessity, lend their ear to the representations made to them by those whom they must naturally consider to be most nearly interested in the business; and the defender is sorry that, by this means, they have been innocently led to lend their names to proceedings which, he is satisfied, will not ultimately meet with their approbation. In respect whereof, etc. Which answers are signed by the defender himself, and by Mr. Alexander Wright, advocate, his procurator, in presence of the Lord Ordinary."

[Lochiel's Trustees succeeding in the action of Reduction and Declarator, the sale of the lands in dispute was declared null and void.]

APPENDIX II.

THE following statement, giving the names of all the tenants, and the total rental paid on the Estates of Lochiel, nearly a century ago, will be found interesting. There were "many cottars, and herds, and sub-tenants," whose names were "not put down" by the factor. A comparison with the present rental, in 1884, would prove instructive.

RENT OF THE ESTATE OF LOCHIEL, FOR MARTINMAS, 1787, AS MADE OUT BY THE FACTOR, EWEN CAMERON OF FASSIEFERN, ON THE 25TH OF JANUARY, 1788.

	£	s.	d.
Drimnasallie, paid by John Cameron,	33	0	0
Kenlochiel, do. Donald Cameron,	11	0	0
Stronlea, two Camerons,	17	6	8
Corrybeg, four M'Masters and three Camerons,	14	0	0
Fassiefern, Ewen Cameron,	34	11	4
Mill of Fassiefern,	8	6	8
Achadalew, John Cumming,	15	14	8
Annat, Collector, Colin Campbell,	22	10	0
Corpach, Alexander Macdonald, Glencoe,	120	0	0
Fishing of Corpach,	2	5	0
Banavie ⅜, Mr. Fraser, Minister, and Patrick Mackinnon,	7	7	7
Muirsherloch, eight Camerons and one Mackintosh,	24	13	4
Strone, John Cameron, a minor, under age,	26	13	4
Barr, five Camerons,	25	6	8
	£362	15	3

	£362	15	3
Inveruiskvullin, two Camerons,	24	2	4
Erracht, Allan Cameron, without augmentation,	25	0	0
Two Moys, twelve Mackinnons, and four Camerons,	57	6	8
Achnacarry, Ewen Cameron, Fassiefern,	26	5	0
Clunes, Donald Cameron,	48	0	0
Achnasoul, eight Camerons,	35	0	0
Crieff, John MacPhie,	12	0	0
Salichan, Cameron and MacPhie,	10	13	4
Muick and ½ Kenmore, Ewen Cameron,	20	0	0
Kenmore ½, John Cameron,	4	0	0
Coanich, three Camerons, one MacPhie,	4	4	0
Callicharth, Donald MacMillan, John MacPhie,	14	13	4
Murlagan, MacMillan, MacIntosh, MacLachlan,	27	18	8
Relenmore, a shealling, Alex. MacMillan,	8	15	0
Invermally, Alexander Cameron,	16	13	4
Kinlocharkik, three Camerons,	13	15	4
Lagganfern ½, Donald Cameron,	5	6	8
Glenpeinbeg ¾, Lagganfern ½, Ocain Cameron,	32	17	7
Glenpeinbeg ¼, two Camerons, two MacMillans,	5	18	2
Glenpeinmore, Allan MacMillan,	32	0	0
Glendissary, ten MacPhies, four MacMillans, four Camerons,	90	0	0
Achintore, Lieutenant Donald Cameron,	40	0	0
Croft of Achintore, Thomas Malcom,	2	7	3
Coruanan, Alexander MacLachlan, a minor,	46	10	10
Corrycherichan, Mrs. Cameron, a widow,	17	6	8
Culchenna, John Cameron, including Milne Croft,	53	6	8
Lundavra, Allan Cameron,	18	13	8
	£1164	8	5

	£1164 8 5
Balichelish, six Mackenzies,	57 6 8
Ferry Balichelish, John Rankin,	10 0 0
Onich, four Mackenzies, and four Camerons,	41 12 0
Fishing of Lochy, his Grace the Duke of Gordon,	29 0 0
Ferry of Lochy, Alexander Robertson,	3 8 8
Mill of Culchenna, Duncan MacKinnes,	6 1 4
Mill Achnacary, Donald Cameron,	5 13 10
Public House, Corpach, Archibald Butter,	3 10 0
Church seat rent, paid by 20 lib., land of Lochiel,	6 9½
	£1212 9 0½

APPENDIX III.

RENTAL OR VALUATION OF THE FARMS UPON THE ESTATE OF LOCHIEL, MADE OUT BY LIEUTENANT ALLAN CAMERON, LATE OF COLONEL TARLETON'S DRAGOONS, IN :—

	Present Rent.	What Worth.
Drimnasallie,	£33 0 0	£110 0 0
Corpach,	120 0 0	160 0 0
Muirshierlich,	24 13 4	40 0 0
Inveruiskvullin,	24 2 4	65 0 0
Achnacary,	26 5 0	30 0 0
Achnasoul,	35 0 0	100 0 0
Crief,	12 0 0	25 0 0
Laggan Fern,	10 13 4	30 0 0
Glendissary,	90 0 0	180 0 0
Achintore,	40 0 0	50 0 0
Corryhurachan,	17 6 8	30 0 0
	£433 0 8	£820 0 0

N.B.—The above farms are all out of lease, and liable to augmentation when you are of age.

	Present Rent.	What Worth.
Kinlochiel,	£11 0 0	£25 0 0
Stronelia,	17 6 8	40 0 0
Corrybeg,	14 0 0	30 0 0
Banavie,	7 7 7	15 0 0
Barr,	25 6 8	60 0 0
Two Moys,	57 6 8	70 0 0
Salachan,	10 13 4	20 0 0
	£576 1 7	£1080 0 0

	£576	1	7	£1080	0	0
Muick and Kenavore,	24	0	0	50	0	0
Coanich,	14	4	0	30	0	0
Callich,	14	13	4	30	0	0
Murlaggan and Riemore,	36	13	8	80	0	0
Invermally,	16	13	4	60	0	0
Kinlocharkaig,	13	15	4	30	0	0
Glenpeanbeg,	23	12	8	60	0	0
Glenpeanmore,	32	0	0	80	0	0
Culchenna,	53	6	8	90	0	0
Ounnich,	41	12	0	65	0	0
Ballyhulish,	57	6	8	100	0	0
	£903	19	3	£1755	0	0

The above are all let at 8 years' lease, and cannot be augmented until that time expire.

	Present Rent.			What Worth.		
Fassiefern and Mill,	£42	18	0	£180	0	0
Achdaloe,	15	14	8	50	0	0
Annat,	22	10	0	60	0	0
Strone and Achnaherry,	26	13	4	120	0	0
Erracht and Glenmally,	25	0	0	150	0	0
Clunes,	48	0	0	180	0	0
Coruanan,	46	10	10	120	0	0
Lundavra,	18	13	8	40	0	0
	£1149	19	9	£2665	0	0

The above are all let at 30 years' lease.

INDEX.

INDEX.

Abercorn, Earl of, 278.
Abercrombie, Sir Ralph, 255, 345, 346, 349.
Aboyne, Earl of, 158.
Achadelew, battle of, 120-8, 196.
Airlie, Earl of, 158.
Albany, Duke of, 22, 43, 264.
Albemarle, Duke of, 150, 157.
Alexander II., 10, 11.
Angus Og of Isla, 2.
Angusson, Donald, of Keppoch, 37.
Argyll, Earl of, 36-8, 40, 45, 47 (n.), 56, 59, 62, 67, 74-6, 78, 79, 87, 91-9, 101, 103, 104, 109, 114, 116, 138, 143, 149, 150, 162, 163, 165-9, 173, 175, 176, 178, 179, 202, 251.
Arros, Lord, 94.
Athole, Earl and Marquis of, 55, 59, 158, 167, 173-6.

Badenoch, 13, 14, 35, 44, 64, 161, 234.
Balcarres, Earl of, 181.
Baligarny, Family of, 12 (n.).
Bancho, 9.
Barclay of Urie, 177, 210, 211.
Barclay, Sir George, 202.
Barclay-Allardice of Urie and Allardice, 211; as one of Lochiel's trustees, 419-57.
Basil, Council of, 20.
Beauclerk, Lord, 268.
Berwick, Duke of, 200.
"Blar-nan-Leine," battle of, 40, 46.
Breadalbane, Earl of, 63, 93, 94, 163, 165, 201, 274, 403.
Bruce, Robert, 2, 11, 27.
Bryan, Col. William, 114, 116, 127, 143.
Buccleuch, Duke of, 258.
Buchan, General, 200, 201, 204.
Buckinghamshire, Earl of, 257.
Busaco, battle of, 356, 376, 413.

Cadogan, General, 207.
Caithness, Earl of, 28, 43, 158.

Callander, Earl of, 150.
Callart, lands of, 17, 18.
Cambro, 6.
Cameron Clan, origin of the name, 7 (*n.*); defeated by the Mackintoshes at Drumlui, 13; battle of Invernahavon, 14, 16; at the North Inch of Perth, 17, 22-4; desert the Lord of the Isles, 26; kill John MacLean of Coll, 26; feud with Clan Chattan, 28; battle with the Mackintoshes, 28; their lands harried by Clan Chattan, 31; battle with Keppoch and Mackintosh, 33; invade the country of the Mackays, 38; skirmish with the Mackintoshes, 50; battle with MacMhicEoin and the MacLeans, 70-2; at the battle of Achadelew, 120-8; Act and Decree of the Court of Session against them, 151; raids upon the Mackintoshes, 159'; settlement with the Mackintoshes, 164; fidelity of two of the clan at Inveraray, 169; skirmish with the Grants, 187, 188; at the battle of Killiecrankie, 193-9; join Prince Charles at Glenfinnan, 220, 221; at the taking of Edinburgh and the battle of Preston, 223, 224; incident at Falkirk, 226, 227; at the seige of Fort William, 229; at the battle of Culloden, 221-3; change in habits and morals, 243, 244; the clan coat-of-arms, 258-60.
Cameron, Major Alexander (Erracht), his bravery at Waterloo, 319, 368, 371.
Cameron, Sir Alexander, of Inverailort, 375-9; his marriage, issue, and death, 379.
Cameron, Alexander Wentworth, of Callart, his marriage and descendants, 383, 384.
Cameron, Alexander, of Glenevis, imprisoned for his share in the Rising of 1745, 392; ill-treatment of his wife by the English soldiery, 393; his marriage and descendants, 394-6.
Cameron, Captain Alexander, of Balvenie, his marriage and issue, 401.
Cameron, Alexander, his marriage, issue, and death, 409.
Cameron, Allan, succeeded his father Donald, and carried on Lochiel line of succession, 9.
Cameron, Allan, or "Allan MacOchtery" IX. of Lochiel, in whose time the feuds between his clan and the Mackintoshes commenced, 12; his marriage, 17; and death, 21.
Cameron, Allan, XII. of Lochiel, known as "Ailein MacDhomh'uill Duibh," becomes a vassal of the Lord of Lochalsh, 32; his death, 33; his marriage and issue, 34.
Cameron, Allan, XVI. of Lochiel, known as "Ailein Mac Ian Duibh," 61; engages in a broil in Appin, 63; makes raids into the Mackintosh country, and joins the Earl of Huntly, 64; at the battle of Glenlivet, 65; victory over the MacLeans, 72; defeats the Macdonalds of Islay, 73; dissensions in his clan, 79, 80; he defeats his opponents, 81; and puts sixteen of them to death, 83; he makes a treaty with the Marquis of Huntly, 84; his marriage and issue, 93.
Cameron, Sir Allan, of Erracht, Colonel of the 79th Cameron Highlanders, 319-20; his early life and education, 321-2; duel with *Fear Mhorsheirlich*, 322-5; a fugitive in Mull and Morvern, 326; becomes a clerk in Greenock, 326; goes to America and joins the "Royal Highland Emigrant Corps," 327; is taken prisoner by the Americans, 328; escapes from prison, 329; returns to England, 330; elopes with Miss Philips and marries her at Gretna Green, 331; reconciliation with his father-in-law, 332; becomes an active member of the Highland Society of London, 332-4; raises the 79th Regiment, 326-40; is made Lieutenant-Colonel of it, 341; and goes with it to Flanders, 342-3; thence to Martinique, 345; returns to Scotland, 346; severely wounded at Egmont-op-Zee, 346; where he prevented disaffection in the

regiment, 348; is present at the battle of Alexandria, 349; is again wounded, 350; raises a second battalion, 350; his opinion of the kilt, 351; is present at Copenhagen, and is thanked by Government, 352; is appointed commandant of Lisbon, 353; severely wounded at Talavera, 355; resigns his command and returns to England, 357; is knighted by George IV., 363; estimate of his character by Col. Sir William Napier, 372, 373; his marriage, issue, and death, 373; action against him by Lochiel's trustees, 419-57.

Cameron, Allan, of Callart, 381.

Cameron, Allan, of Callart, captain in the Lochaber Fencibles, his marriage and descendants, 382, 383.

Cameron, Allan, of Callart, 384.

Cameron, Allan, of Lundavra, his death, 385; his marriage and issue, 386.

Cameron, Allan John Russell Bedford, of Lundavra, 387; his marriage, descendants, and death, 389.

Cameron, Lieut. Allan, of Lundavra, 385.

Cameron, Allan, of Lundavra, 372, 386; his marriage, issue, and death, 387.

Cameron, Allan Ewen Charles, of Lundavra, his marriages and issue, 389, 390.

Cameron, Allan Gordon, III. of Barcaldine and Foxhall, his marriage, issue, and death, 407, 408.

Cameron, Angus, I. of Lochiel, his marriage, 9.

Cameron, Dr. Archibald, 214, 222, 233, 239, 241-3, 251-3; his education, 261; his character, 261-3; at Falkirk and Culloden, 261; escapes to France, 264; charge of embezzlement against him, 265, 266; his apprehension for treason, 268; his trial, sentence, and execution, 269-73; his marriage and issue, 277, 278.

Cameron, Charles MacGilony, 15, 16 (n.).

Cameron, Charles, XXI. of Lochiel, 254.

Cameron, Charles, Governor of the Bahamas, 277; his marriage and issue,

Cameron, Charles Hay, 279; his marriage and issue, 280.

Cameron, Charles, VI. of Worcester, his education, 312; his character, marriage, descendants, and death, 313, 314.

Cameron, Rev. Charles Richard, VII. of Worcester, 314; his marriage and descendants, 314-6.

Cameron, Rev. Charles, VIII. of Worcester, 315; his marriage, issue, and death, 317.

Cameron, Charles Hamilton Hone, IX. of Worcester, his marriage and issue, 317.

Cameron, Dr. Charles A., 415.

Cameron, Dr. Charles, M.P., 415.

Cameron, Christian Helen Jane, of Inverailort, 380.

Cameron, Christina, IV. of Fassiefern, her marriage and issue, 284.

Cameron, Donald Dubh, 7, 8, 9, 15 (n.).

Cameron, Donald, or "Domhnull Dubh MacAilein," XI. of Lochiel, 17; at the battle of Harlaw, 25; joins the Lord of the Isles in 1429, deserts him and flees to Ireland, his estates being forfeited, 26; he returns and chases the MacLeans out of Lochaber, 29; his character, marriage, and issue, 31, 32.

Cameron, Donald, XV. of Lochiel, or "Domhnull Dubh MacDomhnuill," 47; at the battle of Corrichy, 60; his marriage, 61.

Cameron, Donald, XIX. of Lochiel, known as the "Gentle Lochiel," 214; his correspondence with the Chevalier de St. George, and his uncle, 214-17; meeting with Prince Charles at Borrodale, and his advice to the Prince, 219; leads his clan to Glenfinnan, 220, 221; takes the city of Edinburgh, 222,

223 ; at the battle of Preston, 223, 224 ; anecdote, on the march to Derby, 225 ; is wounded at the battle of Falkirk, 225 ; severely wounded at Culloden, 231 ; proceedings after the battle of Culloden, 233-9 ; meeting with Prince Charles in Benalder, 240 ; escapes to France and enters the French service, 241 ; his character, 242-4, 249 ; correspondence with the Chevalier de St. George, 245-9 ; his marriage, issue, and death, 250 ; forfeiture of his estates, 422.

Cameron, Donald, XXII. of Lochiel, 254 ; his marriage and issue, 255 ; Action of Reduction and Declarator at the instance of his trustees against Allan Cameron of Erracht, 419-57.

Cameron, Donald, XXIII. of Lochiel, a captain in the Grenadier Guards, 255, 256 ; his marriage and issue, 257, 258.

Cameron, Donald, XXIV. of Lochiel, M.P. for the county of Inverness, his marriage and issue, 258.

Cameron, Donald, of Erracht, joins Prince Charles at Glenfinnan, 318 ; his marriage and issue, 319.

Cameron, Donald, I. of Inverailort, his marriage and issue, 375.

Cameron, Donald Charles, of Dawnie, his marriage and descendants, 404.

Cameron, Donald Charles, of Dawnie, his marriage and issue, 405.

Cameron, Donald Charles, I. of Barcaldine, 406 ; his marriage, descendants, and death, 407.

Cameron, Donald, banker, one of Lochiel's trustees, 419-57.

Cameron, Sir Duncan, III. of Fassiefern, his marriage, 284.

Cameron, Col. Duncan, 362, 363, 370, 371.

Cameron, Duncan, of Inverailort, his marriage, issue, and death, 379, 380.

Cameron, Duncan, 409 ; sketch of his career, 410 ; his marriage, death, and issue,

Cameron, General Sir Duncan A., K.C.B., sketch of his career, 413, 414.

Cameron, Eugene Hay, Major, R.A., his issue, 280.

Cameron, Ewen, son of Donald Dubh, 8 ; genealogy of, 9.

Cameron, Ewen, X. of Lochiel, in whose time the famous combat on the North Inch of Perth was fought, 17, 21 ; fights a duel for a lady, 25.

Cameron, Ewen, XIII. of Lochiel, known as "Eoghainn MacAilein," joins the Lord of Lochalsh, 34 ; from whom he obtains grants of land, 35, 36, 41 ; joins Donald Dubh of the Isles and is forfeited as a traitor, 37 ; appointed Lieutenant of Lochaber, 38 ; sets out on a pilgrimage to Rome, 39 ; at the battle of "Blar-nan-Leine," 40 ; is apprehended for treason, tried, and executed, 40 ; his part in the "Raid of Urquhart," 45 ; his marriage and descendants, 46-8.

Cameron, Ewen, or "Eoghainn Beag," XIV. of Lochiel, 48 ; is killed by the governor of Inch-Connel Castle, 49.

Cameron, Sir Ewen, XVII. of Lochiel, or "Sir Eoghainn Dubh," 93 ; is placed under the care of Argyll, 94 ; adventure at Stirling, 96 ; visits Sir Robert Spotiswood in prison, 98 ; his kindness to prisoners at Inveraray, 104 ; returns to Lochaber, 105 ; his character at this time, 105, 106 ; his first raid, 107 ; joins the Earl of Glencairn, 110 ; defends the pass of Tullich against the English, 111 ; joins General Middleton, 115 ; attacks the English at Achadalew, 121 ; hand-to-hand struggle with an English officer, 123 ; bites out the officer's throat, 124 ; narrow escape from being shot, 125 ; curious adventure in a London barber's, 129 ; rejoins General Middleton and defeats the garrison of Inverlochy at Achintore, 130 ; defeats the English at Stronenevis, 132 ; his life saved by a dream, 135 ; captures four Colonels sent out to survey by General Monk, 139; treaty with General Monk, 141-3; is present at the Restoration, 148, 149; gets into difficulties, 150, 151, 156; settlement with Mackintosh, 164; attempts to shoot Argyll, and is taken ill, 168; fidelity of two of his clansmen at Inveraray, 169; is knighted by the Duke of York, 170; his stratagem for sending the Sheriff out of Lochaber, 172; joins the Marquis of Athole against Argyll, 173; unfortunate incident, 174; his loyalty impeached, 174-6; he clears his character to the King, 177; the King's kindness to him, 177-9; clever escape from being imprisoned, 181; projects a Confederation of the Clans, 182; his fidelity to Viscount Dundee, 184; his advice to the Council of War, 184-6, 191, 192; at the battle of Killiecrankie, 193-7, 198 (*n.*); amusing anecdote, 196; his appearance at the age of ninety, 205; curious dream and its fulfilment, 206, 207; anecdote, 207 (*n.*); appearance and character, 207, 208; his marriages and descendants, 145, 157, 208.

Cameron, Sir Ewen, II. of Fassiefern, created a Baronet in 1817, 281-2; his marriage and issue, 282; one of Lochiel's Trustees, 419-57.

Cameron, Ewen, I. of Erracht, 318.

Cameron, Ewen, or "Eoghainn Mòr" (Erracht), 319, 337, 339.

Cameron, Ewen, of Glenevis, his marriage, descendants, and death, 396-8; letter to Captain Cameron of Milton of Balvenie, 399-401.

Cameron, Ewen, of Dawnie, his marriage and issue, 404.

Cameron, Gillespick or Archibald, II. of Lochiel, 10.

Cameron, J. A., War Correspondent of the *Standard*, 414.

Cameron, James, of Callart, his marriage and descendants, 382.

Cameron, John, III. of Lochiel, 10.

Cameron, Sir John de, V. of Lochiel, and his issue, 11.

Cameron, John de, VII. of Lochiel, 11.

Cameron, John de, or "John Ochtery," VIII. of Lochiel, was present at the battle of Halidon Hill; his marriage, 11, 12 (*n.*).

Cameron, John, Archbishop of Glasgow; his character, 17; his coat-of-arms, he is made Lord Chancellor of Scotland, 18, 19; he visits John, who had charge of Callart, 17; and who gets the lands of Callart from Lochiel, 18; his death, 21.

Cameron, John, XVIII. of Lochiel, commands the clan after Killiecrankie, 212; makes over the estates to his son Donald, 204; is forfeited and escapes to France, 205, 213; his marriage and issue, 213, 214; his death, 214.

Cameron, Colonel John, of Fassiefern, 211, 213, 282; his early life and education, 284, 285; enters the army, 285, 286; duel with Lieut. MacLean, 286; engaged to a young lady in Ireland, 286; the engagement broken off, 287; severely wounded at Egmont-op-Zee, 287; also at Alexandria, 289; promoted to the rank of Lieut.-Col., 289; extracts from his correspondence, 290, 291; narrow escape at Arroyo del Molino, 291; at the Battle of Maya, where he is wounded, 292-4; at St. Pierre, 294-6; returns to Britain, and is slighted by the Government, 298-301; joins Wellington in 1815, 302; is killed at Quatre-Bras, 303, 304; his funeral in Lochaber, 305; inscription on his monument by Sir Walter Scott, 305, 306; lines upon his death by Scott and Professor Blackie, 307, 308.

Cameron, John, I. of Fassiefern, 213, 218, 219, 221; banished from Scotland, his marriage and issue, 281.

Cameron, John, XX. of Lochiel, an officer in the French army, 250; correspondence regarding him, 250-3; return to Scotland and death, 253.

Cameron, John, a colonel in the French service, 277; his marriage, issue, and death, 278.
Cameron, John, a captain in the army, died unmarried, 378, 379.
Cameron, Rev. John, I. of Worcester, his issue, 309.
Cameron, Rev. John, IV. of Worcester, 309; his marriage and issue, 310.
Cameron, John, of Glenevis, 398.
Cameron, John, of Dawnie, his marriage and issue, 404.
Cameron, John, of Dawnie, 405.
Cameron, John, II. of Barcaldine and Foxhall, 407.
Cameron, General Sir John, K.C.B., sketch of his career, 413.
Cameron, Lieut. Kenneth (Clunes), 358.
Cameron, Nathaniel, of Erracht, Lieut.-Colonel, 2nd Battalion, 79th Regiment, his marriage and descendants, 273, 274.
Cameron, Nathaniel Pryce, of Erracht, his marriage and issue, 274.
Cameron, Patrick, of Glenevis, 398.
Cameron, Patrick, of Speyside, 401; his marriage and descendants, 402.
Cameron, Philips (Erracht), Lieut.-Colonel of the 79th, 373; is killed at Fuentes D'Onor, 359.
Cameron, Robert, IV. of Lochiel, and his issue, 10.
Cameron, Sir Robert de, VI. of Lochiel, made his submission to Edward I., 11.
Cameron, Sir Roderick William, origin and account of his family, 408-12; sketch of his career, his marriage and issue, 411, 412.
Cameron, Thomas, II. of Worcester, his marriage and issue, 309.
Cameron, Thomas, III. of Worcester, his marriage and issue, 309.
Cameron, Dr. Thomas, V. of Worcester, his education, 310; writings and anecdotes of, 311, 312; his marriages, issue, and death, 312.
Cameron, Commander Verney, R.N., 414, 415.
Camerons of Barcaldine, 406-8.
Camerons of Callart, 80, 174, 381-4, 413.
Camerons of Camisky, 414.
Camerons of Clunes, 358, 414.
Camerons of Cuilchenna, 413, 414.
Camerons of Dawnie, 403-5.
Camerons of Dungallon, 93, 210, 233, 277, 394.
Camerons of Erracht, 79, 164, 259, 318-74, 414.
Camerons of Fassiefern, 211, 281-4.
Camerons of Glendesseray, 93, 199, 210, 257, 382.
Camerons of Glenevis, 4, 11, 29, 79, 81, 85, 391-8.
Camerons of Inverailort, 375-80.
Camerons of Invermalie and Strone, 4, 9, 10, 32, 80, 278.
Camerons of Kinlochiel, 79, 414.
Camerons of Letterfinlay, 80, 85.
Camerons of Lochiel, 4, 6, 7, 9, 260.
Camerons of Lundavra, 385-90.
Camerons of Perthshire, 18.
Camerons of Speyside, 399-402.
Camerons of Torcastle, 266.
Camerons of Worcester, 309-17.
Campbell, Clan, 68, 162, 229, 230.
Campbell of Achallader, 211, 213, 281, 283.
Campbell of Ardchattan, 286.

INDEX. 471

Campbell of Ardkinglas, 68.
Campbell of Ardshiel, 282.
Campbell of Auchinbreck, 250.
Campbell of Auchindown, 159.
Campbell of Barcaldine, 210, 282, 284, 305, 406.
Campbell of Caddell, John, 56.
Campbell of Calder, Sir John, 36, 38.
Campbell of Corrie, 282.
Campbell of Edinchip, 211.
Campbell of Glenmore, 394.
Campbell of Glenorchy, 163-5.
Campbell of Glenure, 282, 284, 406.
Campbell of Glenure, Colin, and his descendants, 210, 211.
Campbell of Inverawe, 274, 284, 407.
Campbell, Lieut.-Col., 139, 141.
Campbell of Lochdochart, 209.
Campbell of Lochnell, 213, 266, 275, 281.
Campbell of Melfort, 211.
Campbell of Monzie, 284.
Campbell of Shawfield, 275.
Cannon, Colonel, 193, 199, 200.
Carlisle, Earl of, 388.
Cathcart, Lord, 352.
Charles II., 106, 148, 150, 156, 157.
Charles, Prince, 213, 217-22, 224, 226-31, 233, 234, 236, 239-41, 244-7, 249, 251, 253, 254, 262, 264-7, 272, 274-6, 385, 392, 403, 404.
Chattan, Clan, 1-7, 13, 14, 16, 25 (*n.*), 28, 31, 34, 43, 89, 164.
Cheann-Duibh, Clan, 4.
Chevalier de St. George, 206, 207, 209, 214, 216, 217, 244-7, 249-53, 26
Clare, Lord, 267.
Clarendon, Earl of, 157.
Cope, Sir John, 221, 222.
Cornwallis, Lord, 335, 336.
Craig Cailloch, battle of, 31.
Crawford, Earl of, 22.
Cromwell, Oliver, 103, 108, 136, 144, 185, 385.
Culloden, battle of, 231-3, 243, 244, 248, 263, 272, 275, 381, 392, 404.
Cumberland, Duke of, 230, 231, 233, 236, 237, 251, 275, 392.

Dalnafert, lands of, 5.
Darling, Sir Charles, 279.
David I., 10.
David II., 11, 15.
Davidson, Clan, 4, 14, 15, 23 (*n.*).
Day, Clan, 16.
Donald Balloch, 26, 28, 29.
Douglas, Earl of, 19.
Drumlui, battle of, 13.
Drummond of Balhaldy, 210, 217, 246, 247, 250, 264.
Drummond of Stobhall, 17.
Drummond, Sir John, 181.

Dunbar, Earl of, 74.
Dundas, Rt. Hon. Henry, one of Lochiel's Trustees, 419-57.
Dundee, Earl of, 158.
Dundee, Viscount, 182-95, 198 (*n*.), 199, 381.
Dunfermline, Earl of, 196.
Dunkeld, Archdean of, 10.
Duror, lands of, 38.

Edward I., 11.
Elgin, Lord, 258.
Enzie, Earl of, 79-83, 85, 87, 91.
Errol, Earl of, 158, 279, 386.

Falkirk, battle of, 225, 228, 263.
Farquharson, Clan, 234.
Fear Mhorsheirlich, 323-5.
Fergus II., 1.
Fleance, 9.
Flodden, battle of, 43.
Forbes, Lord, 43.
Forbes, President, 251.
Forbes, of Skellater, 158.
Fraser, Clan, 40, 231, 234.
Fraser of Lovat, 43, 209, 227, 236, 254.
Fuentes D'Onor, battle of, 358, 359, 377.

George I., 223.
George II., 273, 276, 277.
George III., 347.
George IV., 363.
Gillean, Clan, 26.
Gillechattan, Clan, 3.
Gillechattan, Mor, 5.
Gillonie, Clan, 4.
Glencairn, Earl of, 110-12, 114, 115, 155, 202.
Glencoe, lands of, 38.
Glenlivet, battle of, 65.
Glenlui, lands of, 3, 6, 13, 27, 28, 30, 31, 41, 42 (*n*.), 62, 73, 75, 88, 116, 151, 162, 165.
Glenmoriston, 45, 64.
Glenurquhart, 45, 64, 187.
Gloucester, Duke of, 149.
Gordon, Clan, 81, 391, 400.
Gordon, Colonel Nathaniel, 100.
Gordon, Duke of, 176, 178, 179, 364, 404.
Gordon, Lord, 42, 234.
Gordon, Sir William, 266.
Gordon of Aberlour, 401.
Gordon of Glenbucket, 233, 234.
Gow, Clan, 23 (*n*.), 25 (*n*.).
Grant, Clan, 187, 189.

Grant, Sir John, 88, 89.
Grant of Culcabock, 37, 48.
Grant of Freuchie, 37, 47 (*n.*), 48, 64, 65, 73.
Grant of Glenmoriston, 210, 396, 397, 407.
Grant of Grant, Sir James, 47, 90.
Grant of Lurg, 90.
Grant of Mulben, 48.
Grant of Rothiemurchus, 158, 396.

Halidon Hill, battle of, 12.
Hamilton, Hon. George, 278.
Harlaw, battle of, 25, 28, 30.
Hartfell, Earl of, 97.
Hawley, General, 225.
Hay, Lord John, 256.
Haya, John de, 11.
Highland Society of London, 332-5, 410, 411.
Hogarth, 276, 277.
Huntly, Earl and Marquis of, 36, 39, 40, 59, 60, 64, 65, 67, 69, 76, 78, 80, 87, 92, 150, 171, 286, 335 (*n.*), 341, 348, 400.

Inverlochy, battle of, 7, 28, 92, 93, 95, 96.
Invernahavon, battle of, 14, 15, 22.
Inverness, 26, 35, 59, 162, 229-31, 346.
Isla, Angus Og of, 2.
Isla, John of, 13, 27.

James I., 17-19, 26.
James II., 169, 170 (*n.*).
James IV., 35, 36, 41-3, 166.
James V., 36, 41, 43, 45, 78.
James VI., 229.
Johnson, Dr., 276, 277.

Kay, Clan, 4.
Keppoch, lands of, 3, 107, 180.
Killiecrankie, battle of, 193-9, 209-12.
Kilmarnock, Lord, 226, 227.
Kinrara, lands of, 5.
Kintail, Mackenzies of, 41, 87.
Kintail, Lord, 73, 209.
Kishorn, lands of, 32, 41, 64.

Lamberton, Henry de, 10.
Lauder, Bishop, 20.
Lauderdale, Duke of, 150, 151, 157, 158.
Lennox, Earl of, 40, 46.
Leslie, David, 104.
Lichfield, Dowager Countess of, 332.
Lismore, Lord, 249.
Livingstone, Sir Thomas, 201.

Lochaber, Thane of, Kenneth, 9.
Lochalsh, Alexander, Lord of, 34-7, 41-4.
Lochalsh, Celestine, Lord of, 26, 27, 32, 46.
Lochalsh, lands of, 64, 73, 87.
Locharkaig, lands of, 3, 6, 13, 27, 28, 30, 31, 41, 42 (*n.*), 62, 73, 75, 88, 116, 140, 151, 162, 165, 235, 236, 256, 284.
Lochiel, lands of, 6, 26, 27, 35, 36, 38, 45, 73, 78.
Lochiel, lands of, rental of, in 1787, 458-60.
Logan, Adam de, 11.
Loudon, Lord, 229.
Louis XIV., 208.
Lord of the Isles, Alexander, 3, 5, 26, 28, 30, 42 (*n.*).
Lord of the Isles, Angus, 32.
Lord of the Isles, Donald, 25.
Lord of the Isles, Godfrey, 42 (*n.*).
Lord of the Isles, John, 27, 47.
Lord High Steward of Scotland, Alan, 11.
Lorne, Marquis of, 411.

MacAlastair of Loup, 201.
MacAllan of Lundie, 73.
MacBean, Clan, 4.
MacBeth, 9.
MacDonald of Balranald, 404.
MacDonald of Barrisdale, 233-6, 379.
MacDonald of Clanranald, 6, 34, 40, 42, 59, 74, 75, 77, 78, 82, 91, 94, 193, 200, 230, 233-6, 241.
MacDonald of Dalily, 241.
MacDonald of Dunyveg, 40, 77.
MacDonald of Glenaladale, 241.
MacDonald of Glencoe, 65, 162, 167, 282, 283, 305, 375.
MacDonald of Glengarry, 37, 41, 45, 73, 82, 91, 93, 94, 107, 113, 114, 167, 187-91, 193, 204, 220, 230, 233-5, 237, 239, 265, 266, 284, 366.
MacDonald of Greenfield, 210.
MacDonald of Islay, 72, 73.
MacDonald of Keppoch, 33, 34, 37, 40, 94, 107, 113, 114, 167, 180-3, 220, 222, 227, 229, 230, 231 (*n.*), 233, 234, 237, 381, 385.
MacDonald of Kingsburgh, 392.
MacDonald of Largo, 201.
MacDonald of Lochgarry, 222, 227, 241.
MacDonald of Morar, 211.
MacDonald of Scothouse, 227.
MacDonald of Sleat, 77, 145, 200, 209, 210.
MacDonald of Tullich, 180 (*n.*).
MacDonald of Vallay, 210.
MacDonell, Lord, 94.
MacDougall of Fairlochline, 63.
MacDougall of Lorne, 48, 49.
MacDougall of MacDougall, 211.
MacGilleCattan, Dougal Dall, 13.

INDEX. 475

MacGillivray, Clan, 4.
MacGillonie, Clan, 5, 8, 9, 27.
MacGlashan, Clan, 23 (n.).
MacGregor, Clan, 44, 74-6, 82-5, 162, 234, 236.
MacGregor of Balhaldy, 249, 251.
MacIan of Ardnamurchan, 37, 70.
MacKay, Clan, 38.
MacKay of Bighouse, 210, 380.
MacKay, General, 184, 189, 190, 193, 194, 196-9, 209.
MacKay of Island-handa, 211.
MacKenzie, Col. Hugh, 257.
MacKenzie of Kilcoy, Sir Colin, 396.
Mackenzie of Kintail and Seaforth, 41, 51, 87.
MacKenzie of Kintail, John, 48.
MacKenzie of Kintail, Kenneth, 48.
MacKenzie of Rosehaugh, 183.
MacKenzie of Suddie, 176, 180, 355.
MacKinnon, Clan, 233, 234.
MacKinnon of Strathordell, 77.
MacKintosh, Angus, VI. Chief, 13.
MacKintosh of Aberarder, 210.
MacKintosh, Clan, 1-3, 5-7, 13, 17, 21, 23, 24, 26, 28, 30, 33, 50, 62, 64, 65, 67, 70, 83-7, 89, 92, 151, 159-67, 170, 180-2, 231, 234, 236.
MacKintosh, Duncan, 31, 44.
MacKintosh, Farquhar, 44.
MacKintosh, Gillichallum, 31.
MacKintosh, Lachlan, 16, 44, 64, 88, 151.
MacKintosh, Lachlan, "Badenoch," 31.
MacKintosh, Malcolm, 3, 28, 30.
MacKintosh, William, 3, 13, 27, 38, 40, 42, 44, 48, 142.
MacLachlan of Coruanan, 50, 54, 210.
MacLachlan of Strath-Lachlan, 54.
MacLean of Ardgour, 94, 210, 278, 282.
MacLean, Clan, 26, 27, 29, 45, 96, 173-5, 185, 197, 205, 231, 233, 338.
MacLean of Coll, 26, 27, 36, 257.
MacLean of Drimnin, 325, 326.
MacLean of Duart, 37, 62, 70-2, 77, 157, 167, 168, 200, 209.
MacLean, Hector Bui, 29.
MacLean, John Garve, 26.
MacLean, Sir John, 193.
MacLean of Lochbuy, 26, 27, 36, 38, 73, 74, 76, 79.
MacLean of Pennycross, 326.
MacLean of Torloisk, Colonel, 327, 328, 330.
MacLeod, Clan, 234.
MacLeod of Dunvegan, 37.
MacLeod of Hammer, 410.
MacLeod of Harris, 77.
MacLeod of MacLeod, 209, 410.
MacMartin, Clan, 4, 6, 7, 10 (n.), 31, 94, 145.
MacMhicEoin, 70-2.
MacMillan, Clan, 4.

MacMillan, Ewen, foster-brother of Col. John Cameron of Fassiefern, 284; anecdote of, 288; devotion of, 294, 295, 303, 304.
MacNeill of Barra, 283, 286, 305, 341.
MacPherson of Breakachy, 210, 239, 240.
MacPherson, Clan, 2, 4, 5, 14-16, 23 (*n.*), 159, 162, 234.
MacPherson of Cluny, 210, 222, 229, 234-7, 239-41, 265, 283.
MacPherson of Dalraddie, 210.
MacRuari of Moydart, Allan, 37.
Madderty, Lord, 91, 92.
Malcolm, Ceanmore, 10.
Mamore, lands of, 400.
Mar, Earl of, 12 (*n.*), 28, 158.
March, Earl of, 22.
Marischal, Earl, 158.
Mary, Queen, 36, 42, 60, 203.
Melford, Earl of, 17.
Menteith, Earl of, 11.
Menzies, Clan, 234.
Menzies, Major Duncan, 202.
Mhic Govie, Clan, 4.
Middleton, Earl of, 157.
Middleton, General, 114, 115, 130, 131, 133-6, 149, 150, 206.
Monk, General, 110, 115, 116, 138, 141-5, 148-50.
Montrose, Marquis of, 92, 93, 95-8, 102, 103, 106, 108, 118, 119, 144, 158, 185, 381.
Moray, Earl of, 47 (*n.*), 60, 64, 65, 158, 161, 162, 166.
Morgan, General, 115, 134, 135.
Mostyn, Colonel, 330, 331.
Murray, Duke of, 282.
Murray, Clan, 38.
Murray, Lord George, 227, 229, 267.
Murray, Secretary, 230, 233-6.
Murray of Struan, 174.
Murray, William, 100.

Nairne, Lord, 222.
Napoleon, 363, 366-70.
Newry, John, 104.
North Inch of Perth, 1-4, 16, 21, 23.

Ogilvy, Lord, 97, 234, 245, 246, 264, 266, 267.
Ossianic Controversy, 333-5.

Perth, Earl of, 17, 91, 92.
Philipshaugh, battle of, 97.
Pitsligo, Lord, 234.
Preston, battle of, 103, 223, 224, 385.

Quatre-Bras, battle of, 213, 282, 303, 363, 364-6, 378.
Queensferry, Duke of, 258.
Qwhele, Clan, 4.

INDEX.

Randulph, Thomas, 27.
Reay, Lord, 210.
Reginald of the Isles, 27, 28.
Richmond, Duchess of, 263.
Robert Bruce, 2, 11, 27.
Robert II., 27, 28, 380, 385.
Robert III., 17, 21, 22.
Robertson, Struan, 167 (*n.*).
Ross, Earl of, Alexander, 5.
Ross, Earl of, John, 26, 27, 47.
Ross, Earl of, William, 5.
Ross of Urchany, 159.
Rothes, Earl of, 160.

Saxe, Marshal, 219.
Scone, Lord, 76.
Seaforth, MacKenzies of, 41, 91, 200.
Selkirk, Lord, 410.
Sempill, Lord, 245-7, 249, 309.
Sliochd-Gow-chruim, 4.
Smith, Clan, 4, 23 (*n.*), 25 (*n.*).
Smith of Ballvarry, 24 (*n.*).
Soirlie, Clan, 4.
Spotiswood, Sir Robert, 97-100, 102, 103.
Stewart of Appin, 229, 233, 234.
Stewart of Ardshiel, 222, 237.
Stewart, Clan, 38, 93, 230, 231.
Stewart of Duror, 38.
Stewart of Glenbuckie, 386.
Stewart of Invernaheil, 229.
Stirling, Sheriff of, Alexander, 10.
Strathallan, Viscount, 177.
Strathdon, lands of, 12 (*n.*).
Strome, Castle, 32, 41, 47 (*n.*), 64, 73.
Stuart, John Roy, 233, 234, 241.
Sutherland, Earl of, 43.

"Tillear Dubh," 48, 50-8.
Talavera, battle of, 355, 413.
Tarbert, Lord, 175, 180, 181.
Tarrel Clan, 4.
Taylor, Professor, Malcolm Campbell, 54, 56.
Thriepland, Sir Stewart, 239.
Tulliebardine, Earl of, 100, 221.
Tweeddale, Marquis of, 256.

Urquhart, Sir Alexander, 35.

Waterloo, battle of, 256, 306, 319, 366-70, 378, 379.
Wellington, Duke of, 298, 301-3, 305, 354-7, 360-2, 364-6, 369-70, 377-9.

Wemyss, Earl of, 332.
William the Lyon, 10.
William of Orange, 181, 182, 184, 199-202, 204, 221, 310, 311.
Wodehouse, Admiral, descendants of, 279-80.
Wynd, Henry, 23, 24, 25 (*n*.).

York, Duke of, 149, 157, 169-71, 176, 246, 253, 276, 289, 298, 336, 342-7, 374.

www.ingramcontent.com/pod-product-compliance
Lightning Source LLC
Chambersburg PA
CBHW021427300426
44114CB00010B/688